THE DICTATORSHIP OF RELATIVISM

THE DICTATORSHIP OF RELATIVISM

Pope Benedict XVI's Response

GEDIMINAS T. JANKUNAS, STD

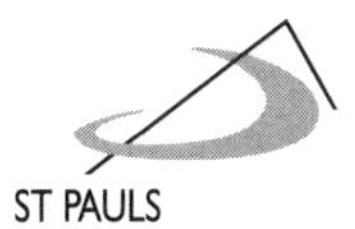

Library of Congress Cataloging-in-Publication Data

Jankunas, Gediminas T.
  The dictatorship of relativism : Pope Benedict XVI's response / by Gediminas T. Jankunas.
      p. cm.
    Includes bibliographical references.
    ISBN 978-0-8189-1316-7
    1. Relativity. 2. Catholic Church and philosophy. 3. Benedict XVI, Pope, 1927- I. Title.
    BX1795.P47.J36 2011
    261.5'1—dc22
                                  2010052472

Nihil Obstat
Rev. Emery de Gaál, Dipl. Theo., Ph.D.
Rev. Edward T. Oakes, S.J., Ph.D.
Censores deputati

Imprimatur
✠ Francis Cardinal George, O.M.I., Ph.D.
Chicago, April 8, 2010

Acknowledgments for permission to use
copyrighted material are on page ix.

Produced and designed in the United States of America by the
Fathers and Brothers of the Society of St. Paul,
2187 Victory Boulevard, Staten Island, New York 10314-6603
as part of their communications apostolate.

ISBN 10: 0-8189-1316-9
ISBN 13: 978-0-8189-1316-7

Printing Information:

| Current Printing - first digit | 1 | 2 | 3 | 4 | 5 | 6 | 7 | 8 | 9 | 10 |

Year of Current Printing - first year shown

| 2011 | 2012 | 2013 | 2014 | 2015 | 2016 | 2017 | 2018 | 2019 | 2020 |

TABLE OF CONTENTS

Chapter 6: Responding to the Challenge of Truth in
Truth and Tolerance* and *Without Roots

ACKNOWLEDGMENTS

Reprinted with the permission of Scribner, Atria, Fireside, a Division of Simon & Schuster, Inc., from THE CLOSING OF THE AMERICAN MIND by Allan Bloom. Copyright © 1987 by Allan Bloom. All rights reserved.

PENSEES & OTHER WRITINGS by Pascal, translated by Honor Levi 656w from pp. 5, 7-8, 24, 35, 38, 62-63, 72-73, 79, 123, 140, 158, 161. By permission of Oxford University Press. New York: Oxford University Press, 1995.

Brief quotes from pp. 140, 151, 163, 211-12, 215-17, 219 from GOD'S CHOICE by GEORGE WEIGEL Copyright © 2005 by George Weigel. Reprinted by permission of HarperCollins Publishers.

Excerpt from "Culture in Crisis" by Michael Novak, *National Review Online*. April 19, 2005. Reprinted with permission.

Material from *Let God's Light Shine Forth: The Spiritual Vision of Pope Benedict XVI* by Robert Moynihan, published by Hutchinson. Reprinted by permission of The Random House Group Ltd.

Approximately 473 words (p. 9, 125, 148, 166) from THE RISE OF POPE BENEDICT XVI: THE INSIDE STORY OF HOW THE POPE WAS ELECTED AND WHERE HE WILL TAKE THE CATHOLIC CHURCH by John L. Allen (Allen Lane The Penguin Press 2005). Copyright © John L. Allen 2005. Reproduced by permission of Penguin Books Ltd. Penguin Group (UK) 80 Strand, London WC2R 0RL

Quotes from "A Remedy for Relativism: The Cosmic, Historical and Eschatological Dimensions of the Liturgy According to the Theologian Joseph Ratzinger" by Geoffrey Wainwright (*Nova et Vetera* Vol. 5, Issue 2 – Spring 2007) used with permission. *Nova et Vetera* is an independent journal published by the Augustine Institute, 3001 S. Federal Blvd., Box 1126, Denver CO 80236.

Various authors, "grouping of small quotes from the entire journal issue," in *Common Knowledge*, Volume 13, no. 2/3, pp. 216-387. Copyright 2007, Duke University Press. All rights reserved. Reprinted by permission of the publisher. Citations from this issue of *Common Knowledge* were taken from the following articles:

Barbara Herrnstein Smith, "Relativism, Today and Yesterday".

David Bloor, "Epistemic Grace: Antirelativism as Theology in Disguise".

Christopher Norris, "Dictatorship of the Professoriate?: Antiobjectivism in Anglo-American Philosophy".

Daniel Boyarin, "The Scandal of Sophism: On the Epistemological Seriousness of Relativism".

Jeffrey M. Perl, "T.S. Eliot's Small Boat of Thought".

Kenneth J. Gergen, "Relativism, Religion, and Relational Being".

Richard Shusterman, "Fallibilism and Faith".

Jeffrey Stout, "A House Founded on the Sea: Is Democracy a Dictatorship of Relativism?".

INTRODUCTION

Joseph Ratzinger began his classic book *Introduction to Christianity* with a story by Kierkegaard about a circus clown sent to a nearby village to warn the people about an approaching fire that had started at the circus. The clown, in full costume, rushed to the village and pleaded with the villagers to come and help put out the fire. However, no one took his message seriously and thought it was all part of his act. The harder the clown tried to explain the problem the more everyone laughed. Eventually, the fire engulfed the circus and spread rapidly to the village. By then it was already too late to do anything about it, and the village burned down to the ground.

Although Cardinal Joseph Ratzinger used this story forty years ago to portray Christianity's position in the modern world, it continues to resonate in the present. As Ratzinger wrote, "It is certainly true that anyone who tries to preach the faith today to people involved in modern life and thought can often be made to feel like a clown."[1] He continues, "Thus anyone who makes an honest effort to give an account of the Christian faith… must realize that he is not just someone in fancy dress who needs only change his clothes in order to be able to impart his teaching successfully."[2] Much more is needed than to change a fancy presentation into something even fancier so that people will grasp the urgency of the message. The reference here is to Ratzinger's lifelong concern with the problem of relativism.

Even though Cardinal Ratzinger had spent his life analyzing and speaking out against relativism,[3] his message was articulated most clearly in his homily *Pro Eligendo Romano Pontifice*. Ratzinger, as Dean of the College of Cardinals, delivered this homily to the cardinals before they entered the conclave that eventually elected him as Pope Benedict XVI:

> Today, having a clear faith based on the Creed of the Church is often labeled as fundamentalism. Whereas relativism – that is, letting oneself be "tossed here and there carried about by every wind of doctrine" – seems the only attitude that can cope with modern times. We are building a dictatorship of relativism that does not recognize anything as definitive and whose ultimate goal consists solely of one's own ego and desires.[4]

This mention of relativism in Ratzinger's homily was printed widely in almost all of the major newspapers of the world. A good number of Catholics were hearing the term *relativism* for the first time. However, more importantly, it was not the term *per se*, but the phenomenon of it – described as the *dictatorship of relativism* – that brought attention to the term.[5] Unfortunately, only the bishops and a small number of scholars from various sciences took significant note of this issue. The rest of the world, Christian or otherwise, paid no further attention, and took no heed. As was mentioned above, Cardinal Ratzinger had predicted such a reaction.

Even though he spoke on a very solemn occasion, visible to both the Christian and the secular world, his message, which was of great importance, was listened to, but not heard; was read, but not understood. John L. Allen, Jr. describes an event that took place during a press conference at the North American College in Rome the morning after the papal election where several American cardinals shared personal impressions of the new pope. He notes, "Perhaps the most perceptive comment in the immediate aftermath of Pope Benedict's election came from Cardinal Francis George of Chicago, one of the few men in the College of

Cardinals who, observers say, can match the new pope in terms of intellectual depth."[6] What did Cardinal George say? Allen says that he drew a kind of historical parallelism between John Paul II and Benedict XVI. "There was a fault line in the Soviet empire that brought it down," Cardinal George observed, "Its concern for social justice was corrupted by the suppression of freedom… in the West, there's also a fault line between concern for personal freedom and the abandonment of objective truth."[7] George also observed that neither contradiction is "sustainable in the long run and that the 'time and tempo' with which Pope Benedict's witness against relativism in the West would gather force are not yet clear."[8] It is obvious that Cardinal George is willing to join forces with the new pope in fighting against the dangers of relativism. He matches the description of those, whom Aidan Nichols cites, stating that Ratzinger "was not the only observer of the Western scene who noted that, by the start of the new millennium, the human faculty for registering comprehensive truth (not simply supernatural but even natural) was at a discount."[9]

What is this *time and tempo* that Cardinal George mentions? Does he mean that Pope Benedict is acting like an Old Testament prophet, or is he like the clown, who tries to deliver an important message of life or death, but no one is taking it seriously? Could it be that the message about the dangerous dictatorship of relativism is just passing news, and the contemporary world is unconcerned about it? Should members of the Catholic Church be concerned? Do they really have to gather their forces and join Pope Benedict XVI in his lifelong campaign against relativism?

To answer any of these questions, we must first clarify in general what the phenomenon of relativism is and from where it comes. As will be seen, it is a multi-faceted phenomenon, where even finding a satisfactory definition is a challenge. Relativism gets more complicated as we try to analyze its origins in the history of human thought. At this juncture, it would suffice to present a brief overview of how relativism is understood by the Magisterium of the Catholic Church, mainly, from Scripture and in dogmatic pronouncements. Considering that the majority of those who study relativism eventually come up with their own understanding of it, this author intends to focus on Joseph Ratzinger and his ideas on this issue.

Joseph Ratzinger's encounters with different forms of relativism, such as National Socialism and Marxism, early in his life were significant in his intellectual formation. What would Joseph Ratzinger be, if not for his intellectual brilliance and education? In the words of his great predecessor John Paul II, he is a "churchman of exceptional theological competence."[10] Cardinal Ratzinger himself acknowledged that for his theology he is grateful for the tradition of the Church and to all of those who worked hard and devoutly throughout the centuries to pass it on to future generations. It was the 19th century Munich School and its heritage of appreciating history, that gave the young Ratzinger his profound reverence for the past, present and future history of humanity as the factual place for the divine Logos to be incarnated. Moreover, it was his studies of Augustine, Bonaventure and other great minds of the early Church that gave him a sense of the Christian understanding of the true meaning and destiny of human existence. In reading how Augustine influenced Ratzinger and what Ratzinger later wrote regarding Bonaventure we recognize certain basic theological predispositions that he gathers and employs in his own theological mindset, especially in his fight against relativism.

The Second Vatican Council constituted a major period in Ratzinger's life. Here he strove to put up protective walls against relativism in *Dei Verbum, Lumen Gentium* and other conciliar documents. His lifelong concern is with the correct meaning and understanding of *Gaudium et Spes*, which set the tenor for relations of the Catholic Church with the modern world. Soon after the Council, the May 1968 student revolts and the continuing rise of liberation theology became areas of battle for Ratzinger because he perceived them as relativism in disguise. When the Soviet Union collapsed and Communism was no longer one of the leading totalitarian ideologies of the Western world, Cardinal

Ratzinger – as Prefect of the Congregation for the Doctrine of Faith – became a major voice in combating relativism as it appeared in the forms of growing popular interest in religious and cultural pluralism. Areas of his concern included ecumenism, inter-religious dialogue and secularized democracies expressed in documents, especially *Fides et Ratio* and *Dominus Iesus*, which were issued to discuss precisely these matters. These certainly are not the easiest questions to be dealt with, particularly as they have "seldom been asked in a sufficiently radical way, for fear of touching wounds that are still open; yet it is still necessary to ask this, just as truth is necessary for love."[11] Ratzinger dedicated a considerable amount of his own study and insight to each of these areas.

This is precisely why, as stated previously, it is imperative to take a closer look at what Ratzinger has said – and to this day is saying – about relativism.[12] We need to get a better understanding of what it is and how relativism may damage the Church and the world, if left unengaged. Thus, the goal of this work is to evaluate properly the issues at stake following the man clad, for some, in *fancy clownish* garments, whom one now calls Pope Benedict XVI. We will attempt to gather the arguments advanced by Joseph Ratzinger in *time and tempo* to provide forceful support and witness to the one who has the prominent responsibility of leading the Church and all humanity to Jesus Christ.

Biblical Abbreviations

OLD TESTAMENT

Genesis	Gn	Nehemiah	Ne	Baruch	Ba
Exodus	Ex	Tobit	Tb	Ezekiel	Ezk
Leviticus	Lv	Judith	Jdt	Daniel	Dn
Numbers	Nb	Esther	Est	Hosea	Ho
Deuteronomy	Dt	1 Maccabees	1 M	Joel	Jl
Joshua	Jos	2 Maccabees	2 M	Amos	Am
Judges	Jg	Job	Jb	Obadiah	Ob
Ruth	Rt	Psalms	Ps	Jonah	Jon
1 Samuel	1 S	Proverbs	Pr	Micah	Mi
2 Samuel	2 S	Ecclesiastes	Ec	Nahum	Na
1 Kings	1 K	Song of Songs	Sg	Habakkuk	Hab
2 Kings	2 K	Wisdom	Ws	Zephaniah	Zp
1 Chronicles	1 Ch	Sirach	Si	Haggai	Hg
2 Chronicles	2 Ch	Isaiah	Is	Malachi	Ml
Ezra	Ezr	Jeremiah	Jr	Zechariah	Zc
		Lamentations	Lm		

NEW TESTAMENT

Matthew	Mt	Ephesians	Eph	Hebrews	Heb
Mark	Mk	Philippians	Ph	James	Jm
Luke	Lk	Colossians	Col	1 Peter	1 P
John	Jn	1 Thessalonians	1 Th	2 Peter	2 P
Acts	Ac	2 Thessalonians	2 Th	1 John	1 Jn
Romans	Rm	1 Timothy	1 Tm	2 John	2 Jn
1 Corinthians	1 Cor	2 Timothy	2 Tm	3 John	3 Jn
2 Corinthians	2 Cor	Titus	Tt	Jude	Jude
Galatians	Gal	Philemon	Phm	Revelation	Rv

1

AN OVERVIEW OF RELATIVISM

1. Defining Relativism

Relativism is a term laden with ambiguity. Barbara Herrnstein Smith writes, "If *relativism* means anything at all, it means a great many things. It is certainly not, though often treated as such, a one-line 'claim' or 'thesis,' for example, 'man is the measure of all things,' 'nothing is absolutely right or wrong,' 'all opinions are equally valid,' and so forth."[13] In her book *Relativism*, Maria Baghramian writes, basically, relativism is "the view that cognitive, moral or aesthetic norms and values are dependent on the social or conceptual systems that underpin them and consequently a neutral standpoint for evaluating them is not available to us."[14] Baghramian also observes that among the circles of analytic philosophy, relativism is either "dismissed readily as an incoherent position or is identified with irrationalism and cognitive anarchy."[15] This still does not answer for the popularity of this doctrine whose supporters insist, "All our standards have the form of conventions sustained by a group of people who are ineluctably fallible, limited and historically situated. The standards will be contingent achievements of the group and no higher kind authority can ever attach to them."[16]

At the same time, Baghramian and others strongly agree that there are other definitions for this term – constructed *relative* to the perspective of the one who is using it. For example, Maurice Mandelbaum (1908-1987) speaks of historical relativism, which he defines as "the view that no historical work grasps the nature of the past (or present) immediately, that whatever 'truth' a historical work contains is relative to the conditioning processes under which it arose and can only be understood with reference to those processes."[17] Another definition is given by sociologist Karl Mannheim, "[Relativism is] the approach that recognizes that all knowledge is socially dependent, bound to the location of the thinker" and he reasons from this to "the inevitable relativity of all human truth."[18] These are just a few examples. As we can see, the definition often depends on the area of study in which the term is used.[19] Therefore one can speak about historical relativism, moral relativism, political relativism, sociological relativism and so forth. For the purpose of this study as well as for its coherence, the definition exercised here will be the one given by Cardinal Ratzinger himself in the above-mentioned homily. Relativism, as defined by Ratzinger, is an attitude of modern times that "does not recognize anything as definitive and whose ultimate goal consists solely of one's ego and desires." It is "letting oneself be 'tossed here and there, carried about by every wind of doctrine.'"

2. A History of Relativism

In relation to when the term *relativism* was first used, Baghramian points us to John Grote (1813-1866) and his *Exploratio Philosophica* (1865), where Grote writes, "the notion of the mask over the face of nature is... *what I have called 'relativism.'* If 'the face of nature' is reality, then the mask over it, which is what theory gives us, is so much *deception* and that is what relativism really comes to [emphasis added]."[20] This notion represents *conceptual relativism*. However, the idea itself has very ancient roots in the history of the development of human thought. A few examples will suffice.

The father of relativism is thought to have been the Sophist

Protagoras of Abdera (481-420 BC), who coined the statement, "Man is the measure of all things, of things that are that they are and of things that are not that they are not."[21] The *homo mensura* doctrine at its basis acknowledges the *deceitfulness* of the senses. It ordinarily has been understood in an epistemological sense and as a statement of the relativity of all human knowledge, of the impossibility of penetrating beyond the appearances of things. This interpretation conforms to the general tendency of the age in which Protagoras lived. Protagoras lived during the end of the Persian Wars and the first decade of the Peloponnesian War and "the political turmoil that ensued cast doubt over the old certainties and introduced the idea that social and ethical rules which had been construed and unchanging, universal or of divine origin were merely transitory and local."[22] However, there were other factors as well, which Baghramian summarizes:

> The first generation of Pre-Socratic philosophers aimed to give all-encompassing metaphysical-cum-scientific explanations of the ultimate constituents and principles of the universe. The various systematic proto-scientific explanatory schemes, however, were in conflict with each other and no single theory emerged as a paradigm for a scientific/philosophical explanation of the world. Irresolvable disagreements among the natural scientists on the constitutive elements and origins of the universe led to disillusionment with the idea of there being a single unifying account. The grand system-building of the Pre-Socratic which led to the multiplication of theories on the nature of reality, where no method was available to adjudicate between them, gave rise to the hypothesis that there may be a variety of non-convergent explanatory systems or world-views on each subject. The diversity of opinions in debates on political and social matters in the Assembly and the law courts cast further doubts on the possibility of finding a unique framework for solving all ethical or political

disputes. The Sophistic approach, as a whole, was an antithesis of the totalizing tendencies of its precursors and Protagorean relativism may, in part, be seen as a reaction to the prevailing disagreements.[23]

Xenophanes (c. 570-475 BC) pointed out that different people have different conceptions of God, and therefore, human knowledge of the Divine is relative, while the Divine and divine knowledge are absolute.[24] Heraclitus' doctrine of flux and the unity of opposites, Parmenides' view that plurality and change are but the semblance of reality, and Democritus' criticism that perception through the senses is subjective were just some of the theories which led philosophers to distrust the deliverance of the senses and instead directed them to rely upon reason or intelligence. Further reflection, however, soon made it clear that rational theories were no more consistent than the data of perceptional experience. The inevitable result of all of this was that the relativism of Protagoras and his followers eventually passed into Skepticism.

Sextus Empiricus (c. 160-210 AD), whose view came to be known as Pyrrhonian skepticism, advocated that the judgment of beliefs be suspended. He explained it thusly: "The objects of perception are relative to those who are sensing them, but even the objects of thought are relative, because they are expressed relative to the one thinking about them."[25] This reasoning was applied by the Greek skeptics to various religions and their practices. However, in this case relativism should not be confused with skepticism, since, "in its strongest sense, (global) skepticism is the denial of the possibility of all knowledge" whereas "relativism is happy to accept local knowledge claims."[26] The Christianization of the Roman Empire and the rest of pagan Europe pushed the relativistic approach aside. It allowed for some variations in rituals and their praxis, but in essential beliefs and practices anything different was considered heretical.[27]

The view of the skeptical-relativists reappeared in new and forceful ways during the Renaissance, with the rediscovery of a wide variety of beliefs and practices of ancient times and with the discoveries of radically different cultures throughout the world. Amerigo Vespucci's (1454-1512) *Mundus Novus* (1503) and André Thevet's (1516-1590) explorations of Asia and the New World raised certain issues regarding what today is known as *ethnocentrism*.[28] In a similar way, the intellectual certainties of the medieval minds were shaken by the Reformation, which presented a challenge "to the dominance of the Catholic Church… not only in matters of faith but also increasingly in all other areas of belief."[29] The rapid development of new practices resulting from the Protestant Reformation also contributed to an emerging view of differences based on cultural factors.

Michel de Montaigne (1533-1592) and his book *Apology for Raymond Sebond* (1580), with its arsenal of Pyrrhonian skepticism, presented a panorama of human beliefs and implied that differences indicated that each set of beliefs and practices were culturally conditioned. He contended that most people's religious views resulted from custom, rather than conviction.[30] He also cited evidence from the ongoing scientific revolution – including Copernicus' heliocentric cosmology – to support relativism. Montaigne's skepticism and cultural relativism were further enhanced by the French skeptics Henri Éstienne (1528-1598) and Pierre Bayle (1647-1706). The latter insisted that a society of atheists could be more moral than a society of Christians, since moral behavior resulted from natural causes such as custom and education and not from religious doctrines. His analysis became incorporated into the Enlightenment's quest for a science of humanity that would explain why people acted, behaved and believed in different ways. In his *Commentaire philosophique*, Bayle showed, "tolerance for all religious views, even those of the heretics, and maintained that 'those who adhere to heretical doctrine sincerely and according to their conscience, are just as much worthy servants of the Lord as those who adhere to true Christian teaching.'"[31]

The major project of Cartesian rationalism was to secure the unchangeable foundations for knowledge and universal reason.

Thus it seemingly did not leave much room for relativism. The best known representative of Cartesian rationalism was its inventor René Descartes (1596-1650) who employed the Cartesian division between the subjective and objective worlds. Eventually, subjectivism was legitimized by the light of reason and thus, "once the possibility of the authority of the subjective view of individuals was accepted and given that the threat of skepticism loomed large, the way was open for subjectivism to become the only credible justification for claims to knowledge."[32]

David Hume's (1711-1776) *Natural History of Religion* (1757) initiated the study of religion as a manifestation of human behavior in which religious activity was relative to individual and cultural conditions. He also thought that "all knowledge was derived from experience and constructed through one's natural capacity to link ideas together and then align one's behavior by negotiating conventions. The resources of human nature alone, unaided by divine intervention, would suffice."[33] Therefore, it follows, for Hume, that "any book not devoted either to mathematics or to 'experimental reasoning concerning matters of fact and existence' (i.e. works of metaphysics or theology), would contain 'nothing but sophistry and illusion' and one should 'commit it then to the flames.'"[34] This relativistic aspect of religion was identified as a crucial feature of the human condition by the 18th century German philosopher Johann Gottfried Herder (1744-1803). He contended that every society or culture develops from its own unique idea and character. Elements of Herder's ideas were refined by Adolf Bastian (1826-1905) and more influentially by Edward Westermarck (1862-1939) who, in his major work *The Origin and Development of Moral Ideas* (1906), asserted that "morality was rooted not in universal principles but in culturally conditioned emotions."[35] His teaching was grounded in historical, sociological and anthropological evidence that no ethical principles are objectively valid.

Hume also discussed the issue of diversity in moral opinion. According to him, sentiments rather than reason were the universal source of morality, since "the sentiments which arise from humanity are not the same in all human creatures" nor do they "produce the same approbation or censure, etc."[36] Hume's most famous contribution to ethical thought was his argument for an unbridgeable gap between facts and value judgments. It has had a formative impact on the development of moral relativism.[37] David Bloor supports this notion, by saying, "Hume definitely identified the non-absolute (i.e., relative) character of all inductive reasoning and hence of all empirical knowledge. For this service alone, Hume might be called the Patron Saint of Relativists."[38]

The ontological dimension of Protagoras' relativism committed Immanuel Kant (1724-1804) to the view that "what appears to each individual is the only reality and therefore the real world differs for each."[39] Kant thought that "the qualities of things may be relative, private and possibly unique to each agent and consequently there is no common shared reality. What is real or exists depends on the judgment of men, nothing is constant, things are continually undergoing change and therefore everything *is* as it appears to the perceiver."[40] The relativist position was further reinforced by various theories of the natural causes for beliefs. The theories of Karl Marx (1818-1883) and Sigmund Freud (1856-1939) offered ways by which one could account for the idea that individuals and groups adhered to beliefs without considering whether or not these beliefs were true. Modern scientists began to consider whether various religious beliefs were beneficial or futile, or in the light of the historical critical method, which will be discussed later, why a particular belief arose at a certain moment in human history. In the late 20th century and to the present, it seems that relativism has become a dominant philosophical position.

Baghramian continues a contemporary discussion on relativism by stating that it comes from existing differences of attitudes and beliefs in the world. In her view, relativism's prominent place in current intellectual ethos has something to do with the rise of political ideologies, which in turn share global and universal aspirations. So what makes this doctrine so plausible, especially in modern times?

Relativism is often defined negatively – in terms of what

it denies, viz., the theses of universalism, objectivism, absolutism and monism.[41] Hilary Putnam (b. 1926), Nelson Goodman (1906-1998), Richard Rorty (1931-2007) and Jacques Derrida (1930-2004) are representatives of these forms of relativism. In addition, there are a number of different types of relativism – whether cognitive, social, conceptual, moral, aesthetic, cultural, religious, alethic (pertaining to the various modalities of truth, such as the possibility or impossibility of something being true), etc. – because they are trying to answer the dual questions: What is being relativized? and What is the context of relativization? Baghramian also presents some of the main philosophical impulses motivating relativism. She speaks of context-dependence; perspectivalism, mind-dependence, philosophical Manichaeism, the underdetermination of empirical theory by data, the collapse of old certainties, cultural diversity, the prominence of social-scientific explanations, the imperative of tolerance and alethic relativism.

Context-dependence can be a motive for relativism because "it is often argued that all our judgments and beliefs are context-sensitive in that they always take place within a social and cultural framework and a background of both personal and collective assumptions, interests and values and if not wholly determined, they are at least influenced by them."[42] Followers of this position argue that

> …beliefs are also situational, i.e., they are formed and held under specific physical and material conditions. Therefore… evaluations of judgments should include a reference to their context and background conditions. But then such evaluations themselves would be influenced by their specific historical, cultural and psychological conditions and hence no neutral ground for surveying beliefs and judgments is available.[43]

A similar view is shared by *perspectivalism*, which goes beyond mere context-dependence by arguing that the truth of one's judgments is relative to the perspective or the point of view one adopts, implying that these judgments are selective and determined by the position one occupies in time and space along with one's interests and background knowledge. This type of reasoning is often found when constructing hypotheses and represents a form of conceptual relativism. Parallel to this view would be the *underdetermination of empirical theory by data*, or the thesis that more than one theory can successfully explain a given body of data. This is a clearly scientific thesis and, if it stays within the compounds of empirical science, it is perfectly legitimate.[44] Supporters of the *mind-dependence* view argue that all of one's knowledge about reality depends on one's mind. In this view, no reality exists outside of human judgment, as Baghramian puts it in her own words, "a God's-eye view or a view from nowhere is not available to us."[45] She also clarifies, that although such anti-realism should not be equated with relativism, often it becomes the starting point for various relativistic positions.

Philosophical Manichaeism represents the assumption of various philosophical dichotomies, such as subjective versus objective, the mind versus the world, fact versus value, etc. Baghramian notes, "Modern philosophy, from Descartes to Kant to the Logical Positivists, has bequeathed a number of dualisms which, despite their absolutist overtones, have contributed greatly to the development of relativistic tendencies in contemporary thought."[46] She explores in detail most of these tendencies in her book and suggests that one of the ways to overcome some of the destructive forms of relativism is by trying to overcome the philosophical Manichaeism inspiring them.

The remaining motives for relativism arise from the philosophical currents of the late 20th century. In terms of *the collapse of old certainties*, Baghramian observes the following:

> The disappearance of old certainties in the religious, political and scientific arenas has been instrumental in the popularity of relativism in recent times. The collapse of a religiously motivated cosmology, which

fixed the position of individual human beings within a larger and immutable framework and provided firm foundations for their ethical outlook, helped to create a climate that was conductive to relativistic views. In science, the discovery of the possibility of non-Euclidean geometries, followed by developments of the early 20th century, particularly Einstein's theory of relativity and the discoveries in quantum physics eroded the confidence placed in what was considered unassailable. The disillusionment with utopian political ideologies that espoused global aspirations and the dismay experienced at the intractability of ethical and political problems also added to the attraction of relativism. As there seems to be neither a decision procedure for solving ideological conflicts nor a neutral ground to adjudicate between incompatible moral viewpoints, the only alternative appears to be either to impose our world-view on others or to grant each person or culture full and incorrigible authority over the truth and justification of her beliefs and convictions.[47]

By sharing these conclusions, Baghramian steps out of the mere philosophical sphere of treating the issue of relativism and enters the existential realm of one's being. In a sense, she follows Edmund Husserl (1859-1938) who argues, "It is not possible to relativize truth and yet maintain the objectivity of being. Clearly the relativization of truth presupposes an objective being as a point of reference and therein lays relativism's inconsistency."[48] However, it will be shown that "no single argument can be used to defeat or rescue this many-headed hydra."[49] It is also important to note that religion is the primary element related to these changes. This makes one raise the question about the Second Vatican Council and its spirit of change. Was it the Council that triggered the spirit which eventually opened the door to relativism, or was it the times which made some of the Council's members subscribe to the already existing currents of relativistic spirit and so, become its victims? This question will be addressed when considering Ratzinger's role in and his thoughts on the Council.

Cultural diversity is another contemporary and very influential motive for choosing relativism as a basic philosophical presupposition. Baghramian comments that increasing awareness of the extent of different cultures, as well as reports by anthropologists about remote peoples, suggest that all normative judgments may have only a limited or local authority. She mentions that opponents to this kind of relativism argue that the scope of diversity is often exaggerated and that beyond the apparent dissimilarities "there are many core similarities which unify all human cultures and systems of beliefs."[50] Related to the anthropological issues is the prominence of *social-scientific explanations*. Thinkers including Karl Marx, Max Weber (1864-1920) and Wilhelm Dilthey (1833-1911) introduced the idea of human beliefs and actions being related to their social, economical and historical backgrounds, which in turn determined the content of these beliefs. The differentiation and specialization of social sciences, promoted these relativistic premises even further, through the work of social anthropologists such as Ruth Benedict (1887-1948) and Margaret Mead (1901-1978), sociologists Émile Durkheim (1858-1917) and Talcott Parsons (1902-1979) and hermeneutic philosophers, such as Hans-Georg Gadamer (1900-2002).

The imperative of tolerance promotes liberation from oppressive, dominant, and often political powers from those who feel excluded or alienated by them – the young, racial minorities, feminists, the political left, etc. Those sympathetic toward relativism argue that "Western ethnocentrism and the intellectual legacy of the Enlightenment prevent us from appreciating or even seeing the uniqueness of different cultures and modes of thought and respecting the legitimacy of their epistemic and ethical claims."[51] The following quote, by Allan Bloom (1930-1992), expresses the somewhat ironic sentiments opposing this view:

> Openness – and the relativism that makes it the only
> plausible stance in the face of various claims to truth

and various ways of life and kinds of human beings – is [treated as] the great insight of our times…. The study of history and of culture [according to this view] teaches that all the world was mad in the past; men always thought they were right and that led to wars, persecutions, slavery, xenophobia, racism and chauvinism. The point is not to correct the mistakes and really be right; rather it is not to think you are right at all.[52]

Another impactful form is *alethic relativism*. According to this type of relativism, truth is dependent upon varying belief systems and attitudes of individuals and their corresponding social, political and cultural background. Alethic relativism is "central to many relativistic positions since the arguments for various subdivisions of cognitive relativism and even ethical relativism, can be recast as a question about the truth of judgments in those particular domains."[53] Plato argued against relativism being a self-refutation of truth, "for if 'truth is relative' it itself is true unconditionally, then there is at least one truth, which is not relative and hence relativism is not true."[54] In other words, "in order for relativism to be an intelligent doctrine, it should exclude non-relativistic doctrines, but to do so would be tantamount to the denial of the truth of relativism."[55]

This work has presented a number of definitions and causes for relativism, but it will focus primarily on the analysis of Ratzinger's thoughts on relativism and its relationship to the Catholic faith.

3. Scripture and Magisterium on Relativism

Though there is no explicit mention of relativism in Scripture, some references might be understood as warning against this phenomenon. Pope John Paul II begins his encyclical *Veritatis Splendor* with a reference to Genesis 1:26: "The splendor of truth shines forth in all the works of the Creator and, in a special way, in man, created in the image and likeness of God."[56] In the Book of Wisdom, there is a reference to the unjust, who decide for themselves: "Let our strength be our norm of justice; for weakness proves itself useless" (2:11). If relativism teaches that there cannot be any absolutes on which to ground one's knowledge, the pericopes about the Two Foundations, found in Luke (6:46-49) and in Matthew (7:21-27) may be seen as providing a different view. The true foundation of one's life, or *house*, must be dug deep with the foundation laid on rock, not sand, in order to overcome the storms and the floods of life. The instability of relativism as a *shifting sand* is often used in the documents of the Holy See.[57]

That same theme might be found in St. Paul's writings, especially in his Letter to the Ephesians. In Eph 4:14, Paul speaks of the maturity of faith, "so that we may no longer be infants, tossed by waves and swept along by every wind of teaching arising from human trickery, from their cunning in the interest of deceitful scheming." In fact, he calls the believers to live the truth in love, growing in every way into him who is the head – Christ. The theme of a relativistic wind arises in the Book of Sirach (5:11-12) who exhorts, "winnow not in every wind and start not in every direction. Be consistent in your thoughts; steadfast be your words." This theme also appears in the Book of Wisdom, when speaking of the unjust, "for even though their branches flourish for a time, they are unsteady and shall be rocked by the wind and by the violence of the winds, uprooted" (4:5). In his Letter to the Colossians (2:4-8), St. Paul warns his brothers and sisters in Christ not to be deceived by specious arguments or "empty, seductive philosophy, according to human tradition, according to the elemental powers of the world and not according to Christ." In Romans 12:2 St. Paul talks about the "patterns of the world" or *Zeitgeist* as it was translated in German theology, where the apostle is warning about not conforming oneself to the spirit of the age. Paul also cautions the young bishop Timothy, "The time will come when people will not tolerate sound doctrine but, following their own desires and insatiable curiosity, will accumulate teachers and will stop listening to the truth and will be diverted to myths" (2 Tm 4:3-4).

It is clear that relativism is essentially related to the question of truth. Therefore, in his First Letter, the Apostle Peter speaks about being purified by "obedience to the truth" (1 P 1:22), which in turn means the truth coming from God in Jesus Christ. The question "What is truth?" was famously raised by Pontius Pilate (Jn 18:38). However, the response was already given by Jesus, earlier to his disciples, when he clearly states: "I am the way and the truth and the life" (Jn 14:6). Nevertheless, men are always tempted by the "liar and the father of lies" (Jn 8:44), the devil, who, as Jesus tells us, "does not stand in truth, because there is no truth in him" (Jn 8:44). Therefore, St. Paul declares, a man is constantly tempted to replace the true living God with idols (cf. 1 Th 1:9) and exchange "the truth about God for a lie" (Rm 1:25).

There are numerous doctrinal pronouncements on the issue of relativism. Maurice Schepers mentions three forms under which relativism is present in theology: historical relativism,[58] immanentism and evolutionism. Consequently, all three had to be addressed and have been opposed by the Magisterium. However, the major type of theological relativism arises from the above-mentioned three forms and constitutes what is known as moral relativism.[59] With this form of relativism, the moral code of Christianity "varies in relation to the circumstances of the age, the degree of penetration achieved by man into the religious psyche, or the stage of progress the human race has reached."[60]

The early dogmatic pronouncements against relativism can be detected in Pope Pius X's decree against modernism *Lamentabili* and the encyclical *Pascendi* (1907) and finally, the *oath against Modernism* (1910). Pope Pius XII explicitly used the term relativism in his encyclical *Humani Generis* (1950) and it was in that work where he commented on contemporary philosophical trends which affected one's theology. He described those who argue that Christian dogma must employ modern philosophy as follows:

Some more audacious affirm that this can and must be done, because they hold that the mysteries of faith are never expressed by truly adequate concepts but only by approximate and ever-changeable notions, in which the truth is to some extent expressed, but is necessarily distorted. Wherefore they do not consider it absurd, but altogether necessary, that theology should substitute new concepts in place of the old ones in keeping with the various philosophies which in the course of time it uses as its instruments, so that it should give human expression to divine truths in various ways which are even somewhat opposed, but still equivalent as they say. They add that the history of dogmas consists in the reporting of the various forms in which revealed truth has been clothed, forms that have succeeded one another in accordance with the different teachings and opinions that have arisen over the course of the centuries (15).[61]

Such argumentation, Pius XII responds, undoubtedly leads into what he calls *dogmatic relativism*:

It is evident from what we have already said, that such tentatives not only lead to what they call dogmatic relativism, but that they actually contain it. The contempt of doctrine commonly taught and of the terms in which it is expressed strongly favors it. Everyone is aware that the terminology employed in the schools and even that used by the Teaching Authority of the Church itself is capable of being perfected and polished; and we know also that the Church itself has not always used the same terms in the same way. It is also manifest that the Church cannot be bound to every system of philosophy that has existed for a short space of time. Nevertheless, the things that have been composed through common effort by Catholic teachers over the course of the centuries to bring about some understanding of dogma are certainly not based on any such weak foundation. These things are based on principles and notions deduced from a true knowledge of created things. In the process of deducing, this knowledge, like a star, gave enlightenment to the human mind through the Church. Hence it is not astonishing that some of these notions have not only been used by the Ecumenical Councils, but even sanctioned by them, so that it is wrong to depart from them.[62]

Pope Paul VI in his encyclical letter *Ecclesiam Suam* (1964) speaks of *false philosophies*. Among them, he mentions, "relativism, too, seeks to justify everything and treats all things as of equal value. It assails the absolute character of Christian principles."[63] However, the Holy Father also raised a crucial contemporary question, asking how the Church can adapt its mission to the particular age, environment, educational and social conditions of the day. He questioned as to how the Church would be best able to fulfill its mission:

> To what extent should the Church adapt itself to the historical and local circumstances in which it has to exercise its mission? How is it to guard against the danger of relativism which would make it untrue to its own dogmas and moral principles? And yet how can it fit itself to approach all men and bring salvation to all, becoming on the example of the Apostle Paul "all things to all men," that all may be saved?[64]

Pope John Paul II blamed religious relativism as the cause for lack of interest in missionary work. Quoting his great predecessor Pope Paul VI,[65] the Holy Father pointed out that a serious reason for the lack of interest in missionary tasks was that there existed widespread indifferentism – even among Christians – based on "incorrect theological perspectives and characterized by a religious relativism, which leads to the belief that 'one religion is as good as another.'"[66]

A year later, Pope John Paul II mentioned relativism in his encyclical *Centesimus annus* (1991) where he argued against those who claim that "agnosticism and skeptical relativism are the philosophy and the basic attitude which correspond to democratic forms of political life."[67] Even more so, observed the Holy Father, "those who are convinced that they know the truth and firmly adhere to it are considered unreliable from a democratic point of view, since they do not accept that truth is determined by the majority, or that it is subject to variation according to different political trends."[68] The Holy Father continues that, "If there is no ultimate truth to guide and direct political activity, then ideas and convictions can easily be manipulated for reasons of power. As history demonstrates, a democracy without values easily turns into an open or thinly disguised totalitarianism."[69] In his own reflections on the papal encyclical *Fides et Ratio* Cardinal Ratzinger reacted to the critique of it which came from the Italian philosopher Paolo Flores d'Arcais. The latter accused the dogmatic tone of papal encyclicals as having *murderous consequences for democracy* and identified the Pope's teachings with the *fundamentalist* version of Islam.[70] To this Ratzinger responds by arguing:

> …such assertions assume that there can be no appeal from the decisions of a majority. The chance occurrence of a majority becomes absolute. For there is still such a thing as something absolute, beyond which there is no appeal. We have been handed over to the rule of positivism and of the erection of what is accidental, what can indeed be manipulated, into an absolute value. When man is shut out from the truth, he can only be dominated by what is accidental and arbitrary. That is why it is not "fundamentalism" but a duty of humanity to protect man from the dictatorship of what is accidental and to restore to him his dignity, which consists precisely in the fact that no human institution can ultimately dominate him, because he is open to the truth.[71]

A few years later, Ratzinger repeated these same thoughts in his now renowned homily *Pro Eligendo Romano Pontifice.*

In the encyclical *Veritatis Splendor* (1993), Pope John Paul II continued to speak out against relativism and its effects on the moral and ethical aspects of one's faith. It is because of original sin that "man's capacity to know the truth is also darkened and his will to submit to it is weakened. Thus, giving himself over to relativism and skepticism (cf. Jn 18:38), he goes off in search of an illusory freedom apart from truth itself."[72] This need of having a correct relationship between freedom and human nature insists that

> ...the human person cannot be reduced to a freedom which is self-designing, but entails a particular spiritual and bodily structure, the primordial moral requirement of loving and respecting the person as an end and never as a mere means also implies, by its very nature, respect for certain fundamental goods, without which one would fall into relativism and arbitrariness.[73]

The Holy Father concludes that, ultimately, the fundamental question about human freedom and God's instituted natural law is the question of the relationship between freedom and truth. This is why he writes: "According to Christian faith and the Church's teaching, only the freedom which submits to the Truth leads the human person to his true good. The good of the person is to be in the Truth and to *do* the Truth."[74] In the following quote, the character and the effects of moral relativism are highlighted even more clearly:

> A comparison between the Church's teaching and today's social and cultural situation immediately makes clear the urgent need *for the Church herself to develop an intense pastoral effort precisely with regard to this fundamental question.* This essential bond between Truth, the Good and Freedom has been largely lost sight of

by present-day culture. As a result, helping man to rediscover it represents nowadays one of the specific requirements of the Church's mission, for the salvation of the world. Pilate's question, "What is truth?" reflects the distressing perplexity of a man who often no longer knows *who he is, whence* he comes and *where* he is going. Hence, we not infrequently witness the fearful plunging of the human person into situations of gradual self-destruction. According to some, it appears that one no longer need acknowledge the enduring absoluteness of any moral value. All around us we encounter contempt for human life after conception and before birth; the ongoing violation of basic rights of the person; the unjust destruction of goods minimally necessary for a human life. Indeed, something more serious has happened: man is no longer convinced that only in the truth can he find salvation. The saving power of the truth is contested and freedom alone, uprooted from any objectivity, is left to decide by itself what is good and what is evil. This relativism becomes, in the field of theology, a lack of trust in the wisdom of God, who guides man with the moral law. Concrete situations are unfavorably contrasted with the precepts of the moral law, nor is it any longer maintained that, when all is said and done, the law of God is always the one true good of man [emphasis in original].[75]

There is also the danger of trying to protect fundamental human rights by political means alone, disregarding the religious source. Pope John Paul II continues in the encyclical by stating: *"The risk of an alliance between democracy and ethical relativism* would remove any sure moral reference point from political and social life and on a deeper level make the acknowledgment of truth impossible" [emphasis in original].[76]

The danger of moral relativism on the value and inviolability of human life was expressed in his encyclical *Evangelium Vitae*

(1995). The major precondition for this relativism was society, which changed the understanding of human freedom by granting the maximum possible amount of freedom to each individual, whereby leaving out the objective responsibility of freedom toward one another. In this case, a great number of individuals are allowed to exercise their freedom to its maximum; but at the same time, the limits of this freedom will inevitably lead to a clash of one individual with another. Therefore, "any reference to common values and to a truth absolutely binding on everyone is lost and social life ventures on to the shifting sands of complete relativism. At that point, everything is negotiable; everything is open to bargaining, even the first of the fundamental rights, the right to life."[77] The saddest part, according to the pope, is that this process of relativization is already happening at the level of politics and government in the name of democracy, which as he says:

> ...the original and inalienable right to life is questioned or denied on the basis of a parliamentary vote or the will of one part of the people – even if it is the majority. This is the sinister result of a relativism which reigns unopposed: the "right" ceases to be such, because it is no longer firmly founded on the inviolable dignity of the person but is made subject to the will of the stronger part. In this way democracy, contradicting its own principles effectively moves towards a form of totalitarianism.[78]

The idea that raises the most concern is that, at the basis of this contemporary understanding of democracy lies ethical relativism and there are those who consider it an essential condition for democracy.[79] Pope John Paul II states that these people dangerously think ethical relativism "alone is held to guarantee tolerance, mutual respect between people and acceptance of the decisions of the majority, whereas moral norms considered to be objective and binding are held to lead to authoritarianism and intolerance."[80] This raises an important question on the true meaning and role of democracy which, if it remains unaccountable, will bring devastating consequences to societies. John Paul II himself states the situation as follows:

> Democracy cannot be idolized to the point of making it a substitute for morality or a panacea for immorality. Fundamentally, democracy is a "system" and as such is a means and not an end. Its "moral" value is not automatic, but depends on conformity to the moral law to which it, like every other form of human behavior, must be subject: in other words, its morality depends on the morality of the ends which it pursues and of the means which it employs.[81]

Therefore, a democracy needs to be founded on moral and objective values, such as the dignity of every human person, the respect for inviolable and inalienable human rights, and the promotion of the *common good*.[82] The basis of these values cannot be "provisional and changeable 'majority' opinions, but only the acknowledgment of an objective moral law which, as the 'natural law' written in the human heart, is the obligatory point of reference for civil law itself."[83] Otherwise, the pope warns, if an attitude of moral relativism and skepticism were to succeed, the democratic system would be shaken at its foundations and at its best, reduced to a means of deciding different empirical interests. The problem with this type of *mechanism* would be, according to Pope John Paul II, "even in participatory systems of government, the regulation of interests often occurring to the advantage of the most powerful, since they are the ones most capable of maneuvering not only the levers of power, but also of shaping the formation of consensus."[84] Additionally, in such a situation, the pope concludes, democracy would easily become an empty word.

Moreover, he says in his apostolic letter *Tertio Millenio Adveniente* (1994), even among the Christians the spiritual life is passing through what he calls *a time of uncertainty*, which in turn affects not only their moral and spiritual life but also the theological correctness of their faith. In John Paul's view, the crisis of faith is also seen in the "crisis of obedience vis-à-vis the Church's Magisterium."[85] The teachings of this and previous papal documents provided the basis for reiterating and expanding the principles of Catholic social doctrine in a *Compendium of the Social Doctrine of the Church* (2004), where among the issues already discussed, the question of love is also observed as being affected by relativism. In illustration, article 223 states:

> *The human being is made for love and cannot live without love.* When it is manifested as the total gift of two persons in their complementarities, love cannot be reduced to emotions or feelings, much less to mere sexual expression. In a society that tends more and more to relativize and trivialize the very experience of love and sexuality, exalting its fleeting aspects and obscuring its fundamental values, it is more urgent than ever to proclaim and bear witness that *the truth* of conjugal love and sexuality exist where there is a full and total gift of persons, with the characteristics of *unity* and *fidelity*. This truth, a source of joy, hope and life, remains impenetrable and unattainable as long as people close themselves off in relativism and skepticism [emphasis in original].[86]

The Church sees relativism as already present in almost all areas of contemporary life. For example, in the year 2000 the Pontifical Council of Social Communication issued a document in which it pointed out the media's role in promoting relativism. It said, "Often, the media popularize the ethical relativism and utilitarianism that underlie today's culture of death. They participate in the contemporary 'conspiracy against life.'"[87] Two years later, the same Council issued another document where it described the internet as having a potential for both good and evil, which required the Church to call for prudence, as well as for fortitude and courage and to stand up for "truth, in the face of religious and moral relativism, for altruism and generosity in the face of individualistic consumerism, for decency in the face of sensuality and sin."[88]

Relativism also affects the educational system. As early as 1977, the Sacred Congregation for Catholic Education stated, "Cultural pluralism leads the Church to reaffirm her mission of education to insure strong character formation. Her children, then, will be capable both of resisting the debilitating influence of relativism and of living up to the demands made on them by their Baptism."[89] The challenges in contemporary society were well described by the same Vatican Congregation:

> On the threshold of the third millennium education faces new challenges which are the result of a new socio-political and cultural context. First and foremost, we have a crisis of values which, in highly developed societies in particular, assumes the form, often exalted by the media, of subjectivism, moral relativism and nihilism. The extreme pluralism pervading contemporary society leads to behavior patterns, which are at times so opposed to one another as to undermine any idea of community identity. Rapid structural changes, profound technical innovations and the globalization of the economy affect human life more and more throughout the world.... The phenomena of multiculturalism and an increasingly multi-ethnic and multi-religious society are at the same time a source of enrichment and a source of further problems. To this we must add, in countries of long-standing evangelization, a growing marginalization of the Christian faith as a reference point and a source of light for an effective and convincing interpretation of existence.[90]

The other two very important doctrinal pronouncements concerning the issue of relativism were John Paul's II encyclical

Fides et Ratio (1998) and the declaration *Dominus Iesus* written by the Congregation for the Doctrine of Faith in 2000. These two documents were directly influenced by Cardinal Ratzinger and will be further discussed in the context of his thoughts and writings. From the above-mentioned references and documents, one can see, the Catholic Church has always been aware of the dangers that relativism might present. This will be expanded further in the following chapters, where the life and work of one of the greatest theologians of modern times – Cardinal Joseph Ratzinger, now Pope Benedict XVI – will be addressed.

2

RATZINGER'S BIOGRAPHICAL BACKGROUND AND HIS EARLY OPPOSITION TO RELATIVISM

1. National Socialism and *Der gerade Weg*

Joseph Alois Ratzinger was born on Holy Saturday, April 16, 1927 in the little town of Marktl am Inn, in the Bavarian diocese of Passau, in southern Germany. He was the third child born to Joseph and Maria, after siblings Georg and Maria, and was baptized on that same day with the newly blessed baptismal water. Ratzinger considered his birth and baptism providential in that it "seems to be fitting for the nature of one's human life, we are still awaiting Easter; we are not yet standing in the full light, but walking toward it full of trust."[91] It was with this kind of faith and trust that Ratzinger lived his entire life.

As was earlier noted by Baghramian, relativism is somehow connected to the rise of totalitarianism. Therefore, one cannot write about Ratzinger without mentioning the political climate of his youth. The Nazi party was rising to power with promises of a Third Reich. Nichols wrote, "In Bavaria, the political climate at the time of Hitler's coming to power was fervently anti-Marxist and particularist," however, "the favor which the Catholic lower middle class bestowed on the Nazis in early 1933 soon drained

25

away."[92] Ratzinger remembers how his father Joseph, a police commissioner, used to take a position against the violence of the Nazis in public meetings. He had subscribed to *Der gerade Weg*, an anti-Nazi newspaper, where Ratzinger remembers the caricatures of Hitler and the *fits of rage* his father would have reading it. Joseph Ratzinger's outspokenness even forced the family to relocate.[93] Moreover, Ratzinger speaks of his father as very well reasoned in his arguments and deliberate, *a reflective believer*, who "always understood clearly at the outset what was going on and always had an astonishingly accurate judgment."[94] Ratzinger recalls:

> My father, even if he had little formal education, was a person who, intellectually speaking, was absolutely superior, of great superiority even in comparison with academics. He had his convictions, which he deepened through study, of course. He was a great Bavarian patriot. That is, he did not willingly accept Bismarck's empire and the incorporation of Bavaria into Prussianized Germany. And one must say that there were always, or for some time, these two currents in Bavaria: one reconciled with this idea of a unified Germany, and the other that did not accept this idea and thought rather in the context of ancient history, back before the French Revolution. They identified with the Holy Roman Empire, that is, with the ideals of friendship or close relations with Austria, and also with France. And my father was oriented this way; above all he was a committed Catholic, and therefore he had a position which was very clear against nationalism. His arguments were so well founded that he simply convinced us.[95]

It was his father's *inner honesty* which, Ratzinger recalls, allowed him to possess an effortless power to convince. This was something his son eventually inherited himself.

Another one of Ratzinger's early memories of Nazism was

the example of a young teacher who, filled with enthusiasm and new ideas, tried to revitalize Germanic culture by bringing back some ancient pagan rituals. He believed that it was Judaism and Christianity which alienated Germans from their own great culture.[96] Ratzinger remembered this from his past as he reflected on the present, "When nowadays I hear how in many parts of the world Christianity is criticized as a destruction of individual cultural identity and an imposition of European values, I am amazed at how similar the types of argumentation are and at how familiar many a turn of phrase sounds."[97] One need only recall the controversy which arose over the European Constitution's mentioning of Christian roots in its text.[98]

One more important biographical note, which sheds light on Ratzinger's later theology, is the incident he recalls about his cousin's death. Allen reports:

> The brutality of the Nazi regime once touched the Ratzinger family personally. A cousin with Downs' syndrome who in 1941 was fourteen years old, just a few months younger than Ratzinger himself, was taken away in that year by the Nazi authorities for "therapy." Not long afterwards, the family received word that he was dead, presumably one of the "undesirables" eliminated during that time.[99]

Nichols writes that "ranging from the enforced closure of monasteries to the removal of crucifixes from schools, its gravest crisis concerned a Nazi attack at the heart of Christian teaching on the sanctity of innocent life, the 'euthanasia action' which accounted for the deaths of more than 70,000 mentally and physically handicapped persons."[100] That explains Ratzinger's preoccupation with the issue of euthanasia and with the value of the life of any human being, especially those seen as useless by the reigning ideology or government.

When Ratzinger's father retired from police work at the age of 60, the family moved to Hufschlag, outside the city of

Traunstein. It was here that Joseph began his studies of the classical languages at a *Gymnasium*. He had no difficulty studying or conversing in Greek or Latin and noticed that his most esteemed teachers showed little interest in supporting the new ideas of the time. He wrote, "In retrospect, it seems to me an education on Greek and Latin antiquity created a mental attitude that resisted seduction by a totalitarian ideology."[101] However, this did not last long, for the educational model soon changed. As Ratzinger explained it, the humanistic *Gymnasium* and the scientific school, which previously existed side by side as two separate institutions, were blended into a new type of school. As a consequence, Greek disappeared, the teaching of Latin diminished and a greater focus was given to the natural sciences. Of course, religion lost its place and was replaced by physical education and sports that were torturous for him as Ratzinger recalled. All of this, he remembers, came at a great loss, since this new type of school with its new generation of teachers was more in step with the New Regime and lacked the integral knowledge of antiquity and its texts. It was in Traunstein that Ratzinger first experienced the horrors of the Third Reich. In the Stadtplatz, the central square of the town, signs were put up calling for a boycott of Jewish businesses. The night of November 9, 1938 became known as *Kristallnacht*, the night of broken glass, when the Nazis initiated the systematic destruction of Jewish-owned property and businesses throughout Germany, arresting approximately twenty thousand Jews, destroying 180 synagogues and murdering an estimated ninety-one Jews.[102]

In 1939, Joseph Ratzinger entered the minor seminary in Traunstein where his older brother Georg was already studying. Even though he preferred the freedom and quiet of his individual studies, there was a positive side to this seminary experience in that he "had to learn how to fit into the group, how to come out of my solitary ways and start building a community with others by giving and by receiving."[103] Another community learning experience occurred when Ratzinger, then being just sixteen years of age, was drafted into the Munich anti-aircraft corps. He remembers that time as a fascinating experience, especially for those like him who came from the small provincial areas into the big city with its multitude of cultural offerings.

In 1944, upon reaching military age, Ratzinger was called into military service. He was drafted into labor detail under the infamous Austrian Legion. It was a time of oppression for him. On one occasion, he was about to be recruited for the SS, but that was terminated after he expressed his wish to become a Roman Catholic priest. This made him and his friends objects of great ridicule. They were to perform the *cult of the spade* ritual, which for the Nazis was a cult of work as a way to redemption. Ratzinger called it a *pseudo-liturgy* which actually ended after Hungary, an ally of Germany, surrendered to the Russians. It was precisely "this fall of the spade from cultic object to banal tool for everyday use that allowed us to perceive the deeper collapse taking place.... A full-scale liturgy and the world behind it were being unmasked as a lie."[104] It was "a world disfigured by ideology and hatred," which before it collapsed, still made its young recruits, like Ratzinger, "march through Traunstein singing war songs, perhaps in order to show the civilian population that the Führer still had young and freshly trained soldiers at his disposal."[105] He had deserted the German troops in the last days of war. However, when the Americans arrived in the spring of 1945, Ratzinger was identified as a soldier and was sent off to a prisoner-of-war camp near Ulm.[106] In the midst of this world in ruins he would look at the majestic contours of the Ulm cathedral and find it as a consoling proclamation of the indestructible humaneness of faith.[107]

In November of 1945, Ratzinger, together with his brother Georg, reentered the seminary. A great sense of gratitude for a chance at a new life, after all the horrors and wounds of war went through the entire seminary community of 120 men. Once again, Ratzinger ascribes this sense of gratitude and hope to the strength of faith preserved in the Church:

> This gratitude now created a common will to make
> up finally for everything we had neglected and to

serve Christ in his Church for new and better times, for a better Germany and for a better world. No one doubted that the Church was the locus of all our hopes. Despite many human failings, the Church was the alternative to the destructive ideology of the brown rulers; in the inferno that had swallowed up the powerful, she had stood firm with a force coming to her from eternity. It had been demonstrated, the gates of hell will not overpower her. From our own experience we now knew what was meant by "the gates of hell" and we could also see with our own eyes that the house built on rock had stood firm.[108]

2. Cardinal Faulhaber, Josef Stelzle and Alfred Delp

Out of his many different seminary experiences, Ratzinger most fondly remembers the hours of silent prayer in the house chapel and the great liturgical celebrations in the cathedral, where he was deeply impressed by the grand and venerable figure of Cardinal Faulhaber. He remembered Faulhaber even from his childhood: "When later Cardinal Faulhaber paid a visit to our region, with his imposing purple, he impressed me all the more, so that I said I would like to become something like that."[109] Cardinal Michael von Faulhaber was born in 1869, in Heidenfeld, the Lower Franconia region of Bavaria and died in 1952, in Munich. He was educated in Rome and was ordained to the priesthood in 1892. After obtaining his doctorate at the University of Würzburg, he taught for a while in Würzburg and from 1903 to 1911 was a professor of Old Testament studies at the University of Strasbourg, until he was named bishop of Speyer. In 1917 Bishop Faulhaber was transferred to the archdiocese of Munich and after four years created a cardinal.

During the first years of the rule of the Third Reich in Germany, it seemed that in Hitler the Catholic Church found a powerful supporter against the perils of Bolshevism. But Cardinal Faulhaber, already in 1938, preached against Hitler in his sermon to commemorate the sixteenth anniversary of Pius XI's election to the papacy. In his sermon he posed the following question concerning an inner similarity between Bolshevism and Nazism: "'As opposed as fire and water' could both be enemies of the Church and, at the same time, be strikingly similar in the methods they employ?"[110] Aside from his continuous efforts to oppose Nazism, starting with the Advent sermons in 1933, his other great deeds were related to his efforts to attack anti-Semitism which were grounded in his understanding of the Jewish background of Christianity. In 1934, a book of these sermons[111] emphasized the Jewish background of Christianity and that "the German tribes had become civilized only after Christianization and asserted that Christian values were fundamental to German culture."[112] Moreover, there are references to Cardinal Faulhaber "as recalled by the woman active in the 'underground railroad' engaged in spiriting Jews into Switzerland... [that he] was generous in his financial contributions to that work."[113] This should not come as a surprise, knowing that Faulhaber had been a professor of the Old Testament and a member of a group called *Amici Israel*, dedicated to fighting anti-Semitism within and outside the Church since 1923. The most vivid example of his respect for the Jewish roots of Christianity would be his bishop's coat of arms, with a menorah on it.[114] Because of his sermons, Cardinal Faulhaber was "publicly and persistently denounced by the Nazis as a political reactionary disloyal to Germany."[115] Ratzinger, speaking of Cardinal Faulhaber in those years, recalls, "you could practically touch the burden of suffering he had to bear during the Nazi period, which now enveloped him with an aura of dignity," but he adds, "what moved me most deeply about him was the awe-inspiring grandeur of his mission, with which he had become fully identified."[116] That sense of identifying with the great mission will prove to be for Ratzinger a major aspect on his own theology of the priesthood.

Ratzinger also recalled the actions taken by the German

bishops. In order to safeguard the existing system of parochial schools, they would issue pastoral letters. He remembers that even then, as he listened to them, it occurred to him that such insistence on preserving institutions was a misreading of reality. What was needed, he thought, were people who would support those institutions from inner conviction and not because of the long tradition of having priests in charge of school inspections. Ratzinger concluded and it has remained his basic lifelong conviction that "it was inane to insist on an institutionally guaranteed Christianity."[117]

Nevertheless, he argues, it was the Catholic Church which strongly opposed the new regime. In 1977, newly appointed Archbishop Ratzinger wrote a response to Hans Küng's book *On Being a Christian*.[118] Küng wrote that during the Nazi years in Germany, a new understanding of the Church developed in both Protestant and Catholic circles. Seemingly, he was charging the episcopate of both sides as being collaborators with the new regime. For the purposes of this work, here is a response that Ratzinger gave in regard to the position of the Catholic Church at the time:

> As far as the Catholic episcopate is concerned, a preliminary but not unimportant task would be to indicate the countless clear judgments given, from Cardinal Faulhaber's famous Advent sermons in December 1933 to the sermons of Bishop von Galen during the war; between these two came the encyclical of Pius XI *Mit brennender Sorge*, the text of which was prepared by Cardinal Faulhaber – all statements which were understood very well by both the Nazis and the faithful and which meant concentration camp for a number of priests and brought practically all of them into conflict with the organs of the State.[119]

Ratzinger further pointed out that the theology of most of the Protestant churches at the time was doctrinally weak and liberally rationalistic, and thus more open to the domination of the new ideology. This eventually created a *German-Christian* movement, of which Ratzinger commented:

> But at a deeper level it must be said that the problem to which the Synod of Barmen and the resulting Confessing Church responded – namely the rise of the "German Christians" who turned Church and Creed to political ends and had begun to make them instruments of Antichrist – could not enter the Catholic sphere in the same manner because the integrity of dogma and its anchoring in a Catholicity concretized in the Pope excluded the possibility of manipulating the Church in that way.[120]

In September of 1947, Ratzinger entered the *Herzögliches Georgianum*, a theological institute associated with the University of Munich. It was here that he was hoping some day to dedicate himself completely to theology as a profession.[121] After the war, Munich's theological faculty had to be reconstituted anew, since it had been abolished by the Nazis in 1938, but "Cardinal Faulhaber refused to give his approval to a professor who was known to be a Hitler sympathizer and whom the authorities wanted to install in the chair for canon law."[122] Again, Ratzinger noticed and admired how this leader of the Church stood firm in his convictions against the Nazi regime.

Nor was Cardinal Faulhaber the only example of Church opposition to the Nazi regime. In Ratzinger's life, there were a number of other, more personal, examples. One of them was Father Josef Stelzle, Traunstein's pastor, where Ratzinger's family moved in 1937. Father Stelzle preached a sermon openly criticizing the National Socialist Party which led to his arrest as well; moreover "a bomb exploded outside the rectory."[123] Eventually he was released and came back to Traunstein, remaining a continual thorn in the flesh for the regime. He providentially survived the war and died in 1947. The local youth, and one may suspect the young Ratzinger, also heard Father Stelzle's sermon, where he told the youth in his parish that their "priorities should be Church first, family second and the State third."[124]

The young priest Ratzinger became acquainted with the stories of two other priests, those of Fathers Alfred Delp and Hermann Joseph Wehrle, both Jesuits. For ten months he lived and served as a chaplain in the parish of Holy Blood in Bogenhausen on the eastern side of Munich where these priests had also served as ministers.[125] Both priests were executed after being accused of supporting the *Putsch* of July 20, 1944, the famous assassination attempt against Hitler. As for Father Wehrle, his only *fault* was that he had been the confessor of Ludwig Freiherr von Leonrod, a member of the parish who was one of the conspirators. Mary Alice Gallin, in her book, cites a special army report of the trial in which Father Wehrle was questioned about the response he gave to Major Leonrod who "had gone to ask if it would be a sin not to reveal knowledge of a plot against the Fuehrer's life."[126] In order to give this type of response, a priest told the court, he consulted the *Lexikon für Theologie und Kirche*[127] on the subject of "Tyrannenmord" – "Tyrannicide" – and after reading it, concluded that keeping the plot a secret was not a sin. However, he warned Leonrod not to take part. Later, when asked in court if Hitler was a tyrant, he responded in the affirmative.[128]

In comparison to Wehrle, Father Alfred Delp had a more extended history of his opposition to the Third Reich. He was born in 1907. A convert to the Catholic faith, he became a Jesuit in 1926. It is said that Delp was "unique among the priesthood… in believing that it was a part of his duty to help to plan for the political future of the country."[129] For that reason, he joined the group of the primarily conservative *Kreisau Circle*, gathered around Count Helmuth von Moltke, a connection that, because of the *Circle's* involvement with the assassination, caused Father Delp to lose his life. He was executed in February of 1945. In 1940, Moltke gave Delp a task, which he accepted, namely to draw up plans for the postwar social order which he wanted to establish on Christian principles. At the time, Delp also was on the staff of the Jesuit journal *Stimmen der Zeit*. Eventually the accusation was made that the Jesuits were *a priori* the enemies of the Reich.[130] Aside from the book he wrote about the Church's universal mission, called *Humanity and History*, Father Delp left another very strong testimony, namely the meditations composed between the time of his arrest and his death, later called *Im Angesicht des Todes* published in 1947.[131] It would be very natural for Ratzinger to have read this book which could have influenced him in his later thoughts as Pursell suggests:

> "Man, created in the image and likeness of God, is at the center of history," Delp wrote, while the Nazi idea of truth being contingent on nationalism, race and individual will was simply false. Views similar to these appeared repeatedly in Joseph Ratzinger's writings over the next half century.... Also from Delp, Ratzinger took special note of a certain saying, "Bread is important, freedom is more important, but most important is unfailing worship." The Church is, first and foremost, neither a charitable institution, nor a proponent for social and political justice around the world, but a community of prayer. Given this fact, whenever and wherever she neglects her worship, even for the sake of concentrating on other, socially relevant activities, she will eventually falter in all.[132]

Certainly, Cardinal Faulhaber, Alfred Delp and Hermann Joseph Wehrle were not the only ones, who as members of the Roman Catholic Church in Germany conflicted with the Third Reich. The real extent of such resistance to Hitler is difficult to measure, but according to most estimates, approximately 5,000 clergy members were sent to German concentration camps where more than 2,000 of them died.[133] From early on in life, Ratzinger knew what totalitarianism looked like and reflected upon the conditions which would bring it about.

3. The Munich School and Ignaz von Döllinger

In order to shed light on Ratzinger's insistence to preserve a historical perspective as a way to oppose relativism, the background of his relationship with the *Munich School* should not be overlooked. At the University of Munich, Ratzinger encountered this old and well-defined tradition. At the end of the 19th century, according to Nichols, the Munich School had shifted its focus from metaphysics and mysticism to a more historical approach to scholarship.[134] This was not an accidental feature, knowing its history. The University itself is an autonomous Bavarian institution of medieval origin, first established in Ingolstadt in 1471 and in 1826 moved to Munich. It counted among its professors some of the most outstanding scholars of its day. Among them was Johann Georg Turmair (1477-1534), also known as Aventinus, whose *Annales Baiorum* (1521) became the first major work of history in the German language. During the Reformation, the university strove to preserve its orthodoxy in the person of Johann Maier-Eck (1486-1543), who became the foremost opponent of Martin Luther (1483-1546) and who, during the Counter Reformation, "succeeded in making Ingolstadt a stronghold of Catholicism in southern Germany just as Wittenberg was the center of Lutheranism in the North."[135] Another renowned scholar was Jesuit theologian, St. Peter Canisius, SJ (1521-1597), a Doctor of the Church and the author of the first Catholic catechism in the German language (1556).

In 1826, the university moved to Munich and Johannes Döllinger, a Roman Catholic priest, was appointed to the chair of Church history. Döllinger was gifted with a phenomenal memory and linguistic ability, and his erudition was vast. His choice of a diverse selection of courses such as history, philosophy, philology, natural sciences with a specialization in botany, mineralogy and entomology in the University of Würzburg, was "undoubtedly also an expression of intellectual gluttony."[136] His key-expressions were *organic growth* and *consistent development*. Not surprisingly, the concept of tradition played a vital role in his work as it did in the more systematic theological constructions of the Catholic Tübingen school and notably in the thought of Johann Adam Möhler, who himself had taught at Munich 1835-1838.[137] It was apparent that he preferred a historical approach to a speculative one on issues of theology, but although he admired Möhler and Newman, he failed to measure up to their level of vision.[138] Eventually, Döllinger joined the Catholic circle in Munich led by Franz von Baader and Joseph von Görres. This circle was influenced by contemporary Romanticism and was politically conservative, anti-capitalistic and monarchist. It sought to restore social and religious life on Catholic principles, much as did the French movement of liberal Catholicism. Döllinger stressed the importance of public opinion and engaged in public affairs because he believed theologians should guide the public. He used his historical knowledge to argue that Protestantism, liberalism and rationalism marked breaks with the historical past, continuity and development.[139]

By 1850 overt nationalism began to affect Döllinger's work. He began to call for episcopal independence from Rome, a Catholic Church in Germany headed by a German metropolitan and education for the priesthood in universities rather than in seminaries. He became so disturbed by what he considered growing papal absolutism that he delivered lectures questioning the further usefulness of the Vatican State and criticizing its current administration. More fundamental, however, was Döllinger's hostility to the revival of scholastic theology, particularly by Roman Jesuits. In 1863, he organized a congress of a hundred Catholic theologians in Munich. In his opening address, Döllinger "blasted scholasticism, a narrow school of theology based on a particular reading of Thomas Aquinas and regarded by Rome as the official theology of the Church. He called for an assertion of scholarly independence from Vatican authority."[140] Döllinger preferred the study of historical theology and feared the tendency of some scholastics to label opinions contrary to their own as heretical. At the same time he also was engaged in the promotion of Christian unity, especially with the lectures of 1872, published as *Über die*

Wiedervereinigung der christlichen Kirchen (1888).[141]

Döllinger was not asked to participate in the First Vatican Council, but he was drawn into the central controversy concerning papal primacy and infallibility. During the Council, under the pseudonym Quirinius, he published 69 Roman letters attacking the conduct of the leaders of the majority group and complained that the bishops of the minority were not entirely free to speak their minds. However, he "overestimated the impact of those letters. Since he had to operate more on the level of council journalism than council theology, his influence among the bishops was less convincing than he had hoped."[142] After Döllinger refused to subscribe to the definitions of papal prerogatives, he was excommunicated and lost his Munich professorship in 1872. For the rest of his life, he remained well connected with the leaders of the Catholic revival in Germany, France and England.[143] He exerted considerable influence by impressing upon Catholic scholars the necessity of developing a historical as well as a speculative approach to theology. In addition, he did much to promote among Catholics an interest in scientific research and the study of Church history.[144] Nichols reflects on how the Munich School might have influenced Ratzinger:

> Ratzinger's theological work constitutes a microcosm of the Munich inheritance. His insistence on the context of theology in ecclesial life is reminiscent of Sailer. The interest in metaphysics, mysticism and social philosophy reflects the peculiar combination of concerns of the 'Munich circle' of Baader and Görres. His belief that systematic theology must be nourished at all times by historic theology, not least for the sake of the organic continuity of Church tradition, echoes Döllinger. Detailed investigation of the patristic corpus (chiefly Augustine) continues the efforts of Bardenhewer. Enquiry into the thought of the mediaevals builds on the achievement of Grabmann and Schmaus.[145]

After all, it was at the University of Munich that Ratzinger received his doctorate in theology with his first important work, regarding Augustine. There he also wrote his postdoctoral thesis on the 13th century Italian Franciscan Cardinal Bonaventure.

Even though post-war German academia was suffering from a lack of available materials and books, Ratzinger recalls, "we wanted not only to do theology in the narrower sense but to listen to the voices of man today."[146] Dostoevsky, Claudel, Bernanos, Mauriac were widely read, along with studying the discoveries by Planck, Heisenberg and Einstein. In the field of theology and philosophy, the writings of Romano Guardini,[147] Josef Pieper, Theodor Häcker and Peter Wust received much attention. Ratzinger was especially fond of his prefect of studies at the time, Alfred Läpple, who introduced him to Cardinal Newman's concept of conscience[148] as well as to the works of his director Theodor Steinbüchel, a moral theologian in Munich. In his memoirs, Ratzinger notes, it was through the reading of Steinbüchel's two volumes on the philosophical foundations of moral theology, that he "found a first-rate introduction to the thought of Heidegger and Jaspers as well as to the philosophies of Nietzsche, Klages and Bergson."[149] However, it was another book of Steinbüchel's, *Der Umbruch des Denkens* that made a greater impact on him:

> …here I read how, just as now we could affirm that physics was abandoning the mechanistic world view and turning toward a new openness to the unknown – and hence also able to know Unknown, namely, God – so, too, in philosophy we could detect a return to metaphysics, which had become inaccessible since Kant. After beginning his career with studies on Hegel and socialism, Steinbüchel was now portraying in this book (under the influence above all of Ferdinand Ebner) his discovery of personalism, which had become a major turning point in his own intellectual development.[150]

Martin Buber's (1878-1965) and Ferdinand Ebner's (1882-1931) personalism left an essential mark on young Ratzinger who "saw that their ideas combined well with those of Augustine, whom he encountered in all of the human passion and depth that came through from the text of the *Confessions*."[151] Ratzinger once mentioned that if he were stranded on a deserted island, the two books he would want with him would be the Bible and the *Confessions*.

Even in his early years in the seminary, Ratzinger was considered to have a discerning mind. One example to illustrate this would be how vividly he retells the story of the faculty's most esteemed professor, Friedrich Wilhelm Maier, a professor of New Testament exegesis. Maier was the one who proposed the *two-source theory*, in which both the Gospel of Mark and the Q source, or *Quelle*, were seen as the sources for the three Synoptic Gospels. This broke with ancient tradition, which placed Matthew as the oldest Gospel and it caused Maier to confront the strongly waged Modernist dispute about the Gospels. Because theories of liberal exegesis were posing a threat to the foundation of faith, it seemed that Maier's theory surrendered to that kind of liberalism and Maier was asked by Rome to step away from teaching theology. Though he was later called back, he never quite got over the trauma of having been dismissed. The fact that Ratzinger even mentions this story shows that it had an impact on him, one that even as the prefect of the Congregation for the Doctrine of Faith, possibly led to a certain sensitivity when it came to silencing some of the theologians of his time.

As time went on, Ratzinger came to realize that Maier's approach to the Scriptures had its weaknesses too, especially in comparison with Rudolph Bultmann (1884-1976) and Karl Barth (1886-1968). For "Maier represents those who look upon dogma, not as a shaping force, but only as a shackle, a negation and a limit in the construction of theology."[152] However, Ratzinger believed, it was still a legitimate approach, as long as it was balanced by obedience to dogma. He credits Maier with making exegesis a center of his theological work and, because of him, Sacred Scripture became *the soul of our theological studies*, as was later understood by the Second Vatican Council.

If Maier was *the* professor of the New Testament, then Friedrich Stummer was the professor of the Old Testament. With him, Ratzinger grew to understand the Old Testament in a new light:

> More and more I came to understand why the New Testament is not a different book of a different religion that, for some reason or other, had appropriated the Holy Scriptures of the Jews as a kind of preliminary structure. The New Testament is nothing other than an interpretation of "the Law, the Prophets and the Writings" found from or contained in the story of Jesus. Now, this "Law, Prophets and Writings" had not yet, at the time of Jesus, grown together to form a definitive canon; rather, they were still open-ended and, as such, offered themselves spontaneously to Jesus' disciples as a testimony to him, as the Sacred Scriptures that revealed his mystery. I have ever more come to the realization that Judaism (which, strictly speaking, begins with the end of the formation of the canon, that is, in the first century after Christ) and the Christian faith described in the New Testament are two ways of appropriating Israel's Scriptures, two ways that, in the end, are both determined by the position one assumes with regard to the figure of Jesus of Nazareth. The Scripture we today call Old Testament is in itself open to both ways.[153]

Another great influence for Ratzinger was Professor Gottlieb Söhngen who had a "passion for truth and the habit of asking unrelenting questions about the foundation and goal of all the real."[154] Ratzinger explained that an important characteristic of Söhngen was the idea that his thought developed directly out of the sources themselves; beginning with Aristotle and Plato;

through Clement and Augustine, Anselm, Bonaventure and Thomas; to Luther and the more recent Tübingen theologians of the 20th century. Moreover, Pascal and Newman were among his favorite writers, who were major influences on Ratzinger as well. However, perhaps the most revealing aspect of Söhngen's influence was that he was never satisfied in theology with the sort of positivism often detected in other subjects but was always asking questions concerning the truth of the matter and thus questions concerning the immediate reality of what is believed. This turned out to be characteristic of Ratzinger himself.[155]

Another influence on Ratzinger was his teacher, the liturgical theologian Joseph Pascher, to whom Ratzinger is indebted to for a heightened appreciation of the liturgical movement. Even as a young man he became enchanted with Catholic liturgy. As he himself recalled, "it was becoming more and more clear to me that here I was encountering a reality that no one had simply thought up, a reality that no official authority or great individual had created."[156] It was the discovery of this other mysterious objective reality that sustained Ratzinger. Faith for him was not just a cluster of intellectual truths or concepts, but foremost an encounter with the Other. It was this great sense of the transcendent as the source of truth which he used to formulate his arguments in matters of faith.

Though he was grateful to this new movement, which made it possible to have a Missal in Latin and German, Ratzinger still had some reservations about it. He felt that many of the representatives of this movement offered "a one-sided rationalism and historicism that concentrated too much on forms and historical origins and exhibited a remarkable coldness when it came to dispositions of mind and heart that allow us to experience the Church as the place where the soul is at home."[157] However, the teachings of Pascher convinced Ratzinger to commit himself to the liturgical movement with the understanding that whereby the Scriptures constituted the soul of theology, the liturgy became its living element. Both were necessary for theology to have a living space and expression.

From reading his memoirs, one may gather that Ratzinger approached his studies with a sober, critical mind. He would initially get excited about the new material, but in his free time would reflect once again on what had been said and would try to discern where the truth actually lies. As fond as he was of his professors, he was also able to see for the most part that they represented the historical school which by then was becoming narrower and more restrictive. Ratzinger illustrated this with an episode he recalled:

> Before Mary's bodily Assumption into heaven was defined, all theological faculties in the world were consulted for their opinion. Our teachers' answer was emphatically negative. What here became evident was the one-sidedness, not only of the historical, but also of the historicist method in theology. "Tradition" was identified with what could be proved on the basis of texts. Altaner, the patrologist… had proven in a scientifically persuasive manner that the doctrine of Mary's bodily Assumption into heaven was unknown before the 5th century; this doctrine, therefore, he argued, could not belong to the "apostolic tradition."… This argument is compelling if you understand "tradition" strictly as the handing down of fixed formulas and texts. This was the position that our teachers represented. But if you conceive of "tradition" as the living process whereby the Holy Spirit introduces us to the fullness of truth and teaches us how to understand what previously we could still not grasp (cf. Jn 16:12-13), then subsequent "remembering" (cf. Jn 16:4, for instance) can come to recognize what it had not caught sight of previously and yet was already handed down in the original Word. But such a perspective was still quite unattainable by German theological thought.[158]

Ratzinger was also pleased that even in the face of criticism his teachers were able to remain faithful to the Church. As an example, when Professor Söhngen was asked what he would do if the Church eventually decided to pronounce the Assumption as dogma, Söhngen responded, "If the dogma comes, then I will remember that the Church is wiser than I and that I must trust her more than my own erudition."[159] This was for Ratzinger, a good lesson in intellectual humility which the theologian or any rational being should preserve and one he learned quite well.

3

FROM AUGUSTINE TO BONAVENTURE

1. Augustine's Ecclesiology

What Augustine meant in Ratzinger's life can be gathered from a remark he made in 1969 when he said, "Augustine has kept me company for more than twenty years. I have developed my theology in a dialogue with Augustine, though naturally I have tried to conduct this dialogue as a man of today."[160] In his work on Augustine, Ratzinger found the *concourse* where antiquity and the Gospel meet. More so, Erich Przywara states that Augustine "conjoins the two 'fundamental motifs' of ancient thought: the movement from what is changing to the Changeless in Parmenides (and Plato) and the syncopated rhythm of finite being in Heraclitus (and Aristotle)."[161] Henry Chadwick, in his book on Augustine as one of the major types of *theological* influences, notes that the theology and philosophy of medieval times were rooted in Augustine's ideas of the relationship between faith and reason, which were interconnected with the centrality of God's love.[162] Ratzinger bases his theology on that same insight, since it was about Augustine that he wrote his doctoral work (in nine months, initially directed toward an academic prize, which Ratzinger won) called *Volk und Haus Gottes in Augustins Lehre von der Kirche* (Munich 1954).[163] The work was written under the supervision of his favorite teacher Professor Gottlieb Söhngen and a major impetus to his dissertation was Henri de Lubac's *Catholicism*,[164] about which Ratzinger recalls:

> This book was for me a key reading event. It gave me not only a new and deeper connection with the thought of the Fathers but also a new way of looking at theology and faith as such. Faith had here become an interior contemplation and, precisely by thinking with the Fathers, a present reality. In this book one could detect a quiet debate going on with both liberalism and Marxism, the dramatic struggle of French Catholicism for a new penetration of the faith into the intellectual life of our time. De Lubac was leading his readers out of a narrowly individualistic and moralistic mode of faith and into the freedom of an essentially social faith, conceived and lived as a *we* – a faith that, precisely as such and according to its nature, was also hope, affecting history as a whole and not only the promise of a private blissfulness to individuals. I then looked around for other works by de Lubac and derived special profit from his book *Corpus Mysticum*, in which a new understanding of the unity of Church and Eucharist opened up to me beyond the insights I had already received from Pascher, Schmaus and Söhngen. Drawing on these perspectives, I could now enter into the required dialogue with Augustine, something I had already been attempting for a long time in different ways.[165]

De Lubac not only highlighted the theme of the Church for him, but it was also a feeling Ratzinger shared with Romano Guardini. They both thought "the 20th century was providing, theologically, the 'century of the Church,' when the idea of the Church was re-awakening in all its breadth and depth."[166] There was no better source for this theme than Augustine, for whom the

Church was at the same time both the people and the house of God. In the preface to his work, Ratzinger acknowledges, his efforts to analyze his theme proved very worthwhile since the study of Augustine touched on a number of vital issues of the patristic times which also proved relevant during the Third Reich. Issues addressed included the relationship between the Old and New Testaments, between law and the sacraments, and the attitude of Christians toward the pagan State and paganism generally.[167]

Ratzinger was very interested in Augustine's conversion and how his conversion led him first to God, then to his Church – where the Incarnate Logos and the Person of Jesus Christ exist. Augustine's conversion became an example for many to follow. Augustine's conversion could be thought of as a philosophical one because, if done seriously, it leads one to the question of religion. One may deduce that Ratzinger believes the same may apply to contemporary philosophy and philosophies, if they were to return to that "ultimate *arche* of things sought by the philosopher."[168] Still, relativist philosophers would not be able to consider such things, since to them; an ultimate principle does not exist. Here is an example of one of the obstacles in Ratzinger's desire to bring people to the Truth. On the other hand, there is always hope for those philosophers who are searching for some ultimate principles.

However, according to Augustine and Ratzinger, those who attained knowledge of the absolutes would not be able to sustain them for long. In time, because of the human condition, those absolutes would dim and so a concentrated effort would be needed to maintain them.[169] That comes in the form of having eyes and hearts fixed on Christ as he reveals himself in his Church where he proclaims his word and administers his sacraments. It is the Church where "God gives us the Invisible to feed upon in visible form, thus leading us ever more towards the Invisible, until we become adults in his presence."[170] This concept of an *adulthood of faith* was expressed in Ratzinger's homily *Pro Eligendo Romano Pontifice*.

Another aspect of Augustine – and to a lesser degree of

Ratzinger – was that traces of Platonism existed in his thought. Nevertheless, as Nichols puts it, "while Ratzinger affirms this quite explicitly, he does not underestimate the claims of Platonism as a philosophical partner to Christian revelation."[171] Platonism has two realities: one is the real and the other is the appearance of the real. It is in the second reality where humans live, because it takes a lot of intellectual effort to distinguish *appearances* from the *real*. Such dualism, although a part of Platonism, can also be found in Christianity: the natural versus the supernatural, or the Transcendent versus the body and the soul. Only the Incarnation took away the dualism when the transcendent God became a part of the natural world. However, as mentioned earlier, those who attained knowledge of the absolutes would not be able to sustain them for long and the danger of dualism continued. Ratzinger's later emphasis on ecclesiology of communion was a way offered to avoid all dualism of the kind "which eventually led Tertullian to contrast the 'Church of the Spirit,' *ecclesia spiritus*, the charismatic community, with the 'episcopal Church,' *ecclesia numerus episcoporum*, the community of the sacraments and the everyday Christian life."[172]

With maturity, Augustine began to describe God as *caritas*, who manifested himself as the third person of the Holy Trinity – the Holy Spirit. It was his understanding that the same happened within the Church: "Through the unifying force of love – which the Holy Spirit, *vinculum amoris*, personally is – the many believers are ushered into the unity of the body of Christ. Whereas earlier, salvation was measured by intellectual insight, it now consists in that being in the Church which is simultaneously a being-in-love."[173] It is through *caritas* that boundaries and limitations are overcome and an individual is able to enter into the mystical Body of Christ,[174] which in turn extends to who one is and how one is. This use of linguistic images nevertheless carries with it some amount of ambiguity; one may even call it linguistic relativism. However, as Ratzinger puts it in his dissertation, "the language of images is admittedly the only means of access here to the authentic reality. But then again, that whole reality is only to be grasped *in via* by images and analogies."[175] Augustine himself saw the danger of any human analogy used for God and that it had a tendency to replace the true reality of God. Nichols explained it thusly:

> For if a people be, as Augustine's definition proposed, "the association of a multitude of rational beings united by a common agreement on the objects of their love" then such aspects of civil religion as Roman belief in the divinity of Romulus sprang from an "error of love": it was because she loved Romulus that Rome believed him to be a god. But the true God, conversely, must precede the *civitas*: love can be humanity's unifying force only if men recognize God as the *summum bonum* of all the world.[176]

This quote refers to the issue of democracy and its temptation to have all of the objectives of common life established by majority vote. Ratzinger, however, makes a clear distinction between the love, which is *responsive co-acting* with God and one another and the falsely creative *self-acting*, which is much promoted by one's modern mindset.[177] As for his understanding of the Church, Ratzinger would often cite the prayer of Jesus at the Last Supper where he prayed for his disciples who were in this world and yet not of this world (cf. Jn 17:11-26). This tension, or in other words the paths taken by the Church through her history to overcome it, especially the modern Catholic Church, will be a point of contention for Ratzinger.

At this time Ratzinger too confesses, he did not find St. Thomas to be as appealing for him as were St. Augustine and others. He says, "St. Augustine interested me very much – precisely also insofar as he was, so to speak, a counterweight to Thomas Aquinas."[178] For him, Aquinas' crystal-clear logic was too impersonal and rote. That same opinion of Aquinas remained for Ratzinger in his entire theological career – although, he clarifies later, it was mostly neo-scholasticism, with its share of speculative theology and often misinterpretation of Aquinas' theology that kept him less interested in this great theologian. Ratzinger, who in his episcopal coat of arms used the Johannine words *co-workers of truth*, comes close to Aquinas' lifelong position to follow the words of Jesus "Consecrate them in the Truth" (cf. Jn 17:9-19). More so, in his own homily on Aquinas, Ratzinger says of him, "his life was a life in the truth and for its sake. A humble and constant service of the truth was the form taken by his consecrated life and his priestly ministry."[179] Here one could say, unknowingly, Ratzinger described his own self. The theme and the thoughts of his dissertation have relevance even today, as Ratzinger himself acknowledges in his foreword to the new edition of it in 1992:

> As for its relation to the theological debate today, the book... acquired an unexpected relevance precisely in the post-conciliar dispute about the Church. The Council... assigned new significance to the concept "People of God" and devoted to it a whole chapter in the Constitution on the Church.... If ones reads this chapter in the context of the entire document, it becomes evident that the "People of God" statements are connected inseparably and organically with all the other great themes of the ecclesiological tradition and are combined with them into a synthesis, in which I find a complete confirmation of the essential conclusions of my book, a fully intrinsic unity in the foundational way of seeing the Church.[180]

2. Bonaventure's Historicity of Revelation

Ratzinger continued to work toward his *habilitation* on St. Bonaventure's theology of history and revelation – once again under the guidance of Professor Söhngen. He had chosen this topic mainly because "the idea of salvation history had moved to the focus of inquiry posed by Catholic theology and this had cast new light on the notion of revelation, which neo-scholasticism had kept too confined to the intellectual realm."[181] In this new notion of revelation, the truth came about not through communication to the intellect but as something gradually revealed as God's action working in history. This new historical understanding of revelation excited Ratzinger and it was his task to discover whether there was any support for it in Bonaventure. Even as he accepted the chair for dogma at the college in Freising in the summer of 1954, a year later the handwritten manuscript of his work on Bonaventure was finished.

That was not the end of it however. The greatest challenge was about to come from one of the readers – Professor Schmaus, who at first rejected the work. Schmaus was a medieval theologian himself and did not like the idea that Ratzinger wrote his work in this area under someone else's tutelage. In addition, Ratzinger's work was rejected because of the different analysis he used in his treatment of the concept of *revelation*. He acknowledges that following the tradition of medieval theologians, especially of the late 13th century, he recovered the understanding of revelation, not just simply as the concept referring to all the revealed contents of the faith, but more as a concept denoting the act. It "refers to the act in which God shows himself, not to the objectified result of this act."[182] Although this understanding of revelation will eventually become the basis for the Second Vatican Council's *Constitution on Divine Revelation*, to which Ratzinger himself contributed a great deal, at the time of his *habilitation*, it still was not accepted.

Ratzinger subsequently revised and improved on his work by using Joachim's controversy as a focal point of his thesis. Joachim of Fiore proposed the understanding of history in relation to salvation not as a locus where it takes place, but as an ultimate form and actual realization of it, thus moving it to the center of revelation itself. In a late two-volume work by Henri de Lubac, Ratzinger recalled that he studied "the subsequent history of Joachim's idea, which reaches out to Hegel and the totalitarian systems of our own century."[183] Ratzinger always remained very cautious of any philosophy or theology which presented itself as making human history and was responsible for the redemption of all. His relationship with Professor Schmaus eventually relaxed, however Ratzinger's earlier experience in the matter made him resolve never to reject dissertations or theses routinely but to respect the integrity of the process by engaging the stronger side of the argument. In February 1957, Ratzinger received his *habilitation* and so was assured of his teaching position and thus was assured of housing for himself and his parents.

In his introduction to the second dissertation on Bonaventure, Ratzinger stated that the concern with the question of history often arises during times of crisis. Naturally, when the world does not turn out as imagined, one begins to look for who is responsible. The understanding of history thus becomes crucial in settling or disturbing one's hopes. Bonaventure himself encountered a crisis when he was elected General of his Franciscan Order. The major figure in the controversy was Joachim of Fiore and his understanding of eschatology as being already in the process of fulfillment in the enveloping of human history. The *Collationes in Hexaemeron* was Bonaventure's answer to the problem posed by Joachim.

However, Ratzinger notes, although Bonaventure was opposed by many others, he tried to interpret Joachim's thoughts back into tradition, not against it. Bonaventure's response to him consisted, not in total rejection of Joachim's teaching, as with Aquinas, but in a corrective interpretation. Whereas the Joachimites were interpreting Joachim against tradition, Bonaventure would interpret him within, indeed back into tradition. Nichols comments that "this ecclesial reinterpretation of deviant divines, rather than their outright condemnation, was evidently something Ratzinger approved of in the Franciscan thinker."[184] That way, there are some elements of truth in almost everything anyone says and those elements must be singled out and preserved, since they create a ground for unity, not separation. This attitude is a counterargument against those who see him as an absolutist, since Ratzinger never leaves out any traces of truth, if there are some, in his opponent's position and argumentation. He instead takes it, or suggests it to be, the starting point and common ground for genuine dialogue.

Bonaventure was a highly educated man of his time. Through the influence of Arabic sciences, the medieval universities were presented with observations coming from the natural sciences and these were not always easily and readily reconcilable with the theological or philosophical thought of the time. Ratzinger makes a comparison of this to the post-Conciliar era in which he is living. Bonaventure himself was somewhat puzzled by this development and after a ten-year absence returned to the university pulpit to find himself an outsider pointing to the limitations of science from a faith-based perspective. Thus, writes Ratzinger, it was "the intention of *Hexaemeron* to hold up the picture of the true Christian wisdom in the face of the intellectual aberrations of the age."[185]

Here Ratzinger makes his major point about Bonaventure; he was a man who believed there is no knowledge disconnected from a historical situation. He was a pioneer of what in the 19th century will be known as the historical-critical method in approaching the Scriptures, since for him the exegesis must be done with the emphasis on the historical character of the scriptural statements, an idea quite antagonistic to the unchangeable and enduring position of Medieval Scholasticism.[186] According to Ratzinger, Bonaventure agrees there is a certain closed objectivity to Scripture, but "as the physical world contains seeds, so also Scripture contains 'seeds'; that is, seeds of meaning. And this meaning develops in a constant process of growth in time."[187]

What then is the role of a learned theologian in interpreting the knowledge coming from Scripture, with such emphasis on history? Here Ratzinger sets forth his major thesis:

> …new knowledge arises constantly from Scripture. Something is taking place; and this happening, this history, continues onward as long as there is history at all. This is of fundamental importance for the theologian who explains Scripture. It makes it clear that the

theologian cannot abstract from history in his explanation of Scripture; neither from the past nor from the future. In this way, the exegesis of Scripture becomes a theology of history; the clarification of the past leads to prophecy concerning the future.[188]

One could see how this would be important for Ratzinger, who observed that a number of contemporary theologians disregarded the past in formulating their present statements. These statements – devoid of historical context – were imperceptive regarding future outcomes. Such is the relativistic way of acquiring knowledge, for it disregards the historical past of that knowledge as irrelevant – and that, in Ratzinger's view, is building the house on sand and not on a solid foundation, historically grounded and gradually unfolding to reveal truth.

Ratzinger in his work also stated that Augustine and Bonaventure have opposing understandings of the theology of history. Whereas for Augustine, the world's history was a place for the great conflict of the two civitates: *civitas Dei* and *civitas terrena*; for Bonaventure, history was a part of bringing about and realizing the victory of the Reign of God and the salvation taking place therein. In other words, "for the Augustinian schema, Christ is the end of the ages; for the Bonaventurian schema, Christ is the center of all ages."[189] Ratzinger thinks that Bonaventure rejects the idea of Christ being the highest degree of inner-historical fulfillment with nothing else left but an eschatological hope of his return, beyond history. On the other hand, for him the eschatological hope of Christ's return is realized within history, not aside from it. Therefore the history that humankind fashions matters regarding salvation. Here one comes close to the important point, which Ratzinger makes about Bonaventure and which eventually becomes a basis for his own ecclesiology:

On the one hand, Bonaventure recognizes the full heavenly glory of the souls of those who have died and have been purified; on the other hand, it remains clear that this heavenly condition is not the final state, but that it is still a part of world-history; it also stands in expectation of that which is to come. Consequently, the mystery of hope remains for Christianity, a concrete hope for a transformation of the world.[190]

This is why in the heavenly Church, those who shared the faith in the past have not disappeared, but continue to remain active participants of the Church on earth. Those who were in the past need to share their knowledge so that those in the present will be able to reach the future. Ratzinger suggested that for Bonaventure, his primary concern of this view of history is precisely the future and what he calls *the seventh age.*

For Bonaventure, unlike Joachim, the New Testament was the eternal covenant and redemption happens in the framework of this Testament. At the same time, Bonaventure remained soberly realistic in his interpretation of what the true meaning of St. Francis' life was in terms of salvation history. From Ratzinger's writings, "Bonaventure recognized [that] Francis' own eschatological form of life could not exist as an institution in this world; it could only be realized as a breakthrough of grace in the individual, until such time as the God-given hour would arrive at which time the world would be transformed into its final form of existence."[191]

It is important to observe how Ratzinger described Bonaventure's understanding of learning and wisdom. For Bonaventure, the main goal of Christian learning was to attain wisdom, which ultimately was attainable not simply by learning, but only through sanctity. For Bonaventure there were four levels of wisdom: *sapientia uniformis, multiformis, omniformis and nulliformis.* The first one, *uniform wisdom,* was the knowledge of basic truths which are given and are not decided by ourselves but are discovered as given. Ratzinger assigns this type of wisdom as proper to the natural sciences. The second form of wisdom, the *sapientia multiformis,* was the wisdom which is derived from an understanding of the truths hidden in Scripture. Thus, here is a wisdom that arises from divine revelation. This type of knowledge is often given to the simple in heart. Thirdly, there was the wisdom of *omniformis*, the wisdom of philosophers since it is that wisdom "which discovers in all things the reflection of the Creator and follows His traces through all of creation."[192] Nichols points out that in his *Commentary on the Sentences*, Bonaventure "had early developed the view that, in the contemporary period, man's contemplative power is so reduced that only the healing and helping grace of God can revive his understanding of the 'book' of creation."[193] Bonaventure further develops this idea of divine grace acting upon humankind as a ladder leading from creation to the Creator in his *Journey of the Mind toward God*.[194] However, here we find a danger for some of the philosophers, to remain focused on what is created instead of the Creator and not finding the way to him. In that case, Bonaventure says, their wisdom becomes folly.

Finally, we come to the fourth kind of wisdom, the *sapientia nulliformis*. This type is the knowledge of the mystic who "approaches in silence to the very threshold of the mystery of the eternal God in the night of the intellect whose light is extinguished at such heights."[195] Ratzinger says it is this type of wisdom, which Bonaventure names *revelation*, not revelation in the contemporary theological understanding of it, but as an individual revelation given to some, which reflects the final stage of salvation. In terms of revelation contained in Scripture, Bonaventure believed "that which truly constitutes revelation is accessible in the word written by the hagiographer, but that it remains to a degree hidden behind the words and must be unveiled anew."[196] For that unveiling, the living spirit is necessary and there are certain stages:

> The stages of faith are also stages of mysticism. And, in such a viewpoint, they are seen quite naturally as stages of *revelation* as well. *Revelatio* refers not to the letter of Scripture, but to the understanding of the letter. And this understanding can be increased. If we were to suppose the possibility of a period of time in which the power of genuine mystical elevation were granted

to all human beings, then – in this perspective – we could refer to such a time as a time of revelation in a quite new sense.[197]

Bonaventure's understanding of revelation was restored in Vatican II. Revelation needed to be contained within both Scripture and tradition homogenously. Ratzinger observes that some might interpret Bonaventure's view of revelation as based on subjectivism. However, that is not true. It is not up to the individual to interpret the true meaning of Scripture. It has to be done in relation to the faith of the Church and her understanding of Scripture. He explains it further as follows:

> The understanding which elevates Scripture to the status of "revelation" is not to be taken as an affair of the individual reader; but it is realized only in the living understanding of Scripture in the Church. In this way the objectivity of the claim of faith is affirmed without any doubt. If we keep this in mind, we can say that without detriment to the objectivity of faith, the true meaning of Scripture will be found only by reaching behind the letters. Consequently, the true understanding of revelation demands of each individual reader an attitude which goes beyond the merely "objective" recognition of what is written. In the deepest sense, this understanding can be called mystical to distinguish it from all natural knowledge. In other words, such an understanding demands the attitude of faith by which man gains entrance into the living understanding of Scripture in the Church. It is in this way that man truly receives "revelation."[198]

Another question, which Ratzinger had to deal with in Bonaventure's *Hexaemeron*, was the relationship between Scripture and history. The ancient concept of history was a flow of individual events, not having anything common or universal behind it.

However, Ratzinger pointed out, "in Christianity this unhistorical mode of thought necessarily had a limited applicability from the very start because of the prophetic interpretation of the Old Testament history given in Scripture."[199] He asserted that in medieval theology the Scriptures were closely connected with the exegesis of the Fathers and they shared an equal authority. Nevertheless, a change happened to scriptural interpretation as represented by the life of St. Francis. This posed a question of possible development in the tradition of interpreting the Scriptures. Bonaventure's aim was precisely to answer this question, but in a different way from how Joachim of Fiore did. For him, "Scripture was full of hidden seeds which are developed only in the course of history and therefore constantly allow new insights which would not have been possible for an earlier age."[200]

Ratzinger also spoke of a danger when remaining only with the letter in the exegesis of Scriptures, or in the knowledge which comes from created things. He alludes to the positivist thought of his times when he writes, "because of our own situation in salvation history, this danger has become particularly acute."[201] This danger became even more prominent with the growth of Aristotelian influence in medieval philosophy. Bonaventure saw the danger of systematization, and thus formulated his antithesis or so-called canon of anti-Aristotelianism, which consists of opposing three errors: the eternity of the world, the necessity of fate, and the unity of the intellect in all men.[202] For Bonaventure, the world consisted of two corresponding movements of *egressus* and *regressus* from the very beginning, where "Christ stands as the turning point of these movements and as the center who both divides and unites."[203] Christ here becomes the center, the medium of all things – that fact fully realized in his Crucifixion:

> The lost middle of the circle is found again by means of two lines that intersect at right angles, that is, by a cross. This means that by His cross, Christ has definitively solved the geometry-problem of world history. With His cross He has uncovered the lost center of the

circle of the world so as to give the true direction and meaning to the movement of the individual life and to the history of mankind as such.[204]

Ratzinger also went into great depth to demonstrate Bonaventure's precaution with the rise of Aristotelian philosophy. Bonaventure went so far as to call reason a *harlot*, "a self-sufficient philosophy, a philosophy that attempts to draw us from the hands of the royal bride that is the Christian wisdom."[205] It should not be understood as condemnation of philosophy as such, but as integration of the truth coming from revelation. For Bonaventure, time was not linear but circular, although ascending as a spiral with the idea of a progressive line, since one always "remains conscious of the unique and unrepeatable character of that which takes place in history."[206] Aristotelian philosophy suggested the eternally cyclical character of the world, which is not accepted by Bonaventure or Ratzinger, because with such a view, history becomes accidental, whereas for Bonaventure and Ratzinger history is a saving time. They both believed that Christ is the center and the meaning of the whole history and that there is no history apart from the economy of salvation in Christ.

Ratzinger's understanding of history has us all participating in the act of salvation. The saints of the past serve as clear examples for us; this salvation should be accepted and lived. One inherits from previous generations of believers the knowledge and the experience of the redeeming works of God. One does not start anew, but accepts experience from the saints in humility and respects and builds upon it and passes it on to future generations. Salvation unfolds in history and one should never stop acknowledging that. Therefore, Ratzinger is discontent with the Aristotelian, singularly speculative theology, which deals only with intellectual concepts and considers historical facts as irrelevant. However, Bonaventure already predicted that there will be a time when reason and theology will fail to exist and the *auctoritas* of faith will take over. It will be the age of contemplative wisdom, expressed in mystical love which was exemplified in the life of St. Francis, "as the *simplex* and *idiota*, Francis knew more about God than all the learned men of his time – because he loved Him more."[207]

In his conclusion, Ratzinger compared Bonaventure to Augustine because they both came to the same point: "The Church, which hopes for peace in the future, is nonetheless, obliged to love in the present; and they both realize that the kingdom of eternal peace is growing in the hearts of those who fulfill Christ's law of love in their particular age."[208] This brings to mind a question: how does one overcome the contemporary attitude with its indifference to absolutes, whether they are about goodness, beauty, truth... essentially God? Ratzinger would say the answer lies in revelation, by finding Christ in each person. The primary location of this encounter, although it may happen anywhere, is the Church and the primary time is during the liturgy: worship or prayer centered on the Eucharist. Study and understanding of who the human being is, along with the study of human history may help us to recognize the extended and sustaining hand of God. First, people need to reclaim their true human dignity which involves the ability to reason, freedom to choose, and willingness to love and to be loved. By learning about the true self, the limitedness of life, and of man's nature, humankind might realize that they are God's creatures dependent on his care and protection. God would never leave humankind alone, for he himself came down from heaven to hold people by the hand and lead them to the true fulfillment of themselves and their lives.[209]

3. Christian Brotherhood

Christian Brotherhood was an essay Ratzinger presented to the Theological Congress of the Austrian Institute for Pastoral Work in Vienna in 1958. Its content provided the source for contemporary debate on ecumenism and inter-religious dialogue. At the time Ratzinger began his essay, he singled out the theme of brotherhood as found in the words of Jesus, "You have but one teacher and you are all brothers" (Mt 23:8). Ratzinger takes these words of Jesus very seriously, saying that they describe the new relationship, the brotherhood of the spirit, which in turn becomes the core of Christian ethos. Starting with sources from Ancient Greece, Ratzinger concluded that brotherhood, being based on some sort of unifying factor, be it blood or any other, ultimately is a union and "all unions involve the separating of those who are united together from others."[210] This in turn created an unavoidable tension, which is also present in Christianity. In the Old Testament, it was clear that the *brother* was the one who belonged to the unity of the unique Chosen People of God. However, as Ratzinger, pointed out, "this God was not just some local national god, but was a supranational, universal God, therefore, this almost implies an impossibility of forming a unity within the brotherhood of one's own nation or else it could – through a false development – lead to a kind of internal ossification."[211] Throughout the Old Testament, especially in the words of the prophets, there is a reminder to Israel; it is not they who have chosen God, but God who has chosen them. Since it was a free choice by God, he could always alter it and that, Ratzinger said, "brought an element of uncertainty into any tendency to separate off the brotherly community of Israel too rigidly."[212] However, with time, Judaism abandoned this *openness* to the universality of their God, but it was still preserved in the Old Testament, especially in the creation account and in the story of Noah.

In the end, Ratzinger noted, one has both unity and duality of the ethos – unity being expressed in the universality of God and duality in exclusive electiveness shown to some by this universal God. Consequently, one has differences in brotherly ethos as well. The responsibility an Israelite took for another Israelite was different from that which he took for a Gentile. However, this duality "could never degenerate into dualism… rather it was held together through the unity of God and the unity of humanity, so that human responsibility went beyond the framework of the brotherly community, as is shown concretely by the Old Testament's laws concerning strangers."[213] One can understand here, Ratzinger wanted to demonstrate the legitimacy of this dual ethos of brotherhood as it was established in the Old Testament and passed on into the New, although not with the relief of the tension inherent in it.

The idea of dual ethos leads to the creation of different sects and the forming of special groups, such as the Essenes, or the Qumran sect. Even Christians were seen as a sect by the Romans because of their secret teachings which were believed to be dangerous to the rest of Roman society. The Roman Empire, Ratzinger observed, strove for political unification and had "its philosophical parallel in Stoic cosmopolitanism which discovered the unity of the world and of men… one basic ethos of brotherliness was appropriate to all men."[214] That same idea of a single universal brotherhood found its best expression in the French Revolution, during the period of Enlightenment. Even more, "the dream of a perfect circle of brothers continued in post-Restoration liberalism, where its characteristic form was that of Freemasonry."[215] The Revolution's slogan *Liberté, Egalité, Fraternité* promoted the equality and universality of human rights; however, its premise was not based on the universal God, but was independent of him. In this case, for revolutionaries, human rights are defined by the commonly shared world, nature and its history.

As appealing as this idea of universal brotherhood might be, Ratzinger suggests that the result was bound to disappoint people. Why? Because, he asserts, "a brotherliness which embraces everyone equally cannot expect to be taken seriously by anyone."[216] Hence, Ratzinger asked, for an ethos to be realizable should it not have some form of duality? Marxism answered this question with a radicalism unparalleled in history. It came down to the idea of dividing the whole of humanity into antithetical classes – the capitalists and the proletariat – and presenting human history as a constant battle between the two. In its final form, Ratzinger pointed out, Marxism came back to that original insight about the concept of brotherhood where "brotherhood toward some involves enmity toward others."[217] Also, as Allen notes "from stories about the horrors of the 1919 Soviet revolution in Bavaria, to the 1968 student radicals and the Baader-Meinhof gang, to repression inside East Germany, Ratzinger associates Marxism with terrorism and violence."[218] Moreover, Marxism did not remain content with this division. It proposed the condition of a classless society. However, such a state could only possibly be achieved by moving beyond the class struggle of human history. Ratzinger ended his brief historical analysis of the non-Christian understanding of universal brotherhood by noting that an understanding of the Christian idea of brotherhood is integral to the proper formulation of the Christian religion. Ratzinger continued his essay by presenting the development of the Christian meaning of brotherhood, which at first reflected the Jewish rabbinic form. Soon, because of Jesus, it developed into a completely new understanding: Jesus' brothers were those who were united with him in the common acceptance of his Father's will. This clearly differs from the Stoic or the Enlightenment idea of brotherhood; in a way, in Christianity, it is not seen "naturalistically, as an original phenomenon of nature, but depends on a decision of the spirit, a saying 'yes' to the will of God"[219] and on acceptance of the Christian faith. Moreover, Ratzinger continued, in the parable of the Last Judgment, in Matthew 25, there is another aspect of the Christian meaning of brotherhood, founded on the lowliness and suffering of those in need. However, there still arises a certain ambiguity:

> On the one hand, it is clear that all those who need help are, irrespective of any barriers, through their very plight the brothers of Jesus. On the other hand, it is also apparent that the coming community of the faithful will form a new fraternal community which will be distinct from those who do not believe. Thus we have a limited conception on one side and a universal one on the other.[220]

One may find this same dualism in St. Paul's writings. In his doctrine of the two Adams, he talks about two different brotherhoods, one being united with an old Adam in evil and sin and the other being united with the New Adam, Christ in salvation. However, the delimitation here is also present. As Ratzinger put it, in Paul, "every man *can* become a Christian, but only he who really does is a brother."[221]

In the second part of his essay, Ratzinger provided a synthesis of the significance and the possibilities a Christian brotherhood could bring today. At the foundation of the Christian brotherhood stands the fatherhood of God. Although the mystical religions, Plato and the Stoics, as well as 18th century deism all spoke of God as father, Ratzinger argues, that when Christians call God *Father* it means something quite different. With the former it is an impersonal creative power behind this universe; whereas for the latter, it is the God who through faith becomes very concrete and personal. Nevertheless, Ratzinger observed, even among those who accept the Bible as the source of their faith, the danger always remained to see this personal, living God in more detached spiritual terms. It is very important to realize as Blaise Pascal in his conversion did:

> This God never becomes a God of the philosophers; he remains the living God, the God of Abraham, of Isaac and of Jacob; more, he becomes the God of Jesus Christ and thus the God who has taken on our flesh and blood and our whole human nature. In Jesus Christ, God has not only spoken to men but has also finally and radically made it possible for them to speak to him; for in him God became man but has also finally stepped out of his totally different being and entered into the dialogic situation of all men. Jesus the *man* stands as such within the community of discourse which unites all men as beings of the same order. The man Jesus can be addressed by every man, but in him it is God who is addressed. Thus the question of how changeable man can address a totally different, unchangeable God is resolved. In Christ, God has taken a piece of this world's time and of changeable creatureliness, drawn

it to himself and finally thrown open the door between himself and his creatures. In Christ, God has become God more concretely, more personally and more "addressably," "a partner of men."[222]

He is saying the true Christian brotherhood is founded in nothing less than man's incorporation into Jesus Christ, who is not a mere idea but a true actuality, a person. One enters this reality through baptism and reestablishes it constantly through the participation and partaking of the Eucharist and, in that way, Christian brotherhood is "grasped in faith and acquired through the sacraments,"[223] and this forms the dogmatic basis for it.

Ratzinger added that the social dimension of faith should not be undermined. For him, it is best expressed in the opening words, "Our Father," where only Christ could say *my Father,* and the rest of us can only call him *our Father* inasmuch as we are part of the community of God's children in Christ. This type of faith, Ratzinger affirms, will lead us to a new relationship with God and one another. Moreover, in people's relationships to one another, it will form the new ethics, where "to become one in Christ means to lose one's 'oneself,' to cease to regard one's ego as an absolute."[224] In relationship to the present attitude of relativism, the true meaning of Christian brotherhood finds the strength of its argument not in an individual's private ego, but in opening up to the history of the *our* being in the Body of Christ. Opening up to the social dimension of *we* in one's life would help to overcome many of the contemporary depressions and anxieties, which result from many people focusing excessively on themselves and their needs, rather than on others.

Ratzinger continued by saying that the union of Christians in Christ also involves a removal of the separating barriers of nature and history and must transcend the necessary divisions of class, nationalism or race. Among these, nationalism is seen as a significant barrier in which every generation must redefine itself.[225] Ratzinger's attempts to overcome nationalism relates to those against relativism. From that perspective, nationalism can be seen as another form of relativism, since it places too much emphasis on the particulars of a nation and does not consider the deeper responsibility for what is universal, what is human. Christianity, however, does not require the removal of all barriers, since Christianity itself creates a new and unavoidable barrier, that of Christians and non-Christians; at the same time, the commitment of love is independent of this division. In the end, Ratzinger returned to the question he raised before: Is the idea of Christian brotherhood as it is realized in the Church grounded on realistic expectations for its fulfillment or not? He himself answers that it *is*, because by going back to the original Christian meaning of *ekklesia* one learns that Christian brotherhood demands "concretely the brotherhood of the individual parish community,"[226] its source and center being the Eucharist.

Ratzinger also addressed the question of those outside the Church. The Enlightenment unsuccessfully tried to erase any possible demarcation between people. However, Ratzinger argued, it is precisely this *Christian line of demarcation* that "ultimately serves a universal openness."[227] Otherwise, one would fall into empty romanticism and to the level of unrealizable expectations. What is realizable for him is sharing in the Eucharistic meal and thus forming the Body of Christ. It is precisely in this concreteness of a Body, the definite brotherhood and separation from the rest is formed, however, not against the whole, but in the service of all. This leads to the missionary factor of Christian activity where through the election of a few, God seeks to save many. In other words, "however important it is for the Church to grow into the unity of a single brotherhood, she must always remember that she is only one of two sons, one brother beside another, and that the mission is not to condemn the wayward brother, but to save him."[228] Here, Ratzinger is explicitly under the influence of Karl Barth[229] and this idea for him is the core of *true universalism*, where one needs to strive to acquire through the Church's missionary work an intelligent proclamation of faith, agape, and vicarious suffering.[230] However, it should be remarked, such universalism, the salvation of everyone, is not part of Christian faith, but of Christian hope. In the end of his book, Ratzinger presented what he believed to be the true state of the Church:

> …the relationship between the "few" and the "many" reveals the true measure of the Church's catholicity. In external numbers it will never be fully "catholic" (that is, all-embracing), but will always remain a small flock – smaller even than statistics suggest, statistics which lie when they call many "brothers" who are in fact merely *pseudadelphoi*, Christians by name only. In her suffering and love, however, she will always stand for the "many," for all. In her love and her suffering she surmounts all frontiers and is truly "catholic."[231]

On January 1, 1958, Ratzinger was named professor of fundamental theology and dogma at the College of Philosophy and Theology in Freising. In 1959, he moved to the University of Bonn and began his lectures as an ordinary professor of fundamental theology. Here he befriended the Indologist Paul Hacker, who was a master of Indian languages. How Ratzinger attributes certain Indian influence to the growth of relativism in the West will be explained later. For now, here are his remarks regarding Hacker:

> When I met him, Hacker was a practicing Lutheran but also a man who was always searching. His search had led him to Indology, but his explorations into the intellectual and spiritual universe of India had brought him back again to Christianity.… His passionate temperament knew no bounds and so, for example, he would spend whole nights with one or more bottles of red wine in conversation with the Fathers or Luther. His road then led him into the Catholic Church, belonging at first to the faction critical of Rome. Later on he became more and more critical of the Council and inveighed especially against Karl Rahner's theology

with a vehemence that, although quite in keeping with his volcanic temperament, nevertheless was not apt to win a hearing for his arguments. Thus, too, his book on Luther, the fruit of many years of inner struggle, was unfortunately brushed aside as the work of an outsider and a dilettante – neither of which he really was; the precision of his textual analyses remained unsurpassable to the end.... It was inevitable that such friendship would include all kind of tensions, but my gratitude to him remains unchanged because, both in the realm of theology and in that of the history of religion, I am much in his debt.... His work is hardly taken into account nowadays, but I am convinced that someday it will be rediscovered and then it will still have much to say.[232]

It was those years and because of this friendship that Ratzinger's interest in the world of religions focused on Hinduism. As Kuhn recalls, some students "complained jokingly about it. They said: 'Ratzinger is totally absorbed in Hinduism, he talks to us only of Rama and of Krishna and we can't take it anymore.'"[233]

4

AGAINST RELATIVISM AT VATICAN II

1. Ratzinger as *peritus* and *Dei Verbum*

Ratzinger wrote a now-famous lecture read by Cardinal Frings in Genoa on November 19, 1961 called "Vatican Council II in the Face of Modern Thought," that summarized the expectations of reform stirred in most European episcopates by the coming ecclesial assembly.[234] He was not impressed with the euphoria surrounding the gathering of the Second Vatican Council (1962-1965). He saw it as a continuation of "the atmosphere of renewal and hope that had reigned in the Church and in theology since the end of the First World War despite the perils of the National Socialist era."[235] It might have been the sober view of the future of the Church preceding the Council that caught the attention of the almost-blind Cardinal Frings of Cologne, who in turn then invited Ratzinger to be his theological adviser and later *peritus* at the Council.[236]

During the Council years, Ratzinger wrote the conciliar journal *Theological Highlights of Vatican II*, where he shared with his fellow compatriots the basic ideas and developments of the Council. In this journal, he often commented on what he thought was the true mission of the Council.[237] Ratzinger wrote as follows: "It is perhaps fair to say that the first real task of the Council was to overcome the indolent, euphoric feeling that all was well with the Church and to bring into open the problems smoldering within."[238] Such optimism reflected the general positivistic philosophy of the age, where it was believed, after the horrors of the two world wars, humanity had finally learned its lesson to value and safeguard the peace. The world was working hard to restore itself and hope for a brighter future using new discoveries in science and of energy sources, while at the same time, the Church remained constant during the years of turbulence. However, Ratzinger thought that times had changed and that there were limits to such a positivistic outlook.[239] He concluded, "The renewal of the Church... cannot mean progress in the sense of technological and economical development. This renewal has rather a twofold intention.[240] Its point of reference is contemporary man in his reality and in his world, taken as it is. But the measure of the renewal is Christ, as Scripture witnesses him."[241] With Christ as the measure of the renewal, Ratzinger set limits to what could be done. The contemporary relativistic mindset does not like to have limits placed upon it.

It would be important to note, during the Council, Ratzinger and Karl Rahner (1904-1984) both worked as *periti* and even had a chance of preparing jointly a new schema on revelation.[242] It was then that Ratzinger realized how much he and Rahner differed theologically. Ratzinger believed that Rahner was influenced in his theology by Suarezian scholasticism, German idealism and by Heidegger and thus, "his was a speculative and philosophical theology in which Scripture and the Fathers in the end did not play an important role and in which the historical dimension was really of little significance."[243] This contrasted with Ratzinger's training, represented by the Munich school, which was shaped by Scripture, the reading of the Fathers and a profoundly historical way of thinking. Ratzinger thought the Council should not engage in scholastic disputation simply for the sake of discussion but its efforts should be directed toward the living realities of this world and the Church.

a) The Primacy of Liturgy

The Council's choice first to address liturgy was an important step. Ratzinger considered it to be a decision that was a "profession of faith in what is truly central to the Church – the ever renewed marriage of the Church with the Lord, actualized in the Eucharistic mystery where the Church, participating in the sacrifice of Jesus Christ, fulfills its innermost mission, the adoration of the triune God."[244] True renewal must emphasize "the objective Mystery, rather than the individual's private devotions."[245] This objectivity of faith can be found in Paul's Letter to the Corinthians: "I give thanks to God that I speak in tongues more than any of you, but in the church I would rather speak five words with my mind, so as to instruct others also, than ten thousand words in a tongue" (1 Cor 14:16-19). Therefore, faith must have an objective communal character; however, the dimension of subjectivity in personal prayer is not disregarded. It is like the old saying, *the Church makes prayer and prayer makes the Church*. Therefore, it should come as no surprise that one of the ways to fight back the relativism creeping into Christian faith is by renewing the Church's commitment to prayer and worship. However, it needs to be God whom one worships and not the community of worshippers.

One issue, which arose during the Council, was the use of Latin. Ratzinger observed, "It can hardly be denied that the sterility to which Catholic theology and philosophy had in many ways been doomed since the end of the Enlightenment was due not least to a language in which the living choices of the human spirit no longer found a place."[246] Therefore theology for the most part was not open to new ideas and remained unable to have an impact upon them. Even though the content of the human spirit and of theology cannot be relativized, language can, because the articulation and communication of content is subject to the cultural and linguistic changes during the course of history. However, there needs to be caution when dismissing words; this should be done only when words no longer convey the meaning entrusted to them.

Ratzinger also commented on the presence of the Eastern bishops of the Uniate Churches. He saw it as a sign for the Church to be more open and to become more of what she ought to be, "the East was able again and again to open up the narrow Latin horizon and to force the Council to think not in a Latin, but in a catholic manner and to avoid the fateful equating of Catholicity with Latinity."[247] He also applauded the presence of non-Catholic observers, who although they had no right to speak on the Council floor, were always felt and stood as an example of the diversity surrounding the Church.

b) *The New Position – Pastoral and Ecumenical*

When the schema on revelation was presented to the Council, Ratzinger noticed a different atmosphere than the one on liturgy. He found it "clearly marked in the Syllabus of Pope Pius IX (1864) in which the Church decisively and uncompromisingly detached itself from the growing error of the *modern mind*, and 'as with every historical necessity, however, it undoubtedly went about this with excessive one-sided zeal.'"[248] At the same time, Ratzinger observed that the Council Fathers had already experienced a different positive spirit of the day and did not want to return to the theology of negations and prohibitions as in the years prior to the Council. He wrote, "The fathers were merely concerned with overcoming neo-scholastic intellectualism, for which revelation chiefly meant a store of mysterious supernatural teachings, which automatically reduces faith very much to an acceptance of these supernatural insights."[249] More so, he observed, the passing of the liturgy schema had given rise to the possibility of a new beginning different from the previous patterns of negation and defensiveness. For him:

> The real question behind the discussion could be put this way: Was the intellectual position of "anti-Mod-

ernism" – the old policy of exclusiveness, condemnation and defense leading to an almost neurotic denial of all that was new – to be continued? Or would the Church, after it had taken all the necessary precautions to protect the faith, turn over a new leaf and move on into a new and positive encounter with its own origins, with its brothers and with the world of today? Since a clear majority of the fathers opted for the second alternative, we may even speak of the Council as a new beginning.[250]

According to Ratzinger, two main arguments were used to defend the new position. They rested upon the intention of Pope John XXIII that the texts should be pastoral and their theology ecumenical.[251] However, he sensed the possible dangers of relativism if progressiveness were to become overemphasized. Thus, it was important to clarify the terms *pastoral* and *ecumenical* and their relationship to the Church:

"Pastoral" should not mean nebulous, without substance, mercly "edifying," a meaning sometimes given to it. Rather what was meant was positive care for the man of today who is not helped by condemnations and who has been told for too long what is false and what he may not do. Modern man really wishes to hear what is true. He has, indeed, not heard enough truth, enough of what the faith has to say to our age. "Pastoral" should not mean something vague and imprecise, but rather something free from wrangling and free also from entanglement in questions that concern scholars alone. It should imply openness to the possibility of discussion in a time which calls for new responses and new obligations. "Pastoral" should mean, finally, speaking in the language of Scripture, of the early Church Fathers and of contemporary man. Technical theological language has its purpose and is indeed necessary, but it does not belong in the kerygma and in our confession of faith.[252]

As for *ecumenical*, Ratzinger wrote the following:

> "Ecumenical" must not mean concealing truth so as not to displease others. What is true must be said openly and without concealment; full truth is part of full love. "Ecumenical" must mean that we cease seeing others as mere adversaries against whom we must defend ourselves. We have pursued such a course long enough. "Ecumenical" means that we must try to recognize as brothers, with whom we can speak and from whom we can also learn, those who do not share our views. "Ecumenical" must mean that we give proper attention to the truth which another has and to another's serious Christian concern in a matter in which he differs from us, or even errs. "Ecumenical" means to consider the whole and not to single out some partial aspect that calls for condemnation or correction. "Ecumenical" means that we present the inner totality of our faith in order to make known to our separated brothers that Catholicism clearly contains all that is truly Christian. "Ecumenical" and "Catholic" in their very etymology say the same thing. Therefore to be a Catholic is not to become entangled in separatism, but to be open to the fullness of Christianity.[253]

c) Pope Paul VI and Christ-centeredness

Although the second session began under the new pope – Paul VI, Ratzinger observed that the he did not differ much from his predecessor. Ratzinger noticed "everything he did afterwards bore this same imprint: 'willingness to welcome change and innovation, but always in keeping with the continuity of history.'"[254] He recalled Pope Paul's first address and was most impressed by how Christ-centered it was. Pope Paul VI mentioned in his address the mosaic in the apse of St. Paul Outside-the-Walls, where Christ the Pantocrator is depicted standing upright with Pope Honorius III prostrated before him. This ancient mosaic, Ratzinger thought, "reflecting as it does early Christian awareness of Christ's primacy, interpreted the present age and as the pope saw it, served as a yardstick by which to measure events."[255] It is in Christ that one finds the measure of all truth and thus genuine renewal, change and life. In Christ, the living person – as revealed by his life, death and resurrection – is the source of revelation.

d) The Limits of Exegesis

However, a controversy arose during the session regarding the role of the historical-critical method, which was taking a ruling stand in theology. The tension was created by the fact that those who apply this method would not allow the authority of the Church to restrict its application. In their understanding, only the historical argument is the final authority. Moreover, seen from this perspective "the concept of *tradition* had itself become questionable, since this method will not allow for an oral tradition running alongside Scripture and reaching back to the apostles – and hence offering another source of historical knowledge besides the Bible."[256]

The invisible key figure in this dispute was Tübingen's dogma specialist, Joseph Geiselmann and his discoveries of a different interpretation of what Trent had to say on the issue of revelation. Geiselmann did not attend the Council. According to his findings, "Trent had wanted to teach that there can be no distribution of the contents of faith into Scripture, on the one hand, and tradition on the other, but rather that both Scripture and tradition, each is complete in itself."[257] If this is true, then Trent was really saying Scripture contains the deposit of faith whole and entire and nothing can be said to be a part of the faith which cannot be found in the Bible – much akin to the Protestant *sola scriptura* principle. Likewise, nothing can be supported by the Scriptures that did not pass the scrutiny of the historical-critical method. What this new theory meant was:

> ...exegesis now had to become the highest authority in the Church; and since, by the very nature of human reason and historical work, no agreement among interpreters can be expected in the case of such difficult texts (since here acknowledged or unacknowledged prejudices are always at work), all of this meant that faith had to retreat into the region of the indeterminate and continually changing that characterizes historical or would-be historical hypotheses. In other words, believing now amounted to having opinions and was in need of constant revision.[258]

Although the Council opposed such a theory, the idea stimulated quite a few minds. Ratzinger attempted to alter Geiselmann's thesis by reading the Trent documents himself where he found the same understanding of tradition as in Bonaventure. Ratzinger writes:

> Revelation, which is to say, God's approach to man, is always greater than what can be contained in human words, greater even than the words of Scripture. As I have already said in connection with my work on Bonaventure, both in the Middle Ages and at Trent it would have been impossible to refer to Scripture simply as "revelation," as is the normal linguistic usage today. Scripture is the essential witness of revelation, but revelation is something alive, something greater and *more*: proper to it is the fact that it *arrives* and *is perceived* – otherwise it could not have become revelation. Revelation is not a meteor fallen to earth that now lies around somewhere as a rock mass from which rock samples can be taken and submitted to laboratory analysis. Revelation has instruments; but it is not sepa-

rable from the living God and it always requires a living person to whom it is communicated. Its goal is always to gather and unite man and this is why the Church is a necessary aspect of revelation. If, however, revelation is more than Scripture, if it transcends Scripture, then the "rock analysis" – which is to say, the historical-critical method – cannot be the last word concerning revelation; rather, the living organism of the faith of all ages is then an intrinsic part of revelation. And what we call "tradition" is precisely that part of revelation that goes above and beyond Scripture and cannot be comprehended within a code of formulas.[259]

For Ratzinger, revelation provides understanding of man as the one who, through dialogue, is able to listen to the word of God, and in this way is able to point to the presence of God. What revelation helps to answer is the life-altering question of who one is and ought to be as a human being. It is that in which:

> the true nature of revelation and its truth becomes apparent: it does not reveal *something*, nor does it reveal various kinds of things, but in the man Jesus, in the man who is God, we are able to understand the whole nature of man. The truth and deception of human existence appear in the light of the man who is truly man because he comes entirely from God and is *una persona* with God himself.[260]

This will be discussed in further detail when covering Ratzinger's commentaries about *Gaudium et Spes*.

e) The Eschatological Perspective

Ratzinger believed the Church's perspective during the Council and especially when discussing the question of revelation should be eschatological. For him, "all knowledge in the time of the Church remains knowledge seen in a mirror – and hence fragmentary. The direct relation to reality, to the face of God itself, is kept for the *eschaton* (cf. 1 Cor 13:12)… this is *theologia negativa*, which necessarily involves the setting of a certain limit to both kerygmatic and ecclesial positivity."[261]

In his comments on the Mariological question, Ratzinger observed, "With Mariology integrated into ecclesiology, the idea of the Church now encompasses the heavenly Church with the result that the eschatological as well as the spiritual aspects of the Church are strengthened."[262] This kind of ecclesiology formed the basis for Ratzinger's opposition to contemporary individualist democracy and its desire to be the center of issues facing humanity and the world. As he himself stated years later, "The Council called for a Church made up of men and women open to the transforming activity of God's grace and united, not by democratic consent, but by the objective, in the one Spirit, and within the one divinely-given structure."[263] This issue will be further analyzed when discussing ecclesiology and the issue of democracy in the Church.

2. The Church's Attempts to Understand Herself – *Lumen Gentium*

Ratzinger comments on the schema on the Church and its nature, defined by the Council as "the continuing history of God's relationship with man – led naturally to what is called the 'eschatological' view of the Church."[264] The Church has to be attentive to developments in history, if she wants to be on the same level as God acting in it. The Church cannot be static, but has to be a living organism open to development and accomplishment, which is finally realized only in the *Eschaton*. However, if the Church is considered to be in a state of pilgrimage, it cannot focus solely on the past, even though it is from the past – as it possesses the unique Christ-event as its unchanging center. In other words:

A Christ-centered Church is thus oriented not merely toward past salvific events; it will always also be a Church moving forward under the sign of hope. Its decisive future and its transformation are still ahead. It must therefore always be open to what comes and always ready to shed fixed formulations with which it was once at home so as to march on toward the Lord who is calling and waiting. So seen, the Church's image assumes a more human aspect.[265]

f) The Structure of the Cross

Another question to consider is how can the Church, which is human and imperfect, have any authority in presenting the truth? However, at the time of the Council, this was not a question to be raised, for the Church ruled with unquestionable authority. Nevertheless, Ratzinger did raise the question suggesting that the Church should have the structure of the Cross – to be at all times vertical with God and horizontal with the world. During that time in speaking of how the sacraments are foundational for Christian existence, Ratzinger wrote, the sacraments "express the *vertical* dimension of human existence. They point to the call of God, which is the thing that, first and foremost, makes the human being human."[266] It is important to note the vertical dimension, which Ratzinger considers having brought about such interplay in the Council. According to him, it was what "had happened during previous decades in fraternal dialogue with separated Christians, in the struggle with the world of atheism and in the Church's own spiritual awakening from country to country."[267] Certainly, all this had a positive effect on the Church in the years of the Council. However, as time went on, the vertical has diminished and the horizontal has become more dominant.

Sadly, in present times, the horizontal has become more pronounced, making the world through technology one big village, whereas the vertical is nearly abandoned. This was also illustrated at the Council, where the assembled bishops introduced themselves to one another and thus were able to hold elections that are more meaningful. But some went even further, proposing the assembly split up into small groups. Yet Ratzinger opposed this idea, "not least on the ground that it might lead to fragmentation into national groupings."[268] Later he praised their decision to stay as one, which for him demonstrated a sense of responsibility toward the unicity of truth. In this sense, no council or party has more authority than each person's conscience and theological convictions. When it came to truth, no group had a right to decide as a majority what truth is, or is not, especially when these groupings would really have been wrong in view of every Council member's special responsibility to truth and the need for each to speak only for himself and his conscience. Ratzinger will employ this last principle when he revisits the authority given to the Bishop's conferences, suggesting, in terms of teaching authority, only the individual bishop and not the majority vote has a right to do so. He points out, "after all, a Council faces tougher problems than determining traffic controls or grain prices" since "here, spiritual changes were underway that needed time to mature."[269]

When exercising responsibility in searching for truth, one needs to be carefully informed of the consequences which their choice might bring about. However:

> Besides the initiation of a living "horizontal Catholicity," we may consider, as a product of this first basic Council decision, the restoration of a fruitful interplay between periphery and center, between the living multiplicity of Catholic life (represented by the episcopacy) and the unity which the primacy must protect. And we might add that the interplay between these two elements is not what a puzzled observer might easily have thought it to be – a kind of embarrassing breakdown in the Church. This interplay, the result of mutual stimulation between multiplicity and unity, was rather part of the Church's vital self-fulfillment. All living realities demand just such a dynamic tension within themselves.[270]

During the Council differences arose among the bishops, partly due to historical differences and partly due to variant encounters with the spiritual needs of the present age. Ratzinger thought the strongest initiatives came from bishops of regions marked by religious pluralism, which were in close contact with the problems of separated Christianity, as well as from bishops who were directly confronted with modern atheism and were looking for the response of faith in present times. He observed the emergence of a new awareness of how the Church could conduct a dialogue in fraternal openness without violating the obedience that belongs to faith. Ratzinger observed, in the second session, that the initiative was more evident in the Latin Church and other missionary Churches, who "had become independent collaborators in the work of renewal from which they expected an answer to urgent needs in a situation both full of danger and full of hope."[271] In time, one of the most controversial articles of this constitution will be contained in section 16, where it reads: "Those also can attain to salvation who through no fault of their own do not know the Gospel of Christ or His Church, yet sincerely seek God and moved by grace strive by their deeds to do His will as it is known to them through the dictates of conscience."[272] Is then not any subjective truth equally true? Philip Kennedy, who teaches theology at the University of Oxford observed, "Section 16 is the most radical turnabout in ecumenical relations for five and one-half centuries. It is a stark counterpoint to the dogmatic teaching of the Council of Florence-Ferrara (1442), which insisted that hell fire is the destiny of those who are not received into the Catholic Church before their life's time."[273]

Another topic discussed by the Council was the Church and how she exerts her authority which she received from Christ. The Council reasoned that the college of bishops was the post-apostolic continuation of the college of the Twelve. Therefore "the Episcopal office is a collegial office; essential here is that the office of the individual bishop be correlated with the office of his fellow bishops."[274] It also emphasized that the individual bishop existed not for his own community alone, but that he shared in the overall responsibility for the Church. Here again Ratzinger speaks of the *horizontal* element of being the Church which, if it abandons the *vertical*, would become unstable. Ratzinger will often come back to this theme of the Cross, especially in his writings on liturgy.[275] Such "inner political" discussions suggest to the outsider that the Church is also subject to change and thus, for some, this confirmed a relativist view of the Church.

g) The Church of the Poor

Ratzinger also observed that "it was especially the Latin countries that developed the idea of *the Church of the Poor.* One of the central ideas that liberation theology speaks about is *the preferential option for the poor,* a phrase coming from the 1968 Medellin document,[276] which is also reflected earlier in Vatican II's *Gaudium et Spes* urging Christian solidarity with humanity, especially the poor. Such an assertion opened itself to many interpretations and misinterpretations. Ratzinger observed that the Church for a long time looked like "a Church of baroque princes... closely identified with the ruling classes,"[277] and that the term *Church of the Poor* unquestionably expressed a project of fundamental importance. However, there is also the question of limits, which will be discussed in more detail with the topic of the relationship of liberation theology and Ratzinger. That is why, in later years, Ratzinger attempted to clarify the initial idea of the Council when he wrote, "Where faith is converted into an earthly messianism that justifies the senselessness of destruction and limits man's hope to what is makeable, there we find also a betrayal of Christianity and a betrayal of mankind."[278]

h) The Quicksand of Ecumenism

The question of truth arose on the Council's floor during the discussion on ecumenism. Archbishop Elchinger of Strasbourg declared that the existence of a partial truth found among and taught by the Christians not in communion with the Catholic

Church, must now be recognized: "Now the time has come to recognize with greater respect that there is also a partial truth – often a profound truth – in every doctrine taught by our separated brethren, which we should profess along with them."[279] More so, Ratzinger acknowledges, the position expressed by Cardinal Léger of Montreal, who spoke against doctrinal *immobilism* and who "demanded of the Church the kind of intellectual humility that would not make an unqualified claim to possess the whole truth, an obstacle in the way of those seeking a deeper understanding of Christ's revelation."[280]

Ratzinger further expanded this position by saying that any Council text would be misunderstood if it were expected to reflect all valid theological viewpoints. Such theological perfection can lead to the following issues:

> The greater the hurry to import the best theology of the moment into a Council's statements, the narrower such statements later seemed. So one can only say: Beware of theological perfection! It might not leave room enough for future development. In general, the texts of a Council are not meant to save work for theologians. Rather, they should stimulate such work and open new horizons. If necessary they should also mark off the boundaries between solid ground and quicksand.[281]

It is this *quicksand* one may fall into when in dialogue with non-Catholic parties.[282] This was the case with Professor Edmund Schlink, one of the non-Catholics present at the Council. During his address on ecumenism, as it was understood by the Catholics, he raised a question: Is not "this kind of ecumenism, as some Protestant Christians suspect, merely a continuation of the Counter-Reformation with other, more accommodating methods?"[283] The idea, which made Schlink ask such a question, was that he thought if Rome acknowledges a relationship between a non-Catholic individual and the Church, Rome presumes that grace and salvation come exclusively through that union. Ratzinger refutes this by stating:

> A starting point is provided by Professor Schlink's view that the ecumenical movement is not supposed to be an effort of absorption of the separated Churches by one of the existing Churches (as in the view of the Catholic Church). This view evidently reflects the conviction that none of the "existing Churches" is *the* Church of Jesus Christ but rather that they are various concretizations of the one Church which does not exist as such. None therefore can claim to be *the* Church. It is certain, however, that a Catholic cannot share Schlink's conviction. Ever since the days of primitive Catholicism which reaches back to the time of the New Testament, it has been considered essential to believe that *the* Church really exists, although with shortcomings and that this has been reflected concretely in the visible Church which celebrates the liturgy. The Catholic is convinced that the visible existence of the Church is not merely an organizational cover for a real Church hidden behind it, but on the contrary that, for all its humanity and insufficiency, the visible Church is the actual dwelling place of God among men, that it is *the* Church itself. To that extent Professor Schlink's contention that there exists an identification of the Catholic Church with the Church of Jesus Christ is valid.[284]

i) The Plurality of Churches

One may think this type of reasoning on Ratzinger's part would have killed any possibility for ecumenical dialogue whatsoever. However, in truth it did not because Catholic theology recognizes a plurality of churches. What it means is that "the Church is a communion of communities, *Église des églises*, not in the sense of a federalism but of a body rendered an organic unity by the Eucharistic bond."[285] In other words, each community of the faithful gathered with its bishop around the altar of the Lord to listen to his Word and partake in his Body exemplifies the essence of the Church and therefore is a *Church*. At the same time, in order to be a Church it cannot exist in isolation but needs to be connected to all other Churches, which in the end make up one single Church of Christ.

However, since the ecumenical question is not addressed in the New Testament, it therefore cannot offer any guidance. At the same time, when Ratzinger discussed unity in plurality, he did not understand it as uniformity – a tendency that existed previous to the Council and so was cause for legitimate opposition from people like Professor Schlink. Ratzinger maintained that to achieve any unity, there exist two criteria: one, Catholics should still hold that they are the historical continuation of the *true* Church of Christ, albeit with some deficiency; and two, the non-Catholic Churches must have the markings of a Church, i.e., be a community of the faithful, hold adherence to the Word of God, have sacramental realities and appropriate ministerial roles.[286] Generally, this would be a great challenge to Protestants who, for the most part, lack the sacramental reality and appropriate ministerial roles which, for the Catholic Church, is based on apostolic succession. Eventually, the Council employed Cardinal König's suggestion to call other Christian denominations by the name of *ecclesiastical communities*. In his final commentaries on the second session of the Council, Ratzinger remarked that no matter how great the ideas are that bring about needed renewal, these matters can only be achieved through the daily routine of the Christian service of daily practice of faith, hope and charity of every believer.

3) The Church in the Modern World – *Gaudium et Spes*

Almost all of the commentators on this Council remarked that the general feeling or mood of the Council considerably changed with time. The enthusiasm that had colored the openings of previous sessions was noticeably lessened at the beginning of the last session. For Ratzinger, such a change of mood had a different meaning. In his mind, the mood deepened, became much more Gospel-oriented. This was eloquently expressed in the opening address of the final session by Pope Paul VI:

> In that final address he [Paul VI] again reviewed the objections which not only conservatives but also some of the observers had meanwhile raised against the Council's "modernism." Pope Paul found the answer in the formula that "the religion of this Council was primarily the religion of love." This, said the pope, was also the answer to the objection that the Council had defected from the gospel. "The Lord said, 'By this shall all men know that you are my disciples, that you love one another'" (John 13:35). The primacy of love overcomes doctrinal doubts. It justifies the Council. Let us add now a word from the pope's speech on September 14, which also shows with how little illusion the pope understood love, "The art of loving is often converted into the art of suffering. Should the Church abandon its duty to love because it has become too dangerous or too difficult?"[287]

Ratzinger himself never forgot that love comes through the Cross and thus suffering is inevitable. Moreover, Ratzinger stressed the primary goal of the Council's undertaking was to find a proper way to witness the truth of the Lord in a contemporary world. The focal point is the truth in Jesus Christ, the primary and the supreme criteria in everything we think or do. He refers to the Council's proceedings as their struggle for truth.

j) On Religious Liberty

As the Council began discussing the document on religious liberty, the question of truth reemerged. Ratzinger observed that there still were those who wanted to approach this question on the level of abstract truth and error. Although he agreed it is correct to insist that error does not have the same prerogative as truth, "this was not a problem about truth and error but about the coexistence of people in whom truth and error are often intermixed."[288] Ratzinger maintained that people can only live together when their assertions about truth are consistent with truth. Another objection was expressed that religious freedom was understood as inconsistent with the revealed truth. Ratzinger objected to this by insisting that religious liberty implies the sacred responsibility of conscience and of the human mind toward truth as well as God's communicating his saving revelation, which is meant for all men in all ages. The question is not the call itself, but the way in which it reaches man's freedom to answer this call. The idea of mission provides the inherent basis for the idea of religious freedom, "a faith which demands, on the basis of its claim to universality, universal freedom to preach its message to all nations in the midst of their traditional religions, must also affirm freedom of belief as a basis for the idea of religious liberty and that this liberty is visibly and intrinsically involved in what is most fundamental in the revealed Christian message."[289]

Here it is also important to mention the speech by Cardinal Frings on the theme of Christian liberty. Frings recognized the self-destructive distortions of liberty. This speech "showed readiness to expose, as man-made and temporal, forms that had been considered sacrosanct and to introduce the positive results of modern legal thinking into ecclesiastical structures. These structures had often taken shape during the age of absolutism and therefore were all too human in origin."[290]

When the text *Dignitatis IIumanae*[291] was finally approved, Ratzinger emphasized three major things it accented. First, the unwavering position of the Catholic Church to be the one true religion.[292] Second, the uncompromising character of truth; and third, a continuity in the statements of the official Church such as those of Pius XI and Pius XII on liberty. Ratzinger wrote as follows:

> ...Religious liberty is a matter of social and political coexistence, which does not affect man's relation to truth but only affects truth's historical concretization. Freedom is a vulnerable thing, which can easily destroy itself if used without restriction. Freedom itself demands that the freedom of the individual be protected against the abuse of freedom in its many forms. Such a requirement, however, can lead in turn to the disregard of freedom. There are no sure norms or standards here. The text sought to formulate the limits of the idea of public good order and to define them in such wise that any restriction on freedom is distinctly seen as a means to protect freedom.[293]

Once again, he emphasizes restrictions or limits even to freedom, in order not to have it destroyed. Therefore, in respect to our humanness as being the creation of God, the one who established limits to his creation, we should never want to overstep those limits. When we do, we disregard the natural order and attempt to start playing God ourself.

k) Struggles over the Preparation of the Schema

Ratzinger continued his commentaries on *Gaudium et Spes* – the longest and most controversial document of Vatican II. The document on the Church had the profound difficulty in defining Christianity's role in the modern world. Giuseppe Alberigo commented, "Ratzinger, for example, maintained that 'one must not expect very much from this schema, which can be nothing other than the beginning of a discussion that must be carried out over the following decades.'"[294] Ratzinger wrote that after the first draft of this text was refused by the Council in 1962, along with the second version, which was chiefly drafted by the German moral theologian and Redemptorist Bernhard Häring, the Council was presented with the new version and the architects of the new text were mostly the French bishops and theologians. Although, in the end it became the actual schema discussed on the Council's floor in the fall of 1965, Ratzinger felt it was lacking in the desired theological precision. He attributed such a lack to the actual length of the text – 83 Latin folio pages and "obviously a document of this size could not have been worked out with the needed precision; it was too large for any real discussion."[295]

However, the major weaknesses to this text were more in its content than anything else. Ratzinger stated:

> This was no doubt the most problematical of all the texts, simply because the theological thought needed to achieve a fully satisfactory statement was still lacking. Theology still oscillated between two extremes. There was the enthusiastic affirmation of the world on the one hand, based on the idea of the incarnation (and carried to its most radical point by Teilhard de Chardin) and, on the other hand, a radical theology of the cross, not by any means lightly to be dismissed as Platonistic or even Manichaean.[296]

This unresolved tension between these two tendencies, one of them being the enthusiastic affirmation to the world in a theology of Incarnation and the other one being a more critical view of the theology of the Cross, enables one to evaluate Ratzinger's so-called *progressivism*. As Nichols remarked, "It was controlled not so much by the imperative of modernization or adaptation, *aggiornamento*, but by that of a return to the biblical, patristic and high mediaeval sources, *ressourcement*" [emphasis in original]."[297] Accordingly, Ratzinger and Henri de Lubac tried to overcome an unbalanced tendency that affirms the world as a part of Incarnation but often forgets that in the act of Incarnation there is not only affirmation, but redemption of the world through the Cross as well.[298]

At the same time, Ratzinger observed, "during this debate there was considerable progress in the discussion of how faith should come to terms with the world and renewed hope arose that the Catholic religion might be freed from its shell of cold abstraction,"[299] which had been the case with Scholastic and Neo-Scholastic speculative theology. Ratzinger also remarked that because of our spiritual inadequacies and lack of genuine Christian commitment, progress may lead us nowhere. True Christian commitment is grounded deeper in faith and must avoid keeping up with the trends of the times for their own sake. The Church's desire to be more acquainted with the world does not allow for abandoning its own identity or disregarding past tradition. It must be accomplished with discernment of spirits and its risks:

> Its [the Church's] obedience to the Lord precisely as such must be obedience to him as *pneuma*, as summons today; it must be accomplished with discernment of spirits and must accept the risk of submitting at all times to such discernment. That is of course necessary in order that the moment of the Holy Spirit may not imperceptibly change into the momentary spirit of the age and what is done under the appearance of obedience to the *pneuma* may not in fact be submission to the dictates of fashion and apostasy from the Lord.[300]

l) Dialogue with the World

In order for dialogue to be possible, Ratzinger thought certain conditions were required. As he put it, "there must be two partners with a certain difference or even opposition between them which the discussion seeks to overcome, but at the same time there must be a minimum of agreement for the conversation to take place at all."[301] However a believer who comes into a dialogue cannot, at the same time, put everything into doubt about what he or she believes. It would make dialogue, a sharing of different views and opinions in search of truth, impossible or irrelevant.

Ratzinger believed the Council was looking for a new, non-authoritative form of pronouncement, distinct in such a way that it would "replace authoritative imperatives with the proclamation of the Gospel."[302] This in turn would mean presenting the faith to non-believers devoid of all authoritative claims except the authority of God's truth, which would be recognized by the receiver of the message. In that same line of argumentation, Ratzinger stated that: "The Christian message is first and foremost a *kerygma*, a proclamation. It is an invitation to reception, not to dialogue. Dialogue follows belief. The Church, it follows, must do more than engage the world in dialogue, it must proclaim the Gospel to it."[303] He suggested the Church return to a missionary state, which would communicate the Gospel in an intelligible way to its listeners.

Ratzinger pointed out that Jesus' dialogues and the preaching of the early Christian missionaries, especially St. Paul, involved dialogue, which was not addressed to total strangers. The dialogue was carried on using commonly accepted knowledge without which it would not be possible. In Ratzinger's view, the Council should direct dialogue in the following terms:

> ...the idea of humanism which present-day atheism opposes to faith can serve as the hinge of the discussion and a means of dialogue. The problem of God is approached in the mirror of the idea of full human development and consequently atheism too is examined from the standpoint of humanism. The whole Pastoral Constitution might therefore be described in this light as a discussion between Christian and unbeliever on the question of who and what man really is.[304]

m) The Reality of Sin

Ratzinger supported the argument made by the French authors of the schema. In order to speak to contemporary man, one needed to step out from behind the protective walls of theology and its jargon. However, in doing so, there should be no change in the fundamentals of faith because in speaking about subduing the world and having freedom to decide one's fate, the Christological idea of a man saved by Christ alone must be preserved. Nichols observed that Ratzinger's anxiety over the final version of the document revolved around the question of *soteriological optimism*, which presents itself by weakening the mystery of iniquity and the price paid by God on the Cross in order to overturn sin into grace.[305] Ratzinger believed:

> One easily got the impression that the authors themselves saw the Christological and centrally Christian statements as only acceptable on faith, that they considered this world of faith a kind of second world alongside the first and immediate world of ordinary daily life and that they felt that people should not be prematurely and unnecessarily bothered with the second world. But looking at the text objectively, it was necessary to say: Either faith in Christ really concerns the center of human existence, either faith is something definitely realistic that goes down into the far reaches of the human heart so that the person who accepts faith can only here begin to describe man realistically, or else the world of faith is a word separate from the ordinary world of experience. But how then could faith make its claim on the center of man's existence? Doesn't this really reduce faith to an ideology for those who need such a refuge apart from reality? If theology is really going to move out from behind the walls of specialized science, it must be courageous enough to do this wholeheartedly. It must not in the name of caution leave its finest values hidden there.[306]

Augustine's theology can be felt in Ratzinger's discussion on human nature. He notes that for Augustine, the idea of man as the image of God has a dynamic aspect, "man is the image of God to the extent in which he directs himself to God; man disfigures his likeness to God by turning away from God."[307] Moreover, Ratzinger observed that the Council adopted two other fundamental concepts of Augustinian thought. The first was the distinction between the *homo interior* and *exterior.* The second was "the concept of 'philosophia cordis,' the biblical concept of the heart which for Augustine expresses the unity of interior life and corporeality,"[308] and later became a key concept of Pascal.[309]

n) Teilhard de Chardin and Technology

Ratzinger also observed another issue the Council Fathers were presented with, was that of a growing technological world. He suggested that those who followed Teilhard de Chardin's position are in error, "attributing to the progressive process of hominization as a process of Christification with the cosmic Christ as the Omega point toward which all evolution moves."[310] For Ratzinger, the Christian hope of bringing about the Kingdom of God, in truth, cannot be realized through technological progress, no matter how appealing it may seem. One of the greatest examples of this was the making and using of the atomic bomb, which being one of the highest achievement of the human mind and technology, proved itself to be so frightening and deadly. Ratzinger thought the schema did not make it clear enough that Teilhard de Chardin's vision of redemption through the achievement of technology cannot be even remotely placed on the same level as redemption through Christ. Ratzinger did not deny that those technological achievements have their legitimacy. However, Christological development cannot be equated with the technological, since it happens on a level of human passions. Latently ambiguous technology serves its mission when it serves in love. "The Christian message cannot have as its purpose the glorification of the technological. The technological needs no such glorification. Yet the Christian message should establish critical norms by which to judge the technological."[311]

As today's world is becoming more dependent on technology, such critical norms must be established and followed. Man has altered his understanding of reality. What in earlier times was approached with wonder and awe is now seen as something functional, something that can be measured. This leads to "religious mystery largely vanishing from things because this mystery cannot be methodologically examined."[312] Such an understanding of reality alters the understanding of the meaning of man and his life as well.

o) The Personalistic View

Another development that occurred at the Council was a change in the understanding of the meaning of marriage. Ratzinger noticed the early Church in her development of moral teaching was mostly dependent on the ethics of Stoicism which stated that the main purpose of marriage was procreation. In his opinion, the Council supplanted the procreative view with a personalistic view, in which the focus shifted to the individual's conscience. Ratzinger writes, "We would have to say that the personalistic stress in the contemporary theology of marriage may sometimes risk overlooking the essentially social significance of marriage."[313] Moreover, a personalist perspective might easily lead to an artificial construction which cannot be connected to reality or revelation. In one of his interviews, Ratzinger explains how he became acquainted with the personalism theories of Heidegger and Jaspers. A key book at the time entitled *The Revolution of Thought* was written by his moral theology professor Theodor Steinbüchel who emphasized the pardigmatic shift from neo-Kantianism to personalism that was taking place.[314] However, a danger arises when this kind of position becomes a norm in itself, because it is a form of relativism.

p) The Crisis of the Missionary Task

One of the final schemas of the Council addressed the issue of missions. Bishops of missionary countries stated that the
very idea of mission was in crisis because of a profound change
in modern thinking. They argued that:

> The motive which had driven missionaries in the past
> to bring other people to Christ had increasingly lost
> its urgency. What drove the great missionaries at the
> beginning of the modern era to go out into the world
> and what filled them with holy unrest, was the convic-
> tion that salvation is in Christ alone. The untold mil-
> lions of people who suddenly emerged from unknown
> worlds beyond the horizon would thus be hopelessly
> doomed to eternal ruin without the message of the
> Gospel. Therefore, the sacred obligation of the faith-
> ful to preach the Gospel everywhere seemed the most
> compelling responsibility of brotherly love, since love
> not only concerned particular earthly needs, but the
> destiny of all men. What was involved was either eter-
> nal salvation or eternal damnation. Meantime, in recent
> generations, the idea had more and more come to pre-
> vail that God can save and wants to save all men even
> though outside the Church, although ultimately not
> without the Church. This idea hitherto only applied by
> way of concession and exception. Moreover, in recent
> times a more optimistic interpretation of the meaning
> of the world religions has been propounded.[315]

Another factor mentioned during the Council, was that missionaries for the most part failed in Asia. The most discouraging
thing, in Ratzinger's view was that another European entity was
more successful in rooting itself throughout the world. Marxism
conquered so much of the world disregarding all of the theories
of adoption and cultural implantation as well as adjustment developed by missionary theology, because Marxism could disregard

missionary adjustments by promising something new and on a different level that people could accept without giving up their ways. That new promise was to create unity based on material wealth, or economy. Though economic unity was a goal, it did not bring about the desired satisfaction and goodness to humanity. Ratzinger predicted this when he commented:

> If it is a fact that human history moves relentlessly toward the unification of mankind, then this unification must not be a mere economic unification through technological achievement. It must become unification in view of human values, unification of the spirit and of what is highest in the human spirit, its relationship to God. A unification which is not unification in spirit would lead mankind to ultimate self-destruction through a conflict between external cooperation and inner antagonism.[316]

It is significant to note, if Ratzinger's thoughts on unification of spirit had been properly understood, there might have been a greater renewal of missionary zeal.

q) Post-Conciliar Observations

Ratzinger ended his commentaries on the Council with a few contemporary observations: "I do not refer to the fact that here and there (and perhaps not so rarely) renewal is mistakenly taken to mean the dilution and cheapening of religion.... I do not mean that here and there people seem to demand not so much truth as modernity and they take this as the sufficient standard for behavior."[317] Ratzinger also warned of what the Council could not achieve. The Council could not take away on its own account the Church's shortcomings originating from man's frailty and therefore constant renewal will be needed until the end of time. He reminded people not to forget their true human situation and its frailty, which in turn required a constant renewal in the

Spirit and in grace. Whereas at the time his perceptions were not of primary urgency, with time and with the increasing dangers caused by the dictatorship of relativism, they will become much more significant in other areas, not simply theology.

The ending note was a signature statement of Ratzinger himself. He spoke of the Church's faith safeguarded, as so many times before, in the faith of simple people. He said, "The faith of those who are simple of heart is the most precious treasure of the Church."[318] He himself always tried to live this way. As archbishop of Munich in his sermon given on December 31, 1979, following the quarrel caused by the silencing of Küng, he stated, "The Christian believer is a simple person: bishops should protect the faith of these little people against the power of intellectuals."[319] For Ratzinger, everything the Council decided is only a starting point. The real importance of its decisions came only when these changes are implemented in the everyday life of the Church. Nichols gives the following summary of Ratzinger's ending comments on the Council's proceedings thusly:

> Ratzinger's 'Epilogue' strikes more than one somber note. Here and there, he thought and perhaps more frequently than this phrase would imply, 'renewal' would be regarded as synonymous with the 'dilution and trivialization of the whole.' Here and there, the pleasure of liturgical experimentation would 'belittle and discredit' the reform in worship. Here and there, people would enquire after modernity, not after truth and make what was contemporary the measure of all they did. Already, he noted, the faithful were complaining of preachers whose sermon pattern was "It was said to you of old – but I say to you...." Amid the joy at the Council's many evangelical achievements, such warning-signs should not, he felt, be overlooked.[320]

Already one may clearly detect in this summary an early warning against the spreading movement of relativism.

In the remaining years of the Council, Ratzinger began to detect a peculiar, and at the same time dangerous, phenomenon. He described it as the growing impression among theologians that nothing was considered stable any more in the Church and everything was open to revision. It appeared that the Council was acting like a secular parliament, divided into parties, where the Council Fathers would be taking sides with one group or the other. However, what was more disturbing was that even faith was now perceived to be dependent upon human decision-making and essential tenets like the Creed – before seen as untouchable – were now subjected to the scrutiny of scholars.[321] In Ratzinger's view, these things were happening because of the role theologians took upon themselves during the Council.[322] Since the bishops allowed themselves to be informed by their advisers in all matters, it gave the impression that from now on nothing can be said by them unless first approved by the experts.

Moreover, Ratzinger observed, behind this tendency was the idea of the ecclesial sovereignty of the people, in that the people determined what it wants to understand by Church, since *Church* already seemed equated with the *People of God*. As one of his students, Vinzenz Pfnür, recalled, "The first signs of chaos appeared not so much in the faculty as in the parishes. The parish priests began to change the liturgy to their own liking and on that he straightaway made very critical judgments."[323] Ratzinger became deeply troubled by these changes in ecclesial climate. In 1966, at the conference held at Bamberg, Ratzinger delivered this analysis of what he saw to be the effects of Vatican II:

> In this address he supported of course liturgical reform, the Church's greater openness to the world and efforts toward Church unity. But the overall assessment is quite grim. In the liturgy he found faulty fascination with the archaic as well as excessive modernization; the Church's relationship with the world had led it to carelessly turn away from the Cross; finally, in the name of Church unity, some are succumbing to a

naïve impetuosity (Voreiligkeit) hoping to eliminate controversial theology.[324]

One could simply connect the above-mentioned concept of *Voreiligkeit* to that of relativism. In later years, during a presentation at the University of Münster, few took note of the warning Ratzinger gave.[325] Some argue that in time there was a noticeable change in Ratzinger's position held during the Council. However, as he himself said, and others would say about him, "It is not Ratzinger who has somehow changed and suddenly become reactionary and conservative. It is the secular culture that has drifted beyond the pale."[326]

Ratzinger's contribution to the theology of Vatican II was soon acknowledged by his appointment as one of some forty theologians to the Vatican International Theological Commission. Additionally, after his withdrawal from the journal *Concilium*, his profound concern for the proper understanding of conciliar theology found its expression in a new theological review *Internationale Katholische Zeitschrift/Communio* (1972), launched together with Hans Urs von Balthasar, Henri de Lubac, Karl Lehmann and others, which one of Ratzinger's former doctoral students Father Vincent Twomey described as a "new international periodical of the highest scholarly standard… characterized by its ethos of *sentire cum ecclesia*, that is, thinking with the Church, remaining true to both tradition and contemporary Church teaching while engaging in an open yet critical dialogue with the world."[327] To the public square it now appeared as if the Church had become driftwood amid a sea of relativism.

5

RATZINGER BRINGING RELATIVISM INTO THE OPEN

1. Liberation Theology and Relativism

When Ratzinger talks about relativism, it is mostly an attempt to name a phenomenon, which already had become a part of the Church's reality and reality at large. It is like giving a name to a disease, which had already spread wide enough to show its effects, but even with a name attached to it, still remains to be studied and explained. When studying these matters, questions arise regarding relativism's origin, cause, range and possible cure. The following questions will be addressed: How does Ratzinger define relativism? What are its effects? Why does it appear that relativism has become the raging philosophy of the day? And how does he intend to overcome it?

No one doubts that Joseph Ratzinger is one of the most prolific writers in the contemporary intellectual world.[328] However, he has acknowledged that, although he touches on a great variety of intriguing and important theological topics, he does not deal with many of them in as systematic and complete a way as he himself and his readers would prefer him to.[329] The topic of relativism is no exception to this tendency. There are many references, most of them indirect and only a handful of texts in

101

which Ratzinger explicitly talks about relativism. These texts, presented chronologically are: (a) "Relativism: The Central Problem for Faith Today" – address given in May 1996; (b) Preface to the New Edition of *Introduction to Christianity* "Yesterday, Today, Tomorrow," 2000; (c) Presentation of *Dominus Iesus* (2000); d) the book *Truth and Tolerance: Christian Belief and World Religions*, 2003; (e) *Without Roots: The West, Relativism, Christianity, Islam* – this book which came out in 2006 was based on lectures given by Ratzinger and Marcello Pera in 2004; and (f) The Homily at the Mass *Pro Eligendo Romano Pontifice*, 2005.[330]

a) Failure of the Marxist Dream

Ratzinger's first major text on relativism was "Relativism: The Central Problem for Faith Today."[331] As the prefect of the Congregation for the Doctrine of Faith, Cardinal Ratzinger gave this address to the presidents of the Doctrinal Commissions of the Bishops' Conferences of Latin America in Guadalajara, Mexico in May of 1996. Not surprisingly, Ratzinger began the address speaking about *liberation*. This topic was particularly salient because it was primarily in Latin America where the "theology of liberation" found its home. Ratzinger asserted that in the 1980's, liberation theology was the most urgent challenge to the faith of the Church.[332] It was a great challenge because it seemed to present a plausible and practical response to the fundamental question of Christianity – that of redemption. He suggested that the word *redemption* was equated and replaced with the word *liberation* following the understanding, "If sin exerts its power over the structures and impoverishment is programmed beforehand by them, then its overthrow will come about not through individual conversions but through struggle against the structures of injustice."[333]

Liberation theology – which took its name from Gustavo Gutiérrez's 1971 book *A Theology of Liberation* – called for a social and thus, political action to alter the existing oppressive structures. However, in doing so, liberation theology had presented politics with a task it could not fulfill.[334] It based itself on the *dream* of Marxist philosophy which suggested that people themselves should strive to transform the world around them to bring about true liberation and happiness. When liberation theology follows Marxism, truth is centered on action and the future. In other words, *orthopraxis* takes the place of orthodoxy and *eschato-practice* becomes more important than eschatology.[335] However, in Ratzinger's view, it is wrong because "when politics are used to bring redemption, they promise too much. When they presume to do God's work they become not divine but diabolical."[336] He also defines liberation theology as being faith in praxis, with a clear political character and with a tendency to have salvation realized here and now. According to Cardinal Ratzinger, there are dangers inherent to such a theology. Nichols' explanation of this precaution is that:

> …Ratzinger found himself unable to accept the medieval Franciscan's belief that prior to history's entry into God's eternity, there will be a 'last age' in which the poverty of the Church's Jerusalem beginnings will blossom again in a reign of the poor on earth. Before the name 'liberation theology' was ever heard of, Ratzinger had to arrive at some judgment about this uncanny 13th century anticipation of liberationist eschatology. He points out that this kind of eschatological thinking does not really reproduce the pattern of eschatology in the New Testament.[337]

A more extensive treatment of this issue can be found in the book called *The Ratzinger Report*.[338] Here, Vittorio Messori presented the full text of the document Ratzinger wrote as a private theologian regarding liberation theology.[339] This occurred just before the official Instruction of the Congregation came out in the Fall of 1984.[340] Since liberation theology has certain premises which are related to the issue of relativism, it would be helpful to read the given text and note the connections.

Ratzinger called liberation theology "a phenomenon with an extraordinary number of layers."[341] Though there are positive and negative sides to it, the document focuses on its negative side, since the theology embraces the Marxist fundamental option. However, liberation theology does not fit the classical mold of heresy and, as such, cannot be called one. Remaining faithful to his own methodology, or epistemology, Ratzinger makes it clear at the very beginning that the aim of this document is to detect the grains of truth, which are present in any error.

He continues in establishing the idea of liberation theology as being a universal phenomenon in three ways: (a) that it affects theology not with a new content, but with a different emphasis on its understanding and implementation in Christian living; (b) that although it is primarily centered in Latin America, it goes beyond to other countries and continents as well, especially to those called *Third World* countries; and (c) it goes beyond denominational borders, "from its own starting point it frequently tries to create a new universality for which the classical church divisions are supposed to have become irrelevant."[342]

b) Bultmann's Hermeneutics

What fundamental concepts make up liberation theology? According to Cardinal Ratzinger, before answering that question certain concepts must be observed. One of them revolves around Bultmann and how he shaped a new understanding of Christ. He used the historical-critical method as the basis for judging what is true or not of Jesus in the Gospels. Ratzinger observed that this altered Christology because it opened it to new interpretations making some previous affirmations no longer matter because they are not historically grounded. At the same time, this discredited the Church's teaching authority, because its doctrines seemed based on scientifically untenable theories.

Ratzinger further explains that hermeneutics, properly defined, "expresses the insight that a real understanding of historical texts does not come about by mere historical interpretation and, indeed, every historical interpretation already includes certain prior decisions."[343] In other words, he says that one treasures Scriptural texts because they are interpreted according to the Church's tradition and "through the divine inspiration of the sacred authors, it preserves for us the fundamental dialogue which God has established with man."[344] However, Bultmann, who distrusts the tradition because of its lack of *scientific credibility*, proposes to interpret the Bible in a completely new way, himself employing the existentialist philosophy of Martin Heidegger. What this leads to is a hermeneutical criterion which is no longer based upon the Catholic Church and its rich tradition but to an interpretation of the Bible as understood by an extra-Christian world-view: in the context of Marxist philosophy or the class struggle, by the community or the so-called *people* according to their experience and praxis. Ratzinger recalls the conciliar statement of the *People of God*, which Marxism transforms into a myth and where *people* become "the antithesis of the hierarchy, the antithesis of all institutions, which are seen as oppressive powers."[345]

Also, the concept of *history* then becomes *a crucial interpretative category* by which it is the real revelation and hence the real interpreter of the Bible. This becomes problematic in that when preaching of *the Kingdom of God*, the concept of *kingdom*, which is at the center of liberation theology, cannot be understood spiritually, or as an eschatological eventuality, but as a concrete and particular action or praxis taken in a historical reality with the attempt to transform it into the Kingdom. In the following passage, Ratzinger aptly summarizes his understanding of liberation theology:

> The Exodus becomes the central image of salvation history; the *paschal mystery* is understood as a revolutionary symbol and consequently the *Eucharist* is interpreted as a celebration of liberation in the sense of politico-messianic hope and praxis. The word *redemption* is largely replaced by *liberation*, which is

seen against the background of history and the class struggle as a process of progressive liberation. Absolutely fundamental, finally, is the stress on *praxis:* truth must not be understood metaphysically, for that would be "idealism." Truth is realized in history and its praxis. *Action is truth.* Hence even the ideas which are employed in such action are ultimately interchangeable. Praxis is the sole deciding factor. The only true *orthodoxy* is therefore *orthopraxy.* It follows that the biblical texts can be treated more loosely, for historical criticism has loosened Scripture from the traditional interpretations which now appear to be unscientific. Tradition itself is treated with the greatest possible scientific strictness along the lines of Bultmann. But as for the historically transmitted content of the Bible, it cannot be exclusively binding. Ultimately, what is normative for interpretation is not historical research but the hermeneutic of history experienced in the community or the political group.[346]

He also believes that post-conciliar theology not only helped to lead people toward liberation theology, but also toward the tendency to overcome every dualism – whether it be that of body and soul, of the natural and supernatural, or of the then and now. What then followed is, "one had ceased to work for the benefit of people in this present time and had begun to destroy the present in the interest of a supposed future: thus the real dualism had broken loose."[347]

However, what makes liberation theology difficult to oppose is how it is logically constructed. It is coherent and comprehensible, especially to the modern man and those who oppose it, who are seen as being out of touch with reality, reason and morality. Ratzinger proposes that in order to successfully contradict this kind of thought, what is needed is to make "the logic of faith visible in an equally compelling manner and in presenting it as a logic of reality, i.e., manifesting the concrete force of a better answer attested in lived experience."[348] Although, he does not mention it here explicitly, he probably had in mind the example of the saints. As Ratzinger wrote in his post-conciliar observations, "Whether or not the Council becomes a positive force in the history of the Church depends only indirectly on texts and organizations; the crucial question is whether there are individuals – saints – who, by their personal willingness, which cannot be forced, are ready to effect something new and living."[349] One must live out one's Christian call to sainthood, which one received in baptism.

c) Democratization of the Church

The pragmatism which forms the theology of liberation affects the Church in such a way in that it attempts to *democratize* it. In other words, relativism emerges as the contemporary supplement of a wish to appear democratic, tolerant and humble about one's ability to grasp truth. In this attitude, democracy is perceived as defending "the right of each person to his or her own viewpoint, so much so, indeed, it seems to imply a toler ance that asks one to relativize one's own positions and to shrink from putting them forward as *true*."[350] Even more, Ratzinger himself observes, "There is the intention, with different degrees of intensity, to extend the principle of the majority to the faith and customs.... What does not seem obvious to the majority can- not be obligatory."[351] However, as Stout argues, numbers alone would not provide us a safety from error, since for achieving true justice, one needs more than procedural democracy.[352] In Ratzinger's view, the problem with this is the very notion that faith is no longer considered an inherited absolute coming from the Other but a decision made by the majority of a living group. Ratzinger states:

> The faith, together with its praxis, either comes to us from the Lord through his Church and the sacramen- tal ministry or it does not exist in the absolute. The abandonment of the faith by many is based on the fact

that it seems to them that the faith should be decided by some requests, which would be like a kind of party program: whoever has power decides what must be part of the faith.[353]

Statistics play a prominent role in this process of *democratization*. To this Ratzinger responded, "In such cases, the Pope may and must not hesitate to speak against statistics and the power of opinion with its pretence of possessing exclusive validity. This should happen the more decisively if, as in the hypothetical case I am imagining, the witness of tradition is strongly behind him."[354] In other words, because religion stirs the deepest passions of the human soul a pope has the capacity to change people's aspirations of themselves and their lives.[355] Cardinal Faulhaber's episcopal motto "*Vox populi, Vox Dei*" must not be inverted and thus the voice of the majority does not always apply as people from democratic societies would expect.

Democratization also dramatically alters the present ecclesiology of the Church and as such, threatens its very foundations. The *catholicity* of the Church is not just geographic and chronological, but *diachronic*, meaning that it extends across time. Therefore, the decisions made by the Church are not just made by the people presently holding the leadership positions in the Church, but includes all the members of both the earthly and the heavenly Church.[356] It this sense, Ratzinger says that "one cannot ascertain the *sensus fidelium*, or 'sense of the faithful' merely by taking into account what a majority of Catholics thinks today. One must consider what the testimony of the Church has been throughout the ages."[357] In that case, what constitutes the *real* majority behind the Church's decision might appear just a small number of actually visible people, when in fact it is the decision by the *great all* extending through the centuries of the Church's life. Therefore, Ratzinger states that it is "the function of the Magisterium to uphold the testimony of every generation of believers over against the tyranny of the present.... [In doing so] the Magisterium reflects a genuinely democratic principle: it honors the witness to the faith of Catholics from every era of Church history."[358] Once again, Ratzinger would support the classic ecclesiological view that authoritative truth does not come from accumulating the majority's opinion, but by accepting it from the greater spheres of the transcendent and incarnated God through revelation as his sovereign self-communication. Democratic processes fall mute in front of divine self-revelation, lest revelation is beholden to relativism.

John Reid suggests that Ratzinger confronts this type of understanding of the Church with Protestantism, which bases its doctrine on the principle of *sola scriptura,* and "the inference is drawn that 'faith comes from one's individual perceptions, from intellectual application along with the contribution of the experts.'"[359] However, this somewhat modern position is not only confined to Protestantism. One could also find it among some Catholic theologians who perceive the Church as a human construction or an instrument of man's own making, which one could easily adapt according to one's present needs.[360] However, Ratzinger would argue that the Catholic Church being a supernatural, God-willed structure, cannot be seen as merely a sociological human-made reality. For him, the Church's "form is regarded as not only providentially emergent (as Rahner), not only as willed by God (*iure divino*), but as dominically (i.e. historically) prescribed."[361] The key issue here is precisely the historical aspect of it.

Reid also points out that Ratzinger makes a connection between the questions of Church and truth. However, as Ratzinger himself observed:

> In a world in which, at bottom, many believers are gripped by skepticism, the conviction of the Church that there is *one truth* and that this one truth can as such be recognized, expressed and also clearly defined within certain bounds, appears scandalous. It is also experienced as offensive by many Catholics who have lost sight of the essence of the Church. The Church

is, however, not only a human organization; she also has a deposit to defend that does not belong to her, the proclamation and transmission of which is guaranteed through a teaching office that brings it close to men of all times in a fitting manner.[362]

For him, revelation is truth and the Church with its hierarchy is entrusted to safeguard and pass on this truth. Following this model, the faithful are then required to submit themselves to *an iron discipline* forbidding any movement away from or around the Church in order to avoid the possibility of error.[363] Whether Cardinal Ratzinger would say it in such a way is somewhat doubtful because though he believes that a certain amount of submission by the faithful is necessary, it is not to demonstrate the Church's dominance over them but to protect and ground the faithful in truth. That is why, in his view, every orthodox effort to confront heresy would lead to some discrepancy, "as the illumination of the necessary truth places others in shadow."[364] One would probably wonder what kind of changes, if any, Ratzinger would allow. However, as Reid observes in Ratzinger's case, change is not "abjured but affirmed and linked with continuity: the Church moves forward out of the past, into the future, but conserving its fruits as it moves forward; not making a 'scorched earth' of what has been; but not slithering back into the comfortable prison house security of the past."[365] In terms of the relationship of the Church with the modern world, Ratzinger agrees that the position taken by the Council was the correct one; however, with time, certain interpretations caused such turmoil that he felt it was time to abjure the "unrestrained and unfiltered opening to the world, that is to say, to the dominant modern mentality."[366]

In that sense, according to Ratzinger, the most pronounced area of reform, and therefore change in the Church, was liturgy. Many different phases of liturgical reform left people with the opinion that liturgy could be changed at random. Even more, certain democratization occurred which allowed for a new ecclesiology by which it became possible for local authority to assume central authority. Using relativistic logic, this can be further extended to the community itself, especially since it is the unit which most closely bonds and expresses itself in liturgy. Therefore, Ratzinger concludes:

> Following the rationalist and puritanical tendency of the 1970s and even the 1980s, today there is weariness with the pure, spoken liturgy and a living liturgy is sought that does not delay in coming closer to the New Age tendencies: the inebriating and ecstatic is sought and not the *logike latreia*, the *rationabilis oblatio* about which Paul speaks and with him the Roman liturgy (cf. Rm 12:1).[367]

Although liberation theology has centered itself in Latin America and other Third World countries, according to Ratzinger, its founders come from the affluent West. It is, he says, an "attempt to test, in a concrete scenario, ideologies that have been invented in the laboratory by European theoreticians.... It is a kind of cultural imperialism, even if it is portrayed as the spontaneous creation of the disenfranchised masses."[368] Where Marxism was a ruling ideology, such as the former Soviet republics, liberation is having an opposite consequence. These countries are trying to liberate themselves from the deleterious effects of Marxist socialism without embracing the capitalism of the West. Ratzinger believes that Marxism is a deadly form of atheism, whose philosophy and moral goals represent:

> ...a more insidious temptation than many practical atheisms which are consequently less ambitious intellectually. For the Marxist ideology actually uses the Jewish-Christian tradition and turns it into a godless prophetic movement; man's religious energies are used as a tool for political ends and directed to a merely earthy hope, which is equivalent to standing the Christian yearning for eternal life on its head. This

perversion of the biblical tradition deludes many believers who are convinced in good faith that the cause
of Christ is the same as that proclaimed by the heralds
of political revolution.[369]

Ratzinger also laments that what often makes dialogue impossible
with the representatives of liberation theology is their predisposi-
tion that human reality could only be understood as divided into
the struggling classes of the oppressors and the oppressed. Any
other point of view is dismissed.

However, as Ratzinger indicated previously, the true root of
every evil and injustice in this world is sin. He tells that personal
sin is at the root of unjust social structures. Therefore, he concludes, "a more human society needs to begin with the root, not
with the trunk and branches, of the tree of injustice."[370] In order
to oppose the force of sin, what is needed is to place one's faith in
God and embrace his Son, Jesus Christ, who redeemed and freed
us from this fatal condition. In the end, one can conclude that in
Ratzinger's view Marxism is just another variation of relativism.

d) Ratzinger defining Relativism

Events of the late 1980s, such as the fall of the Berlin Wall
and the breakdown of the Soviet Union, demonstrated to the
world the ineffectiveness of Marxism. Marxism believed that

> ...it knew the structure of world history and from there
> it tried to show how history could be led definitively
> along the right path. The fact that the presumption
> was based on what was apparently a strictly scientific
> method that totally substituted science for faith and
> made science the praxis gave it a strong appeal. All
> the unfulfilled promises of religions seemed attainable
> through a scientifically based political praxis.[371]

When the Marxist vision failed, Ratzinger observed that a great disillusionment followed which found its expression in the growing fascination with the philosophy of nihilism or, as he called it, *total relativism.* However, he does not see nihilism and relativism as one and the same, "for where relativism is consistently thought through and lived (without clinging secretly to an ultimate trust that comes from faith), either it becomes nihilism or else it expands positivism into the power that dominates everything, thus ending once again in totalitarian conditions."[372] Nevertheless, in Ratzinger's opinion, relativism and nihilism are two possible coping mechanisms for those who became disillusioned with the hopes raised by Marxism. It would also help explain why a good number of college students became attracted to Friedrich Nietzsche and his philosophy of nihilism as well as to relativism.[373]

Though Cardinal Ratzinger presents relativism as a central issue to faith today, he himself never gives a clear definition of the word. Instead, he explains relativism's presence in today's world and formulates it as a kind of phenomenon not only presented as the acceptance before the immensity of the truth but also as a "position defined positively by the concepts of tolerance and knowledge through dialogue and freedom, concepts that would be limited if the existence of one valid truth for all were affirmed."[374] Such a description by Ratzinger seems to indicate there are two kinds of relativism: a positive and negative relativism with the latter being termed *total relativism.*

Relativism can be defined positively, by the ruling concepts of the day, such as tolerance, knowledge, dialogue and freedom. Ratzinger would not have a problem if these concepts were limited by the one and valid truth to all; however, relativism in its positive form falls back to the negative when concepts lose their limits which are established by the objective truth. The legitimacy of some relativism in political or social spheres and even in theology becomes a problem only when the limits of it are overlooked or ignored altogether. According to Cardinal Ratzinger, relativism becomes an issue only if it oversteps its limits established by truth and becomes, in a sense, *total.*[375]

For that, one first needs to know what the truth is. In Ratzinger's view, this question cannot be answered without connecting it to what it means to be a human being. These two questions combined form a more fundamental one. Is there a truth for man that is accessible by all and for all or is it only accessible on the surface, never really getting to know the essence of it? Understanding truth informs man's will and the subsequent action, or praxis, which follows. This is also referred to as ethics and morality. Here Ratzinger follows closely his own master, Romano Guardini, who said, "as time passed, I became less and less concerned… with immediate effect. What I had wanted from the outset, first instinctively and then more and more consciously, was to bring the truth to light. Truth is a power, but only when one does not demand that it have any immediate effect."[376] However, if this praxis is linked with relativism, it leads to what is binding upon no one and renders it – precisely for this reason – superfluous; or, on the other hand, presumes there are absolute standards where in fact they do not exist. In Ratzinger's own words: "When mystery no longer counts for anything, then politics necessarily becomes the religion."[377]

e) Relativism and Politics

Michael Novak, in his article "Culture in Crisis," says the following:

> In today's liberal democracies, Ratzinger has observed, the move to atheism is not as it was in the 19th century, a move toward the objective world of the scientific rationalists. That was the "modern" way and it is now being rejected in favor of a new "post-modern" way. The new way is not toward objectivity, but toward subjectivism; not toward truth as its criterion, but toward power. This, Ratzinger fears, is a move back toward the justification of murder in the name of "tolerance" and subjective choice.[378]

Ratzinger does not deny that, in the realm of politics, a certain amount of relativism is justifiable. Otherwise, it would parallel the error of Marxism, by which the construction of a freely ordered common life for people becomes absolutized, and coexistence between people cannot be absolutized, because it should be a system with a certain amount of freedom. For example, liberal democracy is built on the basis:

> ...that no one can presume to know the true way and it is enriched by the fact that all roads are mutually recognized as fragments of the efforts toward that which is better. Therefore, all roads seek something common in dialogue and they also compete regarding knowledge that cannot be compatible in one common form. A system of freedom ought to be essentially a system of positions that are connected with one another because they are relative, as well as being dependent on historical situations open to new developments. Therefore, a liberal society would be a relativist society: only with that condition could it continue to be free and open to the future.[379]

Ratzinger states, "One single correct political option does not exist," but, if relativism were allowed in politics, there would still be "things that are wrong and can never become right," as well as "things that are right and can never become wrong."[380] Relativism's major problem in politics is that it sees itself as being without limits.

Ratzinger also often speaks of one more important issue, a very urgent one because it is directly related to the political situation of which he himself is a part. It is the question of the European Union and its Constitution, but more so, the "chimerical tolerance," or unruly relativism, implied in its presuppositions. In his words, "the failure to mention Christian roots is not the expression of a superior tolerance that respects all cultures in the same way and chooses not to accord privileges to any one of them."[381] Continues the Cardinal, "rather, it expresses the absolutization of a way of thinking and living that is radically opposed (*inter alia*) to all the other historical cultures of humanity."[382] Ratzinger leads one to that same conclusion:

> Relativism, which is the starting point of this whole process, becomes a dogmatism that believes itself in possession of the definitive knowledge of human reason, with the right to consider everything else merely as a stage in human history that is basically obsolete and deserves to be relativized. In reality, this means that we have need of roots if we are to survive and that we must not lose sight of God if we do not want human dignity to disappear.[383]

f) John Hick's Attenuation of Christology

When Ratzinger speaks of relativism in theology as being the attenuation of Christology, he uses John Hick as an example. Hick is a Presbyterian from England[384] who employs the Kantian distinction between phenomenon and noumenon, which means that reality, "in its infinite mystery, is beyond the scope of the human intellect and [is] reality as known through the 'lenses' of the human mind," and that "our awareness of the Transcendent is necessarily mediated to us through our own conceptual apparatus."[385] After spending a year in India, Hick concluded that Jesus of Nazareth could not have been the only true representation of the living God, but in reality was only one religious leader among others. His reasoning was that:

> The Absolute cannot come into history, but only models and ideal forms that remind us of what can never be grasped as such in history. Therefore, concepts such as the *church, dogma and sacraments* must lose their unconditional character. To make an absolute of such limited forms of mediation or, even more, to consider

them the real encounter with the universally valid truth of God who reveals himself would be the same as elevating oneself to the category of the Absolute, thereby losing the infiniteness of the totally other God.[386]

Hick is refusing to acknowledge the Christian doctrine of the Incarnation – a common position of almost all relativists.[387] The particularity that God can freely choose to come into history and be limited by his own creation is denied. Those who hold this affirm that "there is a binding and valid truth in history in the figure of Jesus Christ and the faith of the Church." They are seen as representatives of fundamentalism, which "constitutes a real attack on the spirit of modernity" especially, against its supreme goods: tolerance and freedom.[388] Ratzinger critiques such thinking by stating, "to return to Hick's thinking, faith in the divinity of one concrete person, as he tells us, leads to fanaticism and particularism, to the dissociation between faith and love and it is precisely this which must be overcome."[389]

g) Recovering the Concept of Dialogue

In the contemporary world, the belief that Jesus Christ is the one valid and binding truth is considered fundamentalistic. A belief in Jesus Christ leads to an "assault upon the spirit of the modern age and, manifested in many forms, as the fundamental threat to the highest good of that age, freedom and tolerance."[390] In order to overcome this assault of fundamentalism, the relativists propose to dialogue. However, as Cardinal Ratzinger notices, the kind of dialogue they propose is not the kind where both parties respect each other's position in trying to acquire the truth:

> ...The dialogue in the relativist sense means setting one's own position or belief on the same level with what the other person believes, ascribing to it, on principle, no more of the truth than to the position of the

other person. Only if my fundamental presupposition is that the other person may be just as much right as I am, or even more so, can any dialogue take place at all. Dialogue, it is said, has to be an exchange between positions that are fundamentally of equal status and thus mutually relative, with the aim of achieving a maximum of cooperation and integration between various religious bodies and entities.[391]

For the relativist it means that "dialogue must be an exchange between positions that have fundamentally the same rank and therefore are mutually relative."[392] However, such a dialogue is a sheer tautology, its outcome at the very best leads toward indifference and at its worst, toward frustration. This new notion of dialogue, which relativists such as Hick, Raimondo Panikkar, Tissa Balasuriya and others[393] propose as a way to reach cooperation and integration between different religions, Ratzinger sees instead as jeopardizing the Christian call for conversion and its missionary work.[394] Instead, he repeats, "mission and dialogue must no longer be antitheses, but must penetrate each other. Dialogue is not random conversation, but aims at persuasion, at discovering the truth. Otherwise it is worthless."[395]

h) Relativism – ex oriente

The works of Hick, and others like him, would not by themselves have been a major influence in promoting contemporary relativism. Cardinal Ratzinger suggests that relativism, as was the case with liberation theology, is "a typical offshoot of the Western world and its forms of philosophical thought."[396] However, he sees that the present historical situation of relativism comes about also from yet another direction – that of the philosophical and religious intuitions of Asia, especially India's Hindu heritage. The Cardinal sees relativism as drawing its force from contact between these two distinct worlds.[397]

Ratzinger suggests that there is a closeness between Europe's post-metaphysical philosophy and Asia's negative theology. In Asia's negative theology, "the divine can never enter unveiled into the world of appearances in which one lives; it always manifests itself in relative reflections and remains beyond all words and notions in an absolute transcendence."[398] Though Ratzinger does not specify what the post-metaphysical philosophy of the West actually looks like, he nevertheless affirms, "the a-religious and pragmatic relativism of Europe and America can get a kind of religious consecration from India, which seems to give its renunciation of dogma the dignity of a greater respect before the mystery of God and man."[399] Here one learns two other features relativism has for Ratzinger – that of being (1) *a-religious* and (2) *pragmatic*. Pragmatization presents a greater concern for theology than being a-religious, which in reality is the nihilistic and atheistic rejection of God's existence.

Referencing the document "Some Tentative Reflections on the Language of Christian Uniqueness: An Indian Perspective,"[400] Ratzinger brings to attention the following observations. In India there is a growing tendency among the Christians to set aside the image of Christ and no longer display it prominently, because he is seen as just another Indian saving myth. However, this is happening not only because of the connection to different religions and their doctrines, but also on a more basic cultural level. Proponents of cultural relativism argue that the meaningfulness of issues comes from "the forms of life in which we collectively engage. All that we take to be significant, sacred, objectively true, or worthy of commitment comes into being through this process."[401] Cardinal Ratzinger states that under the sign of the encounter of cultures, relativism appears to be the real philosophy of humanity, although some would argue that cultural relativism has significant flaws and is greatly overstated.[402] Nevertheless, Ratzinger is led to conclude that in the age of globalization:

Anyone who resists [relativism] not only opposes democracy and tolerance – the basic imperatives of the human community – but also persists obstinately in giving priority to one's Western culture and thus rejects the encounter of cultures, which is well known to be the imperative of the present moment. Those who want to stay with the faith of the Bible and the Church see themselves pushed from the start to a no-man's-land on the cultural level and must as a first measure rediscover the "madness of God" (1 Cor 1:18) to recognize the true wisdom in it.[403]

One may detect Ratzinger expressing his support to those who accept this challenge of the madness of God and live in such a no-man's-land.

i) Orthodoxy and Orthopraxis

As he begins his chapter on orthodoxy and orthopraxis, Cardinal Ratzinger raises the question, where does this new religion of people like Hick lead humankind? Hick in his *Evil and the God of Love*[404] responds, "Man goes from 'self-centeredness,' the existence of the old Adam, to 'reality-centeredness,' the existence of the new man, thus extending from oneself to the otherness of one's neighbor."[405] Ratzinger observes the new development of the concept of person, which now denotes "an individual which has come into being in and through socialization and cannot at all be conceived of independently of society. This individual is produced or made, so to speak, in the mechanism of socialization."[406]

In Ratzinger's judgment, this sounds beautiful, but ultimately it reflects the same emptiness as the call to authenticity proposed by Bultmann, who, in turn, had taken this concept from Heidegger and for which religion is not necessary at all. Ratzinger himself strongly believes that only in and with Jesus Christ, the second Adam begins a new humanity. Here, Christ is not some exceptional human being but rather, *par excellence*, the exemplary human being, in whom God's intention for humanity fully becomes known.[407] In other words:

...he is the restored image of God, "the revelation and the beginning of the definitive mode of human existence," the complete answer to the question "What is the human being?" In him, the second, the definitive Adam (1 Cor 15:14-48; Col 1:15), we are shown what it really is to be human; and we see that, with creation – the first Adam – a preliminary sketch, a rough draft, was given, which means that we are being *en route*, not yet ourselves, but transitioning to what we are to become, as this is revealed in the second Adam.[408]

Ratzinger also questions Paul Knitter, a Catholic theologian and a proponent of relativism with his proposal to overcome the apparent irrelevance of religion as it was expressed by Bultmann and Hick, drawing a new synthesis between Asia and Europe. Knitter joins the theology of pluralist religion with the theology of liberation by suggesting that "interreligious dialogue must be simplified radically and become practically effective by basing it on only one principle: 'the primacy of orthopraxis with regard to orthodoxy.'"[409] Ratzinger immediately makes a connection to Marxism, which also puts praxis above knowledge. However, with Knitter there is something different. Marxism denounces metaphysics altogether, but Knitter proposes that even though the absolute cannot be known, it still can be acted upon. Ratzinger, following his own axiom "mere praxis is not light,"[410] critiques this proposition by questioning how an action can be just if one does not know what the just or unjust is in the first place.

According to Ratzinger, the present understanding of orthopraxis differs from its true meaning. Whereby the religions of India appear not to have a congruent doctrine, in place of doctrine they have a set of ritual acts which need to be followed in order to obtain salvation. Therefore, the correct original meaning of orthopraxis is an exact observance of the ritual, which almost exactly corresponds to the understanding of orthodoxy, especially in the Eastern Christian Churches. There too, "*doxa* was not understood in the sense of 'opinion' (real opinion). From the Greek viewpoint, opinions are always relative."[411] Hence, the real meaning of *doxa* was "glory, glorification," and to be *orthodox* actually means to know and practice the right way in which God wants to be glorified and worshiped. Recognizing this point can lead to dialogue between the East and the West. Ratzinger even speaks of *Neo-Hinduism* which tries to address this same issue from the Indian point of view. Neo-Hinduism looks for the correct praxis, for the right action, at the same time correcting the *theory;* that is its doctrine and "we can see to some extent how 'practical' the Christian belief in God is and how unfair it is to brush these disputed but important distinctions aside as being ultimately irrelevant."[412]

However, as Ratzinger observes, this is not how the term *orthopraxis* is understood in modern theology. By adhering to ritual, a deeper understanding of worship is excluded, thus leaving as *praxis* either *ethics* or *politics*. However, the *ethos* can hardly be a part of a relativist praxis, since it gives no definitive answers to what is good or evil. Instead, what remains is correct political action, which is the primary concern of liberal theology and of Marxism. Ratzinger acknowledges that both follow the original meaning of orthopraxis to the extent that the acceptance of a chosen political action defines who belongs to this group and who does not.

Ratzinger points out that such political action still has the idea of freedom as its guide. Knitter himself follows this principle affirming that "the criterion for differentiating orthopraxis from pseudopraxis is freedom."[413] However, says Ratzinger, Knitter and the other relativists are unable to explain what freedom and the true purpose of human liberation are because "the relativist theories all flow into a state of not being obligatory and thus become superfluous, or else they presume to have an absolute standard that is not found in the praxis, by elevating it to an absolutism that really has no place."[414] It is to this end that mysteries of faith no longer count and therefore politics has to be converted into religion. Ratzinger believes that true freedom and the purpose of human liberation "may awkwardly be described as coming into contact with God, finding him as the basis of our being and all of our acts – discovering that real sense of interiority which gives us an independence from things of this world and a new relationship to them."[415] He adds:

> This union with God is, ultimately, the only real basis on which community with others can rest. Our interior liberty enables us to live in community and serve the needs of all, especially the poor. The type of committed detachment which is the by-product of this interior liberty destroys the roots of all forms of exploitation including the lust for power inherent in political activity; and it opens the eyes to the injustices that are concealed in every system.[416]

i) The Antirationalism of the New Age

Ratzinger notes that such relativists as Hick, Knitter and others, ultimately have to embrace the rationalism which finds its basis in Kant's meaning of reason as they are incapable of metaphysical cognition. Kant referenced St. Augustine as one who renounced the optimism of the Enlightenment by arguing that human nature was distorted by radical evil.[417] However, Kant was not original in his reasoning:

> Greek philosophy deduced, on the basis of the logic inherent in metaphysical thinking, that the immutable God could not enter into mutable relationships and that relationship is proper to mutable man. In the relationship between God and man, therefore, one could speak only of a *relatio non mutua*, a relatedness without reciprocity: man refers to God, but God does not refer to man. The logic seems unavoidable. Infinity requires immutability and immutability excludes relationships that come and go in time and as a result of time.[418]

Therefore, it follows that reason is the only avenue to knowledge and one that does not require the presence *of* or revelation *by* God. This is how the new foundation of religion is sought in the pragmatic anti-rationalism of the *New Age*. The concept of New Age or of the "Age of Aquarius" was introduced in the middle of the past century by Raul Le Cour (1937) and Alice Bailey (1880-1949). Michael Fuss defines New Age as "the result of a mixture of Jewish and Christian elements with the process of secularization, along with Gnosticism and elements of Oriental religions."[419] New Age supporters attempt to solve the problem of relativity by desiring to abandon the subject-object distinction altogether. However:

> Like the old gnosis, this way pretends to be totally at-tuned to all the results of science and to be based on all kinds of scientific knowledge (biology, psychology, sociology and physics). But on the basis of this presup-position, it offers at the same time a considerably anti-rationalist model of religion, a modern "mystic": the Absolute is not to be believed, but to be experienced. God is not a person to be distinguished from the world, but a spiritual energy present in the universe. Religion means the harmony of myself with the cosmic whole, the overcoming of all separation.[420]

It is an attempt to remove all possible limits, which define people and the reality around us. Therefore, redemption is found "in the unbridling of the self, immersion in the exuberance of that which is living and a return to the Whole. Ecstasy is sought; the inebriety of the infinite which can be experienced in inebriating music, rhythm, dance, frenetic lights and dark shadows and the human mass."[421] With this type of relativism, freedom and libera-tion, having no boundaries at all, would be established by nature, culture, society or religion. This also connects to the earlier ques-tion of anthropology – "The New Man" of Hick's – which in this viewpoint becomes no man at all, just a small cloud of spiritual energy entering and disappearing into the Whole.

The New Age movement attempts to re-establish ancient religions and their practices, thereby renouncing the reality of the Living God, who entered peoples' condition and offered his salvation. However, when repeating primitive rituals, liberation is sought and at least for a very short ecstatic moment, man can seemingly become like God. Ratzinger calls it *an anti-rationalist pattern of religion* or "a *modern mysticism* where the absolute is not something to be believed in, but something to be experienced."[422] Here, as in the case of Asiatic religions, God is not a person distinct from the world, but some spiritual energy running through the universe and into which one must merge, thus transcending all possible divisions. Obviously, with such a purpose, reason is not a criterion necessary in becoming "one with the universe." Ratzinger finds it "extraordinary that, at a time when people, not least Christians, are re-discovering the significance of their corporeality, there should be an attempt to save the Christian faith by disembodying it and limiting God to the sole sphere of the spiritual."[423] At this level of mystical experience, "all conflict with scientific reason is excluded from the outset. 'New Age' is, so to speak, the proclamation of the age of mystical religion."[424] One may wonder what makes a modern person so attracted to this type of religiosity:

> ...if the "rational intoxication" of the Christian mystery cannot make us intoxicated with God, then we just have to conjure up the real, concrete intoxication of effective ecstasies, the passionate power of which catches us up and turns us, at least for a moment, into gods, helps us for a moment to sense the pleasure of infinity and to forget the misery of finite existence.[425]

This need for diversion does not satisfy, because it only offers momentary relief. So, what is in the traditional Christian faith that is not satisfying? Cardinal Ratzinger offers some answers.

A number of people abandon the Church community under

the pretext that their faith cannot be decided by some officials or institutions of which they were not a part. This attempt to democratize the faith Ratzinger finds objectionable, because "either the faith or its practice comes to us from the Lord by way of the Church and her sacramental services, or there is no such thing."[426] The Catholic Church is not a democracy, which is a structuring element, but a magisterial, monarchical episcopacy under the universal jurisdiction of the Pope and the College of Bishops.

The type of question raised by relativists, "does the Church have authority to do that?" is like the one Jeffrey Stout raised in his account of the modern flight from authority. He argues that the Enlightenment critique of theism is "strengthened rather than weakened by the non-foundationalist idiom of the modern period."[427] In that regard, the "probabilistic logic of the 17th century carried with it a demand that claims of authority be defended by an appeal to internal evidence."[428] Thomas B. Ommen also observes that not being able to meet such a demand, especially in the context of pluralism, Christianity "either accommodated the modern world or watered down the content of beliefs to a 'thinly disguised atheism' or embraced paradox and an uncritical form of faith."[429]

Peter Berger, the premier scholar in the field of the sociology of knowledge, in his book *A Rumor of Angels*, speaks of that same reality of Christianity, but in a methodological way. He says, the "supernatural has departed from the modern world," and one lives in an age "in which the divine has receded into the background of human concern and consciousness."[430] Even without Berger going to some length to provide enough evidence to demonstrate what he calls "a secularization of consciousness," it is obvious, "those to whom the supernatural is still, or again, a meaningful reality" will find themselves in the status of *a cognitive minority*.[431] Therefore, he concluded, that this "distinctively Christian thought and experience may still be possible in an age largely shaped by social differentiation and the new probability, but only at the margins of public life and in the recesses of private existence."[532] According to Berger, such a minority would eventually become defensive of its *deviant knowledge*,[433] and would have to surrender, ceasing to be plausible to anyone. It is highly unlikely that the present pope will surrender.

j) The Question of Exegesis

Ratzinger wonders what has happened to classical theology that has allowed relativistic and New Age tendencies to become acceptable. What has made it lose credibility? Ratzinger thinks that it was partly due to a changing point in exegesis, which "has proven that Jesus did not consider himself absolutely the Son of God, the incarnate God but that he was made such afterward, in a gradual way, by his disciples."[434] As a response to this take on exegesis, Ratzinger wants to make people understand it does not represent the general position of current exegesis, even though it leaves such an impression. That would be quite impossible, because neither historical research nor hermeneutics can provide this type of certainty, especially since hermeneutics deals with that which is "not purely historical or literary but includes value choices that go beyond a mere verification of the past and a mere interpretation of the texts."[435] Nevertheless, Ratzinger concluded "New Testament exegesis has increasingly relativized Christology."[436] An immediate benefit to that would be the possibility to remove the barrier separating the Jewish or Muslim faiths from Christianity. What would be the cost? Would it be the end of Christianity as such? Ratzinger believes it would be because he is convinced "false simplifications only do damage to the dialogue with the religions."[437] Again, Kant's influence on exegesis can be felt, for he believes the absolute cannot enter or even be adequately recognized in history.[438] Ratzinger refutes this reasoning by stating:

> Many exegetes think like Hick and Knitter and reconstruct the history of Jesus as they do because they share the same philosophy. It is not the exegesis that proves the philosophy, but the philosophy that generates the exegesis. If I know *a priori* (to speak like Kant) that

Jesus cannot be God and that miracles, mysteries and sacraments are three forms of superstition, then I cannot discover what cannot be a fact in the sacred books. I can only describe why and how such affirmations were arrived at and how they were gradually formed.[439]

The way we think generates our opinions and actions and not vice versa. Therefore, it seems logical, in order to correct our actions, we must first endeavor to correct our reason.

Contemporary exegesis employs the historical-critical method. However, Ratzinger points out, because this method is only an instrument and not the goal, it cannot be applied in a completely neutral way. Additionally, when the historical-critical method is applied to the Bible, it is only concerned with the past. Even Eugen Drewermann critiques this method of exegesis since as by definition it "expresses reality, not today's or mine, but yesterday's, another's reality. Therefore, it can never show the Christ of today, tomorrow and always, but only – if it remains faithful to itself – the Christ of yesterday."[440] However, Ratzinger notes, in terms of exegesis and the new meaning of foundations, knowledge can be attained from a careful historical interpretation of text. By doing so, it "helps break the prison of previous philosophical decisions that paralyze interpretation" and "those nets [with which] we want to protect ourselves against God's coming into our lives."[441] Ratzinger cites Brevard S. Childs who acknowledges the 19th century's excitement over the historical-critical method and its promotion as the leading tool of exegesis which led to a separation of theology from the Bible. In order to change this direction, Childs suggests, one must use *canonical criticism*, which means that "the issues encompassed within the cipher 'canon,' namely, Scripture, Church, Word and Spirit, address those basic theological factors – strangely missing in many of the previous debates – without which no truly theological solution to reconcile the Church's Scriptures with modernity can ever be reached."[442] This approach is also closely connected to the community of faith because

Scripture does not bring forth a witness to itself, but points to God's Word calling the Church into existence. Yet the community of faith actively received, shaped and transmitted the Scriptures and the Church provides the context for its correct interpretation for faith and practice. This means that proper interpretation does not consist of an initial stance of seeking a purely objective or neutral reading to which the element of faith is added subsequently, but rather, from the start, the Christian reader receives a particular point of standing from which to identify with the apostolic faith in awaiting a fresh word from God through the Spirit.[443]

Moreover, the new foundation Cardinal Ratzinger speaks about can only be the person of Jesus Christ. As Childs puts it, "True biblical interpretation involves a *Sachkritik*, but one in which the *Sache* is defined in terms of the reality of Jesus Christ."[444]

Ratzinger thinks the crucial point in contemporary theology involves the question of exegesis and the limits of one's reason. However, his primary concern is not so much with theological discourse, but whether it might form a crisis of faith among the simple people. Ratzinger has long admired the faith of what he calls the *little* ones.[445] One of the first to impress him was Konrad of Parzham (1818-1894), a Capuchin brother and porter of his monastery in Altötting, a famous Marian shrine in Bavaria. His beatification and canonization occurred around the time Ratzinger was growing up in that area and he recalls Brother Konrad in his memoirs:

I have often reflected since then on this remarkable disposition of Providence: that, in this century of progress and faith in science, the Church should have found herself represented most clearly in very simple people, in a Bernadette of Lourdes, for instance, or even in a Brother Konrad, who hardly seemed to be touched by the currents of the time. Is this a sign that the Church has lost her power to shape culture and can take root only outside the real current of history? Or is it a sign that the clear view of the essential, which is so often lacking in the "wise and prudent" (see Mt 11:25), is given in our days, too, to little ones?[446]

It is these *little* saints that Ratzinger sees are "a great sign to our time, a sign that moves me ever more deeply, the more I live with and in our time."[447] Ratzinger urges all to "rediscover that luminous trail that is the history of the saints,"[448] especially when one gets discouraged with the "wise and the prudent" in contemporary theology, or the world at large. Aidan Nichols notes that "the mature Ratzinger likewise will speak of theology as subordinate, in the last analysis, to contemplation, charity, holiness and – not least – the attaining of poverty of spirit. As he would put it, writing in 1977, true theology is always 'ordered to the experience of the saints.'"[449] Without such holy correctives, relativism looms as a beguiling alternative.

As already discussed, Cardinal Ratzinger sees the primary source of the crisis in theology as the Kantian treatment of reason. However, he makes it clear, neither reason nor faith could exist without the other: "Faith cannot be liberated if reason itself does not open up again. If the door to metaphysical cognition remains closed, if the limits of human knowledge set by Kant are impassable, faith is destined to atrophy: it simply lacks air to breathe."[450] On the other hand, human reason is not autonomous in the absolute sense, since it always operates in a historical context. However, one is able to cross over only with the help of someone outside history. That is the role of a faith grounded in revelation. Ratzinger expresses his opinion that neo-Scholastic rationalism failed because it tried to reconstruct the *praeambula fidei* with purely rational certainty. Karl Barth was right in opposing this. However, Barth was wrong when he "proposed the faith as a pure paradox that can only exist against reason and totally independent from it."[451] It is with complete confidence that Ratzinger states,

"Reason will not be saved without the faith, but the faith without reason will not be human."[452]

Ratzinger expresses his sincere amazement that in spite of all the challenges the Church and her faith are faced with, she still survives. She does so, because the serene faith of the New Testament and of the Church is still in harmony with what man is. According to Ratzinger, Kant and post-Kantian philosophers have a tendency to portray man as something lesser than he really is and that does not acknowledge that "in man there is an inextinguishable yearning for the infinite."[453] There is only one way to overcome limitations and that is through God, who responded to the question of being by becoming "finite in order to open our finiteness and lead us to the breadth of his infiniteness."[454] It is the Christian faith that is still worthy of today's man, because it addresses the believer and calls the faithful to serve "with a humble spirit and the whole strength of our heart and understanding."[455]

When Cardinal Ratzinger gave this address on relativism in 1996, he spoke of it as not yet being commonplace, but warned us to remain vigilant, so that a "gospel will not be surreptitiously introduced to us – a stone instead of bread – different from the one that the Lord gave us."[456] Focusing on the present tensions in the Church, in terms of its organizational and liturgical aspects, it makes one wonder if the warning given by Ratzinger was ever really heard. It seems to be more like an opening of Pandora's Box – a release of a great variety of issues, with which relativism is connected. In some providential sense, this text may serve as the perfect outline for the present task, which the author of this dissertation has undertaken and that is to explore and to expand in more detail the issues connected to the causes of relativism, as well as to the solutions offered by Joseph Ratzinger in his other writings.

2. *Introduction to Christianity* and the New Millennium

Probably no one would doubt that one of the classical texts of 20th century Catholic theology was *Introduction to Christianity* by Joseph Ratzinger. Published in 1968 as a lecture series, it was directed not so much to theology students as to non-believers. Though Ratzinger believed the book had many flaws, it nevertheless "was able to open a door for many."[457] The book's influence was great, as Balthasarian expert, Edward T. Oakes, SJ explains:

> In 1968, a Professor of theology at the University of Regensburg wrote a modestly sized treatise on the Apostles' Creed called *Introduction to Christianity*. Its impact, however, was anything but modest, for the book so captivated Pope Paul VI that he made its author Archbishop of Munich (and later Cardinal, one of his last appointments to the college); and just a few years later, the new pope, John Paul II, summoned the same man to Rome to head the Congregation for the Doctrine of the Faith. His name, of course, is Joseph Ratzinger.[458]

The impact of this book was so great that when the Soviet Union collapsed in 1988, *Introduction to Christianity* was among the first foreign religious books legally published and sold to the faithful in Lithuania. However, at that time, there was no mention of relativism. It was only in a later edition, published in the year 2000, along with a new preface written by Cardinal Ratzinger, where relativism is specifically mentioned. The universally acknowledged Ratzinger expert, Aidan Nichols finds:

> If there is a single most prominent feature in the new material it would be the sharpening of his critique of relativism and constructivism in all domains. He was not the only observer of the Western scene who noted

that, by the start of the new millennium, the human faculty for registering comprehensive truth (not simply supernatural but even natural) was at a discount.[459]

Something major happened over four decades, something that allowed for the rise of a new phenomenon in religious thought and life. However, this new something did not just appear one day out of nowhere; it was not *creatio ex nihilo*. Every new phenomenon is in some way preconditioned by other factors which contribute to its appearance in human history. As stated earlier, relativism, before it became a part of post-modern reality, had been present in the history of human thought since Hellenistic times: *nihil novi sub sole* – there is nothing new under the sun. Therefore, what are the reasons which allowed relativism to surface now?

a) The year 1968

Cardinal Ratzinger acknowledged in his new preface, since the book was first published in 1968, that world history has moved at an accelerated pace. The same year the book came out marked the rebellion of a new generation which, according to Ratzinger, "not only considered postwar reconstruction in Europe as inadequate, full of injustice, full of selfishness and greed, but also viewed the entire course of history since the triumph of Christianity as a mistake and a failure."[460] Ratzinger recalling this time wrote:

> In my opinion, the events of 1968 and the subsequent development have made clear the direction in which this could go. For the Parisian student revolution, which launched the phenomenon of 1968, did not crash into the Church from outside: rather, it erupted from the post-conciliar fermentations of Catholicism and from earlier trends in revolutionary American Protestant theology. The celebration of the Eucharist on the barricades in Paris as the fraternity of those

struggling for anarchist freedom and as a sign of hope for the political messianism of a new world giving birth to itself in terror shows the essentially religious – or better, pseudo-religious – character of what was going on.[461]

More so, "these young people wanted to improve things at last, to bring about freedom, equality, and justice and they were convinced that they had found the way to this better world in the mainstream of Marxist thought."[462] Where was Ratzinger during these turbulent times and was he personally affected by them?

In 1966, Ratzinger was assigned the second chair of dogmatics at the University of Tübingen. This appointment was strongly supported by Hans Küng, with whom Ratzinger already had developed a personal relationship and inaugurated a new series of books on dogmatic theology. His position in Münster was filled by Johann Baptist Metz,[463] who came there upon Ratzinger's recommendation and whose development of political theology will be an important issue to address for the future prefect of the Congregation for the Doctrine of the Faith. On the onset of his new assignment, everything was going smoothly; however, soon afterward, the ideological paradigm underwent a radical transformation. Ratzinger recalled the shift, "while until now Bultmann's theology and Heidegger's philosophy had determined the frame of reference for thinking, almost overnight the existentialist model collapsed and was replaced by the Marxist."[464] Ernst Bloch and Jürgen Moltmann were the figures behind this change. Ratzinger himself acknowledges that he occasionally had sympathy for Marxist thought, which had its roots in Jewish messianism, to counterbalance the existentialist reduction especially in the doctrine of God; but he was not ready for such a radical shift toward Marxism. In his own words:

> But the destruction of theology that was now occurring (through its politization as conceived by Marxist messianism) was incomparably more radical precisely

because it took biblical hope as its basis but inverted it by keeping the religious ardor but eliminating God and replacing him with the political activity of man. Hope remains, but the party takes the place of God and, along with the party, a totalitarianism that practices an atheistic sort of adoration ready to sacrifice all humanness to its false god. I myself have seen the frightful face of this atheistic piety unveiled, its psychological terror, the abandon with which every moral consideration could be thrown overboard as a bourgeois residue when the ideological goal was at stake. All of this is alarming enough in itself; but it becomes an unrelenting challenge to the theologian when the ideology is presented in the name of the faith and the Church is used as its instrument. The blasphemous manner in which the Cross now came to be despised as a sign of sadomasochism, the hypocrisy with which some still passed themselves off as believers when this was useful, in order not to jeopardize the instruments that were to serve their own private ends: all of this could and should not be made to look harmless or regarded as just another academic quarrel.[465]

Marx did not need God. For him God did not exist. Instead, he adopted the primacy of politics and economics, which for him were the real powers needed to bring about the real change or salvation in people's lives. The "reality in which one had to get involved now was solely the material reality of given historical circumstances, which were to be viewed critically and reformed, redirected to the right goals by using the appropriate means, among which violence was indispensable."[466]

Moreover, the figure of Jesus was interpreted quite differently. He was considered "the embodiment of all the suffering and oppressed and as their spokesman, who calls us to rise up, to change society."[467] Ratzinger observed that what was so appealing about liberation theology was precisely that Christianity once again became part of world history with its *epoch-changing* message. The major problem with this type of thinking, was that "Christian consciousness acquiesced to a great extent – without being aware of it – in the attitude that faith in God is something subjective, which belongs in the private realm and not in the common activities of public life where, in order to be able to get along, we all have to behave now *etsi Deus non daretur*" – as if there were no God.[468] Though God was not rejected outright, he had nothing to do with the daily worries and joys of human life. He was simply reduced to a deistic god whereby man, with his reason and science, was the one who was actually in control. One may see how with a disappearing God, objectivity likewise disappears and the criterion of Protagoras' "man is the measure of all things" takes over as the new dominant mind frame.

b) Progress to "produce" Man

Another concept that Ratzinger discussed was progress. According to him, progress can have at its core such noble ideals as improving the quality of life, but in the process it may reduce man to an object whose purpose would be as mere research material, or as a useful provider of needed organs. In such a case, progress has caused a paradigm shift, where man has lost his humanness and instead has become reduced to a reified object. Coming back to the unrest of 1968, one should also mention the fact that "peals of dissent reverberated through the Church like thunder after Paul VI's encyclical *Humanae Vitae* was issued on July 25, 1968.... Paul's refusal to change the teaching seemed to legitimize a radical skepticism about every claim to truth or authority made by Church authorities."[469] This reaction no doubt to an extent contributed to the appearance of relativism even among the Catholic Christians such as Father Charles Curran.[470] Nevertheless, Ratzinger asks the crucially important question, "If man, in his origin and at his very roots, is only an object to himself, if he is 'produced' and comes off the production line with selected features and accessories, what on earth is man then supposed to think of man?"[471] For such a man to say "I believe" means to lay claim to a new mode of access to reality and one that decisively enlarges the world in which one lives. According to Ratzinger, "in saying *credo* we declare that in this world the receiving of meaning is prior to its making by man – though without denying the value of human creativity. So, far from being irrational, faith is therefore a movement toward meaning and truth, toward the logos."[472]

Ratzinger also observed that with the fall of Marxism, especially in Eastern Europe in 1989, a new interest and search for religion arose:

> In the leaden loneliness of a God-forsaken world, in its interior boredom, the search for mysticism, for any sort of contact with the divine, has sprung up anew. Everywhere there is talk about visions and messages from the other world and wherever there is a report of an apparition, thousands travel there, in order to discover, perhaps, a crack in the world through which heaven might look down on them and send them consolation.[473]

The search for contact with the divine led to a welcomed increase in new lay movements within the Church, which subsequently brought about renewed interest in the different aspects of faith. However, aside from these movements, Ratzinger noticed that Christianity was not a major force in this new search for God, because mass movements have their promises of a new future fulfilled not in numbers, but in concrete persons finding their way to the truth.[474]

c) Jesus, Buddha or Socrates?

The religion with the absolute truth should be a major influence. However, Ratzinger believes, "at a time when we have learned to doubt even whether we can know the transcendent at all and when we are extremely uneasy about the potential for intolerance when claims of truth are made in this area, it seems that the future must belong only to mystical religion."[475] It has become such that the mystical religions of Asia, which offer the *mystical* and not the *doctrinal* aspect of religion and which emphasize experiencing the Other rather than knowing the Other in established ways, are sought. The result is:

> ...individual religions are relativized; for all the differences and, yes, the contradictions among these various sorts of belief, the only thing that matters, ultimately, is the inside of all these different forms, the contact with the ineffable, with the hidden mystery. And to a great extent people agree that this mystery is not completely manifested in any one form of revelation, that it is always glimpsed in random and fragmentary ways and yet is always sought as one and the same thing.... Associated with this relativizing is the notion of a great peace among religions, which recognize each other as different ways of reflecting the one Eternal Being and should leave up to the individual which path he will grope along to find the One who nevertheless unites them all. Through such a relativizing process, the Christian faith is radically changed.[476]

This does not explain what religious relativism is *per se*, but what its effects are. Moreover, as to what becomes radically changed, Ratzinger says it happens in two fundamental places – that of Christology and of the Doctrine of God. The altered understanding of the figure and the role of Jesus Christ has already been discussed to a degree. To that one can only add the relativistic interpretation that Jesus Christ is not the only Son of God, but the one who "has *experienced* God in a special way. He is an enlightened one and therein is no longer fundamentally different from other enlightened individuals, for instance, Buddha."[477]

However, from a Christian Catholic perspective Jesus Christ cannot be compared or seen as equal to other great representatives of world religions. Ratzinger says that the difference lies in the idea, with Buddha or Socrates, that it is not the person that matters, but the way or the path to which figures point. Once the path is found and walked on, Buddha or Socrates should cease to be. That is not the case with Jesus, who presented himself as being the way and the path itself. Ratzinger notes:

> ...With Jesus, what matters is precisely his Person, Christ himself. When he says, "I am he," we hear the tones of the "I AM" on the Mount Horeb. The way consists precisely in following him, for "I am the way and the truth and the life" (Jn 14:6). He himself is the way and there is no way that is independent of him, on which he would no longer matter. Since the real message that he brings is not a doctrine but his very person, we must of course add that this "I" of Jesus refers absolutely to the "Thou" of the Father and is not self-sufficient; rather it is indeed truly a "way."[478]

If Jesus Christ becomes disconnected from leading to the Father then he cannot be *the way*, because the way needs both a point of departure – Jesus' *I*, and a point of destination – the Father's *Thou*. Without this inner dynamic, there occurs a major change in the understanding of the doctrine of God.

d) The Personhood of God

When Jesus' *I* is no longer connected to the Father's *Thou*, the concept of God fundamentally changes. Ratzinger points out, "the question of whether God should be thought of as a person or impersonally now seems to be of secondary importance," and "no longer can an essential difference be noted between theistic and non-theistic forms of religion."[479] Even among Catholics, there arises the tendency to question if it matters whether God is a person or not. These people argue, "The God who speaks and the silent depth of being are, it is suggested, only two different ways of conceiving the ineffable that lies beyond all concepts."[480] However, the Church says it does matter that God is a person, because that is how God revealed himself in the Old Testament and through the person of Jesus Christ. Ratzinger acknowledges that there will always be those who will interpret the personhood of God in a false way, since everything one perceives of him is always less than what the mystery of God contains in itself. Nevertheless, a crucial point to note is, the Christian God has a name, which is not a mere accident, nor an insignificant theological interpretation. It is because God has a name, and therefore is a person, that one is able to communicate and establish a relationship with him:

> When we say that man is the image of God, it means that he is a being designed for relationships; it means that in and through all his relationships, he seeks that relation which is the ground of his existence. In this context, covenant would show us who we are and who God is. And for God, since he is entirely relationship, covenant would not be something external in history, apart from his being, but the manifestation of his self, the "radiance of his countenance."[481]

Therefore, when the Asiatic religions promote a sort of *evaporation* into the mystery of God, an individual has little value and "there is no uniqueness of persons, the inviolable dignity of each individual person has no foundations, either."[482] Cardinal Ratzinger thinks that behind the contemporary fascination with the *mystical* there also is some legitimate spiritual need to rediscover the mysterious aspects of faith in God. No matter what one can say about God, he remains shrouded in mystery, fully inapproachable because of human subjectivity and limitations.

Ratzinger sees a common ground for a possible dialogue with the *mystical* religions, which employ the elements of negative theology, when he observes, "The mystical dimension of the concept of God, which the Asian religions bring with them as a challenge to us, must clearly be decisive for our thinking, too, and for our faith."[483] He reminded his readers that the Christian faith has a mystical and an apophatic side. One of the reasons modern encounters with the religions of Asia will be significant for Christians is they will be reminded once again of this side of their faith; one-sided and hardened positions in statements of Christian faith are broken down.[484] The Greek Orthodox Metropolitan in Germany, Damaskinos, in his letter to Cardinal Ratzinger also spoke about "a keen awareness for the transcendence of the mystery and for the mainly apophatic character that its human expression has to assume."[485] At the same time, one is not kept in complete darkness regarding God's mystery. The light comes to the world in the divine *Logos* and directly communicates to us what God wants us to know about him. This *Logos* presents itself to people in a positive and comprehensible way:

> The God who is *logos* guarantees the intelligibility of the world, the intelligibility of our existence, the aptitude of reason to know God and the reasonableness of God, even though his understanding infinitely surpasses ours and to us may so often appear to be darkness. The world comes from reason and this reason is a Person, is Love – this is what our biblical faith tells us about God. Reason can speak about God; it must speak about God, or else it cuts itself short.[486]

e) The Fear of "Christian imperialism"

Another change in the understanding of Christ is what Ratzinger referred to as "the fear of Christian 'imperialism,' a nostalgia for the beautiful multiplicity of religions and their supposedly primordial cheerfulness."[487] In this case, the term *imperialism* could also rightly be equated with the term *ethnocentrism*. Michael Brown, an anthropologist who teaches at Williams College, observed that ethnocentrism generally means:

> ...each culture is said to constitute a total social world that reproduces itself through enculturation, the process by which values, emotional dispositions and embodied behaviors are transmitted from one generation to the next. These values and practices are usually perceived by members of a society as uniquely satisfying and superior to all others – hence the universality of ethnocentrism.[488]

In this idea, spreading Christianity, i.e., missionary activity, is equated to colonialism in that it deprives the native people of their own cultural and religious identity. A solution to that should be to "finally grant to these lost cultures the right of domicile within the Christian faith and allow them to devise for themselves an aboriginal form of Christianity."[489] However, though all great cultures are open to one another and to the truth and a good number of those cultures have already found their own expression in different Christian popular devotions, to accept their ways within Christianity more fully still requires great effort.

In his book *Many Religions – One Covenant*, Ratzinger addressed the issue of different religions and their true value in relation to Christianity according to the doctrinal teachings found in the *Catechism of the Catholic Church*. As an example, he used the story of the Magi from the East and how they followed the Bethlehem Star. The star symbolized the religions of the world in that "the world religions can become the star that enlightens men's path that leads them in search of the kingdom of God. The star of the religions points to Jerusalem; it is extinguished and lights up anew in the Word of God, in the Sacred Scriptures of Israel."[490]

f) Relativism and Ethics

Ratzinger also remarked that there is a crisis of moral values and *ethics*. He confirms this is not anymore just an academic, but also rather a very practical question. Citing Leszek Kolakowski, a

Polish philosopher and historian of ideas, who stated that "deleting faith in God, however one may try to spin or turn it, ultimately deprives moral values of their grounding."[491] If God is not the source who establishes the measures and gives direction to human existence, then whatever rules are made become subject to modification by the majority. With this view what one comes to is the idea that the good is a matter of pragmatic calculations, or in other words, it may be decided in the light of teleological ethics or proportionalism. The major problem with this approach is determining which ruling group of people has the authority to make pragmatic resolutions for the rest of humanity. How long would such decisions endure, considering how easily opinions change?

Ratzinger believes the understanding of God in the second divine person as *Logos*, as the intelligent Word coming to people, presupposes a certain responsibility in its receivers. Therefore, when in dialogue with other religions, there must be a rational search for a common understanding of responsibility in all of their traditions, because the truth sought and intended by all is one, prefigurations of which can be found to a greater or lesser extent in all of them. This presumes the truth in all its fullness is already present in the Catholic Church, but learning from other religious traditions allows for a better understanding and appreciation of some of the hidden or overlooked aspects of this truth.

g) The Divinity of Jesus Christ

Another fear which modern man seems to have is that Jesus' divinity is a form of alienation. Somehow, modern mentality cannot allow for dependence upon another, or anything aside from oneself. This is a matter of pride. For according to Ratzinger, if Jesus is divinely connected to God and God is thought of as being a remote and distant God, then it only naturally follows that Jesus is also very distant from us. A huge gap is thus perceived between God and man and therefore if Jesus is God, he too is somewhere far away. Ratzinger, however, believes that precisely the opposite is true: "If he were only a man, then he has retreated irrevocably into the past and then only a distant recollection can perceive him more or less clearly."[492] However, God is a living God, one who participates in his own creation, especially in and through the person of Jesus Christ, truly God and truly man, for all ages and generations.

3. Controversies over *Dominus Iesus*

During a press conference on September 5, 2000, Cardinal Ratzinger, prefect of the Congregation for the Doctrine of the Faith, gave a short presentation of the declaration *Dominus Iesus*, which was primarily intended and addressed to the members of the Catholic Church.[493] He began with the following remark:

> In the current lively debate about the relationship of Christianity to other religions, the notion is becoming more and more widespread that all religions are of equal value for their adherents as paths to salvation. This conviction has meanwhile become accepted not only in the realm of theology, but also quite extensively among the Catholic public at large and is being reinforced in particular by a cultural trend currently dominant in the West, that is referred to as relativism.[494]

The Cardinal observed that the *currently dominant cultural trend* has its religious expression in the pluralist theology of religion. Therefore, the major intention of the declaration was precisely to outline some of the philosophical and theological presuppositions underlying the various pluralist theologies of religion as they could be found among the Catholic theologians. What were these presuppositions? Cardinal Ratzinger, citing the text of the declaration, named seven of them:

- the conviction of the elusiveness and inexpressibility of divine truth, even by Christian revelation;
- relativistic attitudes toward truth itself, according to which what is true for some would not be true for others; the radical opposition posited between the logical mentality of the West and the symbolic mentality of the East;
- the subjectivism which, by regarding reason as the only source of knowledge, becomes incapable of raising its 'gaze to the heights, not daring to rise to the truth of being';
- the difficulty in understanding and accepting the presence of definitive and eschatological events in history;
- the metaphysical emptying of the historical incarnation of the Eternal Logos, reduced to a mere appearing of God in history;
- the eclecticism of those who, in theological research, uncritically absorb ideas from a variety of philosophical and theological contexts without regard for consistency, systematic connection, or compatibility with Christian truth;
- and the tendency to read and to interpret Sacred Scripture outside the Tradition and Magisterium of the Church.[495]

Ratzinger summarized this way of thinking by referring to it as "the refusal to identify the unique historical figure of Jesus of Nazareth with the reality of God, the living God himself, since it is held that absolute being, or *the* absolute being, can never be completely and finally revealed in history."[496] This can lead to erroneous notions such as 'other world religions are complementary to the Christian revelation,' which also means, the Church with its dogma and sacraments loses its absolute and necessary relevance to all peoples, cultures and religions.[497]

Moreover, those who still insist on the universality of truth which became flesh in the person of Jesus Christ, are regarded as proponents of fundamentalism and thus threaten the modern spirit and its ideals of tolerance and freedom.[498] However, Ratzinger believes, a wrong concept of tolerance is at work here. He acknowledges that the principle of tolerance was accepted and promoted by the Second Vatican Council as one of the fundamental ethical principles when it referred to respect for freedom of conscience, of thought and of religions (cf. *Dignitatis Humanae*). However, its meaning changed when "extended to include the acceptance of the contents of religious belief," where "it is being maintained that all the contents of the various religions and indeed nonreligious conceptions of life, are of equal value," and that "objective and generally valid truth, on the other hand, does not exist, because it is said that God, or the Absolute, reveals himself under countless names and that all these names are true."[499] The result, in Ratzinger's view, is that it means nothing less than the renunciation of the question of truth as a meaningless question for many in today's world.

More precisely put, Ratzinger questions the validity of the new understanding of dialogue as a modern way to achieve some commonality, a common narrative. He calls it "the ideology of dialogue," which marks a radical change from the meaning of dialogue, which was expressed during the Second Vatican Council as a response to mission and the urgent call to conversion. This modern understanding of dialogue found its way even into the Catholic Church with the deliberate intention to relativize her dogmatic teaching. It involved "setting one's own position, or one's own faith and what the other person believes on the same level, so that everything is reduced to an exchange of opinions that are fundamentally relative and of equal value, with the aim of achieving a maximum of cooperation and integration between the different conceptions of religion."[500]

However, Ratzinger argues that the concept of *dialogue* as it was founded and rooted in the Second Vatican Council "never separated dialogue from proclamation and never did away with the truth in the name of practicing dialogue."[501] The Australian theologian Gerard Hall questions Ratzinger's understanding of the role of dialogue by arguing that "because the latter, viewing the world in which dialogue is to occur as rife with the 'relativistic mentality,' [he] falls consequently into a 'negative – at times even aggressive – tone.'"[502] How is it possible, then, to come to any meaningful conclusion in such a dialogue if absolute truth is no longer considered as objective and universally binding? Ratzinger argues that without standards to truth, one lacks the necessary criterion to distinguish what is positive or negative in any religion and its content, as well as to evaluate all of the other areas of human reason and action.

Cardinal Ratzinger continued by acknowledging that, because the Spirit of God moves both in individual human hearts as well as in religions, there is a mixture of good and evil to be found in all world cultures and religions. However, he observed, an important conclusion has to be maintained: "The good that is present in the various religions offers paths toward salvation and does so as part of the activity of the Spirit in Christ, but the religions themselves do not."[503] This was already stated during the Second Vatican Council in the declaration *Nostra aetate*, which explicitly professes both respect and evangelical responsibility:

> The Catholic Church rejects nothing that is true and holy in these religions. She regards with sincere reverence those ways of conduct and of life, those precepts and teachings which, though differing in many aspects from the ones she holds and sets forth, nonetheless often reflect a ray of that Truth which enlightens all men. Indeed, she proclaims and ever must proclaim Christ "the way, the truth and the life" (John 14:6), in whom men may find the fullness of religious life, in whom God has reconciled all things to Himself.[504]

However, Ratzinger warned to be wary of the errors and illusions present in other religions. Although the various cultures and religions of the world are growing ever closer, incontrovertibly allowing for mutual enrichment, it should not become grounds for dismissing the tenet of the Christian faith: that Christ is the final and complete revelation of the mystery of God's truth and salvation. This universal and thus missionary claim should not be perceived as being rooted in any presumption of superiority of the Catholic Church, but only in the mystery of Christ which was gratuitously revealed to and through his Church. Ratzinger concluded that the declaration *Dominus Iesus* had precisely two tasks to fulfill. One of them was to bear witness once again to the world of the glory of the Gospel of Christ. The second was to affirm officially to the faithful "as obligatory those fundamentals of teaching that can never be surrendered and that must guide, inspire and direct, not only theological research, but also the pastoral and missionary activity of the faithful in the whole Catholic Church."[505]

6

RESPONDING TO THE CHALLENGE OF TRUTH IN *TRUTH AND TOLERANCE* AND *WITHOUT ROOTS*

1. In Search of Truth and *Fides et Ratio*

In the Gospel of John, Jesus stands before Pontius Pilate and says, "I came into the world for this: to bear witness to the truth" (Jn 18:37). Pilate then asks the question: "What is truth?" (Jn 18:38). Is it something knowable, or is it found, as Umberto Eco holds, "in learning to free ourselves from the insane passion for the truth"?[506] Christians believe in Jesus' words to Pilate: "all who are on the side of the truth listen to my voice" (Jn 18:40). However, in the modern world, truth, or rather any claim to know the truth, is widely regarded as a threat to tolerance and freedom. Cardinal Ratzinger, in *Truth and Tolerance*, addresses the interplay of truth, tolerance, religion and culture in the modern world. He presents the difficult challenge of meeting diverse understandings of spiritual truth while defending the Catholic teaching of the uniqueness of the salvation which comes through the person and action of Jesus Christ.[507]

149

a) *Religious Pluralism – Asiatic Religions and Christianity*

In the first part of his book, Ratzinger establishes the place of Christianity in the history of world religions. He presents the classic teaching that "Christ is the only real salvation of man and thus his final salvation."[508] However, the majority of people today think that, even though there are many religions, their differences are only superficial because fundamentally they are all the same. Cardinal Ratzinger believes there are two main reasons which help to explain this modern approach. One reason is that "the concept of religion held by 'the modern man of today' is static; he usually does not foresee any development from one religion to another."[509] The second reason for this approach would be that today's man has a concept of religion "that is always very much a matter of symbols, heavily spiritualized."[510] In other words, "religion appears as a world of symbols, which despite the ultimate unity of the language of human symbols…, vary in many details yet nonetheless mean just the same thing, and we really ought to begin to discover their deep, underlying unity."[511]

If one looks closely enough at the history and the origins of various world religions, however, it will become clear they cannot be equalized, because the basic presuppositions forming the content of these religions are quite different. As an example Cardinal Ratzinger compares Asiatic religions with Christianity. For Asiatic religions, he says, a basic element is the *mystical experience*, which enlightens one's understanding of the divine. Ratzinger observes, "the dogmatic presupposition of the assertion that all religions are equal, with which the Western man of today has so much sympathy, is revealed here [in the Asiatic mystical element] as the claim that God and the world, the Divinity and the depths of the soul, are identical."[512] This is not the case, though, with the monotheistic religions and Christianity. Although the notions of mystical experience and that of unity play important roles in the Christian religion, the foundational element of it is not an impersonal deity and one's disappearance into it, but a true person who seeks to establish a personal relationship with a man. Thus, Ratzinger concludes, the major difference between the Asiatic religions of the East and the monotheistic religions of the West is that, for the former, experience of the divine is seen as the loss of one's personhood in the mystical experience with the impersonal divine, whereas for the latter, it is a unity realized by the relationship of two distinct persons – God and a human being. Ratzinger explains his preference for the religions of the West when he writes: "Over against the unity of merging, with its tendency to eliminate identity, should be set personal experience: unity of love is higher than formless identity."[513]

Another key difference between these two types of religions is the role of time in their religious experience. To demonstrate this difference, Cardinal Ratzinger cites Jean Daniélou (1905-1974) and Mircea Éliade (1907-1986). Christianity, as emphasized by Daniélou, "'is essentially faith in an event,' whereas the great non-Christian religions maintain the existence of an eternal world 'that stands in opposition to the world of time.'"[514] Daniélou adds, "The fact of the eternal breaking into time, which gives it duration and turns it into history, is unknown to them."[515] The understanding of Christian faith as grounded in the history of humanity is what Vatican II also affirms in its Constitution on Divine Revelation *Dei Verbum*:

> Then, after speaking in many and varied ways through the prophets, "now at last in these days God has spoken to us in His Son" (Heb 1:1-2). For He sent His Son, the eternal Word, who enlightens all men, so that He might dwell among men and tell them of the innermost being of God (see John 1:1-18). Jesus Christ, therefore, the Word made flesh was sent as "a man to men." (3) He "speaks the words of God" (John 3:34) and completes the work of salvation which His Father gave Him to do (see John 5:36; John 17:4).[516]

The historical character of the Christian faith is also clearly affirmed in the teaching of the late pope, John Paul II. He begins his first encyclical *Redemptor Hominis*, with the sentence, "The Redeemer of Man, Jesus Christ, is the center of the universe and of history."[517] Time and the particularity of their respective revelations do matter in the understanding of monotheistic religions. Once again, this is not the case with Asiatic religions involving mysticism. The trait of being "unhistorical is something mysticism shares as well with myth and with primitive religions" which are characterized by "their revolt against concrete time, their nostalgia for a periodical return to the mythic time of origins."[518] In terms of metaphysics, the difference with Christianity is that it involves "not primarily the discovery of some truth; rather it is the activity of God himself making history."[519]

If one accepts these differences of the role of time and the concept of the divine, then it becomes impossible to sustain the relativistic understanding of religion by modern man as *static* or as *universal spiritualism expressed in different symbols.* As Ratzinger says, "This would be the point at which to bring out what is *special* about Christianity within the monotheistic way insofar as one might show how it is only here that the historical basis has been developed to its full strength, so that the monotheistic way attains here to the full force of its particularity."[520]

b) The Uniqueness of Jesus Christ

Cardinal Ratzinger refutes the relativistic claim, "all religions are the same."[521] Not all religions are the same, but there is an intelligent development among them leading toward what John Paul II calls "the Redeemer of Man, Jesus Christ, the center of the universe and of history."[522] Though divisions exist among religions, Ratzinger points out that what unites us should also not be forgotten:

> We are all a part of a single history that is in many different fashions on the way toward God. For that was what turned out to be the critical insight: for Christian faith, the history of religions is not a circle of what is

endlessly the same, never touching the essential thing, which itself ever remains outside of history; rather, the Christian holds the history of religions to be a genuine *history*, to be a path whose direction we call progress and whose attitude we call hope.[523]

Christianity possesses this genuine history in the person of Jesus Christ, for he is a unique and unrepeatable revelation of God given to all for the salvation and redemption of all. Ratzinger recalls Karl Rahner as the classical advocate of inclusivism:

> Christianity is present in all religions, or (putting it the other way around) that all religions, without knowing this, are moving toward Christianity. It is from this inner direction that they derive their power to save: they lead to salvation insofar as they carry the mystery of Christ hidden within them. In this view of things, on the one hand, it remains true that only Christ and the relationship with him, has any saving power; on the other, we can ascribe a salvific value – albeit on loan, as it were – to other religions and thus explain the saving of men outside the *ark of salvation* of which the Fathers speak.[524]

However, can such inclusiveness justify relativism? If salvation is present to some extent in all religions, why trouble in being *Christian*? Because, Cardinal Ratzinger points out "what all religions offer only vaguely, beneath obscure symbols and even in part distorted or misrepresented, had become visible in faith in Jesus Christ."[525] Christ alone "purifies religions and leads them toward their proper essence, toward their most profound inner longings."[526] Certainly not all share the same conviction. Ratzinger mentions the Austrian-British philosopher, Ludwig Wittgenstein, who remarked in one of his many notebooks that "it would make no difference to the Christian religion whether or not Christ had actually done some of the things recounted concerning him or whether indeed he had existed at all."[527] For Wittgenstein, "the religious person and the nonreligious live, as it were, in two make-believe worlds and move upon different planes without contradicting one another."[528] In this case, Ratzinger observes, religion would then be interpreted "not in the same way as meaningful sentences with some claim to truth, but in a purely anthropological and entirely subjective sense, like a game that is simply someone's personal preference.[529]

Ratzinger attempted to counter the growing trend of relativism by reminding Christians about the uniqueness and universality of salvation, which is granted to the believer through the person and action of Jesus Christ. It is in the name of supposed religious tolerance and open-mindedness, that an essential constituent of faith and of the whole universe is relinquished. "Can a blind man lead a blind man? Will they not both fall into a pit?" (Lk 6:39). This becomes the lot of those Christians who cannot or do not want to realize the true, singular importance and role of Jesus Christ in their own salvation and the salvation of all. This necessitates the use of trained philosophers, theologians and those in the pastoral field to guide the faithful back to realizing the essence of their being as person is the person Jesus Christ.

c) Cultural Relativism and Globalization

Globalization has brought together different faiths and different cultures, and enlightened people have blended the variances. Ratzinger calls it "the most profound difficulty of our age,"[530] which is brought about by cultural relativism. Cultural relativism becomes a challenge when one tries to have both the preserved primitive religions[531] and modern technological progress. This would be unrealistic in that it forces some people to live in a kind of "nature Conservation Park"[532] which would be for religious and cultural history, but would not allow the modern age to penetrate.

However, Ratzinger thinks the challenge of bringing religion and technology together might be overcome if there is an openness to accept the Christian faith. Ratzinger reasons that Christianity has more in common with the ancient cultures of humankind than with the relativistic and rationalistic world of the Enlightenment that has cut itself loose from the fundamental insights of all of humankind. Breaking these organic bonds has led to a vacuum, devoid of all meaning and with fatal risks. The only solution is Christian faith, which opens us to the Logos, to true reason and could, at the same time, "make possible a real synthesis of technological rationality and religion, something that can only come about, not by a flight into the irrational, but by opening up reason to its true height and breadth."[533]

d) Faith and Reason

Pope John Paul II's encyclical *Fides et Ratio*[534] prompted a reflection by Cardinal Ratzinger:

> ...[It seeks] to rehabilitate the question of truth in a world characterized by relativism; it is trying to reinstate it as a rational and scientific task in the situation of modern science, which does indeed look for truths, but which to a great extent disqualifies the search for the truths as being unscientific; it is attempting this, because otherwise faith loses the air it breathes. The encyclical is quite simply attempting to give us courage for the adventure of truth. It is thereby speaking far beyond the sphere of faith, yet also into the heart of the world of faith.[535]

For John Paul II, if man restricts himself only to the rational and forgets the philosophical/theological, he will never learn the fundamental truths about himself; he will not be able to imagine the future and instead will restrict himself to the elemental. However, Christianity claims to call itself the *religio vera*, or the one with the true answers to fundamental questions. Otherwise, Ratzinger states, without the claim that the Christian faith is truth which concerns all men, the missionary tendency of this faith would be futile. In other words, "A related danger is that relativism deprives Christianity of its missionary impulse, since if truth is relative, then 'imposing' a truth on another culture or person becomes an act of colonial domination."[536]

Recalling a passage from C.S. Lewis' *The Screwtape Letters*, Ratzinger notes "how unmodern it is to ask about truth today."[537] Lewis himself observed that the major reason for this "falling away for modernity" with truth, happens with the exclusive application of the historical-critical perspective to most of the ancient texts, including those of Christianity. Ratzinger cites a close friend, the philosopher Josef Pieper, who in his essay on interpretation, calls attention to this connection: "the editions of Plato, for instance, or Dante produced in Communist countries, always gave an introduction to the works being reprinted which provided the reader a 'historical' understanding of them and was meant thus to preclude the question of truth."[538] This relativistic attitude finds its basis in present-day philosophy, which is no longer concerned with asking "What *is?*" but instead with the question of what people can *do* with the reality surrounding them. As Ratzinger puts it, "It is a matter, not of truth, but of action, of dominating things to our own advantage."[539]

Ratzinger mentions yet another reason for the renunciation of objective truth claims, what can be called the *linguistic turning point*. As the German exegete Marius Reiser describes it, this turning point means that "no one can get back behind language and its images; reason is conditioned by language and restricted to language."[540] In this view, truth cannot be found outside of any subjective words or colored texts; it is placed into by those who use and call it truth. As one example of such a relativistic view in theology, Ratzinger mentions his one-time colleague of Tübingen days, Hans Küng, who according to him "claims all formulations can be both true and false – a statement which ultimately reduces all human language to absurdity."[541] Ratzinger himself thought that a different approach is more fitting to the density of this theme. He argued:

As with every language – for example those of the arts and sciences – the language of the Faith cannot be understood without recognizing its own inherent laws. This wrestling to unearth, grasp and, if necessary, reformulate the nuclei of truth expressed in the Church's formulations is part of the theologian's task. These nuclei of truth are not self-existing elements totally independent and capable of being understood in isolation. Rather they are the immutable elements of an interrelated whole and cannot be understood apart from this "system." The fundamental language of the Faith, however, is not expressed in some idiosyncratic philosophic language but rather in the general human language available to all.[542]

Recalling Plato's story about Thoth and Thutmose,[543] Ratzinger, although appreciative of the new ways of communication, information and writing, nevertheless, shares that same concern Plato had, that often the written down knowledge lacks the true comprehension of reality and the depth of wisdom coming not from the texts itself but from their author living that reality. Ratzinger also attributes the rapid spreading of relativism to the mass media. In *A Turning Point for Europe?* he describes the mass media as a:

...destabilizing factor with respect to dictatorships. They relativize everything with their skepticism, they show countertypes to everything and thus call everything into question. They present the eye with images of the life one would wish to have and thereby set up a criterion that impels opposition to the existing order. They form the consciousness and the subconscious and urge one to put into practice what has been seen and heard. Thus they have certainly made their contribution to the shaping of consciousness that was unchangeable. But without a doubt, another side of this same phenomenon also exists: the power of the images to relativize goes beyond the sphere of dictatorship. They induce a general skepticism. One has the impression that one knows everything and can pass judgment on everything. But this could mean the loss of the ability to perceive the deeper dimensions of existence, a grasping for what is external, a claim made on existence that no longer shakes only dictatorships but destabilizes the human soul itself to its very foundations. There is a danger that it may become incapable of the patience that is required to find the truth that does not bestow itself and without which the response of love cannot grow.[544]

e) *Faith and Culture*

Ratzinger comments that there is a modern tendency to put forward "the relativity of cultures to counter universal claims of Christianity."[545] In light of contemporary cultural relativism, Ratzinger wonders "whether there can ever be a communion of cultures in the one truth – whether truth can be expressed for all men, beyond its cultural forms, or whether it is ultimately to be only dimly perceived as a convergence behind varying or even contradictory cultural forms."[546] Pope John Paul II in his encyclical *Fides et Ratio* speaks of culture as being dynamic and communicative, and willing to be open to the universal and transcendent. These cultures, where individuals are more open to the question of God, tend to be also more open to receiving God's revelation. Ratzinger calls this dynamic interaction the "progression of cultures toward the Logos of God, who became flesh in Jesus Christ."[547] John Paul II in his encyclical *Fides et Ratio* expressed three criteria, observed whenever a non-Christian culture encounters the Christian faith.

The first criterion comes from the universality of the human spirit, whose basic needs are the same in all cultures and in all times. However, the second criterion acknowledges the particularity of the Greco-Latin culture as something to be introduced to other cultures, along with the matters of faith, because, as John Paul II said "to reject this heritage would be to deny the providential plan of God."[548] The third criterion speaks about the nature of culture. The true dynamism and thus openness of the culture to the changes being brought by the acceptance of the Christian faith, should be preserved and not "confused with the idea that a particular cultural tradition should remain closed in its difference and affirm itself by opposing other traditions."[549]

Ratzinger is well aware that modern sensibility would be apprehensive to such directions, especially to the one emphasizing the need to embrace Greco-Latin culture. This would seem to place a Euro-centric character on faith, but Ratzinger points out that the encyclical emphasizes the historical origins of faith. In the Bible, through the people of Israel, man's search for truth revealed itself in the person of Jesus Christ. This faith in Jesus Christ transcends all cultures and brings men into true unity with each other.

Similarly, *cultural transcendence* took place in the Hellenistic culture, which through philosophy and in light of the Christian faith was able to come to terms with the self-critique of its own culture and its own thought. The concentric point of contact between the Christian faith and Hellenistic culture became the latter's search in philosophy for a wider space of truth, common to all and concerning all. As Ratzinger states, "faith cannot of course find points of contact with philosophies that exclude questions concerning the truth, but it can do so with the movements that are trying to break out of the relativistic prison."[550]

f) Faith and Salvation

Ratzinger adds what he thinks to be another important consideration. That is the question of the significance of the religions for salvation. He argues that it is not faithfulness to a closed system of religious beliefs and practices that brings about the desired salvation in these religions, but "rather they bring redemption only when they bring men to the point of 'asking after God' (as Old Testament puts it), 'seeking his face,' 'seeking the kingdom of God and his righteousness.'"[551] Regarding salvation, Cardinal Ratzinger observes the contemporary world does not concern itself with the question of life after death because how can a loving God reject his own creation? Is it a person's fault if he was not exposed to Christianity and thus chose another religion? God being merciful will accept all religions and all worship!

As appealing as this may sound to the modern ear, Ratzinger questions such affirmations about salvation because different religions offer differing positions which are often contrary in their content. However, they are an implicit rejection of relativism. This issue is of little concern to those who do not commit themselves seriously to any religion, because for them:

> ...All contents are basically of equal use. What is actually of any use, we do not know. Everyone just has to go his own way – to become happy in his own "façon" as Frederick II of Prussia used to say. Thus, by way of the various theories of salvation, relativism slips in through the back door again: the question of truth is excised from the question concerning religions and the matter of salvation. Truth is replaced by good intentions; religion remains in the subjective realm because we cannot know what is objectively good or true.[552]

g) Is Relativism our Solitary Option?

Having presented the situation as he sees it, Ratzinger wonders if the only choice for religion is between *dogmatic rigorism* and a *humane, kindly relativism*? However, there are three things which need to be changed before one can subscribe to this type of relativism.

First is the falsehood that all pagan religions and even agnosticism and atheism have in common the same kind of belief. This is not the case because religion demands distinctions – the way to achieve a higher plane. When all content becomes equally valid, nothing can happen:

> Relativism is dangerous in quite particular ways: for the shape of human existence and on an individual level and in society. The renunciation of truth does not heal man. How much evil has been done in history in the name of good opinions and good intentions is something no one can overlook.[553]

In fact, religions, with their moral values, are recognized as sometimes unhealthy. For example, even Christianity was unhealthy when it carried out its crusades and the terrible slaughter of Muslims and Jews in the holy city of Jerusalem.

A second point, which needs to be corrected, is that all religions lead to eternal salvation. Ratzinger objects to this by asserting "heaven begins on earth," and hence, "salvation in the world to come presumes a righteous life in this world."[554] He is saying it is not simply a question of who gets into heaven, but what is heaven, and how does it relate to us living in this world. Ratzinger emphasizes, there is a connection between this life and the afterlife. This in turn involves some standards of proper living, which cannot be relativized at one's will, because there are always right things which can never become wrong, as well as there are wrong things which can never become right. Religion in itself does not contain salvation. It is only a path, which might lead toward or away from salvation – which can only be obtained by being with God, who is truth and love.[555]

Ratzinger contends that a third point is often overlooked by those who adhere to religious relativism: it concerns man's conscience. Citing St. Paul's Letter to the Romans (Rm 2:14-16), Ratzinger observes that all men are capable of listening to their consciences because the Law is written in their hearts. However, in the contemporary world there are two opposing understandings of conscience. Paul expressed the classical concept: the conscience is the organ within all men, *the speech of the heart*, which in turn points to the one God. However, in modern thinking human conscience appears as "an expression of the absolute value of the subjective self, above and beyond which there can be no further judgment in the moral realm."[556] This in turn "represents the canonizing of relativism, of the impossibility of establishing common moral and religious standards."[557]

In his closing thoughts regarding the reflection on *Fides et Ratio*, Cardinal Ratzinger returns to the major objective of Pope John Paul II in writing his encyclical, the relationship between theology and philosophy, or faith and reason. There is a *circular movement* where the starting point for theology must always be the Word of God, but since it is also the truth, it leads to the use of reason in finding truth and thus necessitates dialogue with philosophy. Likewise, the believer's search for truth requires listening to the Word and seeking reason. In saying *credo*, one "declares that in this world the receiving of meaning is prior to its making by man – though without denying the value of human creativity. So far from being irrational, faith is therefore a movement toward meaning and truth, towards the logos."[558] Henri J.M. Nouwen said the same by acknowledging that one's acceptance of truth "requires a long and often slow process in which we enter more and more into the truth, that is, into a true relationship with God and, through Him, with ourselves."[559] Cardinal Ratzinger suggested taking this *circularity* further. For him:

> Philosophy, too, ought not to shut itself in within its own material, within what it has itself thought up. Just as it has to pay heed to empirical perceptions that emerge within the various scientific disciplines, so also it ought to regard the holy traditions of religions and especially the message of the Bible as the source of perception and let itself be made more fertile by this.... When philosophy completely blanks out this dialogue with the thought of faith, it ends – as Jaspers once expressed it – in a "seriousness that is becoming empty." In the end, it finds itself forced to renounce the

question of truth, that is, it is forced to give up itself. For a philosophy that no longer asks who we are, what we are here for, whether there is a God and an eternal life, has abdicated its role as a philosophy.[560]

According to Ratzinger, the current process of dethroning theology and metaphysics in reality leads to dethroning God and man, causing a void of frightful silence. This silence cannot be dismissed, and no amount of noise and shouting in the world can fill the emptiness. It all comes back to the questions about God and man, about sin and grace, about death and eternal life and the answers, which can be provided through a renewed dialogue between theology and philosophy.

2. Ratzinger in Dialogue with Marcello Pera

Among the most recent books written by Cardinal Ratzinger addressing the issue of relativism are the books he wrote with Marcello Pera: *Without Roots: The West, Relativism, Christianity, Islam* (2006) and Jürgen Habermas, *The Dialectics of Secularization* (2006). The question at the heart of both books is "Can a civilization exist without any sense of the sacred?" The first book was born of a dialogue between Cardinal Ratzinger, the prefect of the Congregation for the Doctrine of Faith and Marcello Pera, president of the Italian Senate. They were meant as a challenge for Europe to address its moral and cultural depression. Pera and Ratzinger also spoke about relativism and its impact on the West. They agreed that the influence of the *super-dogma of relativism* is enormous to the extent that it could be seen as a kind of *new denomination*.[561]

a) Pera on Relativism

Pera observed whether it is called relativism, post-enlightenment thinking, post-modernism, deconstructionism, *pensiero debole,* or *weak thought,*[562] the target of this school of philosophy is always the same, "to proclaim that there are no grounds for our values and no solid proof or argument establishing that any one thing is *better* or *more valid* than another."[563] According to Pera, relativism finds itself with a plurality of values, while at the same time in a position whereby it is impossible for all values to coexist. To counteract the plurality of values, a form of self-censorship takes place; it goes by the name of political correctness. *Political correctness* is the term that the West uses "to imply, allude to, or insinuate rather than to affirm or maintain."[564]

Professor Pera gave two concrete examples of relativism. One of them is the *Wittgensteinian approach*, whereby "contents cannot be separated from the criteria by which they are judged."[565] In other words, a community sets the criteria of what is true, beautiful, and good. Because of those standards, "there are no meta-criteria that can establish intrinsic truth, absolute beauty, or universal good. All criteria… are contextual."[566] Pera critiques this relativistic approach by arguing that, in order to be evaluated, two different cultures do not require a meta-criterion, but should instead be willing to enter into a constructive dialogue, using the dialectical method of *elenchos*.[567] Pera is convinced that the relativism of the contextualists collapses because "their relativism has developed such an appetite for the foundations of other doctrines that, in the end, having devoured everything else, it becomes self-destructive and devours itself."[568]

b) Jacques Derrida's Deconstructionism

Professor Pera presented another example of relativism, also known as deconstructionism. Its founder was the German philosopher Friedrich Nietzsche (1844-1900). The deconstructionist approach uses the technique of exposing the loopholes in concepts that are supposedly absolute and universal, also known as *unmasking* or *reversal*. French philosopher Jacques Derrida (1930-2004) is a contemporary exponent of this kind of relativism. However, Pera notes that a deconstructionist put in the position of making a value-based choice cannot make such a choice. As

Pera put it, "If what remains instead is inability or impotence to act, then there has been an unequivocal loss: only philosophers in their classrooms can afford the luxury of not taking practical decisions; not so the man of the street, the politician, the head of the state."[569]

This was well illustrated by Derrida's inability to respond to the September 11 terrorist attacks using his decontructionistic philosophy. In Derrida's appeal to the United Nations he stated, "I continue to believe that it is faith in the possibility of this impossible and in truth, undecidable thing... that must govern all our decisions."[570] Faith and truth were called upon to govern all decisions, but how is it possible for the relativist to settle on whose faith, and whose truth? Pera points out that relativism stands on shaky foundations indeed. Derrida substantiates that fact when he is forced to return to the "starting point, the value choice, from which all else derives."[571] If one does not look for and accept the existence of objective truth and reality, one is left to live in a limbo of hypocrisy, "hypocrisy on the part of people who see no evil and speak no evil to avoid becoming involved; who see no evil and speak no evil to avoid appearing rude, who proclaim half-truths and imply the rest, to avoid assuming responsibility."[572]

Pera also said that in opposing these two types of relativism, he is not being a total extremist. He writes:

> In opposing contextualism, I do not deny the relationship between criteria and contents (a typical mutual reinforcement). What I deny is the thesis of Paul Feyerabend that 'Every theory has its own experience,' or of Thomas Kuhn that 'The proponents of competing paradigms practice their trades in different worlds.' In opposing deconstruction, I do not deny that facts cannot exist independently of their interpretation. What I deny are the theses of Nietzsche that 'There are no facts, only interpretations,' and of Derrida, 'there is nothing outside the text.'[573]

On the contrary, Pera believes that when making judgments there are often factors which, although they may not be facts, serve as fundamental elements for decisions. This would be akin to faith or to the supernatural reality found in Christian religion. Even Christianity is being tested by relativism. Pera questions, "Why… are enlightenment and Christianity regarded today as contradicting each other and even mutually exclusive?"[574] He responds observing:

> The takeover proceeded in the customary manner. The starting point was the phenomenological observation that there is a plurality of creeds and religions. This was followed by a comparison, a loss of hope in meta-criteria. The end point is doubt in the fundamental creeds of Christianity (the final stage, the reinterpretation or deconstruction of religious facts).[575]

c) The Religion of the Modern Man

Pera presents two contemporary examples of Christian theologians subscribing to the "new religion of the modern man," Paul Knitter and John Hick. Knitter is best known for his provocative thesis regarding "the fundamental premise of unitive pluralism" where, according to him, "all religions are or can be equally valid."[576] If this statement is true, then it must follow Jesus Christ is only one among many in the world of saviors and revealers. According to Knitter, this can be justified because New Testament authors use the language "not of analytic philosophers, but rather of enthusiastic believers, not of scientists but of lovers."[577] Pera argues that the "notion of a relativistic Christian is oxymoronic; it leads not to dialogue, but to apostasy."[578]

The other theologian Pera mentions who shares the same relativistic enthusiasm is John Hick. Previously a traditional evangelical, he was pushed toward pluralism by the problem of reconciling God's love with the constructions of cultural and religious diversity. If, as Christianity has traditionally taught, faith in Christ is the only means of salvation, then those who have never heard the Gospel are damned, abandoned by God to their eternal fate. Hick's response to this Protestant dilemma is to view religious truth as relative to cultures and to individuals. He rejects Christian exclusivism as false, seeing different religions as appropriate, if culturally conditioned, responses to the *Real*.

Pluralism leads people to examine the extent to which they believe knowledge and beliefs are situational. Its origins might be traced to the beginning of the scientific revolution when competing scientific parties lost common criteria to which they could appeal, instead settling upon the superiority of one position over the other.[579] The loss of these common criteria may be attributed to science moving to a point where "competing theoretical schemes can make sense of the same phenomena in different ways and the differences cannot be finally adjudicated."[580] The different scientific schemes may be incommensurable, which means incapable of being compared or measured, especially because they lacked any common quality necessary for comparison to be made.

Similar incommensurability also appears in sociology and anthropology. Ludwig Wittgenstein (1889-1951) and his followers like Peter Winch (1926-1997) have stressed the relativity of societies and structures. Winch sternly criticizes those who seek to evaluate non-Western societies by using Western standards.[581] He objects to these notions because "there are no standards of reasoning and truth which overlap all cultures and modes of social life."[582] However, there remain those who try to locate a common factor in all of humanity.[583] It becomes apparent, that for the most part Protestantism adheres to a flawed anthropology because of its refusal of natural law, the *imago Dei* teaching, and the axiom *gratia praesupponit naturam*, which in turn leads to relativism.

d) Pera on Relativism and Christian Revelation

After a theoretical critique of relativism, Pera mentions some important concepts it entails. According to him, exclusiveness of the Christian faith had been replaced with openness to dialogue, which the Second Vatican Council embraced. However, Pera states that although dialogue is an "instrument through which to discover or approach the truth," for a Christian, revelation is the primary source of that truth. In Christianity, "truth is not a process but a *state*, not a becoming but a *being*."[584]

The true purpose of religious dialogue, according to Pera, is twofold, "for believers of various faiths to communicate and to foster mutual understanding; and to preach, spread and advance the message."[585] It should be easy to see where such an approach would run into difficulty. Although mutual understanding and tolerance is an idea very much accepted and promoted, the concept of *evangelization* becomes a pointed issue. For example, in the encyclical letter *Redemptoris Missio*, inter-religious dialogue is seen as part of the Church's evangelizing mission, as "dialogue does not dispense from evangelization."[586] Pera claims this type of official teaching by the Church will be perceived as "a covert form of imperialism and the fear that, in some circumstances, evangelization could also lead to conflict."[587]

Pera also questions the subject of this type of dialogue. Will it be about some secular values, such as tolerance, peace, dignity, the promotion of the human person, emancipation and justice; or will it be about the unique, sole, true transcendence? But that leads one back to our starting point, the point of tension where relativism confronts the Christian faith. Despite the possibility of dialogue being cast into doubt and the risk of conflict, Pera hopes that the Church will not lower her standards. If that were to happen, the consequences would be devastating not just for the Church but for the future of the West as well, and to the future of dialogue. Pera asserts that "dialogue will be a waste of time if one of the two partners to the dialogue states beforehand that one idea is as good as the other."[588]

e) On the Conditions for the Rise of Relativism

What conditions were responsible for the rise of relativism? Ratzinger believes that its beginnings are found in the French

Revolution where the modern era began and not simply in terms of politics. Ratzinger points out that on the eve of the revolution, the spiritual framework, a formative element of Europe, broke apart. This meant "the sacred foundation for history and of the existence of the State was rejected; history was no longer gauged on the basis of an idea of a preexistent God who shaped it; the State was henceforth considered in purely secular terms, founded on reason and on the will of the citizens."[589] This was a major turn for the modern world, because not only was God pushed aside from the public and political spheres of life into the private sector, but more, he was relegated to the sphere of feelings. For that, one can also thank Friedrich Daniel Ernst Schleiermacher (1768-1834) who "attempted to save religion from the fundamental danger to which the enlightenment exposed it, by defining religion as feeling."[590] The influence of his school of thought is still felt today.

If the State becomes shaped by the will of its citizens, then should it not follow that "relativism thus also appears as being the philosophical basis of democracy"?[591] This presently exists because of globalization, brought about by technological progress and a shared global economy, which also contributed to a growth of secularism and self-criticizing tolerance. This in turn gave rise to new nations and nationalism, not based on some preconceived political vision, but "through the formation of uniform linguistic regions."[592] With such a plural subject of history, dire consequences arose among the European nations, each wanting to reign supreme. Also, by letting go of their Judeo-Christian spiritual foundation, European nations entered into military conflicts such as the two world wars – the likes of which history had never witnessed.

Oswald Spengler (1880-1936), an amateur German historian and philosopher, best known for his book *The Decline of the West*,[593] believed that "the West arrived at its final epoch, which runs inexorably toward the death of this cultural continent, despite all efforts to avert it."[594] Ratzinger, however, refutes this pessimistic view[595] and instead accepts the one proposed by Arnold Toynbee (1889-1975), a British historian, whose celebrated twelve-volume analysis of the rise and fall of civilizations, *A Study of History* (1934-1961), was a synthesis of world history, a metahistory based on universal rhythms of rise, flowering, and decline which examined history from a global perspective. Toynbee proposes the reintroduction of the religious factor into the State. He offers as a solution "a voluntaristic view that places its trust in the powers of *creative minorities* and exceptional individuals."[597] Cardinal Ratzinger himself is fond of this view, finding encouragement in the *creative minorities* of the new movements arising in the Church and the *exceptional individuals* such as Mother Teresa, and Pope John Paul II.

Ultimately, Ratzinger believes the question about the future of Europe is not a political or even an economic one, but a philosophical and theological one. It is only by bringing back people's humanness and asking questions such as: "What is there, today and tomorrow that promises human dignity and a life in conformity with it?"[598] that Europe's future can be pondered.

f) The Two Kinds of Socialism

In recounting the development of the European states, Ratzinger speaks of socialism, divided into two different paths: the totalitarian and the democratic. Democratic socialism, which was always much closer to Catholic social teaching, helped form a social consciousness in those Western European countries that adopted it. In the totalitarian model, which adopts Marxism as its foundational doctrine, a greater problem arises. Characteristic of this model, Ratzinger says, is the following:

> ...a rigidly materialistic and atheistic philosophy of history: history was understood deterministically as a process of advancement that passed through a religious and then a liberal phase so as to arrive at the absolute and definitive society, in which religion becomes a superfluous relic from the past and the business of

material production and trade is able to guarantee happiness for all. The scientific appearance of this theory
conceals an intolerant dogmatism: spirit is the product
of matter; morals are the product of circumstances and
must be defined and practiced according to the goals
of society: everything that fosters the coming of that
final state of happiness and morality.[599]

According to Marxist doctrine, the circumstances and the ends
dictate the means and the norms of one's moral behavior. With this
type of mentality, the only goals are those of material progress.
At any given moment, everything can be considered moral and
thus permitted. It was the idea of economical progress as one's
ultimate good that allowed Marxism to creep into the rest of the
Western world.

g) The Epochal Anthropocentric Shift

However, according to Ratzinger, the worst happened in the
anthropological sphere where a change occurred as to how society
treats and understands human beings. Without God present, the
state and its ideology is left to establish primordial certainties
about man and his place in the universe. Nazism provided a vivid
example of the horrors which a State is capable of when human
dignity and fundamental human rights are defiled.[600] Nevertheless, a silent and gradual atrophy is occurring regarding the human
condition. Ratzinger believes that medicine and the institution
of family are areas of great concern. In medicine, using the new
form of rationality, "the human being must be no longer begotten
irrationally but rather produced rationally."[601] The goal is intentionally to produce the perfect man who would live a life free of
suffering and sickness, and where the State with its laws would
allow man to do everything he is capable of doing. This might
result in, and even justify, the exploitation of man, provided that
the result is sufficient to justify the means.

Since the secular state does not recognize any religious foundation but instead centers itself on reason and rational knowledge, what serves as a moral compass? Ratzinger points out that reason in itself is *inherently fragile*, and a secular system can only survive "because elements of the old moral conscience have persevered, even without the earlier foundations, enabling the existence of a basic moral consensus."[602] It appears, as was the case with Pera and Camus,[603] that relativism only becomes a challenge when it begins to question this *old moral conscience.* Accordingly, although there are many kinds of relativism, the type that seems to provoke the most interest and concern about the issue is moral relativism. This is because, as Ratzinger understands it using C.S. Lewis' phrase, such moral relativism directly leads to an *abolition of humanity.* He believes that "to abandon truth, no longer to locate the *ought (das Sollen)* of morality in the *is,* the *being (das Sein)* of the created world, is to abolish humanity, to deliver ourselves up to death."[604] Immanuel Kant may have been correct about the categorical imperative being a part of human nature, but not about where it drew its force.

Cardinal Ratzinger here combines two seemingly contradictory phenomena. On the one hand, he says that secularism, starting with the French Revolution, separates State and religion with the State based on reason alone, and religion left to the realm of a *ghetto of subjectivism.*[605] Alternatively, citing Pope Gelasius' (492-496) vision of the West, "a Church that is separate from the State better guarantees the moral foundation of the country."[606] That is to say, "the promotion of the democratic ideal is seen as a moral duty that is in profound compliance with the faith."[607] However, what happens when morality itself falls under the spell of relativism?

h) Relativism and Morality

Totalitarian socialism can be seen as another major condition for the present lordship of relativism, especially when it relates to the origins and the foundations of morality. According to this type of socialism, which is for the most part associated with a rigid materialism and atheistic philosophy of history, morals are produced by circumstances that "should be defined and practiced on the basis of society's purposes, and everything is deemed moral that helps to usher in the final state of happiness."[608] Such moral philosophy eventually leads to accepting the principle that "the end justifies the means," which for Cardinal Ratzinger and especially for Pope John Paul II, was a major reason for the collapse of the Soviet Union and its communist regime. There had to be a collapse because the people could no longer comply with a system that led them to the "starvation of souls and the destruction of the moral conscience."[609] It would be quite ironic to witness Western democracies collapsing for these same reasons. Ratzinger points out that "the unresolved issue of Marxism lives on: the crumbling of man's original uncertainty about God, himself and the universe. The decline of moral conscience grounded in absolute values is still our problem today."[610]

What are these absolute values? For the Cardinal, they are human rights and human dignity, freedom, equality and solidarity, as well as monogamous marriage – the "special communion of man and woman, which opens itself to children and thus to family."[611] Additionally, it is the value of religion and the "respect for that which another group holds sacred, especially respect for the sacred in the highest sense, for God, which one can reasonably expect to find even among those who are not willing to believe in God."[612] However, Cardinal Ratzinger rightly observes that "in our contemporary society, thank goodness; anyone who dishonors the faith of Israel, its image of God, or its great figures must pay a fine. The same holds true for anyone who dishonors the Koran and the convictions of Islam. But when it comes to Jesus Christ and that which is sacred to Christians instead, freedom of speech becomes the supreme good."[613]

What Pera calls "self-censorship of the West" Cardinal Ratzinger calls a "peculiar Western self-hatred that is nothing short of pathological."[614] Moreover, this pathology of the West, "trying to be more open, to be more understanding of the values of outsiders," amounts to nothing other than the missing capacity of healthy self-love.[615] Contemporary Western society "sees in its own history the despicable and the destructive; it is no longer able to perceive what is great and pure."[616] If the West – especially Europe – wants to survive, it will need a new self-acceptance that is critical and at the same time humble. This might explain why some people were displeased with Pope John Paul's II initiative during the Jubilee Year to ask God's forgiveness for the wrong the Church had done over the course of her history. Such repentance, however, was needed to help break through resentment and so bring about a healing. This was necessary in order to bring out the beauty and the good inherent to the sacramental life of the Church.

Europe seems to have lost the capacity not only of self-love, but it appears to be suffering from an almost pathological *self-hatred*; of anything associated with its historical identity. Ratzinger observes that one cannot dishonor the faith of Israel or the fundamental beliefs and symbols of Islam, but when the question turns to Christianity and what is sacred to them, "suddenly freedom of opinion appears to be the highest good and to limit it would be to endanger tolerance and freedom in general."[617] One reason for this behavior might be connected with the horrific failures Europe lived through in the 20th century. However, this still does not explain why "the West is making a praiseworthy attempt to be completely open to understanding foreign values, but it no longer loves itself; and from now on it sees in its own history only what is blame-worthy and destructive."[618]

Ratzinger suggests Europe should rediscover its cultural and spiritual heritage. By denying its spiritual heritage and instead promoting multiculturalism, the identity of Europe is changed, and maybe even lost. This is why other cultures of the world, such as Islam, strongly believe there is no future for a world without God. Thus the useless society which subscribes to such a world might as well disappear from the face of the earth. Unless, as Cardinal Ratzinger suggests, using Toynbee's idea of the creative minorities, "Christian believers should look upon themselves as just such a creative minority and help Europe [and the whole

Western civilization] to reclaim what is best in its heritage and to thereby place itself at the service of all humankind."[619]

i) Pera's Response to Ratzinger

Pera wonders if Western Judaeo-Christian culture can move in any direction, because it is "infected by an epidemic of relativism."[620] This grip on the West almost leads to paralysis. Because relativism believes that all cultures are equivalent, it refuses to judge. Accepting and defending one's own culture would be considered an act of hegemony or of intolerance, even one of insolence toward the self-determination of other populations and individuals. By contrast, the word *Christian* "is considered unacceptable, because it is an identifying adjective: appropriate, precise and therefore suspected of arrogance."[621] If there is one thing relativism cannot stand, it is the condition of being appropriate and precise. It cannot stand the truth as a fact; it always wants to see it as an option or a choice, but never as an absolute.

However, although it may seem that absolute truths do not exist because all societies and their values are equally valid, in reality some are *more equal and true than others*. According to Pera, it is to one's own disadvantage if one refuses to acknowledge that the tolerance and equality one professes does not apply universally. For that reason, when speaking of multiculturalism and integration, one should not confuse it with aggregation – collection, or a total – which presumes indulgence. True integration does not mean having equal points of departure. Instead, it means, "sharing an equal willingness to accept the common arrival point."[622]

Pera goes so far as to suggest forming a *non-denominational Christian religion*, which would be able to instill its values to society while at the same time bypassing the forces of the State. This would also keep the powers of Church and State separate. Pera thinks such a religion can be independent from the State, but he unintentionally contradicts himself by saying, "Without a civil religion, a society cannot live.... A state is never profane: it is always and also paternalistic and therefore has moral purposes."[623]

Pera sees his proposal of a non-denominational Christian religion as a new religion for the European Union. At the same time, he is trying to be being sensitive to the secularists.

How can a secularist participate in the mission of this new religion? According to Pera, regarding morals, the differences between secularists and believers is slight. However, there is one difference that is not easy to overcome – a hierarchy of values. While a believer accepts the existence of such a hierarchy, the secularist does not. In other words, "while for believers values are ends in themselves that belong to an orderable whole... for secularists they are instruments – ends that serve other ends and there is no single end-in-itself capable of ordering all the others."[624] The danger of following the secularist's approach is that "of rushing to transform their whims into desires and their desires into rights."[625] The same can be said about believers for they run the risk of choosing passages from Scripture and then transforming their interpretations into dogma.

An open and respectful discussion is needed, but the times one lives in make it difficult. The values of both the secularists and believers are subject to the challenges of scientific achievements. To use Bertrand Russell's observation, there is a "dramatic gap between our scientific achievements, which progress rapidly and our moral standards, which crawl along at a slower pace."[626] Pera comes close to Peter Berger's inductive, deductive, reductive methodology[627] when he gives his final evaluation of modern times:

> Rather than engage in reductionism and treat ethics as a historical accident – something the relativists would have us do – it would be useful for European Culture today to remember, perhaps, one of its founding fathers, Aristotle, who to avoid falling into the relativism of the Sophists on one side and the dogmatism of Plato on the other, introduced the concept of practical wisdom, *phrónesis,* that is neither a technique of action nor a science of the good, but rather "the true and reasoned

state or capacity to act with regard to the things that are good or bad for man."[628]

However, this *phrónesis*, this practical wisdom to act with regard to the things that are good or bad, becomes quite a challenge not only for believers but also for a secularist such as Pera himself. The risk of an error remains for both. Pera sincerely acknowledges that "the science of good and evil is something we left behind when we were driven out or went on our way."[629] He also adds, speaking of secularists, "our belief in reason helps, but it does not exonerate us from risk, from the gamble."[630] This last remark is similar to a point made in Cardinal Ratzinger's book *Introduction to Christianity* where he describes the ambiguous situation of both a believer and unbeliever.[631] Pera continues to stress the need to foster discussion, which would produce more responsibility among scientists, lawyers and health workers, resulting in everyone being "less propelled to second their desires, transform them into needs, consider them values and construe them as rights."[632] Because "absolute profanity, supposing that there is such a thing," he says, "is an absolute vacuum in which neither the happy majority nor the creative minorities can exist."[633]

j) Ratzinger's Response to Pera

Ratzinger does not intend to pass judgment on the political realities of the world although he does speak of relativism when commenting on the current pacifism of Europe which tends to assign the same value to everything. "To be in favor of peace on such a basis," he writes, "would signify anarchy which is blind to the foundations of freedom, because if everyone is right, no one is right."[634] Instead, the major purpose of his letter was to respond to Pera's idea of a non-denominational Christian religion.

Ratzinger notices that in the old Catholic countries of Europe, there is a prominent fringe that resolutely denies the right of a public presence to the Christian faith and its values, and he believes the cause lies in history. According to Ratzinger, the historical division of Western Europe, between Catholics and Protestants, as well as the dissimilarity of their relationships to the State, influenced the different responses these two groups had to the ideas of Enlightenment. Whereas "Enlightenment proclaimed the autonomy of reason and its emancipation from traditional faith, the Catholic Church remained strongly attached to its heritage of faith, thereby locking the two in endless conflict."[635]

The direct consequence of the Enlightenment was the birth of the concept *secular,* which for Catholics meant freethinking and freedom from religious constrictions. It naturally followed that the "exclusion of Christian contents and values from public life," would lead to "the tendency on the part of the modern conscience to treat the entire realm of faith and morals as 'subjective'"[636] At the same time, notes Cardinal Ratzinger, the Protestant countries had no such usage of the term *secular* and found it completely incomprehensible, since "from the beginning Protestantism has seen itself as a movement of emancipation, liberation and purification."[637] Therefore, this close link between the Reformation and the Enlightenment might serve as a foundation for this new civil religion. However, statistics indicate that the more a Protestant Church adapts to standards of secularization, the more followers it loses. Yet those which are labeled 'fundamentalist' are able to attract thousands of people who are in search of a solid foundation for their lives. Who or what then is able to bring the sacred into the affairs of the State? Cardinal Ratzinger agrees with Pera on the importance of creative minorities, and in his first thesis he states:

> ...it is so important to have convinced minorities in the Church, for the Church, and above and beyond the Church and for society: human beings who in their encounter with Christ have discovered the precious pearl that gives value to all life (Matthew 13:45ff.), assuring that the Christian imperatives are no longer ballast that immobilizes humanity, but rather wings that carry it upward. Such minorities are formed when

a convincing model of life also becomes an opening toward a knowledge that cannot emerge amid the dreariness of everyday life. Such a life choice, over time, affirms its rationale to a growing extent, opening and healing a reason that has become lazy and tired. There is nothing sectarian about such creative minorities. Through their persuasive capacity and their joy, they reach other people and offer them a different way of seeing things.[638]

The second thesis is concerned with the different forms of belonging to these living communities. Reaffirming the new ecclesiology of Vatican II, Ratzinger cites Matthew 13:32 when he admonishes: "Perhaps the Church has forgotten that the tree of the Kingdom of God reaches beyond the branches of the visible Church, but that this is precisely why it must be a hospitable place in whose branches many guests find solace."[639] Such a statement indicates that Cardinal Ratzinger is not a *fundamentalist*, but *the fundamentalist of the Gospel message*. Thirdly, in response to Pera's idea of civil religion, Ratzinger notes that minorities renew the vitality of the greater community by drawing their force from its hidden life source, which is faith in its divine origins.

The fourth thesis speaks of the need for a new openness that Hans Urs von Balthasar called for in 1952, the *Schleifung der Bastionen* ("breaking down of barriers'). It involves what both secular people and Catholic seekers and believers must have and do in order to find a place on the tree of God's Kingdom.[640] Ratzinger argues that the distinction between Catholics and secularists is relative:

Believers must never stop seeking, while seekers are touched by the truth and thus cannot be classified as people without faith and Christian-inspired moral principles. There are ways of partaking of the truth by which seekers and believers give to and learn from each other. This is why the distinction between Catholics and secularists is relative.... Secular people are not a rigid block. They do not constitute a set denomination, or worse, an "anti-denomination." They are people who do not yet feel able to take the step of ecclesiastical faith with everything that such a step involves. Very often they are people who passionately seek the truth, who are pained *by the lack of truth in humankind.* Consequently, they return to the essential contents of culture and faith and through their commitment often *make these contents even more luminous* than an unquestioned faith, accepted more out of habit than out of suffering of the conscience.[641]

Such words bring to mind the fundamental Gospel message of the Prodigal Son (Lk 15:1-15) for it reflects on the source and power of Christianity. After all, Pera's proposal of a new civil religion for Europe was not totally rejected by Ratzinger. Instead, with some modification, a renewed and transformed Catholic Church would be able to fulfill that role. In Ratzinger's words, "by going beyond borders, beyond rigid classification, one could, God willing, form a Christian civil religion that would not be an artificial construction of something that everybody supposedly finds reasonable, but rather a living partaking of the great spiritual tradition of Christianity, in which these values are actualized and revitalized."[642] Why then is the Christian faith struggling in conveying its great message to the people in the Western world? Cardinal Ratzinger speaks of two major reasons.

The first one would be that the Christian model, especially with its morality, is apparently unconvincing. In his own words, "it seems to place too many restraints on humankind that stifle its *joie de vivre,* that limit its precious freedom and that do not lead it to open pastures – in the language of the Psalms – but rather into want, into deprivation."[643] Therefore, a possible solution would be through creative minorities, who, as in the times of early Christianity, were able to demonstrate the emptiness of paganism, and would now be called upon to show a Christian model of life which would serve as a livable alternative to the increasingly empty lifestyle of a leisure-time society. The livable alternative would draw its force from the ability to manifest the Christian model of life as "a life in all its fullness and freedom, a life that does not experience the bonds of love as dependence and limitation, but rather as an opening to the greatness of life."[644]

Another reason as to why Christianity in the West struggles, according to Cardinal Ratzinger, is that "it seems to have been surpassed by 'science' and to be out-of-step with the rationalism of the modern era."[645] This challenge is not easily brushed aside because scientific and technological progress make *prima facie* the contents of faith look like quaint stories. Rudolf Karl Bultmann (1884-1976) did Christianity no favors when, as an expert of the New Testament, he discredited most of its content, especially that which related to the person of Jesus Christ which he claimed was a myth perpetrated by the early Christians. This is a juncture where the true foundations of faith are questioned and so should serve as the focus for theologians and philosophers. They need to engage in a dialogue with each other and the scientific community to answer the basic questions about the world and human beings living in it.

This kind of dialogue would be worthless, however, if the reigning philosophy of modern times would be – and according to Ratzinger already is – relativism. In his letter, he writes:

> In recent years I find myself noting how the more relativism becomes the generally accepted way of thinking, the more it tends toward intolerance, thereby becoming a new dogmatism. Political correctness... seeks to establish the domain of a single way of thinking and speaking. Its relativism creates the illusion that it has reached greater heights than the loftiest philosophical achievements of the past. It prescribes itself as the only way to think and speak – if, that is, one wishes to stay in fashion. Being faithful to traditional values and to the knowledge that upholds them is labeled intolerance

and relativism becomes the required norm. I think it is vital that we oppose this imposition of a new pseudo-enlightenment, which threatens freedom of thought as well as freedom of religion. In Sweden, a preacher who had presented the Biblical teachings on the question of homosexuality received a prison sentence. This is just one sign of the gains that have been made by relativism as a kind of new "denomination" that places restrictions on religious convictions and seeks to subordinate all religions to the super-dogma of relativism.[646]

Relativism has become a required norm, or a super-dogma in the Western world. It professes freedom of speech and religion and yet the Christian faith and its teachings are not allowed to be presented in a public realm, even as a private opinion. Ratzinger, in both his homily *Pro Eligendo Romano Pontifice* and in this letter, calls for a need to oppose this "imposition of a new pseudo-enlightenment." However, he does not offer a solution there. For this answer, one must investigate his other writings.

Another reason for Christianity's struggles is that the relationship between faith and reason has become *dormant* or *deceased* in current thought. However it is in the tension between faith and reason that "the dilemma of human life emerges fully."[647] What is the dilemma? The dilemma is that both reason and faith interchangeably empower and enable one another to serve the greatness of a human being. Ratzinger says that "there is the true heritage of the faith (e.g., the Trinity, the divinity of Christ, the sacraments), but there is also the knowledge that is later recognized as rational and pertaining to reason as such and thus also implying responsibility toward others."[648] Accepting this rationality and using reason and faith to obtain what the Cardinal calls the "moral minimum accessible to reason that all human beings share" should help "close the gap between secular ethics and religious ethics and found an ethics of reason that goes beyond such distinctions."[649]

3. Jürgen Habermas and Secularization

This dialogue between the two intellectual opposites, which took place on January 19, 2004 in Munich at the invitation of the Catholic Academy of Bavaria, is of immense importance in summarizing Ratzinger's attempts to evaluate the contemporary intellectual situation.[650] Jürgen Habermas is the philosopher, who in his own words "sees himself as 'tone deaf in the religious sphere,'"[651] whereas Cardinal Ratzinger is often described as "the quintessence of Catholic orthodoxy."[652] That being so, what made these two highly public figures, so different from each other in their intellectual stance, come together for this debate on the foundations of the secular West? For Ratzinger, it was an occasion by which to stimulate the debate on the truth of the Christian religion, using reflections which he had developed on the structure of worldwide interreligious dialogue. However, for Habermas, it was the surprise he caused when, shortly after the September 11 terrorist attacks, he gave his speech in Frankfurt am Main at the acceptance of the Peace Prize from German Booksellers. In this speech, Habermas stated, "The secular society acquire a new understanding of religious convictions, which are something more and something other than mere relics of a past with which we are finished."[653] Such a statement became the opening of a door for a further dialogue, which is precisely what happened in Bavaria. The participants, although of the same generation, never met in person before this debate. Though both led parallel lives, in the eyes of the public Ratzinger was considered the very personification of the Catholic faith, whereas Habermas was seen as the standard-bearer of secular thinking. The two speakers agreed to converse on the subject of "The Pre-political Moral Foundations of a Free State," or one could say "About the Bases of a Society Worthy of Men."[654]

a) Law and Its Limitations

By examining the present situation of democratic legislation and its nature, Habermas tries to respond to a question asked by

Ernst Wolfgang Böckenförde: Does the free, secularized State exist because of normative presuppositions that it itself cannot guarantee?[655] According to Habermas, who adheres to the nonreligious and postmetaphysical justification of the normative bases of the democratic constitutional State, this basis is formed through the law and established using democratic legislation brought about by the participation and decision of the majority. However, the law itself does not provide for the motivation needed for an individual citizen to participate in such a process of democratic legislation, especially when it comes to the question of a common good.[656] Furthermore, the reduction of the citizen's field of action to the private realm is intensified by the discouraging processes whereby the democratic formation of a common opinion and will loses its functional relevance. This contemporary tendency to leave the processes of decision making up to the global community as a result depoliticizes the citizens and "in view of the conflicts and the outrageous social injustices of a global community that is profoundly fragmented" prevents it from giving "international law the quality of a constitution."[657]

Ultimately, a radical skepticism vis-à-vis reason could be noted and "the remorseful modern age can find its way out of the blind alley only by means of the religious orientation to a transcendent point of reference."[658] Habermas thinks that one should not wait until the modern age stabilizes itself, "exclusively on the basis of a secular communicative reason," but suggests intensifying the already occurring process of "a post-Hegelian self-reflection of reason," also called *post-secular*, which returns philosophy to its religious-metaphysical origins.[659]

b) Self-reflection of Reason and a Dialogue with Religion

In the process of self-reflection, reason becomes aware of its limitations, and so needs to transcend itself into the direction of something else.[660] That something else could mean various things to different people; however, Habermas states, "philosophy has good reasons to be willing to learn from religious traditions."[661] What are those reasons? For one, there is the "ethical abstinence of a post-metaphysical thinking,"[662] which means there are no universally accepted concepts of good and evil, responsibility, autonomy, history and most importantly – of man himself. Here one encounters the reality of total relativism. Another reason for philosophy opening up to religion is the awareness, "in the post-secular society, there is an increasing consensus that certain phases of the 'modernization of the public consciousness' involve the assimilation and the reflective transformation of both religious and secular mentalities."[663]

Habermas asks, if a dialogue between philosophy and religion is unavoidable, how should it advance in practice? First, Habermas suggests the nonbeliever has to accept that religious consciousness, in its origins, tends to own a *comprehensive doctrine*, claiming the authority to give structure to an entire way of life. Although under the conditions created by secularization, religion was forced to withdraw with its universal claims to the inner circle of the fellowship of its members, nevertheless, those claims, often safeguarding the laws of the ethos, need to be brought back into the society of citizens. Since a neutral state guarantees the same ethical freedom to every citizen, it is

> …incompatible with the political universalization of a secularist world view. When secularized citizens act in their role as citizens of the State, they must not deny in principle that religious images of the world have the potential to express truth. Nor must they refuse their believing fellow citizens the right to make contributions in a religious language to public debates.[664]

Habermas clearly rejects the major presupposition of relativism, when he reminds the secularists that different religious images have the potential to express the truth.[665]

c) Challenges of Globalization

Cardinal Ratzinger acknowledges that there are two factors accelerating historical development in today's world: the formation of the global community, and the development of human possibilities. This in turn "lends great urgency to the question of how cultures that encounter one another can find ethical bases to guide their relationship along the right path, thus permitting them to build up a common structure that tames power and imposes a legally responsible order on the exercise of power."[666] According to Ratzinger there is also a third factor, which does not allow for an easy answer to what Hans Küng proposes and calls a "world ethos." That third factor is the disappearance of ethical certainties, which resulted through the encounter and mutual penetration of different world cultures. In other words, with globalization the fundamental question of what is good or why one must do good goes unanswered. Ratzinger thinks the growth of scientific knowledge caused moral certainties to collapse and thus, he concludes, science as such cannot give birth to a universal ethos, for it can never unfold more than partial aspects of human existence.

Another concern for Ratzinger is contemporary man's ability to produce his own self in a test-tube. No longer is man a gift of nature and of the Creator. Instead, he has "descended into the very well-springs of power, to the sources of his own existence."[667] A scientific disposition such as this, as well as – for example – the creation of the atomic bomb, illustrates that "a mere scientific rationalism cannot generate a satisfactory ethos."[668] However, this poses the question: Should religion and reason restrict each other and remind each other of its limits? Julia Kristeva, too, observes that a new shift was occurring in contemporary anthropology where "a new conception of the human is in the process of being constituted out of contributions from fields in the humanities where transcendence is considered immanent."[669] Therefore, in her perspective, the debate between Ratzinger and Habermas could be seen as an effort on their part to confront this new type of humanism. She writes:

> Having remarked the failure of rationalist humanism to avert or cope with 20th century totalitarianism – and having predicted that it would yet fail to prevent the economic and biological automatization threatening the human species in the new century – Ratzinger and Habermas jointly diagnosed the problem as confusion on the part of the modern democracies in the absence of a reliable "higher" authority to regulate the frenetic expansion of liberty.[670]

Present-day man, if not concerned with the question of God, at the very least is concerned with himself, with the question of who he is, what is the meaning of his existence, and what is to be after death. However, not having a higher authority leaves man to answer these imperative questions using only his own reason, which in turn could be, and indeed is, doubted as well. Eventually, Kristeva concludes, "This joint declaration by the theologian and the philosopher implies that a return to faith is the only way possible to establish the moral stability required for us to face the risks of freedom."[671] In this view, freedom is presented as having certain risks. The contemporary world generally does not speak negatively about freedom, but Ratzinger notes many times in his own writings that freedom, which is not led by higher standards of belief and morality, will tends to overstep its boundaries and become an anarchy or some form of dictatorship.

Ratzinger acknowledges that religion without limits might lead to instances of religious fanaticism which in turn can lead to actions of terrorism. He says, "Terrorism was at first a religious enthusiasm that had been redirected into the earthy realm, a messianic expectation transposed into political fanaticism."[672] When, as in the case of relativism, there is no clear criterion of justice, terrorism easily tends to present itself as just another liberation movement. Allen summarizes what Ratzinger thought of politically engaged theologies in the following words, "At the level of theory, he believes they relativize Christian doctrine; as a practical matter, they lead to various forms of revolutionary terrorism. On both levels, they are a danger to the faith."[673]

d) Respectful Limits of Reason and Religion

In terms of the role of law in being a determining force for human affairs, Cardinal Ratzinger states: "It is not the law of the stronger, but the strength of the law that must hold sway."[674] However, law becomes compromised, or viewed with suspicion and even revolted against, when "law itself appears to be no longer the expression of a justice that is at the service of all, but rather the product of arbitrariness and legislative arrogance on the part of those who have the power for it."[675] In that case, Ratzinger asks, how does law come into being? Or what is its genesis? In a democracy, law comes from the common will of everyone participating in its making. That for Ratzinger is the basic argument which "speaks in favor of democracy as the most appropriate form of political order."[676]

However, this model also has its limitations. A democracy relies on a majority decision, but history has shown that the majority can choose and act unjustly. As George Weigel states, "Ratzinger always remembered, however, that Hitler had come to power by legal means, and that the Nazis' opportunity had come about because of the fatal flaws of the Weimar Republic, a beautifully constructed democratic system. It takes more than systems, though, to make democracies work; it takes virtues."[677] What is needed is an ethical foundation of the law, with "self-subsistent values that flow from the essence of what it is to be a man and therefore inviolable: no other man can infringe them."[678] In ancient Greece, the idea arose that there must be a law that comes from nature itself, from the very being of man himself. Such a law is called natural law, and has remained "the key issue in dialogue with other communities of faith, and the secular society."[679]

The understanding of natural law, however, varies over time as the understanding of nature itself changes. For the purposes of this discussion, Ratzinger attempts during this conversation to maintain an understanding of natural law as it is connected to the concept of human rights. Man, by being *man*, is subject to certain rights, values, and norms which are not to be decided or invented by another man, or group of men, but discovered in man's own nature as applying to all.[680] Ratzinger notes that the doctrine of human rights should also contain within it a doctrine of human obligations and of human limitations. Employing the biblical image of the forbidden fruit (Gn 3:3), Ratzinger says, "Human beings who deny the limitations imposed on them by good and evil, which are the inner standard of creation, deny the truth" and as a result of it, "they are living in untruth and in unreality."[681]

4. The Dictatorship of Relativism

As previously stated, the *Pro Eligendo Romano Pontifice* homily publicized the dangers of relativism to a worldwide audience. David Bloor observes: "Cardinal Ratzinger may have provided the best publicized denunciation of relativism in recent times, but his is only one of many, lesser condemnations."[682] It is worthwhile to have a closer look at what was said in the homily regarding this topic. Ratzinger began by reaffirming Christ's saving role in this world, presenting him not just as the announcer of God's mercy to all, but as being that mercy himself in his own person. Therefore, "encountering Christ means encountering the mercy of God."[683] Once again, we are reminded that faith is not about encountering or choosing certain ideas, but involves the encounter with the real person of Jesus Christ, the living God, in whom all that matters for people to know and to believe is embodied.

Cardinal Ratzinger was in no way naïve when he mentioned evil in his homily. He spoke of God's divine mercy as putting a limit on evil ruling this world: "Christ's mercy is not a cheap grace; it does not presume a trivialization of evil."[684] Addressing the always-burning issue of theodicy, the existence of evil is a way to keep people humble and open to God's care and love.

However, because Jesus died on the Cross and rose to life, evil does not have the final word and therefore our journey through this *valley of tears* is filled with hope.[685] Certainly, the idea of this world being a place of tears disquiets modern thinkers, but on further self-reflective introspection, one comes to the realization that this is not one's true home. Man is just a *homo viator* in this world and not its permanent citizen.

Cardinal Ratzinger continued his homily by quoting St. Paul and what it means to be an infant in faith. It means to be "tossed by waves and swept along by every wind of teaching arising from human trickery (Eph 4:14)."[686] This passage is relevant today, for it points out how relativism first originates in *human trickery*, and thus becomes a product of one's own making, which reflects infantilism found in one's faith.[687] The following passage by Ratzinger gives a brief and accurate summary of what relativism is, where it comes from, and what it actually does in the contemporary world:

> How many winds of doctrine have we known in recent decades, how many ideological currents, how many ways of thinking? The small boat of the thought of many Christians has often been tossed about by these waves – flung from one extreme to another: from Marxism to liberalism, even to libertinism; from collectivism to radical individualism; from atheism to a vague religious mysticism; from agnosticism to syncretism and so forth. Every day new sects are created and what St. Paul says about human trickery comes true, with cunning that tries to draw those into error (cf. Eph 4:14). Today, having a clear faith based on the Creed of the Church is often labeled as fundamentalism. Whereas relativism, that is, letting oneself be "tossed here and there, carried about by every wind of doctrine," seems the only attitude that can cope with modern times. We are building a dictatorship of relativism that does not recognize anything as definitive

and whose ultimate goal consists solely of one's own ego and desires.[688]

Barbara H. Smith observes that, "in contrasting due Christian submission to Church authority with a *dictatorship of relativism*, Ratzinger may also be alluding to the increasing dominance and appeal, in many intellectual circles, of certain more or less specific views identified in secular discourse as relativism."[689] Jeffrey Stout suggests that Ratzinger's use of the term *dictatorship of relativism* is hardly surprising, because he,

> ...who was conscripted into the Hitler-Jugend and then into the Luftwaffenhelfer as a teenager, would use the term "dictatorship" when signaling the dangers of a merely procedural conception of democracy. He surely has in mind how the National Socialists used the democratic procedural apparatus of the Weimar Republic to take power in 1933, shortly before instituting the totalitarian tyranny of the Third Reich.[690]

In speaking about the person of Jesus Christ as the *measure of true humanism*[691] Ratzinger follows the example of Pope Paul VI, who during the Second Vatican Council presented Christ as the only mediator and hope of the Church. In his words, Christ was the true *president* of the Council, which Ratzinger paraphrased by saying, Christ is the "interpreter of the present and the measure of all that is happening."[692] *Adult faith* should follow a search of the truth rather than the waves of today's fashions or the latest novelties, among which one could find contemporary secular philosophies. God, "who addresses us in love, as Love" and through his Church "remains in place to ensure the truth of Christianity, its being in accordance with what is right about us and about our salvation."[693] Again, it is in Christ, that *truth and love coincide*.[694] Truth in itself is not enough; it must be followed by love since love without truth is blind and truth without love is meaningless.

In the Garden of Gethsemane, Jesus "transformed our rebellious human will into a will shaped and united to the divine will."[695] At that hour, the whole experience of human autonomy from God was overturned into the gift of freedom when given to God. Speaking of the rebellious human will, elsewhere Ratzinger observes that "this is also something we are experiencing again today; when man's independence is pushed to the point where he says; I don't want to love at all, because then I make myself dependent and that contradicts my freedom."[696] Jesus demonstrated to all of us that by turning our will to God, we do not lose it, but instead we gain true freedom. It is precisely in that communion of wills, where our "redemption takes place: being friends of Jesus to become friends of God."[697] Human freedom is a "*normed* freedom – not blind and directionless, but guided by the light of what is given to us with our creation,"[698] and can only be realized in the love of God. God as creator of the human, allowing himself to enter into that same condition and to be on that same level where man is, could establish a partnership, a love relationship with his creature. However, by establishing such a connection, God takes the risk of man rejecting him.[699]

Ratzinger ended his homily with a reminder, that all Christians, who were given and have realized in the person of Jesus Christ, the gift of a friendship with God, have now as their beautiful duty to share that gift with the rest of the world. We are called by Jesus "to go and bear fruit" (Jn 15:16). Fulfilling that command might be dangerous, difficult or unpleasant at times, but it is the only human effort that remains forever. Everything else will disappear eventually, except for "the human soul, the human person created by God for eternity."[700] Also, it will be the fruits of human endeavors that will remain, "that what we sowed in human souls: love, knowledge, a gesture capable of touching the heart, words that open the soul to joy in the Lord."[701] This homily was especially significant as a symposium was convened shortly thereafter exclusively dedicated to addressing Ratzinger's issue of the dictatorship of relativism. The symposium and further analyses by Ratzinger on relativism are presented in the following chapters.

7

CRITIQUES OF RATZINGER'S ANTI-RELATIVISTIC POSITION

1. Symposium in Response to Cardinal Ratzinger's Last Homily

There is no doubt that Cardinal Ratzinger's homily *Pro Eligendo Romano Pontifice* had a wide resonance among not only the world media, but also the world intellectuals. In response, a few months later the editors of *Common Knowledge* – a journal published by Duke University Press – devoted a double issue to the contestation of Ratzinger's denunciation of relativism.[702] In the introductory article, Gianni Vattimo observes several contributions to the symposium question – the definition of relativism given by Ratzinger in his homily. For example, Christopher Norris writes, "a scientific realist will naturally find the philosophical evidence for what Joseph Ratzinger calls 'relativism' inherently false and infuriatingly wrongheaded. However, it is less clear why a believing Catholic should wish to do so."[703] Vattimo offers a sort of defense for the Cardinal by saying the following:

> ...but if Ratzinger's intention had been precision of philosophical vocabulary, he would surely have achieved it. He was not referring to philosophical relativism so much as to vaguer social phenomena

193

that cluster around the adage "everything's relative." His reference was to kinds of liberal tolerance for the other's "lifestyle" that can easily become interest in, fascination with, or attraction to it, then participation or conversion. His special objection, judging by tone, was less to permanent conversions than to temporary ones – temporary, that is, until something more fascinating, attractive and fashionable comes along.[704]

Vattimo goes on questioning this type of *vaguer sort of relativism* asking if it really presents such a great risk to civilization, religion and for social cohesion, as Ratzinger makes it sound. He cites Adolf Hitler and George Bush as examples of what he considers a zealous certainty, in that both took their countries to war with strong but mistaken conviction. However, Vattimo thinks, this zeal against the dictatorship of relativism comes from the Church's self-understanding and preoccupation:

> In a world in which so many destroyers, of so many kinds, have believed so zealously in false truths, there remains, undiminished, the desire for a true truth – one that can be trusted without doubts and hesitations, one that guarantees the continuity of interior life, the fidelity to an ideal, the cohesion of the community in which we live. Adherents of the religion revealed and transmitted authoritatively by the Universal Church, with the aid of the Holy Spirit, have no doubts about where and where only, such truth is to be found.[704a]

However, Vattimo argues, a certain type of relativism, following Baghramian's categories – alethic relativism – is already present in the Church. As an example, he recalls the Holy Year of 2000 and the youth gathering at Tor Vergata University in Rome, where after the celebration with Pope John Paul II, "mounds of used condoms were reportedly scattered on the grounds – a most eloquent monument to relativism."[705] Vattimo argues this happened because the pope misinterpreted what draws youth to the Church. It is not the presentation of the one truth, but the appeal to charity and universal friendship, because "in comparison with charity, there is no truth worth affirming."[706] He uses the example of Jesus who constructed a set of ethics based on *caritas*, which he interprets as a way that "frees us of our last idolatry: the adoration of Truth as our god."[707] With his position, Vattimo parallels John Hick's argument: in that the central theme of these gatherings should be the love/compassion to which all the great traditions call us and which "in our sociologically conscious age… is likely to be increasingly a politically conscious and active agape."[708] Therefore, Vattimo concluded, "we need more, rather than less, relativism to accomplish this unfinished (this scarcely commenced) task."[709] He is promoting orthopraxis over orthodoxy, or action first, doctrine second.

Furthermore, Vattimo expresses the opinion that Christians are being uncharitable with their doctrine – that salvation comes only through Christ. Since Christians find themselves living in multi-religious and multicultural societies, such narrow thinking would render a peaceful existence with others impossible. He considers Cardinal Ratzinger and his views about having the truth to be arrogant. Jeffrey M. Perl in his article presented at this symposium, also charges Ratzinger and the Catholic Church, of not being humble enough to allow the necessary openness and change. Perl cites Simon Blackburn's *True Enough* article[710] where the latter writes, "Good relativists must have found it especially hilarious to find themselves attacked by the chief curator of that mausoleum of conspicuously old and peculiar historical furniture, the Roman Catholic Church."[711] Charles Taylor, another person Perl quotes, suggests that "the Church [should] 'align itself' with no 'style of life,' to take no side in 'the *culture wars*,' 'to be present in the culture at large, ready to listen, to accompany and to help people find their way to God.'"[712] The salient word is *their*, because the path to finding God "is not of the Church but of the soul."[713] This accusation notwithstanding, Ratzinger still suggests that the Church, the so-called *mausoleum*, still is a reliable sign and is still capable of providing helping means for the individual soul in finding the way and staying on course, knowing where it eventually leads. Ultimately, Ratzinger argues, "It is the relativist who is arrogant, because it is arrogant to *deny* that God can give us the truth. We must be humble: we do not possess truth, but we are able to *receive* it."[714]

Vattimo ends his introduction with a rhetorical question, "Given Jesus' resounding words about charity, love, peacemaking, humility (indeed meekness) and abstention from judging others, may it not be that, in the makeup of a genuine Christian, Joseph Ratzinger not excluded, a relativist component must necessarily abide?"[715] However, one may ask: does Vattimo even seem to know what makes up a *genuine Christian?* To be a genuine Christian, one cannot exclude the word *truth* from Jesus' words, "I am the way, the truth and the life" (Jn 14:6). Relativism will not be able to avoid the question of truth, and whoever excludes truth, will not fully realize the scope of this polemic or the danger relativism poses.

2. Questioning Ratzinger as a Philosopher

Recalling the history of relativist thought, Barbara Smith points out the ambiguity of the term *relativism*:

> ...Indeed, it may be that relativism, at least in our own era, is nothing at all – a phantom position, a set of tenets without palpable adherents, an urban legend without certifiable occurrence but fearful report of which is circulated continuously. Of course, even a phantom position may be consequential. No matter how protean or elusive relativism may be as a doctrine, it has evident power as a charge or anxiety, even in otherwise dissident quarters and even among those otherwise known for conceptual daring.[716]

In these last words, Smith charges Cardinal Ratzinger of being one of those unnecessarily anxious about relativism. She proposes that a necessary distinction has to be made between Ratzinger's conception of relativism and what she thinks relativism is. Smith understands why Ratzinger as the guardian of the Catholic faith is so cautious of a relativistic approach toward faith; however, she argues that when it comes to secular views and sciences, this type of relativism is necessary for a progression of thought. Such relativism, starting with the end of the 19th century, expresses itself mainly in the *radical questioning* of the prevailing orthodoxy in any science or doctrine. Smith concludes that relativism – as understood in the modern period – appears "to have been a significant strand in much respectable intellectual discourse"[717] whereas Ratzinger's "denunciation of relativism amounts to a demand for dogmatism – for predetermined judgment armored against new thought."[718]

However, to say that relativism was the moving force behind the intellectual discoveries of the 19th and 20th centuries is not to see what it may have also caused: two World Wars, fascism, communism and other evils for world to endure. Cardinal Ratzinger does not deny that a sort of relativism – openness to new thought – is necessary in the progress of sciences, even in theology.[719] He wants to make clear, however, that the proper boundaries must be respected. Smith interprets his position quite differently. She suggests that there is a constant antagonism between scholars who entered their disciplines during the 1950s and early 1960s (Ratzinger among them) and those in succeeding decades. The latter represents the liberal school, or what could be called *postmodern relativism*. Its main premise is to question the very idea of objective knowledge itself.

Smith also recalls one line from the Cardinal's homily, which she uses as an example to explain radical differences of thought – "the Son of God, the true man. He is the measure of true humanism."[720] With that quote, she stresses that Christians think of themselves as different, using not themselves or others as a measure of all things, but instead, the Son of God. For her, this is a position coming from the representative of the Catholic Church which she sees as an *authoritarian warning* she cannot accept since "the Church authorizes itself by what it authorizes as authoritative."[721]

Ratzinger disagrees with this view, arguing that the Church does not authorize these standards of truth herself, but receives them from the Lord. This is where the possibility of a contemporary dialogue becomes problematic, for it becomes impossible to have a dialogue if the participants cannot agree that there exists, independently of their own positions, an objective truth. Smith, being a true relativist, cannot enter into dialogue with Cardinal Ratzinger precisely because she does not accept that there is such truth to be sought in all dialogues and conversations.

David Bloor takes a much more respectful approach to interpreting Ratzinger's view on relativism. By acknowledging a certain respect for the theological rejection of relativism, he argues that "no such respect must be accorded to the philosophical critics."[722] This is because from a philosophical point of view, Bloor claims that no one has absolute knowledge or morality, and therefore it is primarily grounded in the human predicament. Cardinal Ratzinger would strongly agree with this position. Although, as St. Paul states, a human being, because of natural reason, is capable of knowing who God is from his creation, nevertheless often that knowledge is not enough to have a loving relationship with God. That is where and why revelation in a person, Jesus Christ, takes place. It extends knowledge of what is true, good, or moral enabling people to be sure through faith of these fundamental realities. However, states Bloor, "for the relativist, there can be nothing transcendental about the story of human achievement or failure. Neither knowledge nor morality can be supernatural. They are natural phenomena and any attempt to evade this is a lapse into superstition and obscurantism."[723]

Bloor continues to argue that "if questions about the status and limits of human knowledge are under discussion, then choice cannot be evaded. Relativism and absolutism represent a dichotomy that is mutually exclusive and jointly exhaustive."[724]

Without question, even Ratzinger as a philosopher has to agree that his intellectual discoveries and acquired human knowledge are tangible. However, as a theologian and a man of faith, he cannot separate himself from the knowledge given to humankind through revelation in the person of Jesus Christ – the "God of philosophers and God of faith is one."[725] Moreover, although there is a tension between these two modes of coming to know God – faith and reason – in the end, they are mutually intertwined and needed. Bloor concludes that absolutism and relativism are the only available choices. Ratzinger, however, presents another way that is dependent upon what sources are used in acquiring knowledge. If it involves only reason, then no other option exists. However, if one accepts faith and revelation with reason, then a third choice can be experienced involving one's ability to think and to question, and accepting answers when they come, through reason and faith.

So once again, one may ask, how is dialogue between a relativist and a believer possible? What Pascal suggests and Ratzinger repeats, is for a way of reaching the limits of human reason, and then desiring to exceed them. As long as someone is comfortable within those limits, there is no need for anything supernatural, and that is precisely what empowers contemporary agnosticism.[726] Ratzinger laments the fact that too many are comfortable in their present state and have abandoned their greatness. Michelangelo once said, "The greatest danger for most of us lies not in setting our aim too high and falling short; but in setting our aim too low and achieving our mark."[727] What happens to those, who do not have any standards from which to reach or to decide?

For David Bloor it is quite clear that Cardinal Ratzinger's argument against relativism is "grounded in his faith in God as the ultimate source of truth in all matters moral, epistemological and ontological. God is the source of all true standards and these standards are, accordingly, absolute and not relative. Here, in the appeal to God, one has the very archetype of something that is absolute."[728] Bloor relates Ratzinger's acceptance of absolutes with the doctrine of the Incarnation. As he himself says, "to adopt the view that the absolute does not enter into the 'actual world' of human history is like having a God who does not involve himself with the human race – that is, an absent, indifferent, infinitely distant God."[729] He concludes, "For Cardinal Ratzinger such a position would be, in all of its consequences just a form of relativism."[730] However, Bloor writes, no matter how one might feel about relativists, they "can provide a coherent analysis of knowledge and, given a naturalistic approach, the only possible analysis. It is the anti-relativists, not the relativists, who have the real problem with epistemic standards. They have to prove their standards are absolute."[731] Bloor believes that often in contemporary intellectual writing and talk, relativism is greatly stereotyped and misunderstood:

> Relativism, say critics, amounts to a willingness to tolerate almost any nonsense because the relativist position renders its adherents incapable of wielding proper standards of judgment or makes them indifferent to the significance of those standards. The non-relativist, by contrast, is seen as free from such restrictions and as someone capable of discriminating truth from falsity, or good from evil and of issuing praise or blame accordingly. These stereotypes are nonsense.[732]

In support for relativism, he provides a qualifying thesis – to say something is not an absolute truth does not preclude it from being a truth. In other words, "someone could assert, on some occasion, belief in the existence of an absolute right or wrong, but confess that he or she doesn't know what it is."[733] It is not that relativists lack moral conviction; it is just that they have nothing more to ground their convictions in other than custom, convention, feeling and intelligence. In his view, feelings are subjective and morality is objective; but by *objective* he does not mean *absolute*, only that it is something in existence outside the mind of an individual. Austin Dacey explains this another way by saying "between 'absolute moral values' and a relativism of the 'all values are equal' variety, there is a sizeable grey area, at least when one considers *how we actually operate* [emphasis in the original]."[734]

Bloor compares this type of *objective* knowledge with what he calls *gut feeling* knowledge. He says, "a relativist knows that he or she has no ultimate justification for this gut feeling… if we were to map the distribution of supposed absolutes and compare the map with the distribution of gut feelings, the two maps would look remarkably similar."[735] Accordingly, Dacey speaks of the *rule of thumb*, which is an example of how "ethicists have long distinguished between what they call defeasible and indefeasible moral claims. Defeasible claims are rules of thumb that nevertheless can be overruled for countervailing moral reasons."[736] Eventually, Dacey makes a point that doubtfulness and a certain relativizing can be quite appropriate when one recognizes the presence of a genuine uncertainty. Corkery, although not completely convinced by Dacey's argumentation, draws an interesting conclusion himself: "It is one thing to assert the existence of absolute moral values but that it is another to bring these to bear on life-situations in (at least some) contemporary cultural contexts."[737] According to him, Ratzinger often fails to allow for these complexities.

Returning once again to the terms *gut feeling* and *rule of thumb*, are they not what Christians would call *conscience*? And if that is so, then is it not also the metaphysical, transcendental source of creation? Anthropology is able to provide an answer in this case. Bloor thinks morality and *gut feelings* are socially learned. They become objective because they arise from participation in a shared common life, traditions and customs. He finds that there is nothing extraordinary about this, but "that they are embodied in precedents and practice. They are not justified by appeal to any supernatural origin but, instead, because they have emerged historically in the institutions of a particular nation."[738] What does one do when born into a culture which has received the Revelation? Bloor recognizes a major obstacle for the relativist when faced with the Incarnation. If the Absolute has revealed himself among human culture as the Christians say, and remains among us, then it is quite a challenge to avoid the ever-pressing possibility of encountering that Absolute. Nichols presenting Ratzinger's view, writes, "The significance of the creedal and biblical belief in 'one God,' is chiefly, then, an existential renunciation of other ways of conceiving of the Absolute and notably that of polytheism for which, characteristically, cosmic and political powers were erected into objects of worship."[739]

Finally, Bloor closes any possibility for a dialogue between the relativist and anti-relativist by asserting the following: "Just as the atheist need never grant the theologian's premises, so the relativist need never grant the absolutist's premises. This may provide the simplest way to characterize the entire confrontation. Relativism is just epistemological atheism, while anti-relativism is theology in disguise."[740] Bloor adds a note of caution to people like Cardinal Ratzinger: "it is high time the anti-relativists in the academic world learned to moderate their rhetoric and curb their complacency. They might begin by drawing a few simple distinctions and taking more care to understand the positions they denounce."[741]

Julia Kristeva, another contributor to the symposium, and one who does not support the proposal of faith, in recalling the dialogue between Ratzinger and Habermas, calls both of them *apostles of normative conscience*, requiring some "difficult intellectual labors to get beyond."[742] According to her, the true source of the contemporary anthropological crisis lies in the "Freudian discovery of the unconscious and the literary experience that is inseparable from theoretical thought."[743] Therefore, she writes:

> We are confronting a crisis whose source is *pre*-religious (though it is a crisis of belief, of ideals) and *pre*-political (though it affects the foundation of human bonds) – a crisis that, contra Joseph Ratzinger and Jurgen Habermas, who have made clear they understand the crisis, no religion or established moral order or ideal of normative conscience will ever resolve. Resolution will demand understanding of *and for* the human soul, along with generosity that free intellectuals can

acquire but that standards of normative conscience are intended to extinguish.[744]

Kristeva proposes that it should be the task of today's intellectuals to find the formula to overcome that uncertainty in which contemporary man lives. The mistake Kristeva makes is her unwillingness to accept that, because of such things as *Freudian unconscious* and other limitations which human reason encounters, one needs faith. This leads to one of Ratzinger's conclusions: "The Christian faith is not a limitation or paralysis of reason: on the contrary, it is only this faith that sets reason free to perform its own proper work."[745]

Daniel Boyarin raises the question of the epistemological seriousness of relativism, especially as found in Ratzinger's homily. He argues that for Ratzinger relativism is not a doctrine as such to confront, but "only an indecisiveness or lack of will in a world where doctrines are copious and fast proliferating."[746] Boyarin thinks Ratzinger is mistaken in dismissing relativism as a legitimate philosophical doctrine, originating from the times of Protagoras and the Sophists. According to Boyarin, Protagoras formulated his famous statement *man is the measure of all things* only after he made a clear distinction between the knowledge or the possibility of that knowledge to be obtained from gods and that knowledge which man is capable of himself. Protagoras' statement, as found in Diogenes Laertius, reads: "Concerning the gods I cannot know either that they exist or that they do not exist, or what form they might have, for there is much to prevent one's knowing: the obscurity of the subject and the shortness of man's life."[747] In the end, this makes him conclude, "of all things, the human is the measure; of that which is, that it is and of that which is not, that it is not."[748]

Eventually, it becomes clear that Protagoras' relativism amounts to agnosticism which, according to Boyarin, is the true philosophical stance for relativism. However, it is precisely that which Ratzinger sees as the greatest danger in relativism.[749] The danger lies not so much from a philosophical aspect as from a religious one. If "gods are epistemologically irrelevant – there may very well be gods, but one does not know anything about them – there is no criterion other than human perception by which judgments can be made."[750] Once again, one is presented with two different schools of thought which define differently what truth is, depending on how it comes to us or is achieved by us. One school includes Plato and Cardinal Ratzinger, where truth is an objective beyond humankind and needs to be received in relation to the other – in Ratzinger's case, God.[751] Then the other school of Protagoras, the school of Sophists, and thus of relativists and agnostics, perceive truth "as seen from the perspective of an educated *doxa* and in the interests of an educated judgment being made about probabilities in a given situation."[752]

However, in reality it is difficult to keep a clear distinction between these two schools of thought. For example, although Socrates is considered an objectivist, he comes close to Protagoras' position by suggesting that "human actions are objectively right or wrong, apart from what the gods may think, but since the gods are infallibly equipped to tell the difference, their authority is beyond reproach."[753] Protagoras at the same time was not much of an agnostic since he "continued to worship the gods and follow other religious observances."[754] Boyarin himself observes that Protagoras at Athens employs "an early version of Pascal's wager"[755] which, as already illustrated, is the way Cardinal Ratzinger proposes to overcome present-day relativism and agnosticism – *Veluti etsi Deus daretur.* Boyarin concludes that one needs Sophist relativism in order to willfully choose between competing alternatives and not be forcefully coerced into the very many varieties on offer of the "One and Only Absolute Truth."[756] Ratzinger would strongly disagree with Boyarin's proposition.

3. The Dangers of Absolutism

Jeffrey M. Perl considers Ratzinger a strongly opinionated objectivist. Employing the metaphor Ratzinger uses in his homily, he says, "the absolutist is not at rest in port – this 'apostle,' like the unnamed wanderer, is on the move, but with purpose and resolve, 'enlivened by a holy restlessness: a restlessness to bring everyone the gift of faith.'"[757] Perl poses a question: If all relativist thinking is godless, and all absolutist thinking is ultimately theological, how could the relativist and Christian be one and the same? Would not a *Christian relativist* be considered an oxymoron? Perl thinks not:

> ...the relativists in those small boats of his are Christians, even if ill equipped to navigate profound waters.... A relativist Christian would presumably be one who holds that the truths of Christianity, in which he or she does believe, are relative to other truths. A Christian of this sort is not necessarily among those who say that religion must "keep up" with the times, must make room for the findings of psychology, biology, or feminist theory. What a relativist holds is that the idea of absolute truth is an incoherent idea and that, therefore, no truths, including those of Christianity, should be regarded as absolute.[758]

As an example of a Christian relativist, he chooses T.S. Eliot, whose philosophical views were of a relativistic or skeptic nature.[759] Perl describes how later in his life Eliot underwent a radical conversion[760] and changed his beliefs toward a Christian understanding of truth and reality. However, Perl thinks that skeptical inclination did not change with his conversion in 1927. In Eliot's essay "Demon of Doubt,"[761] Perl quotes him as saying that *the demon of doubt* is inseparable from the spirit of belief, and that the proper relationship to one's own beliefs is "a systole and diastole, [a] movement to and from, of approach and withdrawal."[762] Ratzinger would agree that doubt has its legitimate place in human life and faith, but doubt cannot prevail.[763]

Kenneth J. Gergen considers Ratzinger an absolutist whose position will create the "potential for global catastrophe in the name of unwarranted and unsupported claims to foundational truth."[764] He thinks Ratzinger's attack on relativism is unfair – even dangerous – to both sides of the contemporary confrontation:

> ...to replace "our God" with "god as we understand god in our culture," or "is true" with "is true in the context of what we are doing here," or "is moral" with "conforms to our deeply felt protocols of morality," is understood as threatening. The basis for worship (in the first case), scientific experiment (in the second), or institutions of justice (in the third) is understood as threatened.[765]

Ratzinger says, indeed, there is a real threat since, by replacing *God*, *truth*, and *morals* with human conventions, one disconnects these important realities from their true foundation and makes them into mere products of human culture. Gergen states that in the end "all parties concerned agree that moral pluralism is our global condition; that people lack a mutually sustaining understanding of the real, the rational and the good; and finally that, with the democratization of weaponry, these schisms are increasingly perilous to the world's people."[766] So what does he propose that both – relativists and absolutists – should do in order to overcome this perilous situation? The solution comes about by evoking the concept of man as a relational being who is in need of interrelationship or dialogue. What is necessary is to find an original or universal ethic to which all may cling and transcend animosities.[767]

For a psychologist, Gergen thinks quite poorly of people's ability to use conversation and dialogue as the means to reach common peace. He cautions that man has a strong tendency toward conflict, and the challenge arises as how to avoid it. One way might be through *appreciative inquiry* as developed by David Cooperrider, which means that the "focus of dialogue shifts from deficits to positive potentials."[768] Certainly this is not a very original idea since one is often advised to see a glass half full instead of half empty. The Catholic Church can be considered a proponent of this through its ecumenical and inter-religious efforts in finding common ground for dialogue, and fragments of truth in all religions.

Richard Shusterman thinks that, although one may long for certainties in life, at the same time people also need and desire both change and movement. That would not be possible if people were to accept Ratzinger's stance, which he summarizes as follows:

> While the newness of its Testament shows that God can suddenly deliver utterly new knowledge of infinite value, its claim that the redeemer has already arrived with the ultimate soul-saving truth implies that entertaining new religious views is not only unnecessary but also puts at risk the existing deposit of the faith.... It is endemic to Catholicism and other ancient faiths.[769]

In response to that, one may argue that God does not deliver himself suddenly. From the Old Testament, one knows, the Messiah was promised generations ago and was awaited. Ratzinger relates that Revelation develops throughout history. It is not suddenly *new knowledge* which becomes personified in the divine *Logos*, but it is more fulfillment of what already had been given to the people of old, in the guise of various Old Testament characters and symbols. Will Ratzinger's position as an absolutist be able to combat relativism? Geoffrey W. Bromiley, professor of Church history and historical theology, eloquently presents Ratzinger's position:

> Relativism, then, has a proper place in theology as an aid to understanding God's word and work and also as an aid to self-understanding. In its restricted place, it has a salutary function. But if it is allowed unlimited entry into spheres where it does not belong, it destroys

both knowledge and faith, though it may seem to offer dazzling rewards. Relativism is not to be absolutized; it is itself to be relativized by the absolute.[770]

8

RATZINGER'S PROPOSALS TO OVERCOME RELATIVISM

1. To Relativize Relativizers

In today's world, the imperative questions of human existence cannot be answered by just Christianity or Western rationality; they also require an intercultural dimension. The global community questions anyone who claims to possess any universal knowledge, be it through reason or revelation. Cardinal Ratzinger acknowledges that in the present relativistic climate of the world there seems to be no formula that would embrace the whole world and unite all persons. This is why the "so-called *world ethos* remains an abstraction."[771] If this is the case, what does he propose?

In terms of practical consequences, Ratzinger accepts Habermas' proposals whereby different communities are willing to learn from each other, while keeping in mind their self-limitations. At the same time, he presents two theses of his own. The first one states that because of existing pathologies in religion and reason, both must *continually allow themselves to be purified and structured by each other*; because, as Ratzinger pointed out, "reason will not be saved without the faith, but faith without reason will not be human."[772] Ratzinger's second thesis states that although the Christian faith and Western secular rationality "determine the situation of the world to an extent not matched by another cultural force," nevertheless it is important that they both "learn to *listen* and to accept a genuine relatedness to... other cultures, too."[773] Ultimately, if one were to accept these proposals universally or cross-culturally, then those essential values and norms that are ingrained in men would take on a new vitality and would unite the world together once again.

Reason can be understood as the facility of the human mind to come to know the truth as practiced first in Catholic theology by the early Church Fathers and later by the Scholastics and Neo-Scholastics. However, relativism adopts Kant's sense of reason which does not accept any metaphysical knowledge. Ratzinger believes that if metaphysical knowledge is not accepted, and man is forced to remain within the limits of human perception set by Kant, then faith will atrophy. He compares this use of autonomous reason that refuses to know about faith to Baron Münchhausen's attempt to pull himself up by his own hair. For if man cannot use his reason to ask about existential questions, and instead leaves such matters to the realm of feeling, reason loses its magnitude. Ratzinger states:

> All errors contain truths. It is true that religion summons to peace; it is true that feelings, too, belong to religion and that reforms that remove the humus of feelings will not succeed. But these truths retain their power only when they do not lose their own inherent interconnection. This interconnection consists in the fact that faith takes up feeling and redeems it from its indeterminacy by giving it its true ground: the feeling for the infinite is based on the truth that there exists an infinite God and that he addresses us, the finite ones. One will not restore power to faith today by reducing it as much as possible to the indeterminate but only by seeing it in its entire magnitude. Reduction does not save faith; it cheapens it. It becomes meaningful only

when one leaves it its entire power. Then it is no longer
we who save faith but faith that saves us.[774]

Restoring the power to faith is how Cardinal Ratzinger
proposes to overcome relativism. In order to *relativize the relativizers*, scholars must look critically at the philosophy of their own
methods. A curious consequence of post-modernist relativism is
that "skepticism pursued consistently and honestly must end up
by denying itself."[775] In *Theaetetus* (350 BC), Plato's argument
against Protagoras, known as '*perotropē*' (*turning about* or the *reversal argument*), was the first of many attempts throughout the
history of philosophy to show that relativism is self-refuting.[776]
Baghramian remarked that both Plato and Aristotle critiqued
Protagoras' doctrine of relativism in different ways. For Plato, it
implied self-refutation, and for Aristotle it was an unintelligible
doctrine contradicting the law of non-contradiction presupposed
by all.

Richard Bernstein and Thomas B. Ommen propose a notion
of rationality that moves beyond relativism. Their conception is
centered on hermeneutics and "the related themes of dialogue,
conversation and undistorted communication."[777] In terms of
employing hermeneutics to overcome fundamentalism, Ommen
says, "the elimination of foundations means the loss of universally valid criteria which can mediate differences of opinion."[778]
Pluralism, or the belief that more than one religion can teach
truths, cannot be thus resolved by an appeal to a single standard
of rationality and truth, but on the contrary, truth emerges
through conversation. From a hermeneutical perspective, the
conversation "presupposes no disciplinary matrix which unites the
speakers, but where the hope of agreement is never lost so long
as the conversation lasts."[779] In other words, truth is dependent
on an agreement reached during communication and, "given the
absence of foundations, such a conversation has an open-ended,
infinite quality."[780]

Ommen is offering a never-ending conversation, where
there is no acceptable conclusion or truth discerned. Ratzinger

would agree that communication is needed, but at the same time, what principles and goals are achieved through such communication? If one were to converse only for the sake of conversing, what conclusions would be reached? One can only imagine what the implications would be if one applied these hermeneutics to theology! Ommen himself suggests a few, not realizing that he is cutting the branch on which he himself is seated:

> Non-foundational theology involves, above all, a renunciation of a quest for objective and immutable foundations. Historical events, unchanging textual essences and universal anthropological schemes do not ground knowledge and belief. Immutable foundations stand in the way of openness to conversation and a transcendence of fixed positions.[781]

According to both Bernstein and Ommen, hermeneutics is an alternative to relativism, especially the historical form of relativism which "stresses the discontinuity between different moments within a tradition."[782] However, it would be hard to deny that historical events are not merely something of the past. Instead, they form an ongoing living tradition which has an impact on the present. In this regard, hermeneutics effectively undermines the presuppositions of historical relativism: "the meaning of historical sources is not confined to the past and recovered by a leap from present into past. A meaning emerges or comes to expression in historical understanding which reflects both the meaning of the text in its original situation and the present day with its particular needs and concerns."[783]

Nevertheless, Ommen also notes that hermeneutics is less effective in overcoming intercultural or interreligious relativism. The lack of a common factor or incommensurability between different cultures or traditions often results in pluralism and relativism. Ommen, together with Hans-Georg Gadamer,[784] believes that "behind differences of traditions and cultures is the continuing possibility of translation, conversation, communication."[785]

Bernstein is much more realistic with his observation that "the determination of truth, especially in a pluralistic setting, requires more than conversation and understanding."[786] To paraphrase David Tracy from his book *The Analogical Imagination*, the appropriation of tradition is not merely a product of understanding or conversation, but a dialect of understanding, explanation and new understanding.[787]

All this suggests that in place of stable foundations, theology should depend on a "diversity of judgments, principles and theories, each entailing different kinds of justification that come together to support or criticize, to reinforce or to revise."[788] Ommen concludes, "Conversational theology offers an alternative to the abstractness and monism of universal anthropology and the pluralism of unrelated religious traditions."[789] It requires recognition that the formulations of theology are hypotheses being tested in the forum of open and unrestricted discourse. However, this way of understanding dialogue would not lead one closer to the truth, in spite of what Ommen says:

> Theology's central concerns include not only the critical appropriation of tradition, but the transcendence of the insularity that tradition represents. Truth is not only that in which we participate in our various strands of community and history, but that which we anticipate as the goal of expanded human conversation. Such conversation is finally beyond objectivism and relativism.[790]

For Ratzinger, the main argument is found elsewhere. For him, man cannot be restricted in the way various post-Kantian philosophies see him. Man longs for the infinite, and it is only through God, who himself became finite, that the question of being can be addressed. Thus, one can see that the response to relativism is directly related to the question of anthropology. If one denies reason or faith, one denies an important part of a person, specifically, the person's humanness. That is why Ratzinger states, "Reason and religion will have to come together again, without merging into each other. It is not a matter of preserving the interests of all religious bodies. It is for the sake of man and the world. Neither of them, it is clear, can be saved unless God reappears in a convincing fashion."[791]

Ratzinger proposes that faith and reason confront relativism in the following way: faith would allow God's initiative as revealed in the figure of Jesus Christ to invite man into friendship with him, and reason would acknowledge man's ability to respond to the invitation in his longing for truth and the infinite. In this effort to confront and overcome relativism, both faith and reason have to come together, otherwise "faith without reason ends in fideism, but reason without faith ends in nihilism."[792] Will such an effort be successful? It might, since in the middle of growing pluralism and nihilism it adopts an attitude which one could call "the gentle presence of truth," so well reflected in the person of Ratzinger himself. No doubt it will take time, but if the truth is one and wants to be known, it will manifest itself despite the changing fashions of modern times or the shifting of philosophies in human minds.

2. Blaise Pascal and his Wager *Veluti si Deus Daretur*

The friendship between Cardinal Ratzinger and Marcello Pera continued after the publication of *Without Roots*. A few years later they jointly penned a book called *Christianity and the Crisis of Cultures*, and even though the themes were the same, Ratzinger was the major author. Pera, in his introduction, names it as Ratzinger's "proposal to those outside the Church."[793] The proposal *Veluti si Deus daretur* (as if God existed) is to be accepted for one basic reason, "because the one outside the Church who acts *veluti si Deus daretur* becomes *more responsible in moral terms.*"[794]

Ratzinger begins his book with an important observation, which might explain the inexplicable militancy of relativism:

The political moralism of the 1970s, the roots of which
are far from dead, was a moralism that succeeded in
fascinating even young people who were full of ideals.
But it was a moralism that took the wrong direction,
since it lacked the serenity born of rationality. In the
last analysis, it attached a higher value to the political utopia than to the dignity of the individual and it
showed itself capable of despising man in the name of
great objectives.[795]

Consequently, the message of Jesus, and his proclamation of the
Kingdom of God, was reduced to the values of the Kingdom,
which identified itself with "the great slogans of political moralism while at the same time proclaiming that these slogans are the
synthesis of the religions."[796]

How does political moralism, or the synthesis of the religions,
relate to the rise and reinforcement of relativism? It seems there is
a direct correlation, because in both politics and in Christianity,
the true value of ideals becomes jeopardized by unrealistic utopias
and politicized faith.[797] Eventually the "young people who were
full of ideals" came to realize that the authorities who presented
those ideals were not themselves faithful to those ideals and they
insisted on changing them according to their own judgments. In
a world based on calculations, the calculation of consequences
becomes the determinant factor of what is moral and immoral.
For that reason, "the category of the good vanishes... nothing is
good or evil in itself; everything depends on the consequences
that may be thought to ensue upon an action."[798]

Within the framework of philosophy, Ratzinger notes that
modern philosophies, which were inspired by the Enlightenment, are "characterized by their positivist – and therefore anti-
metaphysical – character, so that ultimately there is no place for
God in them."[799] This approach leads to man no longer accepting any moral authority that does not agree with his own use
of reason. The danger which arises from such an approach, if it
is generalized, "entails a mutilation of man."[800] As was already

stated, Ratzinger does not deny the value of reason or the benefit of technological progress brought about by the Enlightenment, but he wants to point out that positive reason, although adequate in the technological sphere, is self-limited in determining the cultural situation of the modern West and the true situation of a man living in it.

If God is the solution to many of the issues one encounters in today's modern world, what happens, then, to those who do not believe or doubt his existence and therefore are not able to accept this kind of a solution? It is precisely to these people outside of the Church and her faith that Ratzinger addresses his proposal. Ratzinger begins in the spirit of *Gaudium et Spes*, the Vatican II Pastoral Constitution on the Church in the Modern World, acknowledging that philosophy, and its investigation of the rational element had always been a positive element in Christianity. However, the voice of reason has been quieted by New Age anti-rationalism and the modern tendency to have less space and time to reason. Reason, however, cannot be silenced because it is part of the rational element of faith which cannot be overlooked or ignored. By being the religion of the *Logos*, and thus of creative reason, Christianity needs philosophy to explain

> ...whether the world comes from an irrational source, so that the reason would be nothing but a "by-product" (perhaps even a harmful by-product) of the development of the world, or whether the world comes from reason, so that its criterion and its goal is reason. The Christian faith opts for this second thesis and has good arguments to back it up, even from a purely philosophical point of view, despite the fact that so many people today consider the first thesis the only "rational" and modern view. A reason that has its origin in the irrational and is itself ultimately irrational does not offer a solution to our problems.[801]

Making philosophy a common ground for a possible conversation between a believer and a nonbeliever involves the ancient practice of explaining and defending the Christian faith, which goes back to St. Paul and the early Church Fathers. This is why reason, according to Ratzinger, should not be excluded from its service to the understanding and deepening of the faith. Therefore, Ratzinger presents the following proposal to those of modern times who see themselves as being outside of the Church and her faith:

> In the age of the Enlightenment, the attempt was made to understand and define the essential norms of morality by saying that these would be valid *etsi Deus non daretur*, even if God did not exist.... We must, therefore, reverse the axiom of the Enlightenment and say: Even the one who does not succeed in finding the path to accepting the existence of God ought nevertheless to try to live and to direct his life *veluti si Deus daretur*, as if God did indeed exist.[802]

Ratzinger acknowledges its origins. It is indeed a proposal Blaise Pascal (1623-1662) presented to his non-believing friends. Pascal's influence on Ratzinger is very evident in this book, and also can be observed when treating the issue of relativism.

Blaise Pascal was a French mathematician, physicist and religious thinker. At one point in his life, he aspired to write a book on apologetics and his remarkable attempts to do so were recorded in what now has come to be known as *Pensées*. Since the time it was first published in 1670, this book seemed to speak to all generations – until now. Some even argue that Pascal is a *modern Christian*, or even the first modern Christian.[803] When Pascal was writing his apologetics in the 17th century, he "aimed to effect the conversion not only of *libertines* and atheists – few in number in his experience – but also and more importantly, the conversion of upright individuals for whom religion was a respectable appendage to their existence rather than its warp and woof."[804] Therefore, Pascal's motive for his apologetics was not to defend Christianity as a system of beliefs, but rather to evangelize especially those who were "to be insensitive to the point of looking down on things which concern us and to become insensitive to the matter which concerns us most."[805]

What is "the matter which concerns us most," and who are those *insensitive ones* he talks about? The matter is religion and the insensitive ones are those who greet us with a maxim of relativism – "It is all the same God anyway." Hence, how does one confront such a relativistic attitude, or in this case, how does Pascal confront it? If the insensitive ones care to listen, Pascal's starting point and the point of contact for apologetics becomes the understanding of the human condition as both exalted and fallen. In the very beginning of his *Pensées* he states, "We want truth and find only uncertainty in ourselves. One searches for happiness and finds only wretchedness and death. One is unable not to want truth and happiness and is incapable of either certainty or happiness. This desire has been left in us as much to punish us as to make us realize where we have fallen from."[806]

That being the case, how many would accept such a description of the human condition? There are those who claim they are certain of their truth, no matter how narrowly it might be applied – Fundamentalism. There are those who say they know what and where true happiness is, but at least for the present moment they are still just a bit short of money to finally possess it – Materialism. People share that same desire or restlessness, which according to Pascal helps them to realize their inability to be self-sufficient and self-reliant – Secularism. Pascal also tried to explain the phenomenon of resistance where "Man finds nothing so intolerable as to be in a state of complete rest, without passions, without occupations, without diversion, without effort. Then he faces nullity, loneliness, inadequacy, dependence, helplessness, emptiness. And at once there wells up from the depths of his soul boredom, gloom, depression, chagrin, resentment, despair."[807]

If this is the true condition of man, then it should come as no surprise that one would want to escape from it. As Pascal points out, the usual means to achieve that are through diversion and indifference. Pascal describes these attitudes in the following way:

> As I do not know where I came from, so I do not know where I am going. All I know is that when I leave this world I shall fall forever into oblivion, or into the hands of an angry God, without knowing which of the two will be my lot or eternity. Such is my state of mind, full of weakness and uncertainty. The only conclusion I can draw from all this is that I must pass my days without a thought of trying to find out what is going to happen to me.[808]

Pascal did not choose to unveil the human condition just to make people nervous and upset. His intention is to awaken people from their slumber and make them think about eternity. However, in order to do so, they must also be ready to embrace the true religion, which would teach the cure for man's helplessness, and is also the means for obtaining this cure. Thus, even though Pascal speaks about human lowliness, he also speaks about human greatness, which arises from the idea, "we know that we are wretched. Therefore, we are wretched, because we are. But we are indeed great because we know it."[809] This idea becomes even clearer when he compares a human being to a *thinking reed*:

> A human being is only a reed, the weakest in nature, but he is a thinking reed. To crush him, the whole universe does not have to arm itself. A mist, a drop of water, is enough to kill him. But if the universe were to crush the reed, the man would be nobler than his killer, since he knows that he is dying and knows that the universe has the advantage over him. The universe knows nothing about this.[810]

Pascal's apologetics deals with the human ability to reason. He lived in the time of the rise of rationalism where man's reason became the final source of truth. That being the case, which reflects current times as well, many people in the realm of religion exalted reason and consequently adopted a deistic (Clockmaker) view of God, whereas some others became skeptics – or using contemporary terms, relativists – who doubted the competence of both revelation and reason. Pascal does not side with either of these groups. Moreover, instead of arguing that revelation was a better source of truth than reason, he focuses on the limitations of reason itself.[811] In this respect, Ratzinger concurs.

Being a mathematician and scientist himself, Pascal acknowledges some legitimacy and grandeur to reason and, as Frederick Copleston notes, "reason has its own sphere, mathematics and the natural sciences or natural philosophy; but the truths which it is really important for man to know, his nature and his supernatural destiny, these cannot be discovered by the philosopher or the scientist."[812] Therefore, in Pascal's own words, "Reason's last step is to recognize that there are an infinite number of things which surpass it. It is simply feeble if it does not go as far as realizing that. If natural things surpass it, what will we say about supernatural things?"[813] However, if for Pascal reason is limited in its understanding of natural things, what then helps us to overcome those limits of reason and enables us to know where to find the remedy for human wretchedness?

Pascal answers, "We know the truth not only by means of reason but also by means of the heart."[814] He believed that people really do know some things to be true even if they cannot comprehend them rationally, because "the heart has its reasons which reason itself does not know."[815] For it is in the heart where one discovers a mysterious presence, which is "an experiential faculty competent to furnish those first principles from which all reasoning necessarily derives."[816] This knowledge of the heart and the knowledge of reason do not offer any remedy for man's fallen condition, unless one knows the source from which it flows into one's heart and mind. Ratzinger speaks of God as this source, because only those who have been enlightened by God are capable of speaking intelligently of others. It is only those whose hearts have been opened by God, who are able to touch the hearts of others.

So how does one who is finite, sinful, and wretched come to know the true God and his intentions? Pascal points out that God chooses to be both hidden and revealed because "if there were no obscurity, man would not feel his corruption; if there were no light, man could not hope for cure."[817] Therefore, God presents "enough light to enlighten the elect and enough darkness to humble them. There is enough darkness to blind the damned and enough light to condemn them and leave them without excuses."[818]

Eventually Pascal wants it understood that "since nature was corrupted, [God] has left men to their blindness from which they can escape only through Jesus Christ, without whom all communication with God is broken off."[819] It is clear that Pascal's apologetic is intentionally Christocentric. True knowledge of God is not just an intellectual assent toward the reality of a divine being; at some point it must include knowledge of Christ in whom God chose to reveal himself:

> All who have claimed to know God and to prove his existence without Jesus Christ have done so ineffectively.... Apart from him and without Scripture, without original sin, without the necessary Mediator who was promised and who came, it is impossible to prove absolutely that God exists, or to teach sound doctrine and sound morality. But through Jesus Christ we can prove God's existence and teach both doctrine and morality.[820]

For Pascal, as for Ratzinger, knowledge of God without Christ is incomplete, for it is through Jesus Christ alone that one knows God, and it is only through Jesus Christ that one knows about oneself. However, what Pascal is trying to avoid is "proclaiming a deistic God who stands remote and expects from us only that we live good, moral lives."[821] Belief in a distant and indifferent God does not provide humankind with a redeemer. Even in Christ, God remains somewhat hidden in order not to overwhelm people and make them believe, thus infringing on their freedom.

However, knowledge of God as revealed in Jesus Christ also requires faith. As Jim Corkery, SJ, puts it, "Pascal saw that we have no rational criterion to determine what is just or unjust. Our reason is not the gateway for morality; faith is. Faith as gift – preached, proposed, listened to – is that gateway. We can know the truly good only by means of revelation."[822] For Pascal, faith is the knowledge of the heart that only God gives, while at the same time using proof as the instrument. Though ultimately faith is the gift of God freely given, one should not stop verifying this gift through the ability to reason. Ratzinger in *Truth and Tolerance* speaks of that very same idea – "without faith, philosophy cannot be whole, but faith without reason cannot be human."[823] More than in people's efforts to overcome relativism, "the act of faith opens out onto the distant horizon, breaking down the barriers of my subjectivity."[824]

This remarkable example of ambiguous use of faith and reason is known as *Pascal's Wager*. Here he tells us that reason's inadequacy to find God still requires us to make a choice, even though some data is lacking. Living in a society which is soaked in relativism, does one need to choose anything? In other words, does it matter what one chooses after all? Pascal responds that people do, because a middle ground does not exist between believing in God and not believing. However, if one chooses Christianity, one is better off in the end, even if it turns out not to be true, because "I should be more frightened of being wrong and finding out that the Christian religion was true than of not being wrong in believing it to be true."[825] Additionally, if people choose to believe in God, eventually he will bestow faith upon them.

This still leaves people with a very important question: If one must choose a religion, why Christianity? In other words, if God is the same anyway, why is not one person's choice of religion equally good as another's? Many scholars have disputed over the validity of Pascal's Wager, but arguably this is precisely its strength, because it challenges one to choose and at the same time to choose the right course. Pascal's apologetics do give people legitimate reasons to evaluate the plurality of the world's religions and the truths they claim to possess. If, after all, truth is one, it cannot be equally divided among all religions, nor can the ways in which those religions lead to the truth be equally direct and unequivocal. Therefore, in the search for truth, only Christianity is able to satisfy with answers.[826]

Finally, what if even after following Pascal's apologetics some will not come to the same conclusions about their religion as he did? Pascal does not worry much about that, because he "can only approve those who search in anguish."[827] For if one truly searches, "all these contradictions which used most to keep me away from the knowledge of any religion are what have led me soonest to the true religion."[828] Thomas V. Morris puts it another way: "Marks of the truth are all around us, sufficient to support the life of faith from a rational perspective but insufficient to arrest those who do not seek to know."[829] Even St. Paul in his Letter to the Romans stated that the truth is accessible to the Romans, but they do not want to accept it because of the demands that truth would make on them (Rm 1:18-20).

That is why both Pascal and Ratzinger object to there being a loss of truth, which is so readily accepted by those who share in contemporary relativism. Why? Because for both Pascal and Ratzinger, the danger is, "true nature having been lost, everything becomes natural. In the same way, the true good having been lost, everything becomes their true good."[830] Following this axiom, one can even go further by saying if the truth is lost, everything becomes true and if the true God is lost, everything becomes god. In Ratzinger's words, "Where nothing can be taken for granted, everything becomes possible and nothing is impossible any longer."[831] Thus, in one's "quest for the true nature of man, his true good, true virtue and true religion – cannot be known separately."[832] Knowing one requires knowing the others as well. In the end of *Christianity and the Crisis of Cultures*, Ratzinger gives an apposite summary of Pascal and the method of his apologetics, which Ratzinger himself employs:

> As in the questions of everyday, so too in our relationship with God, we can find a path forward only by sharing in the knowledge of others. In our relationship with God, those who see and those who experience are present and we can rely on them in our own faith. In some way, they bestow their own certainty on us. We make up the multitude, but we are not simply blind vis-à-vis God. Relying on those who see, we advance gradually toward him and the buried memory of God, which is written on the heart of every man, awakens more and more to life in the depths of our own being. When we live close to God, our sight is restored: when we use our eyes, they bear witness to his truth. Pascal's advice to his friends may seem skeptical, but it is correct: begin with the folly of faith and you will attain knowledge. This folly is wisdom; this folly is the path of truth.[833]

3. The Response: Through Prayer and Worship

Early on in his life, the young Ratzinger became enchanted with liturgy. As he recalls, "It was becoming clearer and clearer to me that here I was encountering a reality that no one had simply thought up, a reality that no official authority or great individual had created."[834] It was the discovery of this other mysterious reality that sustained Ratzinger through his entire life. Faith was not just a cluster of intellectual truths or concepts, but primarily an encounter with the Other. The truth and commitment to it were present in that transcendence. That is why reason alone as it is expressed in the sciences cannot offer complete answers. Ratzinger believes that art and science are the highest gifts God has given man.[835] For Ratzinger:

...the liturgy must be seen as the most concrete and definitive form of God's breaking-through to man, drawing man into Himself and closer to others at the deepest level of human existence. The medium used by God is the only medium suitable to man: his total humanity – that is, his material, intellectual and spiritual nature. Symbol, word, song, action, even the material world, all combine to draw man into the eternal cosmic liturgy in which alone man can experience his true dignity and calling.[836]

That is why Ratzinger suggests liturgy as one of the ways to overcome this type of relativism. As an example he cites the Decalogue, where "the work of the Law shows clearly enough that the worship of God is completely inseparable from morals, cult and ethos."[837] It is also through faith and prayer that the Church will once more "recognize its true centre and experience the sacraments again as the worship of God and not as a subject for liturgical scholarship."[838] Geoffrey Wainwright, in his article on Ratzinger, pointed out that there is a relativism found even in the arts, which "runs counter to the Christian faith, for which truth, goodness and beauty are permanently and universally grounded in the triune God who is the maker of all things and who has a final purpose for his human creatures."[839] At the same time, Wainwright thinks, in Ratzinger's theological vision, where the cosmic, historical and eschatological dimensions of Christian worship are present, there is also a remedy to such relativism.

Wainwright analyzes Ratzinger's treatment of the crisis in contemporary culture by presenting the views of Orthodox thinker Paul Evdokimov. Evdokimov suggests that there was an important turn in the history of Christian art which took place during the 13th century and was directly correlated to the turn in philosophy from Platonism to Aristotelianism. Recalling the Gothic period, Ratzinger was very impressed with the magnificent art of stained glass in which "the walls of the church, in interplay with the sun, become an image in their own right, the iconostasis of the West, lending the place a sense of the sacred that can touch the hearts even of agnostics."[840]

However, the Renaissance brought with itself a new tendency, that of the emancipation of man. It is also brought about in the development of the 'aesthetic' in the modern sense where beauty no longer points beyond itself, but is content in the end with itself; and "man experiences himself in his autonomy, in all his grandeur."[841] This anthropocentric tendency in art intensified even further during the Enlightenment, pushing faith into "a kind of intellectual and even social ghetto," and leaving a crisis of art of *unprecedented proportions*, symptomatic of the crisis of man's very existence.[842] In Ratzinger's own words:

> The immense growth in man's mastery of the material world has left him blind to the questions of life's meaning that transcend the material world. We might almost call it a blindness of the spirit. The question of how we ought to live, how we can overcome death, whether existence has a purpose and what it is – to all these questions there is no longer a common answer. Positivism, formulated in the name of scientific seriousness, narrows the horizon to what is verifiable, to what can be proved by experiment; it renders the world opaque.... Art turns into experimenting with self-created worlds, empty "creativity," which no longer perceives the *Creator Spiritus*, the Creator Spirit. It attempts to take his place and yet, in doing so, it manages to produce only what is arbitrary and vacuous, bringing home to man the absurdity of his role as creator.[843]

What was said about art could also be said about liturgical music. Here too, the subjectivism and autonomy of human making can be observed. Ratzinger thought that with the change from solely vocal music in liturgy to the introduction of instruments, music moved from the direction of service to the Word, to self-praise, and to mere entertainment. That is why the Council of

Trent had to affirm the difference between secular and sacred music. Although the cosmic character of music was characterized as being grounded in the Pythagorean theory of numbers, "the subjective experience and passion are still held in check by the order of the musical universe, reflecting as it does the order of the divine creation itself."[844] This however, leads to a threat of the virtuoso mentality and its vanity of technique, whereby the composer considers himself no longer a servant to the whole, but instead wants to push the music itself to the front. The above-mentioned threat did not take much time to become a full-scale reality. Ratzinger even associated the 19th century music movement away from metaphysics to the similar move in the arising philosophies of the day:

> Hegel now tried to interpret music as just an expression of the subject and of subjectivity. But whereas Hegel still adhered to the fundamental idea of reason as the starting point and destination of the whole enterprise, a change of direction took place with Schopenhauer that was to have momentous consequences. For him, the world is no longer grounded in reason but in "*Wille und Vorstellung.*" The will precedes reason. And music is the primordial expression of being human as such, the pure expression of the will – anterior to reason – that creates the world.[845]

In more contemporary times, Ratzinger views rock music as an expression of the new form of worship, a cult in opposition to Christian worship. Such as anarchistic stance coincides with *decontructionism*, which in turn is related to the *dissolution of the subject* and an attempt to "overcome the unbounded inflation of subjectivity."[846] It is only through the principles of art as created for divine worship that one recognizes "a relationship with the Logos who was at the beginning, brings salvation to the subject, that is, to the person… and puts us into a true relationship of communion that is ultimately grounded in trinitarian love."[847]

The vision of man's life can be summed up in St. Irenaeus' famous dictum: "The glory of God is man alive and the life of man is the vision of God."[848] In Christian worship, the cosmic vision becomes revealed and realized in the course of human history by the triune God and the decisive event of the Incarnation, Life, Death and Resurrection of the Son, Jesus Christ. Although the Resurrection of Christ secures the eschatological dimension of the new world, nevertheless suffering, pain and sin speak of that world as being *already and not yet*.

Wainwright suggests that Ratzinger's fundamental understanding of worship, which is that of the *reasonable service* of God,[849] means to achieve two things. The first is to solve the tension between "animal sacrifices at the temple-altar and the spiritual sacrifice of heart and lips." The second he borrows from the Greek, "the idea of a mystical union with the Logos, the very meaning of all things," at the same time avoiding the Hellenistic tendencies that "allow the body to fall into insubstantiality."[850] Wainwright concludes, on those terms, that a Christologically grounded "worship in spirit and in truth" (Jn 4:23) becomes "the Christian response to the cultic crisis of the whole ancient world" and "continues to offer a means to contain and counter the disorder of relativism at all levels."[851]

In Ratzinger's view, relativism in post-Vatican II liturgy mainly appears under the old form of Gnosticism, which disconnects the body from the spirit. Because of this separation, the way man reacts to the Word of God takes on a particular perspective:

> We live in a very sensate and sensualist society. We are in some ways absorbed in our senses, a people defined by materialism and sexuality. Yet in other ways we are curiously detached from our bodies, as though we were not really affected by what happens to us in our bodies or what we do in them. The contradiction between indulging our senses and disowning our bodies is only an apparent one. If our bodies are not us, then we are

not responsible in and for them; and that irresponsibility may assume the character of license or, indeed, of withdrawal. The same phenomenon occurred in the Gnosticism of the 2nd century. St. Irenaeus countered its threat to Christianity by retelling the authentic biblical tale of the divine Word's history *ad extra* as the single sweep of universal creation, the making of humankind, the incarnation in Jesus the Christ, the constitution of the Church, the institution and practice of the sacraments and the awaited resurrection of the body.[852]

Both Ratzinger and Wainwright are saying that the proclamation of the Christian faith and its message, as well as reliving it in the liturgy, helps to overcome the dangerous tendencies of Gnosticism and relativism alike. Ratzinger argues that in liturgy, law and ethics are intertwined. Even at the covenant on Sinai, "people received not only instructions about worship, but also an all-embracing rule of law and life,"[853] and it was thus that they became a people. Without such interconnection between law and ethics, which takes place in true worship, man is being degraded:

> When morality and law do not originate in a God-ward perspective, they degrade man, because they rob him of his highest measure and his highest capacity, deprive him of any vision of the infinite and eternal. This seeming liberation subjects him to the dictatorship of the ruling majority, to shifting human standards, which inevitably end up doing him violence.[854]

In an article on Romano Guardini, Ratzinger speaks of the modern attempt to replace orthodoxy with orthopraxis:

> As we are taught by Guardini, the essence of Christianity is not an idea, not a system of thought, not a plan of action. The essence of Christianity is a person:

Jesus Christ himself. That which is essential is the one who is essential. To become truly real means to come to know Jesus Christ and to learn from him what it means to be human.… Our time is in many respects far different from that in which Romano Guardini lived and worked. But it is as true now as in his day that the peril of the Church, indeed of humanity, consists in bleaching out the image of Jesus Christ in an attempt to shape a Jesus according to our own standards, so that we do not follow him in obedient discipleship but rather recreate him in our own image! Yet still in our own day, salvation consists only in our becoming "truly real." And we can do that only when we discover anew the true reality of Jesus Christ and through him discover the way to an upright and just life.[855]

Wainwright raises another very pertinent question: How in the liturgy as Ratzinger speaks about it is one to distinguish between legitimate diversity, problematic pluralism, and the castigated relativism in matters of religion and culture? In an attempt to provide a response to this question, he recalls the text of the declaration *Dominus Iesus*, where the Church acknowledges that her "constant missionary proclamation is endangered today by relativistic theories which seek to justify religious pluralism, not only *de facto* but also *de iure*," thus trying to lose "the definitive and complete character of the revelation of Jesus Christ."[856] That being the case, Wainwright goes even further in asking: How is all that to be properly dealt with and countered in the realm of liturgy – and, through liturgy, in the realm of an entire culture? How, at this particular time and place, are the distinctions to be drawn between diversity-in-unity and an ideologically affirmed pluralism that amounts to relativism?

In his understanding, Ratzinger responds to these questions by detecting an early Christian realization that "the paths of religious history converged on Christ, philosophy and religion gave faith the images and concepts in which alone it could understand itself."[857] Ratzinger is trying to provide an alternative understanding to what some of the contemporary liturgists have in mind with *inculturation*:

> The first and most fundamental way in which inculturation takes place is the unfolding of a Christian culture and all its different dimensions: a culture of cooperation, of social concern, of respect for the poor, of the overcoming of class differences, of care for the suffering and dying; a culture of law; a culture of dialogue, of reverence for life and so on. This kind of authentic inculturation of Christianity then creates culture in the stricter sense of the word, that is, it leads to artistic work that interprets the world anew in the light of God.[858]

Once again, Ratzinger believes, even artistic expressions which find their way into liturgy, would it be in art, music or the different forms of religious piety, must have magisterial control over them as it was stated in Pope Pius XII's encyclical *Mediator Dei* (1947), with the principle, "*Lex credendi legem statuat supplicandi* – let the rule of belief determine the rule of prayer."[859] In terms of opening up Christian worship to the authentic cultural achievement of other non-Christian cultures, there remains the principle as it was expressed in Scripture, "whatever is true, honorable, just, pure, lovely, gracious" (Ph 4:8) – may find a proper place among "the glory and the honor of the nations" (cf. Rv 21:22-27) that will adorn the City of God.[860] To illustrate this point further, Wainwright himself adapts H. Richard Niebuhr's classic book *Christ and Culture*[861] suggesting:

> Whereas a particular cultural configuration may appear as predominately positive or negative in relation to the saving purposes of God, it is likely that most cultures will contain some elements to be affirmed; some to be negated, resisted and even fought; some to

be purified and elevated; some to be held provision-
ally in tension; and some susceptible to a radical and
profound transformation toward God's kingdom. The
liturgy can function not only to sift but also to inspire
a surrounding public culture.[862]

The last sentence from the above quote can be found in Ratzinger's argument and belief that the Church's liturgy, which is divinely instituted, if it is responsibly celebrated, "has the potential to operate in those ways toward a contemporary culture that is marked by a false and debilitating relativism at the intellectual, social, moral and religious levels."[863] This type of *remedy* as Wainwright calls it, is not meant to be a quick fix, but instead, if done in the proper sense of service and worship in the true liturgy, would bring about the needed redemption and transformation of humankind and the world as it liberates from relativism.

9

BENEDICT XVI AND RELATIVISM

It was George Weigel who observed that in Joseph Ratzinger's pre-conclave homily "he didn't use the phrase 'dictatorship of relativism' to be provocative; he used it because it seemed to him the truth of the matter.... Ratzinger let everyone with a vote know precisely where he stood, and what kind of analysis he would bring to the Church's task in the modern world."[864] Columnist E.J. Dionne, Jr. of the *Washington Post*, suggested that Ratzinger's focus on relativism primarily concerned those in Europe and North America, whereas the many cardinals from the Third World countries were more concerned with poverty and its effects.[865] However, the election of Pope Benedict XVI demonstrated that Dionne had misjudged. Weigel noted: "The African cardinals, some of them first-generation Christians, knew that the greatest poverty human beings can suffer is the lack of that hope and joy that come from conversion to Christ."[866] If there exists no common truth to serve as a guide as to what constitutes a public good, then

> what we call "society" becomes impossible. Life in the desert of radical relativism and skepticism is not a truly human life, for skepticism about the truth of anything, including the truths of how we ought to live together, can neither promote nor sustain genuine hu-

233

man communities. Neither, however, can a drastically diminished view of the human. If human beings come to think of themselves as mere accidents, chance by-products of cosmic chemistry, something is crushed in the human soul. And a soulless humanity will either turn on itself in the kinds of self-destructive behavior that had marred the 20th century, or it will attempt to reinvent itself, perhaps not through politics – that had been tried, and had failed – but now, in the 21st century, through science unfettered from any notion of the good.[867]

From my research on this subject it has become clear to me that Ratzinger's mention of relativism in this homily was not an accident. Ratzinger's own exposure to the terrors of the Second World War, the excitement of the Second Vatican Council, the rise of liberation theology and the constant threat of Marxist ideology were reasons enough to openly address the issue in front of the world. However, now that Cardinal Ratzinger has been elected Pope Benedict XVI, one may question whether he is still as concerned with the issue of relativism as before. The answer to that is in the affirmative. In fact, after reading a number of recent papal texts, one can see that in some cases, Pope Benedict even contributes further insights into his lifelong debate on the question of relativism.

Weigel makes another interesting observation regarding Ratzinger's choice of the papal name with the story and meaning of the life and works of St. Benedict of Nursia. He argues that both foresaw the possibility of a Dark Age on the horizon – St. Benedict with the collapse of the Roman Empire and Pope Benedict with the historically unprecedented rise of the "dictatorship of relativism."[868] What would the rise of relativism accomplish? Weigel, in summarizing Benedict XVI, names the following realities as imperiled: "The rule of law and equality before the law; tolerance and civility; religious freedom and the legitimate rights of conscience; the method of persuasion in politics and democratic self-governance."[869] If these things lose their grounding, and if the human being becomes the measure of his own self, then the horizon of human aspirations will be "drastically foreshortened and the spiritual boredom that comes from self-absorption and ultra mundane aspirations can be lethal to a culture – no matter how materially wealthy it is."[870] Pope Benedict himself argues that "the contemporary 'crisis of truth' is rooted in a 'crisis of faith.' Only through faith can we really give our assent to God's testimony and acknowledge him as the transcendent guarantor of the truth he reveals."[871] Such lack of faith brings about a new Dark Age not only to the Church and the society in the West, but in these times of globalization, to the entire world.

Alasdair MacIntyre, in his book *After Virtue*, a study of the moral confusion of the West, makes a comparison of the Dark Ages with "the barbarianism of a culture in which relativism had been married to willfulness, and emotion had replaced reason as the arbiter of judgment."[872] Even back in 1981, when the book was first published, MacIntyre expressed his concern and his hope: "This time, the barbarians are not waiting beyond the frontiers; they have already been governing us for quite some time. And it is our lack of consciousness of this that constitutes part of our predicament. We are waiting not for a Godot, but for another – doubtless very different – St. Benedict."[873] One might say that this prophecy has been fulfilled in the person of our present Pope Benedict, who acknowledges and is eager to confront the darkness being brought about by relativism and its adherers. Weigel has observed that this *new Benedict* is "a man thoroughly convinced that ideas have real-world consequences and that decent human societies cannot be built upon a foundation of falsehoods."[874]

During the first five years of his papacy, Pope Benedict XVI has mentioned relativism in no less than 60 papal texts. Such occasions and texts include: a papal encyclical, the Sunday Angelus, Wednesday Audiences, and various addresses to bishops, diplomats, ambassadors, members of the Roman Curia and the Rota.[875] Not all these records equally discuss relativism; however, the mere mention of the issue so frequently shows its importance to him, and the following examples will further illustrate this point.

Ratzinger was elected Pope Benedict XVI on April 19, 2005. In his address to the participants in the ecclesial Diocesan Convention of Rome on June 6, 2005 at the Basilica of St. John Lateran, the Pope acknowledged:

> Today, a *particularly insidious obstacle* to the task of educating is the massive presence in our society and culture of that relativism which, recognizing nothing as definitive, leaves as the ultimate criterion only the self with its desires. And under the semblance of freedom it becomes a prison for each one, for it separates people from one another, locking each person into his or her own "ego." With such a relativistic horizon, therefore, real education is not possible without the light of the truth; sooner or later, every person is in fact condemned to doubting in the goodness of his or her own life and the relationships of which it consists, the validity of his or her commitment to build with others something in common. Consequently, it is clear that not only must we seek to get the better of relativism in our work of forming people, but we are also called to counter its destructive predominance in society and culture.[876]

In the above mentioned text, one may recognize Ratzinger's basic definition of relativism found in the *Pro Eligendo Romano Pontifice* homily. Relativism is once again described as a contemporary attitude which does not recognize anything as definitive, leaving man to his own "ego" with its desires to be set as the ultimate criteria of what is true and good. This once again relates to the four major kinds of relativism, which predominantly concerned Joseph Ratzinger: moral/ethical, religious, cultural and epistemic or intellectual.

An even more revealing example of his concern regarding relativism was through the thoughts he shared with the people at St. Peter's Square during the *Angelus* on the Second Sunday of Advent (December 4, 2005). In the *Angelus,* the Holy Father reminded his audience of the role each one shares with the Blessed Mother during the Advent season when they listen to the Word of God and open themselves to receive it. In other words, all are called to be the believers who live searching for God; and in searching for that truth, one's freedom is exercised. Recalling the Second Vatican Council's Declaration on Religious Freedom *Dignitatis Humanae,* the Holy Father once again repeated its statement: "It is in accordance with their dignity that all men, because they are persons, that is beings endowed with reason and free will..., are both impelled by their nature and bound by a moral obligation to seek the truth, especially religious truth."[877] However, nowadays this natural right and obligation to seek the truth is not effectively guaranteed everywhere. As Benedict XVI points out: "In certain cases it is denied for religious or ideological reasons; at other times, although it may be recognizable on paper, it is hindered in effect by political power or, more cunningly, by the cultural predomination of agnosticism and relativism."[878] Although here he does not expand on relativism as such, the Holy Father clearly states that it is related and affects the natural rights of human freedom and moral obligations following that freedom.

Benedict XVI and Youth

In his Christmas Address to the members of the Roman Curia on December 22, 2005, Benedict XVI touched on the issue of relativism in a more detailed and extended manner. When summarizing the major points of the previous year, he mentioned World Youth Day celebrated in Cologne and the Synod of Bishops on the Eucharist. Both these events where initiated by the late Pope John Paul II, who chose the theme and set the agenda. Pope Benedict indicated in his address that a way to overcome the contemporary *tarnish of relativism*[879] is to remember the motto chosen by World Youth Day: "We have come to worship Him!"[880] In other words, the Holy Father proposed worship as a guide and the criteria for our action. To further stress worship as a way to overcome relativism, Pope Benedict XVI recalled Father Alfred Delp, SJ, whose tragic but heroic life under the Nazi regime influenced Ratzinger's earlier formation:

> We are often so oppressed, understandably oppressed, by the immense social needs of the world and by all the organizational and structural problems that exist that we set aside worship as something for later. Fr. Delp once said that nothing is more important than worship. He said so in the context of his time, when it was evident that to destroy worship, destroyed man. Nonetheless, in our new context in which worship, and thus also the face of human dignity, has been lost, it is once again up to us to understand the priority of worship. We must make youth, ourselves and our communities, aware of the fact that it is not a luxury of our confused epoch that we cannot permit ourselves but a priority. Wherever worship is no longer, wherever it is not a priority to pay honor to God, human realities can make no headway. We must therefore endeavor to make the face of Christ visible, the face of the living God, so that like the Magi we may spontaneously fall to our knees and adore him.[881]

Once again the Christocentric and Eucharist-centered vision of Pope Benedict's theology surfaces. However, it is important to note that Benedict recognizes faith as a continuous process in the human search for God, and everyone should respect each one's search because it is "not merely a dogmatism complete in itself that puts an end to seeking that extinguishes man's great thirst, but that it directs the great pilgrimage towards the infinite."[882] He presented a similar message to the youth during his 2008 apostolic journeys to the 23rd World Youth Day in Australia and to the United States. In his address during the welcoming celebration in Barangaroo, Sydney Harbor, on July 17, 2008, the Holy Father spoke of the beauty of God's creation and how all are called to approach that beauty with gratitude and awe. More so, *the apex of God's creation* is man with his achievements in medicine, technology and art.[883] At the same time, Pope Benedict noted that there are also *scars* that mark the surface of the earth, the life of man and his social environment. Among the most obvious ones are the insatiable consumption of natural resources, "alcohol and drug abuse, and the exaltation of violence and sexual degradation, often-presented through television and the internet as entertainment."[884] A less obvious *scar* and threat is the fact that:

> ...freedom and tolerance are so often separated from truth. This is fuelled by the notion, widely held today, that there are no absolute truths to guide our lives. Relativism, by indiscriminately giving value to practically everything, has made "experience" all-important. Yet, experiences, detached from any consideration of what is good or true, can lead, not to genuine freedom, but to moral or intellectual confusion, to a lowering of standards, to a loss of self-respect, and even to despair.[885]

The Pope anticipated this message by presenting a foretaste of things to come in his speech to Anne Maree Plunkett, new ambassador of Australia to the Holy See on May 18, 2006:

> Your Excellency, as I welcome you to the Vatican my thoughts turn with joy to the visit I shall make, God willing, to Sydney for World Youth Day 2008.... More than an event, World Youth Day is a time of deep ecclesial renewal, especially among the young, the fruits of which will benefit the whole of your society. In countries such as yours, where the disquieting process of secularization is much advanced, many young

people are themselves coming to realize that it is the transcendent order that steers all life along the path of authentic freedom and happiness. Against the tide of moral relativism which, by recognizing nothing as definitive, traps people within a futile and insatiable bid for novelty, the young generation is rediscovering the satisfying quest for goodness and truth. In so doing they look to both Church and civil leaders to dispel any eclipse of the sense of God and to allow the light of truth to shine forth, giving purpose to all life and making joy and contentment possible for everyone.[886]

In Australia, Pope Benedict XVI, also reminded the young people that life is not governed by chance, but by conscious choices which seek to find what is true, good and beautiful. In that sense, freedom is not something exercised randomly for one's own pleasure, but it is a responsible gift whose purpose is to lead towards the Giver. The Pope admonished the young people to not be fooled by those "who seek you as just another consumer in a market of undifferentiated possibilities, where choice itself becomes the good, novelty usurps beauty, and subjective experience displaces truth."[887] It is only in encountering Jesus Christ, where one finds the Truth and the Way leading to a meaningful, fulfilled and joyous life. In his own words: "It is necessary to enter into real friendship with Jesus in a personal relationship with him and not to know who Jesus is only from others or from books, but to live an ever deeper personal relationship with Jesus, where we can begin to understand what he is asking of us."[888]

This also requires humility and an honest look at the world and one's own true self. However, the challenges and difficulties awaiting a believer are not easy:

There are many today who claim that God should be left on the sidelines, and that religion and faith, while fine for individuals, should either be excluded from the public forum altogether or included only in the pursuit of limited pragmatic goals. This secularist vision seeks to explain human life and shape society with little or no reference to the Creator. It presents itself as neutral, impartial and inclusive of everyone. But in reality, like every ideology, secularism imposes a world-view. If God is irrelevant to public life, then society will be shaped in a godless image. When God is eclipsed, our ability to recognize the natural order, purpose, and the "good" begins to wane. What was ostensibly promoted as human ingenuity soon manifests itself as folly, greed and selfish exploitation.[889]

This challenge is no less difficult for those preparing for the priesthood. In an address at St. Joseph Seminary in New York on April 19, 2008, the Holy Father acknowledged the many positive achievements the American culture contributed to the growth and development of so many people, but there are also areas of darkness where danger lies waiting to devour man's dignity and take away his freedom. One such area is that of manipulation, where human beings are treated as mere objects for pleasure or financial gain. Another area, which often goes unnoticed, is through the subtle manipulation of truth. As Benedict XVI pointed out:

> Have you noticed how often the call for freedom is made without ever referring to the truth of the human person? Some today argue that respect for freedom of the individual makes it wrong to seek truth, including the truth about what is good. In some circles to speak of truth is seen as controversial or divisive, and consequently best kept in the private sphere. And in truth's place – or better said its absence – an idea has spread which, in giving value to everything indiscriminately, claims to assure freedom and to liberate conscience. This we call relativism. But what purpose has a "freedom" which, in disregarding truth, pursues what is false or wrong? How many young people have

been offered a hand which in the name of freedom or experience has led them to addiction, to moral or intellectual confusion, to hurt, to a loss of self-respect, even to despair and so tragically and sadly to the taking of their own life?[890]

Giving value to everything indiscriminately, claiming to assure freedom and to liberate conscience is the definition for moral relativism. It does not give freedom or liberate conscience; moreover, it "disregards the full horizon of truth... fails to see the whole picture."[891] Whereby truth is not an imposition or a set of rules, but instead a discovery of the divine Person who never fails us and leads us to authentic freedom and everlasting happiness. It is in Christ where the truth is found. That is the message Pope Benedict wishes the youth to follow.

Mutilation of Christology

During his pastoral visit to Poland in 2006, the Holy Father spoke about the present obstacles in living and preaching the Gospel of Jesus Christ. He noted:

> As in past centuries, so also today there are people or groups who obscure this centuries-old Tradition, seeking to falsify the Word of Christ and to remove from the Gospel those truths which in their view are too uncomfortable for modern man. They try to give the impression that everything is relative: even the truths of faith would depend on the historical situation and on human evaluation.[892]

But the actual source of truth for the Church is not the Church herself, but the Spirit of Truth dwelling in her, as it was promised by the Resurrected Jesus. The Church and her leaders along with all of her members share a responsibility to accept the truth of the Gospel and pass it on to other people and generations.

At times, as the Holy Father noted, the teachings of the Gospel and of the Church's Tradition might even be hard to comprehend, nevertheless we are called to remain faithful and not "yield to the temptation of relativism or of a subjectivist and selective interpretation of Sacred Scripture."[893] Benedict XVI reminded his audience that our faith and hope do not consist of accepting a certain number of abstract truths about God, man, life, death and what happens thereafter, but a love-relationship with a person, Jesus Christ and staying in that relationship.

Also on another occasion the Pope noted that even coming to that essential relationship with Christ might be problematic for those who understand Christ differently from what he truly is. Therefore, during his visit to Assisi, addressing the clergy and men and women religious, Benedict XVI lamented *a sort of mutilation* of both Christ and St. Francis even among Christian believers:

> Christians of our time are more and more confronted by the trend to accept a diminished Christ, whose extraordinary humanity is admired but whose divinity in its profound mystery is rejected. Francis himself suffers a sort of mutilation when he is cast as a witness of albeit important values appreciated by contemporary culture, which overlooks the fact that his profound decision, we might say the heart of his life, was his choice for Christ.[894]

In other words, relativism promotes so-called *low* Christology where the primary focus in understanding the person and the action of Jesus Christ is not his divinity, but merely his humanity. And once Jesus is separated from Christ, he cannot be any more a source of truth than, for example, Socrates, Buddha or some other great human figure. Recalling the commentaries Ratzinger wrote during the Second Vatican Council, St. Francis' true mission, as well as the mission of the Church, whom he was called to "rebuild" in Benedict's view, will not be truly understood and accepted, if the "horizontal" dimension is removed from the "vertical."

Benedict XVI on Vatican II

It is important to note that Pope Benedict is among the few people left alive who was an active participant in the Second Vatican Council. He has observed that, even 40 years after the Second Vatican Council, the two contrary hermeneutics which arose at the time of this Council are still in existence today.

One of them he calls a *hermeneutic of discontinuity and rupture*, which frequently availed itself to the sympathies of the mass media and also found a trend in modern theology. More, the adherents of this type of hermeneutics to this day would argue that "because the text would only imperfectly reflect the true spirit of the Council and its newness, it would be necessary to go courageously beyond the texts and make room for the newness in which the Council's deepest intention would be expressed, even if it were still vague."[895] In other words, one needs to follow the spirit of the Council and not the texts. Summarizing such a conciliar and post-conciliar attitude, Benedict XVI eventually concluded that in this way "a vast margin was left open for the question on how this spirit should subsequently be defined and room was consequently made for every whim."[896] The mention of *every whim* directly connects Benedict XVI to his concern as *peritus* of relativism being present in the Council.

Pope Benedict also mentions the *hermeneutic of reform* as being opposed to the hermeneutic of discontinuity. This type of hermeneutic was proposed and supported by both popes of the Council era: John XXIII and Paul VI. According to them, the reform comes not from a new interpretation or alteration of the authentic doctrine, but by the faithful preservation of it, and at the same time, finding the ways of presenting it to the contemporary world through the *methods and research and through the literary forms of modern thought.*[897] In other words, a synthesis of fidelity and dynamism is in demand. As Benedict XVI said:

> This commitment to expressing a specific truth in a
> new way demands new thinking on this truth and a

new and vital relationship with it; it is also clear that new words can only develop if they come from an informed understanding of the truth expressed, and on the other hand, that a reflection on faith also requires that this faith be lived.[898]

One should not misunderstand this to mean that Pope Benedict has any regrets about the Council as such and its value to the present Church. However, having lived through the turbulent years since 1968, he personally knew that the hermeneutics of discontinuity taken to the extremes might lead to some painful consequences, one example being the anthropological shift which occurred during the modern era. As a result of the many historical dynamics, especially the rise of the modern era, the Council was expected to address a number of issues. Some of the main ones revolved around the relationship between faith and the modern sciences, the relationship between the Church and the modern State, and ecumenical relationships. Benedict XVI agrees that when addressing these issues during the Second Vatican Council, the Church used a combination of the two kinds of hermeneutics – continuity and discontinuity – since both were elements by the very nature of true reform. The complete abolishment of relativism was never Pope Benedict's intention, since it possesses some very legitimate forms:

It is precisely in this combination of continuity and discontinuity at different levels that the very nature of true reform consists. In this process of innovation in continuity we must learn to understand more practically than before that the Church's decisions on contingent matters – for example, certain practical forms of liberalism or a free interpretation of the Bible – should necessarily be contingent themselves, precisely because they refer to a specific reality that is changeable in itself. It was necessary to learn to recognize that in these decisions it is only the principles that express the permanent aspect, since they remain as an undercurrent, motivating decisions from within. On the other hand, not so permanent are the practical forms that depend on the historical situation and are therefore subject to change.[899]

But there are also the destructive forms of relativism, such as can be found in religion:

> Thus, for example, if religious freedom were to be considered an expression of the human inability to discover the truth and thus become a canonization of relativism, then this social and historical necessity is raised inappropriately to the metaphysical level and thus stripped of its true meaning. Consequently, it cannot be accepted by those who believe that the human person is capable of knowing the truth about God and, on the basis of the inner dignity of the truth, is bound to this knowledge. It is quite different, on the other hand, to perceive religious freedom as a need that derives from human coexistence, or indeed, as an intrinsic consequence of the truth that cannot be externally imposed but that the person must adopt only through the process of conviction.[900]

The Holy Father noticed that what happened during the Council in terms of setting up a proper relationship between the Church and the modern world reflects a recurrent problem of the relationship between faith and reason. He used as an example what happened when Aristotelian thought came into contact with medieval Christianity. What might have led to irreconcilable contradiction, instead because of the mediating efforts by St. Thomas Aquinas, became a new and positive encounter between these two sources of knowledge. Similarly, the time was such that the Second Vatican Council was needed to develop dialogue between modern reason and the Christian faith.

Faith and Reason

One may argue that what St. Thomas Aquinas was for the medieval Church, Ratzinger-Benedict XVI is for the modern Church. Both felt that dialogue was necessary for negotiations, and in matters between faith and reason served as an important tool. For reason without faith lacks a space to breathe and faith without reason becomes superficial. It is by bringing the two together that the true potential of the human being as well as his openness to the Transcendent is appropriated and exercised. Ratzinger saw this dialogue as one way to overcome the dictatorship of relativism; and, as Pope Benedict XVI, he continues to propound this issue.

Another example of faith and reason was presented by the Holy Father when he spoke about St. Justin, philosopher and martyr (c. 100-165), the most important apologist of the 2nd century. He explained that the early apologists had a twofold concern – one of defending the new religion from both pagans and Jews, and secondly, a missionary concern, "to explain the content of the faith in a language and on a wavelength comprehensible to their contemporaries."[901] St. Justin was a seeker of truth, who was not satisfied until he arrived at the Christian faith. In his surviving texts (the two *Apologies* and the *Dialogue with the Hebrew, Tryphon*), Justin illustrated the divine plan of creation and salvation which is fulfilled in Jesus Christ, the *Logos*, the eternal Word, creative and eternal Reason. He also argued that because the divine *Logos* took on human flesh, we too, in our human rational nature, bear the "seeds of truth" which could also be found partially manifested in the Old Testament Law and Greek philosophy. However, the fullness of truth only resides in the person of Jesus Christ and can be reached through our faith in him. Benedict XVI himself concluded that, according to Justin "these two realities, the Old Testament and Greek philosophy, are like two paths that lead to Christ, to the *Logos*. This is why Greek philosophy cannot be opposed to Gospel truth and Christians can draw from it confidently as from a good of their own."[902]

However, the Holy Father also noted that what was true about Greek philosophy and the Old Testament was perceived and addressed quite differently by Justin and the other early Christians when it came to pagan religions and their myths. Justin *mercilessly criticized* the pagan religions; from both the perspective of Christian faith as well as the philosophy because pagan religions clung to their myths and therefore were "devoid of consistency with the truth."[903] The early Christians and the Greek philosophers saw in pagan religions an artificial collection of ceremonies, conventions and customs detached from the truth of being. What they had was "the choice of the *truth* being against the myth of *custom*" (emphasis in the original)[904] and, as Tertullian said: "*Dominus noster Christus veritatem se, non consuetudinem, cognominavit* – Christ has said that he is truth not fashion" (*De Virgin. Vel.* 1, 1). And "in a time like ours marked by relativism in the discussion on values and on religion – as well as in interreligious dialogue – this is a lesson that should not be forgotten."[905] Pope Benedict XVI does not forget that lesson himself. For example, during his journey to Brazil he defined how the phenomenon of the authentic cultures needs to be understood. He said:

> Authentic cultures are not closed in upon themselves, nor are they set in stone at a particular point in history, but they are open, or better still, they are seeking an encounter with other cultures, hoping to reach universality through encounter and dialogue with other ways of life and with elements that can lead to a new synthesis, in which the diversity of expressions is always respected as well as the diversity of their particular cultural embodiment.[906]

One such very important encounter for a culture is with the Christian faith and thus with the person of Jesus Christ. Such an encounter does not bring alienation, disruption or extinction to any particular culture or person but instead leads them to their true identity and genuine authentic progress. It is through the Incarnation of the divine Logos that human history and culture become incorporated into God's salvific act. Any call to return to the pre-Christian life of the indigenous cultures would be a human and cultural regress. However, bringing the Christian message to missionary lands must not be mistakenly perceived as a message of secularism and materialism coming from the Enlightenment of the West. On the contrary, as the Pope reminded the bishops of Malaysia, Brunei and Singapore:

> By "speaking the truth in love" (Eph 4:15) you can help your fellow citizens to distinguish the wheat of the Gospel from the chaff of materialism and relativism. You can help them to respond to the urgent challenges posed by the Enlightenment, familiar to Western Christianity for over two centuries, but only now beginning to have a significant impact upon other parts of the world.[907]

At the same time, they must resist the *dictatorship of positivist reason* which tries to exclude God from a public realm and, instead, focus on the positive accomplishments of the Enlightenment, such as the promotion of the universality of human rights, the freedom of religion and its practice.[908]

However, this universality does not depend only on the civil law which merely is there to safeguard it, but also draws its origin and essence from the dignity of the human person created in God's image and likeness. That is the core message of Christian foundation which must be present in any society or culture. Otherwise, "the task of preserving the transcendent dimension present in every culture and of strengthening the authentic exercise of individual freedom against relativism becomes increasingly difficult."[909]

On de-Hellenization in Regensburg

In his Regensburg Lecture, the Holy Father expanded on the issue of faith and reason. He observed that throughout Christian history there have been some attempts to separate faith and reason from each other. However, the major process of *de-Hellenization*, according to Benedict XVI, occurred at the beginning of the modern age and in three stages.

The first stage was during the Reformation, and its principle of *sola scriptura* which attempted to purify faith from overreaching scholasticism and its understanding of faith as a superior philosophical system. Eventually, the philosophers like Kant "stated that he needed to set thinking aside in order to make room for faith… thus [he] anchored faith exclusively in practical reason, denying it access to reality as a whole."[910]

Then the second stage came with the liberal theology of the 19th and 20th centuries. Pope Benedict uses as an example Adolf von Harnack whose central idea was "to return simply to the man Jesus and to his simple message, underneath the accretions of theology and indeed of Hellenization."[911] In other words, Jesus' divinity was sacrificed for his humanity as an example *par excellence* of what true humanity should be. In fact, as the Pope observed, Harnack's idea was seen as a way to bring theology back into the university through the introduction of historical-critical exegesis, seeing theology in solely historical and therefore strictly scientific terms. By that same token, he also noted that this modern approach not only stripped theology from faith but also placed limitations on reason as well. In other words, the Holy Father was saying that the modern concept of reason is based "on a synthesis between Platonism (Cartesianism) and empiricism, a synthesis confirmed by the success of technology."[912] Only practical reason counts or *praxis* over *doxa*. This type of reduction has far-reaching consequences:

> In the meantime, it must be observed that from this
> standpoint any attempt to maintain theology's claim

to be "scientific" would end up reducing Christianity to a mere fragment of its former self. But we must say more: if science as a whole is this and this alone, then it is man himself who ends up being reduced, for the specifically human questions about our origin and destiny, the questions raised by religion and ethics, then have no place within the purview of collective reason as defined by "science" so understood, and must thus be relegated to the realm of the subjective. The subject then decides, on the basis of his experiences, what he considers tenable in matters of religion, and the subjective "conscience" becomes the sole arbiter of what is ethical. In this way, though, ethics and religion lose their power to create a community and become a completely personal matter. This is a dangerous state of affairs for humanity, as we see from the disturbing pathologies of religion and reason which necessarily erupt when reason is so reduced that questions of religion and ethics no longer concern it. Attempts to construct an ethic from the rules of evolution or from psychology and sociology, end up being simply inadequate.[913]

The third stage of de-Hellenization is happening now. Here Pope Benedict mentions the contemporary attempts in the light of cultural pluralism to declare that the Christian faith in its fusion with the Greek culture went through the simple process of inculturation which, in order to get to the essence of the Christian message requires one to disregard this process. Benedict XVI strongly argues that this thesis is simply wrong. It is true that the New Testament was written in Greek and bears the imprint of the Greek spirit. However, "the fundamental decisions made about the relationship between faith and the use of human reason are part of the faith itself; they are developments consonant with the nature of faith itself."[914]

Pope Benedict's intent was not meant to play down the positive achievements of the Enlightenment or modernity. The reason for this lecture was "broadening our concept of reason and its application."[915] If faith and reason do not come together again in a mutual dialogue, then any evaluation of new advances in the modern sciences and technology will lack accuracy and the truth will not be able to correspond with reason. It is only when faith and reason open to one another that a genuine dialogue between cultures and religions is possible. Pope Benedict concluded:

> The West has long been endangered by this aversion to the questions which underlie its rationality, and can only suffer great harm thereby. The courage to engage the whole breadth of reason, and not the denial of its grandeur – this is the programme with which a theology grounded in Biblical faith enters into the debates of our time. "Not to act reasonably, not to act with *logos*, is contrary to the nature of God," said Manuel II, according to his Christian understanding of God, in response to his Persian interlocutor. It is to this great *logos*, to this breadth of reason, that we invite our partners in the dialogue of cultures. To rediscover it constantly is the great task of the university.[916]

There is also the growing concern of intellectual relativism in the sciences where "research is subject only to the laws that it chooses for itself and… is limited only by its own possibilities. This is the case, for example, in attempts to legitimize human cloning for supposedly therapeutic ends."[917] "In effect, the development of subjectivism, which makes each one tend to consider himself as the only point of reference and to hold that what he thinks has the character of truth, exhorts us to form conscience on fundamental values that cannot be mocked without putting man and society itself in danger, and upon the objective criteria of a decision that presupposes an act of reason."[918] In other words, the Pope is concerned with relativism not as an intellectual instrument being legitimately used in the search of truth, but an attempt by some people to make it be the *rule unto themselves*.[919]

As one of the means to overcome such subjectivist rule, especially among the young, Pope Benedict recalled the life of Andrei Sakharov, of whom he said: "This outstanding personality reminds us that it is necessary, in private and public life, to have the courage to say the truth and to follow it, to be free with respect to the surrounding world that often tends to impose its viewpoints and the behavior to adopt."[920] It is the development of a strong interior life which safeguards a person's inner integrity, convictions and freedom, in spite of *exterior chains such as relativism* and other maladies of the age.[921] It is the rediscovery of the inner dimension of every human being and coming to the realization that the Creator has gifted every man with the capacity to reason and exercise his freedom.

Media and Relativism

In his message for the 42nd World Communications Day, May 4, 2008, the Holy Father chose the theme· "The Media: At the Crossroads between Self-Promotion and Service. Searching for the Truth in Order to Share it with Others."[922] Acknowledging that there are many positive elements in the area of communications, Benedict XVI also expressed his concern over the media's increasing claims "not simply to represent reality, but to determine it, owing to the power and the force of suggestion that it possesses."[923] Since the mass media has such a profound effect on all areas of human life, the subjective misconstruction of facts and information might endanger the good of a person. Just because something is technically possible does not always make it ethically permissible. Therefore, the media, along with other fields of human endeavor such as medicine or scientific research, must realize that as an integral part of the *anthropological* question it must seek and preserve the truth about humanity, its true dignity and call. The media must avoid

> …becoming spokesmen for economic materialism and
> ethical relativism, true scourges of our time. Instead,

they can and must contribute to making known the truth about humanity, and defending it against those who tend to deny or destroy it. One might even say that seeking and presenting the truth about humanity constitutes the highest vocation of social communication. Utilizing for this purpose the many refined and engaging techniques that the media have at their disposal is an exciting task, entrusted in the first place to managers and operators in the sector. Yet it is a task which to some degree concerns us all, because we are all consumers and operators of social communications in this era of globalization.[924]

An example of the media's misconstruing of the truth and how the self-dynamics of the mass media play to relativism was very pronounced in reporting on the Pope's address at the University of Regensburg. It was there that the Holy Father used an unfavorable remark about Islam made in the 14th century by Byzantine emperor Manuel II Paleologus to an educated Persian.[925] Though the Holy Father did not refute the religion of Islam, this citation sparked an international controversy, even leading to violence in some Islamic countries. Cardinal Jean-Marie Lustiger summarized the incident in the French daily *Le Monde*: "We are faced with a media-driven phenomenon bordering on the absurd…. If the game consists in unleashing the crowd's vindictiveness on words that it has not understood, then the conditions for dialogue with Islam are no longer met."[926] Benedict XVI's intent was to present the fact that rationality is understood differently by Christianity and Islam. For Christians, the nature of God is revealed in the Incarnation of the divine *Logos*, whereas for Islam, God is so transcendent that no human category, including rationality, can be credibly attributed to God.

That the secular press would misinterpret the Pope's meaning might be understandable, so it becomes essential for the Catholic media to "increase its dialogue with the contemporary culture in order to open it to the perennial values of Transcendence."[927] It is in this dialogue that the Catholic media must spread the Christian faith, be in "fidelity to the Magisterium of the Church, and to defend without polemics the truth that is sometimes distorted by unfounded accusations directed at the Ecclesial Community."[928]

Relativism and Democracy

Another area of concern for the Holy Father is the fast-growing secularization of Europe and the Western world. In his own words: "It seems to me that the great challenge of our time… is secularization; that is, a way of living and presenting the world *'etsi Deus non daretur,'* in other words, as if God did not exist."[929] Since secularization is prevalent in many democratic countries, the Holy Father warned that "moral relativism undermines the workings of democracy, which by itself is not enough to guarantee tolerance and respect among peoples."[930] In fact, a democracy without values "turns into a tyranny of relativism with the loss of its own identity and, in the long run, can degenerate into open or insidious totalitarianism, as history has frequently shown."[931] Vincent Twomey, former doctoral student of Pope Benedict, said the following about him: "His theological concerns were often dictated by current developments in politics and society in general but in particular by the pervasive moral relativism that undermines human well-being and erodes human communities."[932] This degeneration is the result of the imperfections found within both individuals and society. It is the recognition of these limits of reason which calls for a relationship with faith; and it is the Church, with its truth, that

> serves all members of society by shedding light on the foundation of morality and ethics, and by purifying reason, ensuring that it remains open to the consideration of ultimate truths and draws upon wisdom. Far from threatening the tolerance of differences or cul-

tural plurality, or usurping the role of the State, such a contribution illuminates the very truth which makes consensus possible and keeps public debate rational, honest and accountable. When truth is disregarded, relativism takes its place: instead of being governed by principles, political choices are determined more and more by public opinion, values are overshadowed by procedures and targets, and indeed the very categories of good and evil, and right and wrong, give way to the pragmatic calculation of advantage and disadvantage.[933]

This pragmatic calculation of advantage and disadvantage has led to a Western society driven by consumerism, hedonism, secularism and relativism. Therefore, the Holy Father calls us back from the individualistic and cafeteria-style pick and choose mentality to a Catholic approach of *thinking with the Church*, and *living one's faith in the Church* as an integral part of interior conversion to the law of Christ.[934]

Natural Moral Law

During his meeting with the members of the International Theological Commission on October 5, 2007, Pope Benedict XVI addressed the theme of natural moral law. The aim of that commission is "above all to justify and describe the foundation of a universal ethics that is part of the great patrimony of human knowledge which in a certain way constitutes the rational creature's participation in the eternal law of God,"[935] and even though it is not exclusively a *denominational* issue, it finds its full developments and understanding in the light of Christian revelation. As the *Catechism of the Catholic Church* points out:

The natural law states the first and essential precepts which govern the moral life. It hinges upon the desire for God and submission to him, who is the source and judge of all that is good, as well as upon the sense that the other is one's equal. Its principal precepts are expressed in the Decalogue. This law is called "natural," not in reference to the nature of irrational beings, but because reason which decrees it properly belongs to human nature.[936]

There are two essential goals which are reached with the doctrine of natural law: First of all, that the ethical content of the Christian faith is not an imposition on human conscience from outside of human nature but inherent in it. Secondly, the basis of natural law in itself is accessible to any rational creature. Therefore, "with this doctrine the foundations are laid to enter into dialogue with all people of good will and more generally, with a civil and secular society."[937] George Weigel describes the malady which affects today's Western world as "a deliberate, willful forgetting of the truth that the human person 'does not himself *invent* morality on the basis of calculations of expediency but rather *finds* it already present in the essence of things.'"[938]

A problem in today's secularized Western society is that it subscribes to the dominance of a positivist conception of law where humanity, or the majority of the citizens, becomes the ultimate source of any law. Though often thought of as the principal condition for democracy, it does not always protect the common good but instead becomes a search for power. There must be a balance between the "intrinsic relationship between the Gospel and the natural law on the one hand, and, on the other, the pursuit of authentic human good, as embodied in civil law and in personal decisions";[939] otherwise, if true rationality is not based on a connection with creative reason as its source, majority decision can and often will err. As Benedict XVI stated, "If, by tragically blotting out the collective conscience, skepticism and ethical relativism were to succeed in deleting the fundamental principles of the natural moral law, the foundations of the democratic order itself would be radically damaged."[940] Consequently, if and when the inalienable value of the natural moral law is fully understood in culture and in civil and political society, then the advance of individuals and society towards authentic progress will be truly achievable.

The Historical Dimension

From his studies of St. Bonaventure early in his life, Joseph Ratzinger developed a high sensitivity towards the historical dimension of our faith. The contemporary idea of progress – which does not see any value in the past and only in the future – leaves many confused and unable to make the right choices. That is because, Pope Benedict states: "In spite of the necessary willingness to move forward and even leave behind other things that were dear to us, there is something that does not change because it is the human being himself, his being as a creature."[941] However, at the same time, one needs to remember that man is not completely historical either. This would lead to another dangerous extreme – the absolutizing of history – "historicism," meaning that man is only and always a creature and therefore the product of a certain period.[942] Man, Benedict XVI argues, is a creature of God, placed as such in time and space and thus in history, which also becomes the chosen place for God to reveal himself definitively and to offer an abiding relationship with man. This relationship is lived in the Church, which is the Church by celebrating daily in time and space the one presence of the God-man, Jesus Christ, in the same Eucharist – in 30 A.D. and 2010 A.D. Our faith, Benedict XVI confirms, is *historical* to the extent that it is *diachronic* as well as *eschatological* and therefore "combines the two things: respect for otherness and newness and the continuity of our being, communicability between people and between times."[943]

Caritas in Veritate

Of the three encyclicals which Benedict XVI has written, it is in *Caritas in Veritate* (2009) that he explicitly mentions relativism. Concerned with the true human development and well aware of the confusion present in today's anthropology, the Pope begins his encyclical by saying: "Charity in truth, to which Jesus Christ bore witness by his earthly life and especially by his death and resurrection, is the principal driving force behind the authentic development of every person and of all humanity."[944] It is in Jesus Christ that human beings are called to live in the truth and reflect the face of Christ in their own lives. This face of Christ must be found in charity, but "charity, in its turn, needs to be understood, confirmed and practiced in the light of truth."[945] Otherwise, without a practiced charity, the authentic Christian witness to the truth would lack credibility and would be easily dismissed by today's cultural and social standards which tend to relativize any truth.

Another risk found in modern times is what Pope Benedict termed *cultural eclecticism*, which uncritically places cultures alongside one another in such a way that they are considered substantially equivalent and interchangeable. The result of such action is "a relativism that does not serve true intercultural dialogue; on the social plane, cultural relativism has the effect that cultural groups coexist side by side, but remain separate, with no authentic dialogue and therefore with no true integration."[946]

According to the Pope, true dialogue requires not only the exchange of different positions but also involves true listening, leading to encounter, relationship and understanding. Therefore, Pope Benedict argues that dialogue does not "only concern the field of knowledge and what we are able to do,"[947] but more, it allows the truth, that is also a person, to speak in our midst. At the same time, he observed, "In a world marked by relativism and too often excluding the transcendence and universality of reason, we are in great need of an authentic dialogue between religions and cultures."[948] This does not advocate relativism let alone syncretism, but a missionary zeal which takes steps to ensure the inculturation of the Gospel message so that it is expressed and lived in the languages and practices of local cultures and traditions.[949] Relativism and syncretism appear where a compromise is sought, often at the expense of watering down the essential elements of Christian doctrine. Pope Benedict strongly believes that such erroneous practice among missionaries must cease and the faithfulness to proclaiming the whole truth of the Christian faith needs to increase, even if at first certain parts of our faith are better comprehended and accepted by and in another culture.[950]

There is also another danger in the now prevalent cultural relativism, which Benedict XVI calls *cultural leveling*: the indiscriminate acceptance of all types of conduct and life-styles. As a result of both *cultural eclecticism* and *cultural leveling*, a separation occurs between culture and human nature. Therefore, "cultures can no longer define themselves within a nature that transcends them, and man ends up being reduced to a mere cultural statistic,"[951] running new risks of enslavement and manipulation.

After this brief overview of the papal texts one may see that the prediction made by James Corkery about a consistency from Ratzinger to Benedict XVI is accurate: "Just as there is no striking discontinuity between the pre- and post- conciliar Ratzinger, neither will there be a striking discontinuity between Cardinal Ratzinger and Pope Benedict."[952] The present Pope has remained consistent in naming the dangers coming from relativism and proposing ways of overcoming it. Whether he will succeed depends in part on how the rest of the members of the Catholic Church will understand and respond to their Shepherd's concern. After all, the victory won would recover the truth concerning us all – the truth about man and the meaning and destiny of his life. By combating relativism, Ratzinger/Benedict XVI is defending the truth of every human being, namely, that true light and fulfillment come in the relationship God is offering through his Son Jesus Christ, who eternally is the Truth, the Way and the Life.

CONCLUSION

Relativism appears early in Western philosophy in Xenophanes and Protagoras and has been with us ever since, despite the efforts of Plato to refute the idea. Though a multifaceted and nuanced phenomenon, its essence lies in questioning the absolute and objective nature of truth and its existence. Many in the contemporary world have embraced this mindset in the name of tolerance and progress. Joseph Ratzinger has found this to be extremely disturbing – so much so, that it has preoccupied him for most of his adult life, as I have tried to demonstrate in this text.

Joseph Ratzinger does not question relativism in all of its forms, but focuses most of his attention on moral and religious relativism. Though he acknowledges relativism as a legitimate tool in questioning philosophical propositions that search for the truth, relativism has progressed beyond a mere tool to a position of authority. The limits of its application have been ignored, and what was once a simple tool has now become a weapon of manipulation behind the various forms of totalitarianism. Ratzinger himself experienced this early in his life, growing up in Nazi Germany where truth was determined by the party leaders. John Allen observed:

> Fundamentally, Ratzinger has long been concerned with the Christian message, that God entered history in the person of Jesus Christ in order to mark out a path to salvation, one that does not vary with time and

fashion, becomes jeopardized in a cultural environment that has largely abandoned the concept of objective truth. He witnessed that in Nazi Germany, when mistaken ideas about human nature led to the disasters of the Second World War, including the horrors of the Holocaust. His concern for maintaining the truths of the faith is therefore not simply an authoritarian desire to police the limits of acceptable thought; it has much deeper roots.[953]

An ancient dictum by Cicero says that *historia magistra vitae est* ["history is life's teacher"].[954] Ratzinger is one of those people who certainly agrees that this is true. His Bavarian background and the respected tradition of the Munich School of Theology have taught him to appreciate and understand history, not as a chain of accidental events, but as a process of human and divine exchange. Real truth is beyond the makings of history, but at the same time history becomes meaningful only if truth realizes itself in history.

During his academic studies, Ratzinger developed a profound appreciation for the sources of truth as found in Christian revelation and the traditions of the Church. The writings of St. Augustine raised within Ratzinger an awareness of the reality of the human condition and destiny; where every individual has the freedom to choose either the eternal city of God, or the one of this world. A hint of Augustine's pessimism also permeated Ratzinger's earlier theology, but this was later offset by Bonaventure's eschatological vision. Ratzinger always reminded others that the primordial damage brought about by sin has been transformed by redemption. However, although the process of healing the world already started with the Incarnation and Resurrection of our Lord Jesus Christ, it will not be fully realized until the end of time through the mission and ministry of the Church. That is why, in this life, one must follow the path to redemption as found in the person of Jesus Christ.

Contemporary relativism began to manifest itself strongly

during the Enlightenment, finding its way not only among the faculties of philosophy and world politics, but as Ratzinger observed, also in Catholic theology and the daily life of the Church. Under the name of pluralism, and so-called inculturation, it entered the realm of faith and relativized the truth about Jesus Christ and his uniqueness in providing the world with salvation. Ratzinger strongly believes that the Church is the means by which to guide humanity through the dangerous tendencies of this world. This is why the goals of the Second Vatican Council are so essential to achieve and to implement.

However, even during the Council, Ratzinger became acutely aware that under the pretext of ecumenism and inter-religious dialogue, certain fundamental tenets of Christology as well as Christian anthropology were being altered. With time, these important beliefs were further weakened. Ratzinger felt it was very important to once again restate the true meaning of Christian revelation as found in the role of Jesus Christ. For if Jesus is put aside in favor of human endeavors as a means of salvation, the world, in fact, will turn upon itself and bring damage to itself. With God no longer the source of meaning, man himself becomes the criterion of truth.

Marxism and liberal capitalism were able to perpetuate such an illusion, so too did liberation theology, but eventually what transpired was that man lost his freedom and instead became a prisoner of manipulation, violence and terrorism. If man forgets God, he also distances himself from the knowledge of his true self and his nature. Man was created in the image of God, and if this true origin becomes lost in a world of man's own making, then truth will never be properly known.

Ratzinger is well aware of Christian anthropology which teaches that, because of the reality of sin, man can only find his true bearings through the *vertical* and *horizontal* dimensions of Jesus' Cross. It is man's nature to reason and to discover, just as there exists within him a true longing and ability to go beyond the self and this world into the realm of transcendence. Since man is both a natural and spiritual being, he acquires the necessary information about himself through both reason and faith – reason residing in his intellect and faith residing in his heart.

Recent globalization and technological progress brought about a rapid spread of ideas and an *end* to isolation. "Members of different cultures become aware of other cultures, other world views, other ways of conceptualizing themselves and their environments."[955] Because of this, a growing number of not only Christians, but more disturbingly Catholics no longer think it is necessary to preserve the foundations of the Church, and instead believe the Church should accept the diversity of human cultures and beliefs. The global economy, with its efforts to fight global warming as well as social difficulties of the world, becomes the final true criterion of any political, social, or even religious success. At the threshold of the New Millennium, Ratzinger detects the world falling under a new dictatorship, one that he calls a *dictatorship of relativism.*

In his proposals to confront this relativism and to overcome the dictatorship of relativism, Ratzinger first uses the philosophical methodology of relativizing relativizers, i.e. refuting relativism with its own arguments. To an extent, this logical methodology is able to achieve some success in confronting relativism or in weakening its argumentation; however, predominantly it remains just an intellectual exercise. It might win the argument, but it seldom effects a change. Ratzinger knows that relativism approached just from an intellectual position, will rarely yield to true conversion of the whole human person.

That is why he proposes using Pascal's Wager as a method of overcoming relativism. *Veluti etsi Deus daretur* – act as if God exists and is the source of ultimate truth – is directed toward those who are not completely deaf to the question of God, but for the most part describe themselves as agnostics. Ratzinger uses Pascal's argument that the heart and reason are jointly the major factors in judging the reality of God and of man. Both offer direction, safety and life's stability, especially in matters of the afterlife. However, this proposal also has its limitations. Though it acknowledges the constitutive usage of both reason and faith, the faith is not based on transcendent reality but on the experience of human feelings. Human feelings do not open up the true source of truth, which lies beyond human feelings and subjectivity.

Another way to overcome relativism is through participation in Christian liturgy. In this way, real communication is formed between God and man. Ratzinger argues that an honest participation in a well-executed Christian liturgy opens man up into an intimate relationship with God through the mediation of the divine *Logos* – Jesus Christ in the mystery of the Eucharist. Furthermore, the personhood of Jesus Christ resides in his Church, which through the proclamation of the Word of God and the sacraments, especially through the celebration of the Eucharist, becomes the true *locus* of that mutual communication and dialogue. The use of art and music in worship also profoundly affects one's being in such a way that there can be no indifference to the hypothetical existence and actual presence of God. Therefore, Ratzinger urges a renewal of the Church's commitment to prayer and worship as a way to overcome relativism. Active participation in the Eucharist liberates the human being from the dictatorship of relativism and towards full rediscovery of his/her God-given personhood.

He also proposes that Christians bear witness to their faith as a means of attracting those who do not come to church, or have not had the chance to observe or to participate in the Church's liturgies. It is the faithful who need to convince the world of the uniqueness of Jesus Christ and of the true freedom and salvation he brings to men and women and all of creation. If the world were to recognize the effects of true freedom, goodness, and joy, which a relationship with the triune God brings to those in such a relationship, then its source would not so easily be dismissed. At the same time, Ratzinger urges Christians to regain their confidence and ability to talk about their faith in an intelligent matter, or as St. Peter says in his First Letter 3:15: "Be always ready to explain about the hope living in you." In this way, faith and reason together proclaim and live the Christian Gospel. The purpose of this work has been to demonstrate Ratzinger's lifelong preoccupation with relativism and its effects. Although Ratzinger has now become Pope Benedict XVI, his message to the Church and to the world has not changed. It is Jesus who is the way, the truth and the life, and it is through him that salvation can be found.

However, Ratzinger also believes there are traces of the Real Truth found in every human being, and the challenge of the world today is to recognize it. However, it is also up to the Christian to be the "voice heard decisively and unmistakably at this very hour,"[956] and it is the present Pope whose voice speaks most loudly. It is up to him to challenge the world to recover its confidence in the power of the human intellect and to recognize the revealed truth. Ratzinger does it joyfully, in a spirit of service rather than power, an attitude he takes from the time of his priesthood ordination (June 29, 1951), where on the special card to commemorate the occasion he chose a line from Paul's Second Letter to the Corinthians: "We aim not to lord over your faith, but to serve your joy" (1:21).[957] However, at the same time he remains uncompromising and clear in his beliefs and his positions. According to him:

> The point of departure of Christian universalism was not the drive to power, but the certainty of having received the saving knowledge and redeeming love which all men had a claim to and were yearning for in the inmost recesses of their beings. Mission was not perceived as expansion for the wielding of power, but as the obligatory transmission of what was intended for everyone and which everyone needed.[958]

In the end, the winning power against the dictatorship of relativism is the strength of faith of each Catholic Christian, especially the young ones.[959] The world will not accept the universal validity of Christianity's truth unless it witnesses its attractiveness in the joyous and peaceful lives of ordinary Catholic people. It is not only important to have the truth, but also to be able to communicate that truth to others. This requires the renewal of

Christian faith and intelligent commitment to the Gospel of Jesus Christ, which is the only secure basis of authentic humanism.

However, in the end, Revelation must have the last word, as St. Paul acknowledges in his First Letter to the Corinthians: "After all, what is Apollos? And what is Paul? We are only the ministers through whom you came to believe – we each simply performed the task assigned to us by the Lord. I planted the seed, Apollos watered it, but it was God who caused the growth. Thus, neither the one who planted nor the one who watered amounts to anything – only God who caused the growth" (1 Cor 3:5-7). Cardinal Ratzinger, the present Pope Benedict XVI, is highly aware of this truth. He himself is in a constant search for the truth and the truth for him is Jesus Christ, the only and unique revelation of God (Christological concern). That is why in the midst of relativism, pluralism, indifferentism and other *-isms*, it is a challenge to maintain that Truth is one, that Revelation is one, that salvation only comes through the dying and rising of Jesus Christ. The *mysterium paschale* must serve as the life-pattern for every human being, because "man can only rightly be understood from the viewpoint of God."[960] If the existence of God is denied or simply forgotten, then man separates himself from the truth, and hence loses his freedom. Only the truth makes one free.

This separation from the truth is why relativism is such a threat not only to the Catholic Church and its members, but also to every person. That is why it is clear that for the present leader of the Catholic Church, the search for the truth about man and the truth about God remains an unshaken objective:

> We, however, have a different goal: the Son of God, the true man. He is the measure of true humanism. An "adult" faith is not a faith that follows the trends of fashion and the latest novelty; a mature adult faith is deeply rooted in friendship with Christ. It is this friendship that opens us up to all that is good and gives us a criterion by which to distinguish the true from the false and deceit from truth.[961]

BIBLIOGRAPHY

Ratzinger, Joseph. "Relativism: The Central Problem for Faith Today" in *The Essential Pope Benedict XVI: His Central Writings and Speeches*, John F. Thornton and Susan B. Varenne, eds., 227-228. New York: HarperCollins Publishers, 2007.

Ratzinger, Cardinal Joseph and Jürgen Habermas. *Dialectics of Secularization: On Reason and Religion.* Foreword by Florian Schuller. Translated by Brian McNeil. San Francisco: Ignatius Press, 2006.

Ratzinger, Cardinal Joseph and Marcello Pera. *Without Roots: The West, Relativism, Christianity, Islam.* Foreword by George Weigel. Translated by Michael F. Moore. New York: Basic Books, 2006.

Ratzinger, Joseph. *Christianity and the Crisis of Cultures.* Introduction by Marcello Pera. Translated by Brian McNeil. San Francisco: Ignatius Press, 2006.

Ratzinger, Joseph. "Presentation of the Declaration *Dominus Iesus*" in *Pilgrim Fellowship of Faith: The Church as Communion*, Stephan Otto Horn and Vinzenz Pfnür, eds. Translated by Henry Taylor, 209-216. San Francisco: Ignatius Press, 2005.

Ratzinger, Joseph. *Introduction to Christianity.* Translated by J.R. Foster, with a new Preface translated by Michael J. Miller. San Francisco: Ignatius Press, 2004.

Ratzinger, Joseph. *Truth and Tolerance: Christian Belief and World Religions.* Translated by Henry Taylor. San Francisco: Ignatius Press, 2003.

Ratzinger, Joseph. *A Turning Point for Europe? The Church in the Modern World: Assessment and Forecast.* Translated by Brian McNeil. San Francisco: Ignatius Press, 1994.

ENDNOTES

1 Cardinal Joseph Ratzinger, *Introduction to Christianity*, trans. J.R. Foster, with a new Preface, trans. Michael J. Miller (San Francisco: Ignatius Press, 2004), 41. John L. Allen in his book *Pope Benedict XVI. A Biography of Joseph Ratzinger* (New York and London: Continuum, 2005), 94 notes "Ratzinger uses the story to declare his purpose in the book: To meet the challenge of Christian belief head on, without watering it down or making it seem more 'reasonable.'"

2 Ratzinger, *Introduction to Christianity*, 41; Aidan Nichols, *The Thought of Pope Benedict XVI: An Introduction to the Theology of Joseph Ratzinger* (New York: Burns & Oates, 2007) wrote: "And yet, Ratzinger insists, it is not enough for the preacher, or the theologian, simply to doff his antique dress in order for him to be taken *au sérieux*. We live in a world where unbelief presses upon the believer, just as belief presses upon the unbeliever, whose 'Perhaps it *is* true' mirrors the believer's 'Perhaps it is *not*.'" 74.

3 Jim Corkery describes this tendency in Ratzinger as follows: "His will be a theology less inclined to seek for 'seeds of the Word' or for the grace hidden in the human mess of things and more inclined to identify the pollutants that distort and seduce a humanity that is constantly in need of healing and conversion. It will, on the whole, be a theology more attuned to the tensions between what is godly and what is worldly rather than to the harmonies between the two." In the following text, one finds Corkery's critical evaluation of Ratzinger's theological approach in Jim Corkery, SJ, "Joseph Ratzinger's Theological Ideas 1–Origins: A Theologian Emerges," *Doctrine and Life* 56:2 (February, 2006), 6-14, here 13.

4 The Holy See, *Homily of His Eminence Cardinal Joseph Ratzinger: Mass 'Pro Eligendo Romano Pontifice,'* http://www.vatican.va/gpII/documents/homily-pro-eligendo-pontifice_20050418 (11 February 2009), from this homily a summary of a contemporary situation: "How many winds of doctrine have we known in recent decades, how many ideological currents, how many ways of thinking? The small boat of the thought of many Christians has often been tossed about by these waves – flung from one extreme to another: from Marxism to liberalism, even to libertinism; from collectivism to radical individualism; from atheism to a vague religious mysticism; from agnosticism to syncretism and so forth."

5 George Weigel, *God's Choice. Pope Benedict XVI and the Future of the Catholic Church* (New York: Harper Perennial, 2006) noted: "Cardinal Ratzinger is no fool. He knew that 'dictatorship of relativism' would be the sound bite taken from his homily by the world press. He must also have known that many of his brother-cardinals were seriously thinking of casting their votes for him, and he had a message for them, too – here is what I think, unvarnished. He did not use the phrase 'dictatorship of relativism' to be provocative; he used it because it seemed to him the truth of the matter, and if others regarded it as provocative, that was, so to speak, their problem. Prior to this afternoon's entry into the conclave proper, Joseph Ratzinger let everyone with a vote know precisely where he stood, and precisely what kind of analysis he would bring to the Church's task in the modern world." 140.

6   John L. Allen, Jr., *The Rise of Benedict XVI: The Inside Story of How the Pope Was Elected and Where He Will Take the Catholic Church* (New York: Doubleday, 2005), 166.

7   Allen, *The Rise of Benedict XVI*, 166. Another comparison Allen drew between the two popes was his thought, "Whether there will be the single dramatic moments that characterized John Paul's moral crusade against the Soviet domination of the East, such as his stirring 1979 return to Poland, is unknowable; relativism is a much more diffuse, amorphous, unsystematic opponent. In the East, Soviet oppression produced explicit political resistance, such as the Solidarity movement, which could be endorsed and assisted by the Pope; in the West, relativism tends to produce ennui and purposelessness rather than organized opposition, which means that the first thing the Pope must do is convince people that there *is* a dictatorship to be resisted, a preliminary challenge John Paul II never faced." 166. Similarly, René Girard, a prominent Roman Catholic thinker and emeritus professor of anthropology at Stanford University notes, "This formula – the dictatorship of relativism – is excellent. It is going to establish a new discourse in the same way that John Paul II's idea of recovering 'a culture of life' from the 'culture of death' has framed a whole set of issues, from abortion to stem research, capital punishment and war." René Girard, "Ratzinger is Right," *New Perspective Quarterly* (Summer 2005), 43-48, here 43.

8   Allen, *The Rise of Benedict XVI*, 166. Allen also noted, "No one in the College of Cardinals understands the Western intellectual tradition better, no one has spent more time reflecting on the phenomenon of relativism, and no one seems to be more forceful in challenging the relativistic mindset of the contemporary West on its own turf – that is, which world-view best protects human freedom and happiness." 125.

9   Nichols, *The Thought of Pope Benedict XVI*, vii.

10 John Paul II. *Rise, Let Us Be On Our Way*, trans. by Walter Ziemba (New York: Warner Books, 2004) 165; Gianni Vattimo makes the following reference: "Eamon Duffy called Ratzinger, upon his election, the most accomplished theological scholar to hold the papacy in a thousand years" in his introduction "Surtout Pas de Zéle," in *A "Dictatorship of Relativism"? Symposium in Response to Cardinal Ratzinger's Last Homily*, Vol. 13, *Common Knowledge* (2007), 215; One of Ratzinger's doctoral students, Vincent Twomey SVD, in the introduction to *The Essential Pope Benedict XVI: His Central Writings & Speeches*, John F. Thornton and Susan B. Varenne, eds. (New York: HarperCollins Publishers, 2007) writes, "Joseph Ratzinger is, to the best of my knowledge, the first academic theologian in two centuries to fill the shoes of the Fisherman, just as his immediate predecessor was the first professional philosopher ever to do so." xvii.

11 Joseph Ratzinger, *The Meaning of Christian Brotherhood*, Foreword by Scott Hahn (San Francisco: Ignatius Press, 1993), 87. Allen recalls Bishop Culligane of Permerston, New Zealand, sharing the following words about Ratzinger, during his visit to Menlo Park, in February, 1999: "I regret very much that Cardinal Ratzinger gets a bad press because I think people, due to a lot of prejudices or their own theological positions, don't always give themselves the opportunity to really hear the man, to really hear what he's got to say. He is a man of tremendous faith, of great integrity, very great intellect and great dedication. I just wish people would allow themselves the opportunity to listen more carefully to what he's saying, what's behind what he's saying, where he's coming from,

what theology really means to him. I think if people really did that they would find that one of the big barriers slips away." Allen, *Pope Benedict XVI*, xi. Joseph Ratzinger, *"Deus locutus est nobis in Filio:* Some Reflections on Subjectivity, Christology, and the Church," in *Proclaiming the Truth of Jesus Christ: Papers from the Vallambrosa Meeting* (Washington, DC: United States Conference of Catholic Bishops, 2000).

12   In order not to exceed the proper length of this book and to remain more focused on Joseph Ratzinger as a theologian, I chose not to cover many other aspects of his thought unless they were related to the issue of relativism.

13   Barbara Herrnstein Smith, "Relativism, Today and Yesterday," in *Symposium in Response to Cardinal Ratzinger's Last Homily*, 228; In the Encarta Dictionary, available at http://encarta.msn.com/dictionary_/a.html; accessed 14 May 2007, the word *relativism* means a "belief in changeable standards," or, in broader terms it is "the belief that concepts such as right and wrong, goodness and badness, or truth and falsehood are not absolute, but change from culture to culture and situation to situation." In his article "Epistemic Grace: Antirelativism as Theology in Disguise," in *Symposium in Response to Cardinal Ratzinger's Last Homily*, 256-257, footnote 13, David Bloor notes, "For now, the important point is that each of the dichotomies, the relative/absolute, the material/ideal, the objective/subjective and the general/particular, has a specific job of work to do. Running them together merely produces confusion. Deplorably, the practice of conflating these different distinctions is now endemic in the philosophical literature. It has become institutionalized in the entries on relativism to be found in the *Oxford Companion to Philosophy* and the *Cambridge Dictionary of Philosophy*," 256-257.

14   Maria Baghramian, *Relativism* (New York: Routledge, 2004), 1.

15   Baghramian, *Relativism*, 1. Here she also quotes Popper, who says: "One of the more disturbing aspects of the intellectual life of our time is the way in which irrationalism is so widely advocated and the way in which irrationalist doctrines are taken for granted. One of the components of modern irrationalism is relativism (the doctrine that truth is relative to our intellectual background)." Cf. Karl R. Popper, *The Myth of the Framework: In Defense of Science and Rationality* (London: Routledge, 1994), 33.

16   Bloor, "Epistemic Grace: Antirelativism as Theology in Disguise," 257.

17   Maurice Mandelbaum, *The Problem of Historical Knowledge: An Answer to Relativism* (New York: Liveright Publishing Corporation, 1938), 19.

18   Gregory Baum, *Truth Beyond Relativism: Karl Mannheim's Sociology of Knowledge* (Milwaukee, WI: Marquette University Press, 1977), 36.

19   Smith, "Relativism, Today and Yesterday," 228, in footnote 3, states, "Harré and Krausz identify, define, distinguish and assess a dozen or more such varieties, e.g., 'moral relativism,' 'epistemic relativism,' and 'ontological relativism,' each with its 'anti-objectivist,' 'anti-universalist,' and 'anti-absolutist' variants and each of those with its 'strong' and 'weak' or 'moderate' and 'extreme' versions." This references Rom Harré and Michael Krausz, *Varieties of Relativism* (Oxford: Blackwell, 1996). Also, Michael F. Brown in his article "Cultural Relativism," *Current Anthropology* 49:3 (June, 2008), 363-384, here page 367 mentions the work of Jack W. Meiland and Michael Krausz, *Relativism, Cognitive and Moral* (Notre Dame, IN: University of Notre Dame Press, 1982), listing 20 types of relativism in its index.

20   Baghramian, *Relativism*, 14, quotes John Grote: *Exploratio Philosophica: Rough*

Notes on Modern Intellectual Science (Cambridge: Deighton, Bell and Co., 1865), 229.

21 Joseph Margolis, *The Truth About Relativism* (Cambridge: Blackwell, 1991), 2. This dictum of Protagoras is recorded by Plato, in his *Theaetetus*, trans. by M.J. Levett and Myles Burnyeat, in *Plato: Complete Works*, ed. John M. Cooper and D.S. Hutchinson (Cambridge: Hackett Publishing Co., 1997), 152a 1-3.

22 Baghramian, *Relativism*, 21.

23 Baghramian, *Relativism*, 22.

24 Baghramian, *Relativism*, 23.

25 Baghramian, *Relativism*, 48. Quotes Sextus Empiricus, *Outlines of Pyrrhonism*, trans. by J. Annas and J. Barnes (Cambridge: Cambridge University Press, 1994), 163.

26 Baghramian, *Relativism*, 47.

27 Jean-Yves Lacoste, ed. *The Encyclopedia of Christian Theology*, Vol. 3 (New York: Routledge, 2005), s.v. "Relativism," by Michael Banner, 1355-1356.

28 Michael Brown, an anthropologist teaching at Williams College, MA in footnote 5 states, the term *ethnocentrism* can be attributed to sociologist William Graham Sumner (1840-1910). For discussion of how ethnocentrism and relativism fit into Sumner's work, see Steve J. Shone, "Cultural Relativism and the Savage: The alleged inconsistency of William Graham Sumner," *American Journal of Economics and Sociology* 63 (July, 2004), 697-715; Brown, "Cultural Relativism," 365.

29 Baghramian, *Relativism*, 50.

30 Lindsay Jones, ed., *The Encyclopedia of Religion*, Vol. 11 (Farmington Hills, MI: Thomson Gale, 2005), s.v. "Relativism," by Richard H. Popkin, pp. 7685-7686.

31 Baghramian, *Relativism*, 54.

32 Baghramian, *Relativism*, 55.

33 Bloor, "Epistemic Grace: Antirelativism as Theology in Disguise," 268.

34 *The New Catholic Encyclopedia*, 1967 ed., Vol. 12, s.v. "Relativism" by R.L. Cunningham, 221.

35 Brown, "Cultural Relativism," 365. In footnote 8, Brown states, "As early as the 1830's, Auguste Comte argued that one of the ways positivist sociology differed from theology and metaphysics was that it has a 'tendency to render relative the ideas which were at first absolute.' This transition from the absolute to the relative was for Comte a decisive step in the creation of social science."

36 David Hume, *Essays and Treatises on Several Subjects* (London: T. Cadell, 1972), 362.

37 Baghramian, *Relativism*, 57. Ratzinger refers to this also, in his *A Turning Point for Europe? The Church in the Modern World: Assessment and Forecast*, trans. by Brian McNeil (San Francisco: Ignatius Press, 1994) where he writes, "it is characteristic of thought marked by the natural sciences to posit a gulf between the world of feelings and the world of facts" and "the consequence of this reduction of nature to facts that can be completely grasped and therefore controlled is that no moral message outside ourselves can now come to us." 31.

38 Bloor, "Epistemic Grace: Antirelativism as Theology in Disguise," 270, footnote 34.

39 William K.C. Guthrie, *The Sophists* (Cambridge: Cambridge University Press, 1971), 171.

40 Guthrie, *The Sophists*, 171.

41 In defining monism Baghramian states, "Relativism is compatible with local but not universal monism, for a relativist may accept that in any given culture or society there can be no more than one correct view on any topic but deny that one single correct norm or belief can apply cross-culturally." Baghramian, *Relativism*, 2.

42 Baghramian, *Relativism*, 10.

43 Baghramian, *Relativism*, 10.

44 Ratzinger also concludes, "Relativism unites easily with positivism; it is indeed positivism's own philosophical basis. We do not wish to dispute the fact that in many situations a dash of relativism, a bit of skepticism, can be useful; but certainly does not suffice as a common ground on which we can live." *A Turning Point for Europe*, 102.

45 Baghramian, *Relativism*, 10.

46 Baghramian, *Relativism*, 11. Brown observes, "Dialogical morality is consistent with the 'rationalism' identified by Mark Taylor (2007), a scholar of religion, as a key element in an emerging, globally networked moral order that duels with absolutes rooted in exhausted dichotomies: God and Satan, right and wrong, individual and group, cooperation and competition. Taylor is convinced that absolutes must be replaced by 'creative co-dependence' and fluid decision making that embrace the relatedness of everything and promote an 'ethic of life.'" Brown, "Cultural Relativism," 370.

47 Baghramian, *Relativism*, 12.

48 Edmund Husserl, *Prolegomena to the Logical Investigations* (London: Routledge, 1970), 132.

49 Baghramian, *Relativism*, 48.

50 Baghramian, *Relativism*, 13.

51 Baghramian, *Relativism*, 13-14.

52 Allan Bloom, *The Closing of the American Mind*, Foreword by Saul Bellow (London: Penguin, 1987), 25-26.

53 Baghramian, *Relativism*, 16.

54 Baghramian, *Relativism*, 16.

55 Baghramian, *Relativism*, 32.

56 John Paul II, *Veritatis Splendor* (August 6, 1993), available at http://www.vatican.va/holy-father/john_paul_ii/encyclicals/documents/hf_jp-ii_enc_06081993_veritatis-splendor_en.html; accessed 30 June 2009.

57 Cf. John Paul II, *Evangelium Vitae* (25 March 1995), 20 (used later in this text); available from http://www.vatican.va/holy_father/john_paul_ii/encyclicals/documents/hf_jp-ii_enc_25031995_evangelium-vitae_en.html; accessed 2 July 2009; also; Giovanni Lajolo, *Address of Archbishop Giovanni Lajolo, Secretary for the Holy See's Relations with States at the Pontifical Gregorian University of Rome* (3 December 2004), available from http://www.vatican.va/roman_curia/secretariat_state/2004/documents/rc_seg-st_20041203_lajolo-gregorian-univ_en.html; accessed 2 July 2009; where he says, "It was thus during the time of antagonism between East and West and it is thus today, before phenomena of intolerance and violence, sometimes connected with a religious fundamentalism closed to rational dialogue, or with an ideological vision that precludes the transcendental dimension of man or that abandons him on the shifting sands of relativism."

58 *The New Catholic Encyclopedia*, 1967 ed., Vol. 12, s.v. "Relativism (Theological Aspects)" by Maurice Schepers, 223. For more information on historical

relativism, see Geoffrey W. Bromiley, "The Limits of Theological Relativism," *Christianity Today* 12:17 (May 24, 1968), 822-823.

[59] Brown argues that moral relativism is "the insistence that each people's values are sui generis and self-validating, requiring that outsiders assess them by that group's own standard rather than by a universal one." Brown, "Cultural Relativism," 368.

[60] *The New Catholic Encyclopedia*, Vol. 12, s.v. "Relativism (Theological Aspects)," by M.B. Schepers, 223.

[61] Encyclical of His Holiness Pius XII, *Humani Generis* (12 August 1950), 15; available from http://www.vatican.va/holy_father/pius_xii/encyclicals/documents/hf_p-xii_enc_12081950_humani-generis_en.html; accessed 30 June 2009.

[62] Pius XII, *Humani Generis*, 16.

[63] Encyclical of His Holiness Paul VI, *Ecclesiam Suam* (6 August 1964), 49; available from http://www.vatican.va/holy_father/paul_vi/encyclicals/documents/hf_p-vi_enc_06081964_ecclesiam_en.html; accessed 2 July 2009.

[64] Paul VI, *Ecclesiam Suam*, 87.

[65] Apostolic Exhortation of His Holiness Paul VI, *Evangelii Nuntiandi* (8 December 1975), 80, says, "the lack of fervor [which] is all the more serious because it comes from within. It is manifested in fatigue, disenchantment, compromise, lack of interest and above all lack of joy and hope." Available from http://www.vatican.va/holy_father/paul_vi/apost_exhortations/documents/hf_p-vi_exh_19751208_evangelii-nuntiandi_en.html; accessed 30 June 2009.

[66] Encyclical of His Holiness John Paul II, *Redemptoris Missio* (7 December 1990), 36; available from http://www.vatican.va/holy_father/john_paul_ii/encyclicals/documents/hf_jp-ii_enc_07121990_redemptoris-missio_en.html; accessed 30 June 2009. In his comments on *Dominus Iesus*, Robert P. Imbelli also states, "The declaration's much criticized insistence on the universal significance of the salvation offered through Christ is not a retreat from ecumenical dialogue or tolerance. It only restates the very first words of *Lumen Gentium*, which confesses that Christ is 'the light of all peoples' and that all are called to union with Christ. Hence, the council's recognition that God's grace is operative outside the visible boundaries of the Catholic Church in no way lessens the missionary imperative to 'preach the gospel to every creature.'" In "Rome & Relativism: 'Dominus Iesus' & the CDF," *Commonweal* 27:18 (October 20, 2000), 12-14.

[67] Encyclical of His Holiness John Paul II, *Centesimus annus* (1 May 1991), 46; available from http://www.vatican.va/holy_father/john_paul_ii/encyclicals/documents/hf_jp-ii_enc_01051991_centesimus-annus_en.html; accessed 30 June 2009.

[68] John Paul II, *Centesimus annus*, 46.

[69] John Paul II, *Centesimus annus*, 46; Cf. Pontifical Council for Justice and Peace, *Compendium of the Social Doctrine of the Church* (29 June 2004), 407; available from http://www.vatican.va/roman_curia/pontifical_councils/justpeace/documents/rc_pc_justpeace_doc_20060526_compendio_dott-soc_en.html; accessed 25 March 2009; where in addition to what was said by John Paul II, it states, "The Church's social doctrine sees ethical relativism, which maintains that there are no objective or universal criteria for establishing the foundations of a correct hierarchy of values, as one of the greatest threats to modern-day democracies"; also in *Letter of John Paul II to Card. Camillo Ruini on the Occasion of the 44ᵗʰ Italian Catholic Social Week* (4 October 2004), 4; available from

http://www.vatican.va/holy_father/john_paul_ii/letters/2004/documents/
hf_jp-ii_let_20041004_ruini-social-weeks_en.html; accessed 30 June 2009,
Pope John Paul writes, "If political action is not confronted by a *superior ethical
body*, illuminated in turn by an *integral vision of the human person and of society*, it
ends by being subjected to ends that are inappropriate if not illicit. On the other
hand, the truth is the best *antidote to ideological fanaticism* in scientific, political
and even religious circles. Indeed, the Gospel message offers the centrality of
the person as an anchorage above ideology and to which all may refer. Without
being rooted in the truth in this way, the human person and society are exposed
to the open or thinly-disguised violence of passions and conditioning."

70 Paolo Flores d'Arcais, "Die Frage ist die Antwort: Zur Enzyklika *Fides et Ratio*"
[The Question is the Answer: On the Encyclical *Fides et Ratio*], *Frankfurter
Allgemeine Zeitung*, 51 (March 2, 1999), 47.

71 Ratzinger, *Truth and Tolerance: Christian Belief and World Religions*, trans.
by Henry Taylor (San Francisco: Ignatius Press, 2004), 190. Also in the first
edition of *Communio* (1972), Ratzinger noted the "new mentality which is
based on increasingly 'sociologising' of the question of truth," and recalled the
Church's special task, "of keeping open the question of truth, or insisting on
its acceptance, as opposed to the retreat into, positivism and sociology." Joseph
Ratzinger, "What Unites and Divides Denominations?" *Communio* 1 (1972),
115-119, here 116. See also Ratzinger's "Christian Faith as The Way: An Introduction to *Veritatis Splendor*," *Communio* 21:2 (1994), 199-207.

72 John Paul II, *Veritatis Splendor*, 1.

73 John Paul II, *Veritatis Splendor*, 48.

74 John Paul II, *Veritatis Splendor*, 84; Ratzinger had expressed the same view, when
in his *Seek That Which is Above: Meditations Through the Year* (San Francisco:
Ignatius Press, 1986), 32 he writes: "God is not the enemy of our freedom but
its ground." On the linkage of freedom and truth, see Ratzinger's "Freedom
and Liberation: The Anthropological Vision of the 1986 Instruction *Libertatis
Conscientiae*," in *The Church, Ecumenism and Politics: New Essays in Ecclesiology* (New York: Crossroad, 1988), 255-275; also Corkery points out in his
"Joseph Ratzinger's Theological Ideas 3–On Being Human," *Doctrine and Life*
56:7 (September, 2006), 7-24, here 11, footnote 21, that, "for his ideas on how
freedom and truth go together, Ratzinger draws on Romano Guardini, also and
more fundamentally, on St. Augustine." Also, Joseph Ratzinger, "The Renewal
of Moral Theology: Perspectives on Vatican II," *Communio* 32:2 (2005), 357-
368.

75 John Paul II, *Veritatis Splendor*, 84.

76 John Paul II, *Veritatis Splendor*, 101.

77 John Paul II, *Evangelium Vitae*, 20.

78 John Paul II, *Evangelium Vitae*, 20.

79 Cf. *Letter of John Paul II to Card. Camillo Ruini on the Occasion of the 44th Italian
Catholic Social Week* (4 October 2004), 4; where the Pope writes, "For example,
there is still a tendency to consider *relativism* as the mental approach that most
closely corresponds to political forms of democracy, as if knowledge of the *truth*
and adherence to it were a hindrance."

80 John Paul II, *Evangelium Vitae*, 70.

81 John Paul II, *Evangelium Vitae*, 70; cf. *Compendium of the Social Doctrine of
the Church* (29 June 2004), 407, which says, "An authentic democracy is not
merely the result of a formal observation of a set of rules but is the fruit of a

convinced acceptance of the values that inspire democratic procedures: the dignity of every human person, the respect of human rights, commitment to the common good as the purpose and guiding criterion for political life. If there is no general consensus on these values, the deepest meaning of democracy is lost and its stability is compromised."

[82] Cf. John Paul II, *Address of His Holiness Pope John Paul II to H.E. Mr. Esteban Juan Caselli, Ambassador of Argentina to the Holy See* (20 June 1997), 3; available from http://www.vatican.va/holy_father/john_paul_ii/speeches/1997/june/documents/hf_jp-ii_spe_19970620_argentina_en.html; accessed 2 July 2009; where the Pope states: "The Church considers that the constitutional State and the application of democratic principles, by which conflicts can be solved through negotiation and dialogue, are important for the preservation and exercise of human rights in the contemporary world, since they are never based on the moral relativism which has regrettably spread in our time. This relativism seeks to reject all certainty about the meaning of man's life and his basic dignity, which must be respected by all social institutions and it fails to oppose the various ways this life and dignity are manipulated and disparaged, causing people to lose sight of what constitutes the noblest quality of democracy: the defense of the human person's incomparable value."

[83] John Paul II, *Evangelium Vitae*, 70; cf. Apostolic letter of His Holiness John Paul II, *Dilecti Amici* (31 March 1985), available at http://www.vatican.va/holy_father/john_paul_ii/apost_letters/documents/hf_jp-ii_apl_31031985_delecti-amici_en.html; accessed 7 July 2009, where the Pope writes: "The upright conscience responds with an interior reaction to man's corresponding deeds: it accuses or excuses. But the conscience must not be distorted; the fundamental formulation of the principles of morality must not surrender to deformation by any kind of relativism or utilitarianism."

[84] John Paul II, *Evangelium Vitae*, 70.

[85] Apostolic letter of His Holiness John Paul II, *Tertio Millennio Adveniente* (10 November 1994), 36, available from http://www.vatican.va/holy_father/john_paul_ii/apost_letters/documents/hf_jp-ii_apl_10111994_tertio-millennio-adveniente_en.html; accessed 7 July 2009.

[86] *Compendium of the Social Doctrine of the Church*, 223.

[87] Pontifical Council for Social Communications, "Ethics in Communication" (2 June 2000), 15; available from http://www.vatican.va/roman_curia/pontifical_councils/pccs/docments/rc_pc pccs_doc_20000530_ethics-communications_en.html; accessed 7 July 2009.

[88] Pontifical Council for Social Communications, "The Church and Internet" (22 February 2002); available from http://www.vatican.va/roman_curia/pontifical_councils/pccs/documents/rc_pc_ pccs_doc_20020228_church-internet_en.html; accessed 7 July 2009. The English cultural critic Richard Hoggart observed that in societies organized around conspicuous consumption relativism offers "perfect soil for their endless and always changing urges." Richard Hoggart, *The Tyranny of Relativism: Culture and Politics in Contemporary English Society* (New Brunswick, NJ: Transaction Publishers, 1998), 6.

[89] The Sacred Congregation for Catholic Education, "The Catholic School" (19 March 1977), 12; available from http.//www.vatican.va/roman_curia/congregations/ccatheduc_doc_19770319_catholic-school_en.html; accessed 7 July 2009.

[90] The Sacred Congregation for Catholic Education, "The Catholic School on the Threshold of the Third Millennium" (27 April 1998), 1; available from

http://www.vatican.va/roman_curia/congregations/ccatheduc/documents/ rc_con_ccatheduc_doc_27041998_school2000_en.html; accessed 7 July 2009.

91 Joseph Ratzinger, *Milestones. Memoirs: 1927-1977*, trans. by Erasmo Leiva-Merkakis (San Francisco: Ignatius Press, 1998), 8.

92 Nichols, *The Thought of Pope Benedict XVI*, 7. The anti-Marxist sentiment was still felt from the 1919 Communist uprising and the declaration of the Soviet Republic of Bavaria, the only such Soviet government ever erected in Western Europe, which in fact lasted for a less than a year. Allen pointed out that "Ratzinger was born only eight years later, and the instinctive fear of Marxist-inspired violence was still fresh in the minds of his countrymen." *Pope Benedict XVI*, 4.

93 Relocations were directly related to young Joseph's father's resistance to Nazism, which resulted in demotions and transfers in his work as a police officer. "Our father was a bitter enemy of Nazism because he believed it was in conflict with our faith, the Pope's brother, Georg, has said." In Robert Moynihan, ed., *The Spiritual Vision of Pope Benedict XVI: Let God's Light Shine Forth* (New York: Doubleday, 2005), 10.

94 Joseph Ratzinger, *Salt of the Earth. The Church at the End of the Millennium. An Interview with Peter Seewald*, trans. by Adrian Walker (San Francisco: Ignatius Press, 1997), 44.

95 Moynihan, *The Spiritual Vision of Pope Benedict XVI*, 12-13.

96 Joseph Ratzinger, in *Many Religions – One Covenant: Israel, the Church, and the World*, with a Foreword by Scott Hahn, trans. by Graham Harrison (San Francisco: Ignatius Press, 1999), 22 writes: "Auschwitz is the gruesome expression of an ideology that not only wanted to destroy Judaism but also hated and sought to eradicate from Christianity its Jewish heritage."

97 Ratzinger, *Milestones*, 16.

98 Sandro Magister, "Europe is Christian, but Turkey's Crescent Moon Shines in Its Skies," *Chiesa* (October 15, 2004), available from http://chiesa.espresso. republic.it/articolo/19629?eng=y; accessed 5 July 2009. Also, Éric Fassin, "The Geopolitics of Vatican Theology," *Public Culture* 19:2 (2007), 233-237, here 236. Weigel observes, "What the drafters of Europe's new constitution were determined to do was to declare secularism – and the skepticism and relativism that inform secularism – as the official creed, so to speak, of the newly expanded European Union." Weigel, *God's Choice*, 221.

99 Allen, *The Rise of Benedict XVI*, 148; "Ratzinger revealed the episode on November 28, 1996, at a Vatican conference organized by the Pontifical Council for Health Care. He cited it to illustrate the danger of ideological systems that define certain classes of human beings as unworthy of protection."

100 Nichols, *The Thought of Pope Benedict XVI*, 10; J.S. Conway in *The Nazi Persecution of the Churches 1933-45* (New York: Basic Books, Inc., Publishers, 1968), 267 gives a number of one hundred people in a five-year period.

101 Ratzinger, *Milestones*, 23. Brennan Pursell adds, "Who could be impressed by Hitler's idiotic tirades, his stupid slogans and banal rhetoric, when one is used to speeches by Cicero, Seneca, and a host of other brilliant ancient minds? None of the Greek or Latin teachers at Joseph's school were proponents of Nazism." Brennan Pursell, *Benedict of Bavaria: An Intimate Portrait of the Pope and His Homeland* (North Haven, CT: Circle Press, 2008), 54.

102 Marco Bardazzi, *In the Vineyard of the Lord: The Life, Faith and Teachings of Joseph Ratzinger/Pope Benedict XVI*, trans. by Michael F. Moore (New York: Rizzoli International Publications, 2005), 18.

[103] Ratzinger, *Milestones*, 27.

[104] Ratzinger, *Milestones*, 23.

[105] Ratzinger, *Milestones*, 35.

[106] Ratzinger compares himself to fellow theologian J.B. Metz because "he was a prisoner-of-war in the United States where he learned fluent English." In Desmond O'Grady, "The Ratzinger Round," *The Month* 6:12 (December 1973), 409-412, here 409.

[107] Cf. Ratzinger, *Milestones*, 38; In describing this period of Ratzinger's life, Corkery makes the following observation, "Thus his was a twilight (literally a two-light) childhood and adolescence, in which there existed a communal reality that could be trusted and a communal reality that could clearly not be trusted. The first, of course, was the Church, the second the Nazi authorities. The first was ever more experienced as the guarantor of human freedom, the second, however, as its indisputable enemy. The first embodied the wisdom of God and told the truth about human beings; the second embodied the false wisdom of a destructive ideology that completely effaced the truth about human beings." In Corkery, "Joseph Ratzinger's Theological Ideas 1–Origins: A Theologian Emerges," 9.

[108] Ratzinger, *Milestones*, 42; Jim Corkery, SJ, notes in his article: "The horrors of Nazism furnished him [Ratzinger] with an abiding trust in the Church as the guarantor of truth and freedom," and for that reason he puts Ratzinger in the same line of thought with Schlier and Guardini; in Jim Corkery, SJ, "Joseph Ratzinger's Theological Ideas 5–*Questiones Disputatae* 2: Theological Dissent," *Doctrine and Life*, Vol. 57:1 (January, 2007), 35-48, here 44.

[109] Ratzinger, *Salt of the Earth*, 52-53.

[110] Franklin H. Littell and Hubert G. Locke eds., *The German Church's Struggle and the Holocaust* (Detroit, MI: Wayne State University Press, 1974), 209.

[111] Michael von Faulhaber, *Judaism, Christianity and Germany*, trans. by George D. Smith (New York: Macmillan Co., 1934).

[112] *The New Encyclopedia Britannica*, Vol. 4, s.v., "Faulhaber, Michael von," 699.

[113] Littell and Locke, *The German Church Struggle and the Holocaust*, 227.

[114] Pursell, *Benedict of Bavaria*, 71-72.

[115] Conway, *The Nazi Persecution of the Churches 1933-45*, 69.

[116] Ratzinger, *Milestones*, 45.

[117] Ratzinger, *Milestones*, 15.

[118] Hans Küng, *On Being a Christian*, trans. by Edward Quinn (New York: Image/ Doubleday, 1976).

[119] Joseph Ratzinger, "On Hans Küng's Being a Christian," *Doctrine and Life* 27.5 (May, 1977), 3-17, here 15; another source supporting Ratzinger's position – Arthur C. Cochrane, *The Church's Confession Under Hitler* (Philadelphia, PA: The Westminster Press, 1962), 38, notes that a strong delegation of bishops, consisting of three cardinals – Faulhaber, Archbishop of Munich; Schulte, Bishop of Cologne; and Bertram, Bishop of Breslau – and Graf von Galen, Bishop of Münster and Graf von Preysing, Bishop of Berlin, interviewed the Pope himself and persuaded him that Bolshevism was not the only enemy. At last, the Pope broke his silence and issued the encyclical *Mit brennender Sorge* ("With Burning Anxiety") on March 4, 1937. It constituted an outright break with Nazism. This papal document demonstrated a new understanding of Hitler, who at first in Rome and Germany, was seen as "the first statesman to have spoken against Bolshevism," cf. Klaus Scholder, *The Churches and the Third Reich: Preliminary*

History and the Time of Illusions 1918-1934, Vol. 1 (Philadelphia: Fortress Press, 1988) 242-243; Conway in his book *The Nazi Persecution of the Churches 1933-45*, xxii, tells in terms of Hitler's opposition to Bolshevism "Cardinal Faulhaber, indeed, sent a letter of congratulations to Hitler, praising him for achieving in six months what the old parties and parliaments had failed to achieve in sixty years."

120 Ratzinger, "On Hans Küng's Being a Christian," 15.

121 Ratzinger, *Milestones*, 47.

122 Ratzinger, *Milestones*, 48-49.

123 Pursell, *Benedict of Bavaria*, 55. Allen gives a citation from one of Father Stelzle's sermons: "Christ was born for all and died for all, white, yellow, and black. Today there are movements who do not want this to be true, who want a falsified Aryan Christ. These populist movements preach a so-called positive Christianity, a sham Christianity, a German Christianity which gives the overlords credibility, and which brings disease over the people. Beware these false prophets! Ask yourself whether they mean the real Christ, the child of Jews, who was born in Bethlehem." Allen, *Pope Benedict XVI*, 21.

124 Allen, *Pope Benedict XVI*, 21.

125 Mary Frances Coady in her book *With Bound Hands/A Jesuit in Nazi Germany: The Life and Selected Prison Letters of Alfred Delp* (Chicago: Loyola Press, 2003), 37 writes, "Delp was not the pastor of the Holy Blood parish, but was a rector of St. Georg's Church, which has been integrated into the larger Precious Blood parish."

126 Mary Alice Gallin, *Ethical and Religious Factors in the German Resistance to Hitler* (Washington, DC: The Catholic University of America Press, 1955), 30-31.

127 The first edition of the *Lexikon* was published by Michael Buchberger, Bishop of Regensburg, between 1930 and 1938. It was an emended and expanded version of an earlier work in two volumes entitled *Kirchliches Handlexikon* (Freiburg im Breisgau, 1907-1912). The editor's goal was to create a modern "summa theologiae," i.e., a reference work that would cover all aspects of Catholic teaching, life and practice. This edition contained 10 volumes.

128 Gallin, *Ethical and Religious Factors in the German Resistance to Hitler*, 31-32.

129 Terence Prittie, *Germans against Hitler* (Boston and Toronto: An Atlantic Monthly Press Book and Little, Brown & Company, 1964), 88.

130 Conway, *The Nazi Persecution of the Churches 1933-45*, 290.

131 *The Prison Meditations of Father Delp* was the first English version of Delp's writings, with an Introduction by Thomas Merton (New York: Herder and Herder, 1963); the second edition was retitled *Prison Writings* (Maryknoll, NY: Orbis Books, 2004) and then Ignatius Press published *Alfred Delp – Priest and Martyr: Advent of the Heart: Seasonal Sermons and Prison Writings 1941-1944*, trans. by Abtei St. Walburg (San Francisco: Ignatius Press, 2006).

132 Pursell, *Benedict of Bavaria*, 79. See also Joseph Ratzinger, "Peace and Justice in Crisis: The Task of Religion," *Communio* 16:4 (1989), 540-551.

133 Prittie, *Germans against Hitler*, 89; "There were certainly more Roman Catholic priests than Evangelical pastors in German concentration camps, chiefly because a proportion of them were Poles (no Protestant country occupied by the Nazis was treated with the same ruthlessness as Catholic Poland). The numbers of German Roman Catholic clergy imprisoned in the camps ran at least, into many hundreds; and scores of them died there." More on this topic in Jean Bernard's *Priesterblock 25487: A Memoir of Dachau*, trans. by Deborah Lucas Schneider

(Maryland, MD: Zaccheus Press, 2007). Allen states: "The Nazi assault on the Catholic Church is inarguable; some twelve thousand priests and male religious were victims of persecution and harassment during the Hitler era, representing 36 percent of the diocesan clergy at the time." *The Rise of Pope Benedict XVI*, 148.

[134] Nichols, *The Thought of Pope Benedict XVI*, 13.

[135] *The New Catholic Encyclopedia*, 1967 ed., Vol. 10, s.v. "Munich, University of" by M.B. Murphy, 76-77.

[136] Alfred Plummer, *Alfred Plummer: Conversations with Dr. Döllinger, 1870-1890*, with introduction and notes by Robrecht Boudens (Leuven, Belgium: Leuven University Press/Peeters, 1985), xi.

[137] Cf. Nichols, *The Thought of Pope Benedict XVI*, 13.

[138] Plummer, *Alfred Plummer: Conversations with Dr. Döllinger, 1870-1890*, xii-xiii.

[139] *The New Catholic Encyclopedia*, 1967 ed., Vol. 4, s.v. "Döllinger, Johannes Joseph Ignaz von," by S.J. Tonsor, 959-960.

[140] Allen, *Pope Benedict XVI*, 6.

[141] Cf. *The New Catholic Encyclopedia*, 1967 ed., Vol. 4, s.v. "Döllinger, Johannes Joseph Ignaz von," by S.J. Tonsor, 959-960.

[142] Plummer, *Alfred Plummer: Conversations with Dr. Döllinger, 1870-1890*, xx-xxi.

[143] Cf. Plummer, *Alfred Plummer: Conversations with Dr. Döllinger, 1870-1890*, xv.

[144] *The New Catholic Encyclopedia*, s.v. "Döllinger, Johannes Joseph Ignaz von," 959-960.

[145] Nichols, *The Thought of Pope Benedict XVI*, 14.

[146] Ratzinger, *Milestones*, 42.

[147] Later in life, Ratzinger will write: "Romano Guardini's book *The Lord* has helped more than one generation of Christians enter into a deeper relationship with Jesus Christ. When the book first appeared, it offered a new approach to the spiritual interpretation of Scripture for which young people in particular longed – a longing, I might add, that is being felt again in our day," in his article "Guardini on Christ in Our Century," in *The Essential Pope Benedict XVI: His Central Writings and Speeches*, John F. Thornton and Susan B. Varenne, eds. (New York: HarperCollins Publishers, 2007), 53. Michael Fahey notes in his article "Joseph Ratzinger as Ecclesiologist and Pastor," *Concilium* 141 (January, 1981), 76-83, during his studies in theology at the University of Munich, Ratzinger studied under Romano Guardini.

[148] See Joseph Ratzinger, "Newman Belongs to the Great Teachers of the Church: Introductory Words for the Third Day of the Newman Symposium in Rome [28 April 1990]," in *Benedict XVI and Cardinal Newman*, ed. by Peter Jennings (Oxford: Family Publications, 2005), 33-35.

[149] Ratzinger, *Milestones*, 43.

[150] Ratzinger, *Milestones*, 44.

[151] Corkery, SJ, "Joseph Ratzinger's Theological Ideas 1–Origins: A Theologian Emerges," 11; also cf. Ratzinger, *Milestones*, 44. Weigel too, noted, "The young Ratzinger immediately made an intuitive connection between the personalism of Buber and Jaspers and 'the thought of St. Augustine, who in his *Confessions* had struck me with the power of all human passion and depth.'" Weigel, *God's Choice*, 164.

¹⁵² Ratzinger, *Milestones*, 52.

¹⁵³ Ratzinger, *Milestones*, 53-54.

¹⁵⁴ Ratzinger, *Milestones*, 55; Corkery states: "In his essay, a *Festschrift* article for Söhngen's seventieth birthday… Ratzinger points out that Professor Söhngen's writings on the analogy of being and the analogy of faith sought to do justice to Karl Barth's critique of a superficially-held optimism about nature based on Thomas Aquinas's positive concept of nature. Söhngen had attempted to hold fast to the biblically-based seriousness of the Reformed critique, while at the same time not giving up the claim of creation-faith, which Catholic theology expresses in a yes to the ontological dimension. Ratzinger said that he would follow the same basic direction." In Corkery, "Joseph Ratzinger's Theological Ideas 3–On Being Human," 16-17, citing Joseph Ratzinger, "Gratia praesupponit naturam. Erwägungen über Sinn und Grenze eines scholastischen Axioms" in *Dogma und Verkündigung* (Munich: Erich Wewel Verlag, 1973), 178-180, here 161.

¹⁵⁵ Corkery, "Joseph Ratzinger's Theological Ideas 1–Origins: A Theologian Emerges," 7 where Corkery summed up Ratzinger's life with the following words: "a life of study, prayer, ecclesial service, writing and speaking, all dominated by unrelenting passion for truth."

¹⁵⁶ Ratzinger, *Milestones*, 20.

¹⁵⁷ Ratzinger, *Milestones*, 56.

¹⁵⁸ Ratzinger, *Milestones*, 58-59.

¹⁵⁹ Ratzinger, *Milestones*, 59.

¹⁶⁰ Joseph Ratzinger, "Glaube, Geschichte und Philosophie. Zum Echo auf *Einführung in das Christentum*," *Hochland* 61 (1969), 533-543, here 543 as found in Nichols, *The Thought of Pope Benedict XVI*, 17.

¹⁶¹ Nichols, *The Thought of Pope Benedict XVI*, 18

¹⁶² Cf. Henry Chadwick, *Augustine* (Oxford: Oxford University Press, 1986), 1-2; reference given by Nichols in his *The Thought of Pope Benedict XVI*, 17.

¹⁶³ Joseph Ratzinger, *Volk und Haus Gottes in Augustins Lehre von der Kirche* (Munich, Germany: K. Zink, 1954); Jim Corkery says, with this work "one sees emerging a preference in Ratzinger's thought for people who write in a more personalist – one could almost say a more 'existentialist'– style rather than for the approach of someone like Aquinas." In Corkery, "Joseph Ratzinger's Theological Ideas 1–Origins: A Theologian Emerges," 11; more on Augustinian and Bonaventurian influence see: Roberto Tura, "La Teologia di J. Ratzinger: Saggio Introduttiva" in *Studia Patavina* 21 (1974): 145-182.

¹⁶⁴ Henri de Lubac, *Catholicism: Christ and the Common Destiny of Man*, Foreword by Joseph Ratzinger (San Francisco: Ignatius Press, 1988).

¹⁶⁵ Ratzinger, *Milestones*, 98.

¹⁶⁶ Nichols, *The Thought of Pope Benedict XVI*, 18.

¹⁶⁷ Nichols, *The Thought of Pope Benedict XVI*, 19.

¹⁶⁸ Nichols, *The Thought of Pope Benedict XVI*, 20. Archē, Αρχη = Beginning.

¹⁶⁹ Corkery notes that Augustine was to have a lifelong effect on Ratzinger and his theology, in which "Augustinian footprints are highly discernible: a preferring of the humility of faith over the pride of philosophy; a defense of the 'city of God' against the powers of the 'earthly city'; and a recognition of the duality that lies deep within human beings who, even when desiring the good, cannot embrace it" in Corkery, "Joseph Ratzinger's Theological Ideas 1–Origins: A Theologian Emerges," 12-13.

[170] Nichols, *The Thought of Benedict XVI*, 21.

[171] Nichols, *The Thought of Benedict XVI*, 23. Jim Corkery argues that Ratzinger was a man "with a heart attuned to 'dualities' and with an antecedent inclination toward writers with a similar feel for contrast." In Corkery, "Joseph Ratzinger's Theological Ideas 1–Origins: A Theologian Emerges," 12.

[172] Nichols, *The Thought of Pope Benedict XVI*, 25. Tracey Rowland states: "The *Communio* scholars argue that, at least since the Reformation, Catholic theology has been set on several dualist trajectories. Nature and grace, faith and reason, the secular and the sacred, Scripture and Tradition, have tended to be isolated and analyzed in separate compartments. They tend to regard the most important causes of the post-Conciliar chaos as the dualist trajectories of the pre-Conciliar theological establishment for which corrections were sought in the Conciliar documents." Tracey Rowland, *Ratzinger's Faith: The Theology of Pope Benedict XVI* (New York: Oxford University Press, 2008), 25-26.

[173] Nichols, *The Thought of Pope Benedict XVI*, 29.

[174] Allen mentions Romano Guardini, Ratzinger's favorite modern theologian, who in turn "saw the 'mystical body' model navigating between two extremes: the neoscholastic definition of the Church in purely institutional terms, and the liberal Protestant congregationalist understanding of the Church as a social contract." *Pope Benedict XVI*, 39.

[175] Nichols, *The Thought of Pope Benedict XVI*, 29.

[176] Nichols, *The Thought of Pope Benedict XVI*, 32.

[177] Nichols, *The Thought of Pope Benedict XVI*, 32.

[178] Ratzinger, *Salt of the Earth*, 60. Nichols states that Ratzinger's "sympathy for Bonaventure and the Franciscan school should not be regarded as anti-Thomist. Indeed, Ratzinger has expressed himself on the subject of Thomas with a good deal more warmth than formal ceremony requires." Nichols, *The Thought of Pope Benedict XVI*, 42. He had in mind Ratzinger's "'Consecrate them in the truth': a homily for St. Thomas' day," *New Blackfriars* 68:803 (March, 1987), 112-115.

[179] Ratzinger, "'Consecrate them in the truth': a homily for St. Thomas' Day," 112-113.

[180] Cited in Maximilian Heinrich Heim, *Joseph Ratzinger: Life in the Church and Living Theology/Fundamentals of Ecclesiology with Reference to Lumen Gentium*, Foreword by Joseph Ratzinger, trans. by Michael J. Miller (San Francisco: Ignatius Press, 2007), 159.

[181] Ratzinger, *Milestones*, 104.

[182] Ratzinger, *Milestones*, 108.

[183] Ratzinger, *Milestones*, 110. Twomey wrote, "As Eric Voegelin has shown, the speculations of Joachim of Fiore are in large part the source of modernity. They effectively helped replace the Augustinian concept of history that had informed Western Christendom up to then, namely, that history was something *transitory*, the rise and fall of empires. Empires pass away; only the eternal *Civitas Dei* (the 'citizenry of God,' as Ratzinger translates it) lasts forever. Its sacramental expression is the Church, understood as mankind in the process of redemption. Joachim proposed an exciting new conception of world history as a divine *progression* within three distinct eras, that of the Father (Old Testament, or the period of the laity or patriarchs), that of the Son (the Church since the New Testament, or the period of the clerics), and a third era, that of the Holy Spirit, the period of the ascetic monks or spirituals, which was about to break into history. In the third period, all structures (Church and State) would give

way to the perfect society of autonomous men moved only from within by the Spirit. This understanding of history is based on what Voegelin calls 'the immanentization of the eschaton,' in other words, the assumption that the end of history is immanent to itself, is an inner-worldly manifestation, the product of history's own inner movement toward ever greater perfection, the kingdom of God *on earth*. It is at the root of what we mean today by 'progress.'" Vincent Twomey, *Pope Benedict XVI. The Conscience of Our Age: A Theological Portrait* (San Francisco: Ignatius Press, 2007), 52-53.

184 Nichols, *The Thought of Pope Benedict XVI*, 36; also "In a remark which anticipates [Ratzinger's] mature evaluation of Martin Luther, he reflects that, whilst something once rightly condemned as heresy cannot subsequently become true, it may nonetheless gradually develop its own positive ecclesial nature, so that the individual lives from a schismatic tradition 'as a believer, not as a heretic'" 51.

185 Ratzinger, *The Theology of History in St. Bonaventure* (Chicago, IL: Franciscan Press, 1971), 6.

186 Colt Anderson in his book *A Call to Piety: St. Bonaventure's Collations on the Six Days* (Quincy, IL: Franciscan Press, 2002), xii, notes that more recent developments in historical research would alter Ratzinger's conclusion. Anderson, giving an extensive number of sources, writes, "Ratzinger assumes Bonaventure must have been drawing upon Joachim's theology of history because, at the time when he was writing, the theological tradition in the 12th and 13th century was viewed as having a static understanding of exegesis and ecclesiology. Subsequent studies of medieval exegesis and ecclesiology have indicated many medieval churchmen such as Gregory the Great, Rupert of Deutz and Hugh of St. Victor also had what can be termed a progressive view."

187 Ratzinger, *The Theology of History in St. Bonaventure*, 9.

188 Ratzinger, *The Theology of History in St. Bonaventure*, 9. See Joseph Ratzinger, "100 Years: The Magisterium and Exegesis," *Theology Digest* 51:1 (2004), 3-8.

189 Ratzinger, *The Theology of History in St. Bonaventure*, 17.

190 Ratzinger, *The Theology of History in St. Bonaventure*, 16.

191 Ratzinger, *The Theology of History in St. Bonaventure*, 51.

192 Ratzinger, *The Theology of History in St. Bonaventure*, 61.

193 Nichols, *The Thought of Pope Benedict XVI*, 40.

194 Bonaventure, *Journey of the Mind toward God*, trans. Philotheus Boehner, ed. with introduction and notes by Stephen F. Brown (Indianapolis, IN: Hackett Publishing Company, 1993).

195 Ratzinger, *The Theology of History in St. Bonaventure*, 61.

196 Ratzinger, *The Theology of History in St. Bonaventure*, 66.

197 Ratzinger, *The Theology of History in St. Bonaventure*, 68.

198 Ratzinger, *The Theology of History in St. Bonaventure*, 67-68. Corkery argued that the faith of the Church remained pivotal for Ratzinger's entire theological journey. "That is why he will always start from the faith of the Church, opposing it, indeed, to the pseudo-wisdoms of this world. This method is rooted in his [Ratzinger's] history and leads him at times to much skepticism regarding the world and too much idealism regarding the Church." Corkery, "Joseph Ratzinger's Theological Ideas 1–Origins: A Theologian Emerges," 10. See also Joseph Ratzinger, "Sources and Transmission of the Faith," *Communio* 10 (Spring 1983), 17-34.

[199] Ratzinger, *The Theology of History in St. Bonaventure*, 76.

[200] Ratzinger, *The Theology of History in St. Bonaventure*, 83.

[201] Ratzinger, *The Theology of History in St. Bonaventure*, 84-85.

[202] Ratzinger, *The Theology of History in St. Bonaventure*, 134.

[203] Ratzinger, *The Theology of History in St. Bonaventure*, 142-143. Nichols notes: "Through Bonaventure's work, Ratzinger here encountered and appropriated, the Christocentricity which was being discovered anew by Catholic dogmaticians in the 1950s"; and he continues: "It also makes it plain why Ratzinger could find himself in due course so sympathetic to the principal prophet of a renewed Christocentrism in Catholic theology: Hans Urs von Balthasar," in *The Thought of Pope Benedict XVI*, 42-43.

[204] Ratzinger, *The Theology of History in St. Bonaventure*, 146. Rowland recalls, "In the mid-sixties, before the crisis of '68, Ratzinger wrote, that 'if the Church were to accommodate herself to the world in any way that would entail a turning away from the Cross, this would not lead to a renewal of the Church, but only to her death.'" Rowland's *Ratzinger's Faith*, xi. See also Joseph Ratzinger, "Jesus Christ Today," *Communio* 17:1 (1990), 68-87.

[205] Ratzinger, *The Theology of History in St. Bonaventure*, 155.

[206] Ratzinger, *The Theology of History in St. Bonaventure*, 147.

[207] Ratzinger, *The Theology of History in St. Bonaventure*, 157. Nichols suggests, "But the revelation of the seventh age will far exceed such modest advantages. It will go beyond the *sapientia multiformis*, the 'multiform wisdom' of the present age, whose model is Augustine. It will transform itself into a *sapientia nulliformis*, a wisdom which is formless to the degree that it lies beyond all forms. The exemplar of this non-discursive, non-Scholastic acquaintance with the mystery of the Word of God, simpler, inner, familiar, is Denys the Areopagite. Bonaventure predicts an end to rational theology." In *The Thought of Pope Benedict XVI*, 40. A similar example could be found in the mystical wisdom of St. Teresa of Avila.

[208] Ratzinger, *The Theology of History in St. Bonaventure*, 163.

[209] Corkery notes that in Ratzinger's understanding of the human situation "ensnared the human being would remain, were the history not broken through by the saving history of the life and death of Jesus Christ, which is at once concrete-historical and, at the same time, if entered into, is able to pull us beyond the prison of the horizontal into a repaired, restored dialogue with our Father, who has never forgotten us." In Corkery, "Joseph Ratzinger's Theological Ideas 3–On Being Human," 10.

[210] Ratzinger, *The Meaning of Christian Brotherhood*, 5.

[211] Ratzinger, *The Meaning of Christian Brotherhood*, 7.

[212] Ratzinger, *The Meaning of Christian Brotherhood*, 8.

[213] Ratzinger, *The Meaning of Christian Brotherhood*, 11.

[214] Ratzinger, *The Meaning of Christian Brotherhood*, 14.

[215] Nichols, *The Thought of Pope Benedict XVI*, 47.

[216] Ratzinger, *The Meaning of Christian Brotherhood*, 16.

[217] Ratzinger, *The Meaning of Christian Brotherhood*, 17.

[218] Allen, *Pope Benedict XVI*, 139.

[219] Ratzinger, *The Meaning of Christian Brotherhood*, 26-27.

[220] Ratzinger, *The Meaning of Christian Brotherhood*, 29.

[221] Ratzinger, *The Meaning of Christian Brotherhood*, 34.

[222] Ratzinger, *The Meaning of Christian Brotherhood*, 46-47; cf. Blaise Pascal, *Pensées*

and other Writings, trans. Honor Levi (New York: Oxford University Press, 1995).

223 Ratzinger, *The Meaning of Christian Brotherhood*, 50.

224 Ratzinger, *The Meaning of Christian Brotherhood*, 54-55.

225 Nichols, *The Thought of Pope Benedict XVI*, 49.

226 Ratzinger, *The Meaning of Christian Brotherhood*, 68. See also Joseph Ratzinger, "The Meaning of Sunday," *Communio* 21:1 (1994), 5-26.

227 Ratzinger, *The Meaning of Christian Brotherhood*, 70.

228 Ratzinger, *The Meaning of Christian Brotherhood*, 80.

229 Nichols, *The Thought of Pope Benedict XVI*, 50.

230 Nichols, *The Thought of Pope Benedict XVI*, 50.

231 Ratzinger, *The Meaning of Christian Brotherhood*, 84.

232 Ratzinger, *Milestones*, 118.

233 Gianni Valente, "Tradition and freedom: the lectures of the young Joseph," *30 Days*, Nr. 3 (2006), available from http://www.30giorni.it/us/articolo_stampa.asp?id=10284; accessed 24 March 2009.

234 Valente, "Tradition and Freedom: The Lectures of the Young Joseph," on internet. Also, as Michael Fahey in his article notes, "As early as 1960 while in Bonn, Ratzinger composed an important essay entitled 'Theologia perennis?' which includes remarks about his uneasiness concerning contemporary Catholic thought, one so highly westernized, European in character that it appeared to people of other cultures as a foreign import. Too much of theology, he wrote, had become confined, extremely complicated, petrified, because of stultifying philosophical and cultural systems devoid of vitality. He hoped that the coming council would waken the dogmas of faith out of their systematized paralysis without removing what is truly valid." Cited "Theologia perennis?" *Wort und Wahrheit* 15 (1960), 179-188. English summary in *Theol. Dig* 10 (1962), 71-76. Michael Fahey, "Joseph Ratzinger as Ecclesiologist and Pastor," 77.

235 Ratzinger, *Milestones*, 120. See also Joseph Ratzinger, "Free Expression and Obedience in the Church," *The Church: Readings in Theology* (New York, 1963), 194-217, especially 212 and 215, where Ratzinger explaining the New Testament concept of *parrhesia* (free expression, boldness), found in Acts 2:29, 4:13, etc. wrote: "The servility of the sycophants (branded by the genuine prophets of the Old Testament as 'false prophets'), of those who shy from and shun every collision, who prize above all their calm complacency, is not true obedience.... What the Church needs today as always, are not adulators to extol the *status quo*, but men whose humility and obedience are not less than their passion for truth: men who face every misunderstanding and attack as they bear witness; men who, in a word, love the Church more than ease and the unruffled course of their personal destiny."

236 Joseph Ratzinger, *Pilgrim Fellowship of Faith: The Church as Communion*, Stephen Otto and Vinzenz Pfnür, eds. (San Francisco: Ignatius Press, 2005), 10. His former students commented, "Joseph Ratzinger had indeed as a young man, just a few years after his qualifying as a professor, helped determine, in a decisive, though still often underrated way, the course and the statements of the Second Vatican Council through his activity as a theological advisor." See also Joseph Ratzinger, "Cardinal Frings' Speeches during the Second Vatican Council: Apropos of M. Muggeridge's The Desolate City," *Communio* 15:1 (1988), 131-147.

237 See Jared Wicks, "Six Texts by Prof. Joseph Ratzinger as peritus before and

during Vatican Council II," *Gregorianum* 89:2 (2008), 233-311.

[238] Joseph Ratzinger, *Theological Highlights of Vatican II* (New York: Paulist Press, 1966), 83.

[239] Joseph Ratzinger, "Dogmatic Constitution on Divine Revelation: Origin and Background," *Commentary on the Documents of Vatican II*, Vol. 3, ed. by Herbert Vorgrimler (New York: Herder and Herder, 1967), 155-167, here 162. In footnote 16 he says: "An impressive warning of the danger of an ecclesiological positivism is given in H. de Lubac in G. Baraúna, ed., *De Ecclesia*, I (German ed., 1966), pp. 15-22"; In 1975 Ratzinger came back to the issue of ecclesial positivism as it was expressed during the Council, as he saw it influencing even the post-conciliar era, to the extent, that he concluded "it was the Council that first urged man on and then disappointed him, just as the public examination of conscience at first enlightened and then alienated him." In Joseph Ratzinger, "Review of the Post-conciliar Era – Failures, Tasks, Hopes," in *Principles of Catholic Theology: Building Stones for a Fundamental Theology*, trans. by Mary Frances McCarthy (San Francisco: Ignatius Press, 1989), 367-377, here 372f.

[240] See Joseph Ratzinger, "Culture, Identity and Church Unity," *Ecumenical Review* 57:2 (2005), 358-360.

[241] Ratzinger, *Theological Highlights of Vatican II*, 2.

[242] Desmond O'Grady notes, "At the time of the Second Vatican Council, it was said the bishops were learning their two R's: Rahner and Ratzinger." O'Grady, "The Ratzinger Round," 409. The major ideas of both theologians can be found in *Revelation and Tradition* (New York: Herder and Herder, 1966) and about the proceedings of the Council on the document on Revelation in Brendan J. Cahill, *The Renewal of Revelation Theology (1960-1962): The Development and Responses to the Fourth Chapter of the Preparatory Schema* De deposito Fidei (Rome: Editrice Pontificia Università Gregoriana, 1999).

[243] Ratzinger, *Milestones*, 128; See Jim Corkery's article "Pope Benedict's Theological Approach May Limit his Pastoral Outreach" *Irish Times* (Tuesday, April 26, 2005), 16, where he argues that opposition to existentialism, idealism, materialism and positivism is characteristic of Ratzinger's writings.

[244] Ratzinger, *Theological Highlights of Vatican II*, 14.

[245] Nichols, *The Thought of Pope Benedict XVI*, 55.

[246] Ratzinger, *Theological Highlights of Vatican II*, 18.

[247] Ratzinger, *Theological Highlights of Vatican II*, 19.

[248] Ratzinger, *Theological Highlights of Vatican II*, 20.

[249] Joseph Ratzinger, "Chapter I: Revelation Itself," *Commentary on the Documents of Vatican II*, Vol. 3, ed. by Herbert Vorgrimler (New York: Herder and Herder, 1967), 184-190, here 172.

[250] Ratzinger, *Theological Highlights of Vatican II*, 23.

[251] Robert P. Imbelli, a Catholic priest who teaches theology at Boston College, notes, "The rejection of the 'traditionalist' preliminary draft of the constitution three years before had marked the effective beginning of Pope John's council and the beginning of the end of Tridentine Catholicism, with its undeniable beauties and banalities. *Dei Verbum* was justly celebrated for recovering a more vibrant, personalist understanding of God's revelation, whose fullness is given in the person of Jesus Christ," in "Rome & Relativism: *'Dominus Iesus'* & the CDF," 12.

[252] Ratzinger, *Theological Highlights of Vatican II*, 24.

[253] Ratzinger, *Theological Highlights of Vatican II*, 24.

254 Ratzinger, *Theological Highlights of Vatican II*, 35.

255 Ratzinger, *Theological Highlights of Vatican II*, 40. Imbelli notes that "the robust Christocentrism of *Dei Verbum* – indeed, of all the council's documents – now seems to evoke embarrassment in certain 'progressive' theological and missionary circles." in "Rome & Relativism: *'Dominus Iesus'* & the CDF," 13.

256 Ratzinger, *Milestones*, 124.

257 Ratzinger, *Milestones*, 125.

258 Ratzinger, *Milestones*, 125-126; Ronald D. Witherup in his book *Scripture: Dei Verbum* (New York/Mahwah, NJ: Paulist Press, 2006), 84, recalls Cardinal Ratzinger participating in a symposium on biblical studies (New York, 1988), where he warned of the excesses of the historical-critical method: "The historical method can even serve as a cloak for such maneuvers insofar as it dissects the Bible into discontinuous pieces, which are then able to be put to new use and inserted into a new montage (altogether different from the original biblical context)."

259 Ratzinger, *Milestones*, 127.

260 Ratzinger, "Chapter I: Revelation Itself," 175-176.

261 Joseph Ratzinger, "Chapter II: The Transmission of Divine Revelation," *Commentary on the Documents of Vatican II*, Vol. 3, ed. by Herbert Vorgrimler (New York: Herder and Herder, 1967), 170-180, here 177.

262 Ratzinger, *Theological Highlights of Vatican II*, 60. See also Joseph Ratzinger, "Thoughts on the Place of Marian Doctrine and Piety in Faith and Theology as a Whole," *Communio* 30:1 (2003), 147-160.

263 O'Grady, "The Ratzinger Round," 409.

264 Ratzinger, *Theological Highlights of Vatican II*, 46; this reflects Ratzinger's eschatological interests, dating back to his earlier work on Bonaventure. Allen noted, "In the mind of Ratzinger, the most important document of Vatican II is the Dogmatic Constitution on the Church, *Lumen Gentium*. It capped the decades-long effort to restore a doctrine of the Church based on Scripture and the Fathers, and it attempted to restore a balance between pope and bishops that many felt had been lost after the declaration of papal infallibility at Vatican I." *Pope Benedict XVI*, 56.

265 Ratzinger, *Theological Highlights of Vatican II*, 47. See also Tracey Rowland, "Variations on the Theme of Christian Hope in the Work of Joseph Ratzinger-Benedict XVI," *Communio* 35:2 (2008), 200-220.

266 Joseph Ratzinger, *Die sakramentale Begründung christlicher Existenz* (Meitingen/Freising: Kyrios-Verlag, 1966), 19; cited in Jim Corkery, "Joseph Ratzinger's Theological Ideas 3–On Being Human," *Doctrine and Life* 56:7 (September 2006), 7-24, here 8.

267 Ratzinger, *Theological Highlights of Vatican II*, 10.

268 Nichols, *The Thought of Pope Benedict XVI*, 54.

269 Ratzinger, *Theological Highlights of Vatican II*, 39.

270 Ratzinger, *Theological Highlights of Vatican II*, 10. More so, as Murphy stated, "Christianity teaches us that the ultimate value is not the unnamable but that mysterious unity created by love and which is represented, beyond all our categories, in the Trinity and unity of God, which for its part is the highest picture of the reconciliation of unity and multiplicity." Joseph Murphy, *Christ Our Joy: The Theological Vision of Pope Benedict XVI* (San Francisco: Ignatius Press, 2008), 53.

271 Ratzinger, *Theological Highlights of Vatican II*, 55.

272 The Dogmatic Constitution on the Church *Lumen Gentium*, 16; available at http://www.vatican.va/archive/hist_councils/ii_vatican_council/documents/vat-ii_const_19641121_lumen-gentium_en.html; accessed 12 November 2009.

273 Philip Kennedy, OP, "Rome & Relativism: *'Dominus Iesus'* & the CDF," *Commonweal* 27:18 (October 20, 2000), 15.

274 Ratzinger, *Theological Highlights of Vatican II*, 51.

275 Joseph Ratzinger, *The Spirit of the Liturgy*, trans. by John Saward (San Francisco, Ignatius Press, 2000), 181f. Geoffrey Wainwright, "A Remedy for Relativism: The Cosmic, Historical and Eschatological Dimensions of the Liturgy according to the Theologian Joseph Ratzinger," *Nova et Vetera* 5 (2007), 403-429. Also, Ratzinger's former student, Francis Schüssler Fiorenza, "From Theologian to Pope: A personal view back, past the public portrayals," *Harvard Divinity Bulletin* 33 (Autumn 2005), 56-62.

276 Latin American Bishops, "Poverty of the Church," Medellin, Colombia (September 6, 1968), available from: http://www.shc.edu/theolibrary/resources/medpov.htm; accessed 4 February 2009.

277 Ratzinger, *Theological Highlights of Vatican II*, 48.

278 Ratzinger, "Review of the Post-conciliar Era – Failures, Tasks, Hopes," 376.

279 Ratzinger, *Theological Highlights of Vatican II*, 62.

280 Ratzinger, *Theological Highlights of Vatican II*, 62.

281 Ratzinger, *Theological Highlights of Vatican II*, 68.

282 Nichols observed that in *Introduction to Christianity*, p. 31, Ratzinger is seeking a "comparison for the contemporary theologian who, rather too often, if for the best of pastoral motives, waters down the content of the faith for the easier consumption of his hearers. The comparison he lights on is with 'Lucky Jack,' a folk-character whose lump of gold was so heavy that he was prevailed on to exchange it for increasingly valueless substitutes. Eventually, finishing up with a whetstone, Lucky Jack has no hesitation about chucking it away altogether." In *The Thought of Pope Benedict XVI*, 73.

283 Ratzinger, *Theological Highlights of Vatican II*, 70.

284 Ratzinger, *Theological Highlights of Vatican II*, 69.

285 Nichols, *The Thought of Pope Benedict XVI*, 97. Ratzinger, *Theological Highlights of Vatican II*, 71. In a radio interview in 1973 Ratzinger spoke of the "essence of the Church," where he said: "While the Church's essential structure, her uniqueness cannot be confined to or totally expressed by any human structure yet, since the Church is to a certain sense the product of history, this structure cannot be discovered in the abstract. It must be found in the form in which it has existed and continued to exist. Harnack, the great liberal Protestant theologian, once linked the attempts to establish the 'essence of Christianity' to the effort of the man who, trying to find the essence of a rose, removed the petals one by one until the rose disappeared; the essence was in the petals. The 'essence of the Church' is to be found in the community of hope, prayer and sacraments." O'Grady, "The Ratzinger Round," 410.

286 Ratzinger, *Theological Highlights of Vatican II*, 71.

287 Ratzinger, *Theological Highlights of Vatican II*, 139.

288 Ratzinger, *Theological Highlights of Vatican II*, 143.

289 Ratzinger, *Theological Highlights of Vatican II*, 145.

290 Ratzinger, *Theological Highlights of Vatican II*, 59.

291 Second Vatican Council, *Dignitatis Humanae*, Declaration on Religious Freedom (December 7, 1965); available from: http://www.ewtn.com/library/COUNCILS/v2relfre.htm; accessed 23 May 2009.

292 Ratzinger, *Theological Highlights of Vatican II*, 146, more on the issue of "the one true religion" see Paolo Gamberini, "'Subsistit' in Ecumenical Ecclesiology: J. Ratzinger and E. Jüngel," in *Irish Theological Quarterly* 72 (2007), 61-73. Also in Heim's *Joseph Ratzinger: Life in the Church and Living Theology/Fundamentals of Ecclesiology with Reference to Lumen Gentium*, 310-330.

293 Ratzinger, *Theological Highlights of Vatican II*, 146-147. Allen summarizes Ratzinger's view in the following words, "Ratzinger makes an urgently important point about submission to the truth. As sons and daughters of consumer culture conditioned to seek gratification, we are too often tempted to repress or rationalize truths that get in our way. We recoil at limits on our freedom, failing to distinguish between those limits that imprison because they are arbitrary, and those that liberate because they are rooted in our nature. We break faith and abandon commitments, and rationalize doing so on the basis of 'growth' or 'change'; we choose the path of least resistance and then exalt 'choice' into a moral principle. No one who listens to our political discourse, where content has been replaced by spin, can escape the sense that something toxic has been unleashed in this society. Ratzinger is right that a culture of lies reaches its apogee in Auschwitz, because when truth no longer puts limits to power, everyone is at risk. We need to recover faith in a standard beyond ourselves, in a truth that exists beyond the reach of our own subjectivity." *Pope Benedict XVI*, 304.

294 Giuseppe Alberigo, *A Brief History of Vatican II*, foreword by John W. O'Malley, SJ, trans. by Matthew Sherry (Maryknoll, NY: Orbis Books, 2006), 79.

295 Ratzinger, *Theological Highlights of Vatican II*, 151.

296 Ratzinger, *Theological Highlights of Vatican II*, 100.

297 Nichols, *The Thought of Pope Benedict XVI*, 68; Virgil Nemoianu suggests, "It is clear that Ratzinger's thinking derives from that of Hans Urs von Balthasar: a mode of thought that is extremely difficult to assign to either ecclesiastical 'conservatives' or 'liberals,' a thinking that goes back to the Patristic sources of Christianity, beyond its medieval structures and somewhat distanced from the pre-Vatican II neo-Thomism (though not necessarily hostile to it) and a mode of thought that admits the importance of the Beautiful at the level of the True and of the Good. However, unlike Balthasar and even his close counterpart the Jesuit priest (and eventually cardinal) Henri de Lubac, Ratzinger was more decisively steeped in the socio-historical issues of contemporaneity"; in Virgil Nemoianu, "The Church and the Secular Establishment: A Philosophical Dialog between Joseph Ratzinger and Jürgen Habermas," *Logos: A Journal of Catholic Thought and Culture*. Vol. 9:2 (Spring 2006), 16-42. Also Allen states, "On the other hand, defenders of Ratzinger often draw a distinction between two schools of thought at the council: *aggiornamento* and *ressourcement*, the latter being a 'return to the sources' impulse that found its primary expression in the liturgical movement, in the recovery of the Church fathers, and in a new appreciation for Scripture. Both scholars agreed on the need to break out of the Church's neoscholastic rut in the 1950s, but the *aggiornamento* people wanted to 'modernize' the Church and bring her into dialogue with the culture, whereas the *ressourcement* circle wanted to recover elements of tradition that had been lost." *Pope Benedict XVI*, 57.

[298] Jim Corkery in his article "Joseph Ratzinger's Theological Ideas 2–The Facial Features of a Theological *Corpus*," *Doctrine and Life* 56:4 (April, 2006), 2-12, here 9 argues, "Ratzinger's celebrated book *Introduction to Christianity* presented not so much an *incarnational theology* but rather a newly emphasized *theology of the cross* that, in Walter Kasper's view, deserved further unfolding," and therefore Kasper, aside from the initial review of *Introduction to Christianity* wrote another article, "Theorie und Praxis innerhalb einer theologia cruces: Antwort auf J. Ratzinger's 'Glaube, Geschichte und Philosophie'" in *Hochland* 62 (March/April 1970), 152-157; more on this dispute see, Jim Corkery, "Joseph Ratzinger's Theological Ideas 4–*Quaestiones Disputatae* 1," *Doctrine and Life* 56:10 (December 2006), 12-24.

[299] Ratzinger, *Theological Highlights of Vatican II*, 102.

[300] Joseph Ratzinger, "The Dignity of the Human Person," *Commentary on the Documents of Vatican II*, Vol. 5, ed. by Herbert Vorgrimler (New York: Herder and Herder, 1967), 116-117.

[301] Ratzinger, "The Dignity of the Human Person," 117.

[302] Ratzinger, *Theological Highlights of Vatican II*, 157. Allen states, "The modern revolt against objectivity was, in its origins, partly a rebellion against ecclesiastical authority that abused the concept of truth to secure its own power. One can argue that Ratzinger's concern for truth is not fully consistent unless he renounces the inquisitorial abuses that helped make skepticism seem plausible in the first place." *Pope Benedict XVI*, 304.

[303] Allen, *Pope Benedict XVI*, 100.

[304] Ratzinger, "The Dignity of the Human Person," 118.

[305] Nichols, *The Thought of Pope Benedict XVI*, 57.

[306] Ratzinger, *Theological Highlights of Vatican II*, 155; Ratzinger also says: "In the background here, there is not only the thought of the actual contradictions in modern thought and in the attempts made in all ages to construct a doctrine of man, but also of Pascal's saying about the mysterious polarity of man between 'grandeur' and 'misère.'" In Ratzinger's "The Dignity of the Human Person," 120.

[307] Ratzinger, "The Dignity of the Human Person," 121; Allen notes, "Ratzinger disassociated himself from the document's language [*Gaudium et Spes*] on the human being as the image of God, arguing that strictly speaking the human person is the image of God only through Christ and thus it refers more to a future promise than an essential endowment." *Pope Benedict XVI*, 80. More on this issue of sin in Corkery's "Joseph Ratzinger's Theological Ideas 2–The Facial Features of a Theological *Corpus*," 9, footnote 16, where he suggested seeing Ratzinger's "Gratia praesupponit naturam," 178-180.

[308] Ratzinger, "The Dignity of the Human Person," 128.

[309] Rowland states, "Newman's choice of motto was the very Augustinian *Cor ad cor loquitur* (Heart speaks to the heart) and it was to this very Pascalian respect for the 'reasons of heart' that Ratzinger was drawn." Rowland's *Ratzinger's Faith*, 3.

[310] Ratzinger, *Theological Highlights of Vatican II*, 159. See Joseph Ratzinger, "Eschatology and Utopia," *Communio* 5:3 (1978), 211-227.

[311] Ratzinger, *Theological Highlights of Vatican II*, 160. Ernest Geller in his book *Postmodernism, Reason and Religion* (London and New York: Routledge, 1992), 58-60 argues, "The relentless spread of science and technology throughout the world is the strongest evidence of positivism's transcultural validity. Key ele-

ments of science may have arisen in the West, but its logic is available to members of all societies and is generally recognized by them as superior (materially, if not morally) when they become fully conversant with it." As it was found in Brown, "Cultural Relativism," 367. See also Joseph Ratzinger, "Technology and Security as a Problem of Social Ethics," *Communio* 9:3 (1982), 238-246.

312 Ratzinger, *Theological Highlights of Vatican II*, 162. Almost thirty years later Ratzinger is still arguing, "While mystery is not thereby abolished, relativism, to be sure, is excluded, for relativism cuts man off from truth, making him a slave. Man's real poverty is darkness to truth. He becomes free for the first time when he is obliged to serve truth alone." In "Christ, Faith, and the Challenge of Cultures," available from: http://www.ewtn.com/library/CURIA/RATZHONG.HTM; accessed 14 November 2009. Allen pointed out that: "Ratzinger remarks that too many modern Christians have been enchanted by the 'cheerful romanticism of progress.' Indeed, Ratzinger says, looking at the crucified one tells us what sort of 'openness' to the world Christians should expect and embrace – the openness of sacrifice." 96, and in the ending remarks of his book Allen says himself: "But in his [Ratzinger's] insistence that Christian spirituality must not skip from Incarnation to Resurrection without passing through the Passion, that Christians must sometimes invite scorn and embrace sacrifice in order to be faithful, Ratzinger is striking exactly the note his Church needs to hear." *Pope Benedict XVI*, 306.

313 Ratzinger, *Theological Highlights of Vatican II*, 167.

314 Ratzinger, *Salt of the Earth*, 60.

315 Ratzinger, *Theological Highlights of Vatican II*, 173.

316 Ratzinger, *Theological Highlights of Vatican II*, 174. Pursell noted that years later, "When discussing the stupendous economic growth experienced in the latter half of the 20th century, the Cardinal stated that this was not necessarily and purely a good thing. In the newfound wealth and the so-called ethics of market capitalism, he saw 'a sign of the Satanic in the way in which people exploit the market for pornography and drugs in the West.'" Pursell, *Benedict of Bavaria*, 67. See also Joseph Ratzinger, "Church and Economy: Responsibility for the Future of the World Economy," *Communio* 13:3 (1986), 199-204.

317 Ratzinger, *Theological Highlights of Vatican II*, 184.

318 Ratzinger, *Theological Highlights of Vatican II*, 185.

319 Found in Fahey's article "Joseph Ratzinger as Ecclesiologist and Pastor," 78, where he references footnote 7, C. Modehn in *Informations Catholiques Internationales*. 547 (14 February 1980), 18.

320 Nichols, *The Thought of Pope Benedict XVI*, 71.

321 Ratzinger, *Milestones*, 133-134.

322 In a radio interview given to Desmond O'Grady, "The Ratzinger Round," Ratzinger acknowledged "theologians were sought for interviews by mass-circulation magazines and television. For another, Küng propounded a theory that there were two forms of leadership in the Church: the bishops, who are mainly pastors and the theologians, who are prophets. Ratzinger commented: 'Küng's theory was really a fairly accurate description of the new, rather exaggerated self-consciousness of the theologians immediately after the council. The experience of addressing scores of bishops – and being listened to – proved rather heady wine. This theory, however, is neither true to the theologian's function nor does it do justice to the total concept of the bishop's office – which cannot be simply opposed to the role of the theologian.'" O'Grady, "The Ratzinger Round," 409-410.

323 Gianni Valente, "Tradition and Freedom: The Lectures of the Young Joseph," *30 Days*, Nr. 3 (2006), available from http://www.30giorni.it/us/articolo_stampa. asp?id=10284; accessed 24 March 2009.

324 Fahey, "Joseph Ratzinger as Ecclesiologist and Pastor," 78. Cites Ratzinger "Catholicism after the Council," *Furrow* 18 (1967), 3-23, here 4. Gregory Baum observed that it was parapraph 44 in *Gaudium et Spes*, that allowed relativism to enter the Church which, he also said, "under the influence of bishops and theologians from the industrialized nations, affirmed the modern world in its development toward greater freedom, greater prosperity, greater technological achievements, and greater participation of people in the making of public decisions." Baum, *Truth beyond Relativism*, 2.

325 Ratzinger, *Milestones*, 134; Ratzinger gives an extensive treatment of the postconciliar time in his "Church and World: An inquiry into the Reception of Vatican Council II," in Joseph Ratzinger, *Principles of Catholic Theology: Building Stones for a Fundamental Theology*, trans. by Mary Frances McCarthy, SND (San Francisco: Ignatius Press, 1989), 378-393.

326 Girard, "Ratzinger is Right," 45. Girard also adds, "Remember, Ratzinger was a supporter of the Second Vatican Council that reformed the Church in the 1960s. He opposed the idea that the Church should stand still in a modernizing world. For him, to be a Roman Catholic is to accept that the Church has something to learn from the world. At the same time, there is a Truth that doesn't change the Gospel. Today, he is just reaffirming his position. He is just standing his ground." See also Avery Cardinal Dulles, SJ, "From Ratzinger to Benedict," *First Things* 160 (Fall 2006), 24-29.

327 Twomey, *Pope Benedict XVI. The Conscience of Our Age: A Theological Portrait*, 33. See also Vincent D. Twomey, SVD, "The Mind of Benedict XVI," *Claremont Review of Books*, (Fall 2005), 66-71.

328 Virgil Nemoianu notes, "it is somewhat difficult to assess accurately the number of publications by Ratzinger, since some of them tend to overlap and the versions in different languages are not always identical"; "The Church and the Secular Establishment: A Philosophical Dialog between Joseph Ratzinger and Jürgen Habermas," 18. The most recent complete bibliography of Ratzinger's writings up to his election to the papacy came out in German under the title *Joseph Ratzinger/Papst Benedikt XVI. Das Werk: Veröffentlichungen bis zur PAPSTWAHL*, ed. by Vinzenz Pfnür, published by his students (Augsburg: Sankt Ulrich Verlag, 2009). A fairly good English bibliography may be found in Joseph Ratzinger, *Pilgrim Fellowship of Faith: The Church as Communion*, Stephen Otto and Vinzenz Pfnür, eds. (San Francisco: Ignatius Press, 2005).

329 The last exception would be his book on eschatology *Eschatologie – Tod und ewiges Leben* (Regensburg, 1977). E.T. *Eschatology, Death and Eternal Life* (Washington DC, 1988). As for the rest cf. Joseph Ratzinger, *Values in a Time of Upheaval*, trans. by Brian McNeil (San Francisco: Ignatius Press, 2006), 7-8; where Ratzinger wrote: "Much in this book is a mere sketch, more question than answer. But perhaps it is precisely the incomplete character of these essays that may provide a spur to further thinking on these subjects." Also in his *Principles of Catholic Theology: Building Stones for a Fundamental Theology*, he notes, "What a collection of these works can offer is but a tentative sketch, a preliminary draft, of a great theme which it approaches from the variety of angles. I am well aware of the fragmentary and unfinished nature of these efforts." 11.

330 Jim Corkery, SJ in his article "Joseph Ratzinger's Theological Ideas 6–Resist-

ing the 'Dictatorship of Relativism,'" *Doctrine and Life* 57:6 (2007), 2-20, here 6, footnote 14 referenced Robert Moynihan, ed., *Let God's Light Shine Forth: The Spiritual Vision of Pope Benedict XVI*. Part I: "The Man and His Life," by Robert Moynihan (London: Hutchinson, 2005) 3-75, at page 54. Corkery notes "Moynihan dates the anti-relativism writings from 1982, but it was in the 1990s that they really flourished."

331 Found in *The Essential Pope Benedict XVI: His Central Writings and Speeches*, 227-240; also appears in the first chapter of part two in Ratzinger's *Truth and Tolerance: Christian Belief and World Religions*, trans. by Henry Taylor (San Francisco: Ignatius Press, 2004), 115-137.

332 Avery Cardinal Dulles notes, "Throughout the 1980s Cardinal Ratzinger was one of the outstanding opponents of this kind of reductionism. In the language of Augustine, he maintained that the city of man can never become the city of God. In the name of Christianity, he opposed the myth that depicts the kingdom of God as the product of politics. Faith, for him, must seek to prevent the political from dominating the whole life." Avery Cardinal Dulles, SJ, "John F. Scarpa Conference on Law, Politics and Culture: The Indirect Mission of the Church to Politics," *Villanova Law Review* 52:2 (2007), 241-252, here 244.

333 Ratzinger, "Relativism: The Central Problem for Faith Today,"in *The Essential Pope Benedict XVI: His Central Writings and Speeches*, John F. Thornton and Susan B. Varenne, eds., 227-228 (New York: HarperCollins Publishers, 2007).

334 Ratzinger, *Many Religions – One Covenant*, 17.

335 Cf. Joseph Ratzinger, *Faith and the Future*, trans. by Ronald Walls (Chicago, IL: Franciscan Herald Press, 1970), 81-83. Allen speaks of Ratzinger's book *Death and Eternal Life*, trans. by Michael Waldstein (Washington, DC: Catholic University of America Press, 1988) in which "Ratzinger argues for the need to 'detach eschatology from politics,' to never construe the Reign of God with some this-worldly social or political order. This, he argues, does not mean disengagement from politics, but rather a relativization of politics that sets limits to power and ultimately upends totalitarianism." *The Rise of Pope Benedict XVI*, 152. See also Jim Corkery, SJ, "Joseph Ratzinger's Theological Ideas 4–*Quaestiones Disputatae* 1," especially 18-24.

336 Ratzinger, "Relativism: The Central Problem for Faith Today," 228.

337 Nichols, *The Thought of Pope Benedict XVI*, 43.

338 Joseph Cardinal Ratzinger with Vittorio Messori, *The Ratzinger Report: An Exclusive Interview on the State of the Church*, trans. by Salvator Attanasio and Graham Harrison (San Francisco: Ignatius Press, 1986); David Gibson notes the appearance of *The Ratzinger Report* was "a bombshell" where "Ratzinger's blunt observations and criticism created headlines and cemented his hardline reputation." In David Gibson, *The Rule of Benedict: Pope Benedict XVI and his Battle with the Modern World* (San Francisco: Harper, 2006), 370; as cited by Jim Corkery in his article "Joseph Ratzinger's Theological Ideas 5–*Questiones Disputatae* 2: Theological Dissent," 35-48.

339 Allen states "The formal debut of Ratzinger as a critic of liberation theology came in 1978, when Pope John Paul II made Ratzinger, then the cardinal of Munich, his legate to a national Marian congress in Guayaquil, Ecuador. 'It would be a terrible misfortune,' Ratzinger said in this September 1978 address, if America 'sold out its soul,' bewitched by European economic and technological achievements, and gave itself over to a 'culture of having.' This culture, Ratzinger warned, is most likely to present itself in the guise of Marxism. He

said that both of the 'great rationalisms' of the age – Western-positivist and Eastern-Marxist – have led the world into a deep crisis." *Pope Benedict XVI*, 148; Allen also argues, that since both Ratzinger and Balthasar sat on the International Commission in the 1970's and helped to shape its 1977 statement "Human Development and Christian Salvation," one can assume that Ratzinger shared at least part of Balthasar's critique, which Allen gives a summary of in pages 141-142 of his book *Pope Benedict XVI*. See also Michael Sharkey, ed., *International Theological Commission: Texts and Documents 1969-1985*. Preface by Joseph Cardinal Ratzinger (San Francisco: Ignatius Press, 1989).

[340] Congregation for the Doctrine of the Faith, "Instruction on Certain Aspects of the 'Theology of Liberation'" (6 August 1984); available from: http://www.vatican.va/roman-curia/congregations/cfaith/documents/rc_con_cfaith_doc_19840806_theology-liberation_en.html; accessed 23 July 2009.

[341] Ratzinger and Messori, *The Ratzinger Report*, 174.

[342] Ratzinger and Messori, *The Ratzinger Report*, 176.

[343] Ratzinger and Messori, *The Ratzinger Report*, 179-180. The term *Hermeneutics*, "while seeking to establish the original meaning of a text in its historical context and to express that meaning today, recognizes that a text can contain and convey meaning that goes beyond the original author's explicit intention." Gerald O'Collins and Edward G. Ferrugia, *A Concise Dictionary of Theology* (New York: Paulist Press, 2000), s.v. "Hermeneutics," 103.

[344] Nichols, *The Thought of Pope Benedict XVI*, 58.

[345] Ratzinger and Messori, *The Ratzinger Report*, 181.

[346] Ratzinger and Messori, *The Ratzinger Report*, 184-185. Elsewhere, presenting his understanding of the fourth world assembly of the World Council of Churches in Upsala in 1968, Ratzinger sees them employing the perspective where "truth is considered as unattainable and its proclamation only an alibi for group interests which are thus consolidated. Only praxis can decide the value or lack of value of theories." Ratzinger, "Magisterium of the Church, Faith and Morality," *Problems of the Church Today* (Washington, 1976), 74-83, here 74. Jim Corkery critiques what he calls "Ratzinger's legendary nervousness about praxis theologies – and an excessive emphasis on the *divine* side in the divine-human reality that is grace, incarnation, even Church." Corkery thinks that in this tendency to *spiritualize* and to be *world-wary*, Ratzinger is greatly influenced by Bonaventure and Augustine. Corkery, "Joseph Ratzinger's Theological Ideas 3–On Being Human," 19.

[347] Ratzinger and Messori, *The Ratzinger Report*, 184.

[348] Ratzinger and Messori, *The Ratzinger Report*, 186.

[349] Ratzinger, "Review of the Post-conciliar Era – Failures, Tasks, Hopes," 377.

[350] Jim Corkery, "Joseph Ratzinger's Theological Ideas 6–Resisting the 'Dictatorship of Relativism,'" 3; Corkery wrote a doctoral dissertation on Ratzinger's theology. See James Corkery, *The Relationship between Human Existence and Christian Salvation in the Theology of Joseph Ratzinger* (Washington DC: The Catholic University of America, 1991). Authorized facsimile available from University Microfilms International, Ann Arbor, Michigan, 1992.

[351] Ratzinger, "Relativism: The Central Problem for Faith Today," 235. See also Heim, *Joseph Ratzinger: Life in the Church and Living Theology/Fundamentals of Ecclesiology with Reference to Lumen Gentium*, 389-395.

[352] Jeffrey Stout, "A House Founded on the Sea: Is Democracy a Dictatorship of Relativism?" in *A "Dictatorship of Relativism"? Symposium in Response to Cardi-*

nal Ratzinger's Last Homily. Common Knowledge 13:2-3 (2007), 385-403, here 387.

353 Ratzinger, "Relativism: The Central Problem for Faith Today," 235-236.

354 Joseph Ratzinger *Das neue Volk Gottes. Entwürfe zur Ekklesiologie* (Düsseldorf, 1969), 144; as cited by Nichols in his *The Thought of Pope Benedict XVI*, 100. Also on this issue, see Joseph Ratzinger and Hans Meier, *Demokratie in der Kirche. Möglichkeiten, Grenzen, Gefahren* (Limburg, 1970) where Ratzinger criticized Rahner's views developed in *Freiheit und Manipulation in Gesellschaft und Kirche* (1970). This reference is taken from Fahey, "Joseph Ratzinger as Ecclesiologist and Pastor," 81.

355 Allen, *The Rise of Benedict XVI*, 2.

356 Pursell states, "*Communio sanctorum*, in the original Latin, first denotes holy *things:* 'the faith, the sacraments, especially the Eucharist, the charisms, and the other spiritual gifts.' In addition, the same phrase refers to 'all the faithful of Christ,' living *and* dead, 'all together forming one Church.' We, the living, must remember that we worship Christ *with* and *for* the departed." Pursell, *Benedict of Bavaria*, 33. See also *Catechism of the Catholic Church*, 2nd ed. (New York: Doubleday, 1995). 272.

357 Allen, *Pope Benedict XVI*, 99.

358 Allen, *Pope Benedict XVI*, 264. Allan also adds, "Ratzinger is right when he talks about the diachronic nature of the sense of the faithful. I am reminded of G.K. Chesterton's argument that tradition is nothing more than democracy extended through time, that it is precisely a sense of tradition that protects the Church against the tyranny of the present." 304.

359 John K.S. Reid, "The Ratzinger Report," *Scottish Journal of Theology* 40.1: (1987), 126-133, here 126.

360 Ratzinger and Messori, *The Ratzinger Report*, 45. For example Philip Kennedy, OP, who teaches theology at the University of Oxford and who argues, "The contemporary hierarchically constituted Catholic Church is unable to regard itself as directly historically continuous with the ministry of Jesus Christ because he did not establish a Church with bishops and diocesan structures to break away from Judaism. Rather, he preached the Kingdom of God to rejuvenate Israel's religious life and enlisted the help of twelve primary Apostles in his mission to Israel. The Church evolved over time after his death and in response to him." In Philip Kennedy, OP, "Rome & Relativism: '*Dominus Iesus*' & the CDF," 15.

361 Reid, "The Ratzinger Report," 126.

362 Ratzinger and Messori, *The Ratzinger Report*, 24. See Ratzinger, "Sources and Transmission of the Faith," 17-34.

363 Reid, "The Ratzinger Report," 127.

364 Nichols, *The Thought of Pope Benedict XVI*, 56.

365 Reid, "The Ratzinger Report," 129.

366 Ratzinger and Messori, *The Ratzinger Report*, 36.

367 Ratzinger, "Relativism: The Central Problem for Faith Today," 236.

368 Ratzinger and Messori, *The Ratzinger Report*, 187.

369 Ratzinger and Messori, *The Ratzinger Report*, 188.

370 Ratzinger and Messori, *The Ratzinger Report*, 190.

371 Ratzinger, "Relativism: The Central Problem for Faith Today," 228.

372 Ratzinger, *A Turning Point for Europe*, 103. Larry Laudan, in his *Beyond Positivism and Relativism: Theory, Method, and Evidence* (Boulder, CO: Westview

Press, 1996), 3, wrote, "By the mid-1970s, however, the general philosophical climate had changed considerably. In part as a result of the influential ideas of my teacher Thomas Kuhn and my (sometime) colleague Paul Feyerabend, positivism had become passé in many circles, only to be replaced by various forms of epistemological and methodological relativism."

373 Ratzinger observed, "One who abandons Marxism has not thereby automatically found a new foundation on which to base his life. The loss of a hitherto life-supporting ideology can very easily result in nihilism." *A Turning Point for Europe*, 147. See also Brown, "Cultural Relativism," where Brown notes, "Nowhere is relativism's stock higher than among undergraduates. I am not alone in having observed a steady shift in student values toward uncritical acceptance of almost any behavior that can be justified in terms of the actor's culture." 363. For more on the issue of Nietzsche, nihilism and relativism see Phillip E. Devine, *Relativism, Nihilism and God* (Notre Dame, IN: Notre Dame University Press, 1989).

374 Ratzinger, "Relativism: The Central Problem for Faith Today," 228.

375 In his article "Joseph Ratzinger's Theological Ideas 6–Resisting the 'Dictatorship of Relativism'" Corkery notes that Ratzinger "sees *analogy* as keeping us ever mindful of the human being's limitations with regard to truth, but he points out that, within the human boundaries that do obtain, analogy (which 'can always be broadened and deepened') does declare truth and is not to be equated with 'metaphor.' Thus, while Ratzinger rejects relativism, he has no difficulty saying that our statements about God admit of a certain *relativising*. The words of St. Augustine are never far from his thoughts; and it was Augustine who remarked that, if we have understood, then it is not God." 6; he also cites Ratzinger's essay "The Spiritual Basis and Ecclesial Identity of Theology" in *The Nature and Mission of Theology. Approaches to Understanding its Role in the Light of Present Controversy* (San Francisco: Ignatius Press, 1995), 45-72, here 56. See also Joseph Cardinal Ratzinger, *God and the World: A Conversation with Peter Seewald* (San Francisco: Ignatius Press, 2002), 34.

376 Romano Guardini, *Bericht über mein Leben: Autobiographische Aufzeichnungen* (Düsseldorf, 1984), 111, as it was found in Ratzinger's *A Turning Point for Europe*, 66. After citing Guardini, Ratzinger concludes "These sentences of this great teacher seem to be a completely appropriate indication of the true essence of a new distinction between the secular order and faith, as well as the essence of a correct praxeology, a correct statement of the relationship between faith and praxis." 66.

377 Ratzinger, *Truth and Tolerance*, 126.

378 Michael Novak, "Culture in Crisis" available at: www.nationalreview.com/novak/novak-archive.asp; accessed 19 May 2006; also in *Salt of the Earth*, Ratzinger says, "It seems to modern man undemocratic, intolerant and also incompatible with the scientist's necessary skepticism to say that we have the truth and that something else is not the truth, or is only fragmentary truth. Precisely this democratic understanding of life and the concomitant idea of toleration has made the question of whether we are entitled to go on with our Christian self-understanding a burning one" 134. For more on the issue of toleration see Alasdair MacIntyre, "Toleration and the goods of conflict," in *The politics of toleration in modern life*, ed. Susan Mendus (Durham, NY: Duke University Press, 2000), 133-155.

379 Ratzinger, "Relativism: The Central Problem for Faith Today," 229. Also, Ratz-

inger adds, "Freedom is equated with the absence of ties and everything that removes ties appears to be progress," where "The word 'progress' has become a satellite of the post-Hegelian philosophy of history." *A Turning Point for Europe*, 88.

380 Ratzinger, *Truth and Tolerance*, 117-118.

381 Joseph Ratzinger, *Christianity and the Crisis of Cultures*, Introduction by Marcello Pera, trans. by Brian McNeil (San Francisco: Ignatius Press, 2006), 44. Allen notes, "Ratzinger argues that for Europe to build a human civilization, it must rediscover two elements of its past: its classical Greek heritage and its common Christian identity.... From the classical era, Europe should rediscover objective and eternal values that stand above politics, placing limits on power. Ratzinger uses the Greek term *eunomia* to describe this concept of the good; in that sense, one could say that Ratzinger is proposing a eunomic, rather than economic, model of European integration.... Christian anthropology, Ratzinger argues, should provide the values for this new eunomic European civilization. It is in the effort to build such a new Europe that Ratzinger holds out the most hope for ecumenical cooperation." *Pope Benedict XVI*, 224- 225.

382 Ratzinger, *Christianity and the Crisis of Cultures*, 44.

383 Ratzinger, *Christianity and the Crisis of Cultures*, 45.

384 In an article "Ratzinger absolutely wrong on relativism," which John Hick wrote after having read the text of "Relativism: The Central Problem for Faith Today," he corrects Ratzinger by saying, "what he calls an American Presbyterian (I am not in fact an American, although I taught for a number of years, very happily, in the United States." Also, he writes "my regret, however, is that internal evidence reveals that he [Ratzinger] has relied on secondary sources that have provided him with a misleading version of what I have written." John Hick, "Ratzinger absolutely wrong on relativism," *National Catholic Reporter* (October 24, 1997). See also Allen's *Pope Benedict XVI*, 240.

385 Hick, "Ratzinger absolutely wrong on relativism." He also quotes St. Thomas Aquinas' maxim, "Things known are in the knower according to the mode of the knower" (S.T. II/II, Q. 1, art. 2). See John Hick, *An Interpretation of Religion: Human Responses to the Transcendent* (New Haven and London: Yale University Press, 1989), 236-245. Francis X. Clooney, "Relativism in perspective: rereading Ratzinger," *Commonweal* (January 31, 1997), 9-10, on page 9, summarizes Hick's position on pluralism: "It is philosophically and theologically necessary to distinguish between reality and our perceptions of it and, accordingly, it is also necessary to expect an enduring plurality of religious view points."

386 Ratzinger, "Relativism: The Central Problem for Faith Today," 230.

387 See John Hick, ed., *The Myth of God Incarnate* (Philadelphia, PA: The Westminster Press, 1977). See also Ernst Troeltsch (1865-1923), who "spent his career arguing against (as he called one of his books) *The Absoluteness of Christianity*. For him an 'absolute' Christology would be the theological equivalent of geocentrism in astronomy or anthropocentrism in evolutionary biology (two telling analogies)." In Edward T. Oakes, SJ, "On Relativism," *First Things* (September 2007), available from: www.firstthings.com/onthesquare/?p=840; accessed 6 March 2009.

388 Ratzinger, "Relativism: The Central Problem for Faith Today," 230. Philip Kennedy, OP, argues for religious pluralism in the same line as Hick, saying, "Yet religious pluralism is unavoidable because of the ineffability or complexity of God. Because God is illimitable, no historical reality can manifest the full

richness of God. Jesus Christ is not the complete revelation of God in history, but a partial manifestation of what God may be like. Since Jesus is not the unveiling of the fullness of God in the world, other religions may have their say about God's salvific nature. Even according to classical dogmatic theology, Jesus Christ is the enfleshment in history of the Second Person of the Trinity. The fullness of the Trinity is not incarnate in Jesus. Consequently, there is more to God, so to speak, than had been shown in Jesus Christ." Kennedy, "Rome & Relativism: 'Dominus Iesus' & the CDF," 15.

389 Ratzinger, "Relativism: The Central Problem for Faith Today," 231; Allen notes, "Of Hick, Ratzinger says that in his thinking 'concepts such as Church, dogma and sacraments must lose their unconditional character.... The notion of dialogue becomes the quintessence of the relativist creed and the antithesis of conversion and mission.... The relativist dissolution of Christology, and even more eschatology, thus becomes a central commandment of religion.'" *Pope Benedict XVI*, 240.

390 Ratzinger, *Truth and Tolerance*, 120.

391 Ratzinger, *Truth and Tolerance*, 120.

392 Ratzinger, "Relativism: The Central Problem for Faith Today," 230.

393 Ratzinger, "Relativism: The Central Problem for Faith Today," 231; in footnote 2, Ratzinger refers to "Il christianesimo e le altre religione," in *Civiltà Cattolica* 1 (January 20, 1996): 107-120. See also Raimundo Panikkar, "The Jordan, the Tiber and the Ganges: Three Kairological Moments of Christic Self-Consciousness," in *The Myth of Christian Uniqueness: Toward a Pluralistic Theology of Religion*, John Hick and Paul F. Knitter eds. (Maryknoll, NY: Orbis Books, 1987), 89-116. Allen states, "Of Panikkar's argument that Christological formulas are not reversible – for example, that Jesus is Christ, but Christ is not only Jesus – Ratzinger says this must be rejected. One cannot argue that 'Christ' is also found in Buddhism, Hinduism, and so on, because to do so is to posit a discarnate Christ." *Pope Benedict XVI*, 238. On Balasuria see Clooney's "Relativism in perpective: rereading Ratzinger," p. 9.

394 Ratzinger wrote, "The real content of Christianity is not the discussion of its Christian content and of ways of realizing it.... The dream of making one's whole life a series of discussions, which, for a time, brought even our universities to the brink of paralysis, also exercised an influence on the Church under the label of the conciliar idea." In Ratzinger, "Review of the Post-conciliar Era–Failures, Tasks, Hopes," 374.

395 Joseph Ratzinger, "Interreligious Dialogue and Relations," a text prepared for a session of the *Académie des sciences morales et politiques* (Paris) and published in *Communio* 25:1 (Spring 1998), 29-41, here 34. See also Martin E. Marty, "Rome & Relativism: 'Dominus Iesus' & the CDF," *Commonweal* 27:18 (October 20, 2000), 12-14, here 12, where Marty notes, "Anyone who cares about spreading the truth of Christ, a.k.a. evangelism and about dialogue among the religions, has to know that you can 'give the store away' in dealings with other faiths on an open market."

396 Ratzinger, "Relativism: The Central Problem for Faith Today," 229. René Girard accordingly argues, "Western civilization is, no doubt, predominantly on the side of secular relativism. That is not true in the Islamic world, where faith dominates. This victory of relativism is precisely why Pope Benedict has made defending the Christian Truth his central mission." Girard, "Ratzinger is Right," 44.

397 See Joseph Cardinal Ratzinger, "Christ, Faith and the Challenge of Cultures," available from: http://www.ewtn.com/library/CURIA/RATZHONG.HTM, accessed 14 November 2009.

398 Ratzinger, "Relativism: The Central Problem for Faith Today," 231. Allen observed that Ratzinger "worries that Hindu 'negative theology' lends support to relativism. In his 1991 book *The Nature and Mission of Theology*, Ratzinger approvingly quotes psychologist Albert Görres about the 'Hinduization' of Catholicism, in which doctrinal propositions no longer matter because the important thing is contact with a spiritual atmosphere that leads beyond everything that can be said." Also, "Ratzinger's concern with Eastern contamination of Christianity was expressed in a December 14, 1989, document of the doctrinal congregation on *Some aspects of Christian meditation*. Its purpose was to establish guidelines for the use of prayer and meditation methods 'inspired by Hinduism and Buddhism, such as Zen, transcendental meditation, or yoga.'" *Pope Benedict XVI*, 254. See "Some aspects of Christian meditation," available at: http://www.ewtn.com/library/curia/cdfmed.htm; accessed 11 March 2009.

399 Ratzinger, "Relativism: The Central Problem for Faith Today," 231.

400 Felix Wilfred, *Beyond Settled Foundations: The Journey of Indian Theology* (Madras (India): University of Madras, 1993); the document prepared by the Pontifical Council for Interreligious Dialogue: *Pro Dialogo*, Bulletin, 85-86 (1994/1), 40-57.

401 Kenneth J. Gergen, "Relativism, Religion and Relational Being," in *A "Dictatorship of Relativism"? Symposium in Response to Cardinal Ratzinger's Last Homily. Common Knowledge* 13:2-3 (2007), 362-378, here 367.

402 Brown states, "Today's consensus is that, as originally conceived, cultural relativism has significant flaws. It tends to exaggerate the internal coherence of individual cultures. It overstates differences between societies and underestimates the possibility of transcending these differences. Its totalizing quality invites moral minimalism and fosters hostility to comparative analysis. The logic of relativism is so inherently powerful that when used indiscriminately it can subvert almost any argument." Brown, "Cultural Relativism," 371.

403 Ratzinger, "Relativism: The Central Problem for Faith Today," 231-232.

404 John Hick, *Evil and the God of Love* (New York: Harper & Row, 1966).

405 Ratzinger, "Relativism: The Central Problem for Faith Today," 232. Hick in his article "Ratzinger absolutely wrong on relativism," argues that Ratzinger aside from citing the wrong pages (it is on p. 300), also misinterpreted what he was referring to on a given point. Hick states that Ratzinger "then goes on to misrepresent it by missing the vertical dimension of transcendence and reducing it to a purely horizontal horizon.... But any reader of *An interpretation of Religion* knows that by 'the transformation of human existence from self-centeredness to reality-centeredness,' I am referring to a radically new orientation centered in the divine reality as mediated to us in our religion." However, Hick also acknowledges, "such a suggestion will of course be totally unacceptable from the standpoint of a Christian absolutism that insists upon the unique superiority of Christianity, or of the Church, as the sole channel of divine saving grace."

406 Ratzinger, *A Turning Point for Europe*, 87.

407 Ratzinger, *Introduction to Christianity*, 175-176. See also Joseph Ratzinger, "Retrieving the Tradition: Concerning the Notion of Person in Theology," *Communio* 17 (Fall 1990), 439-454, especially 445-450.

408 Corkery, "Joseph Ratzinger's Theological Ideas 3–On Being Human," 14-15,

cites Ratzinger's *The God of Jesus Christ* (Chicago, IL: Franciscan Herald Press, 1979), 47; "Salvation History, Metaphysics and Eschatology," in Ratzinger's *Principles of Catholic Theology: Building Stones for a Fundamental Theology* (San Francisco: Ignatius Press, 1987), 171-179, at 187; also Joseph Ratzinger, *"In the Beginning…": A Catholic Understanding of the Story of Creation and the Fall* (Edinburgh: T&T Clark, 1995), 48-49.

[409] Ratzinger, "Relativism: The Central Problem for Faith Today," 232; Ratzinger cites Paul Knitter, *No Other Name?: A Critical Survey of Christian Attitudes Toward the World Religions* (Maryknoll, NY: Orbis Books, 1985). Francis X. Clooney notes that in his *No Other Name?* Knitter "argued on several grounds (including intellectual consistency, the sheer fact of religious diversity, and the values implied in a commitment to honest dialogue) that narrow views of religion – only Christ saves, all salvation is channeled through Christ – must give way before the realization that God, not any particular naming of God, is the core of religious faith. What matters most is that all religious persons share a commitment to the just transformation of the world." In Clooney, "Relativism in perspective: rereading Ratzinger," 10.

[410] Ratzinger, "Relativism: The Central Problem for Faith Today," 232. Allen observes, "Ratzinger sees Knitter as the primary exponent of the pluralist view that praxis is more important than dogma. Interreligious dialogue should focus on building the kingdom, not on points of doctrine. Thus for Knitter, according to Ratzinger, interreligious dialogue reduces to an ethical or political program. This, Ratzinger says, is a self-contradictory stance, because if one abandons objective truth, then who is to say any particular ethics or politics is correct? 'The relativist theories all flow into a state of non being obligatorily and thus become superfluous, or else they presume to have an absolute standard which is not found in the praxis, by elevating it to an absolutism that has really no place.'" *Pope Benedict XVI*, 240.

[411] Ratzinger, "Relativism: The Central Problem for Faith Today," 233.

[412] Ratzinger, *Introduction to Christianity*, 24. See also Ratzinger's mention of Neo-Hinduism, in his address "Christ, Faith, and the Challenge of Cultures," where he notes, "Neo-Hinduism, as represented for example by Radhakrishnan, rests on the fusion of traditional Indian traditions with a late form of Western Christianity. One can no doubt see it as a synthesis of culture and religion, but perhaps it would even be better categorized as a type of philosophy of religion in which modern Western relativism combines with traditional Eastern spirituality, offering a kind of rational basis for religious and cultic perspectives which, to be sure, have largely lost their original sense in this new vision." Available from: http://www.ewtn.com/library/CURIA/RATZHONG.HTM; accessed 14 November 2009. Clooney suggests that contrary to the European "traditional" characterization of Indians and Hindus as "denying the reality of the world and being ambigious about religious truth and tolerant of all religious view points… a century of Indological scholarship shows that the Hindu traditions are often exceedingly precise and developed in their doctrines of truth claims, and that, for the most part, they are quite willing to speak positively about the world, our responsibilities, and divine involvement in human affairs." In Clooney's "Relativism in perspective: rereading Ratzinger," 10.

[413] Ratzinger, "Relativism: The Central Problem for Faith Today," 233.

[414] Ratzinger, "Relativism: The Central Problem for Faith Today," 233-234.

[415] O'Grandy, "The Ratzinger Round," 411. Cf. Joseph Cardinal Ratzinger, "Inter-

pretation, contemplation, action," *Communio* 13:2 (Summer 1986), 139-155, especially 146-148.

416 O'Grandy, "The Ratzinger Round," 411.

417 Nichols, *The Thought of Pope Benedict XVI*, 17.

418 Ratzinger, *Many Religions – One Covenant*, 51-52.

419 Ratzinger, "Relativism: The Central Problem for Faith Today," 4-36, footnote, 11; Michael Fuss, "New Age: *Supermarket alternativer Spiritualität*," *Communio*, 20 (1991), 148-157.

420 Ratzinger, "Relativism: The Central Problem for Faith Today," 234. In *A Turning Point for Europe*, Ratzinger describes the New Age movement, by saying, "New mythologies are formed, as we see with particular clarity in the many-faceted phenomenon that is offered up for sale under the collective name 'New Age.' The parallels to the gnosis of the ancient world are striking: in both, abstruse themes of mythology are linked to the ambitious claim to possess the key of knowledge and to have found an all-embracing interpretation of reality, in which the mysteries of the universe are uncovered and knowledge becomes redemption. The Living God sinks down into the spiritual depths of existence in which man bathes and ultimately is dissolved in order to become one with the All out of which he has come. Karl Barth's observation that religion can become a kind of self-satisfying process that does not lead to God, but rather confirms man in himself and closes him against God, takes on a new contemporary relevance." 101-102.

421 Ratzinger, "Relativism: The Central Problem for Faith Today," 234; in his book *The Spirit of the Liturgy*, Ratzinger writes, "With all of today's empiricism and pragmatism, with its loss of soul, we have good reason to learn again from Asia. But however open Christian faith may be, must be, to the wisdom of Asia, the difference between the personal and the a-personal understandings of God remains," 197. Also Joseph Murphy observes, "In contrast to the rationalist approaches of Hick and Knitter, there also exists a consciously antirationalist response to the notion that all is relative, namely, the complex reality of 'New Age,' whose practitioners seek to overcome subjective consciousness 'in re-entry into the dance of the cosmos through ecstasy.' According to this form of modern 'mysticism,' God is not a personal reality, distinct from the world, but the spiritual energy at work throughout the universe.... In order to be free, man must let himself be dissolved." Murphy, *Christ Our Joy*, 48.

422 Ratzinger, *Truth and Tolerance*, 127.

423 Nichols, *The Thought of Pope Benedict XVI*, 91.

424 Ratzinger, *Many Religions – One Covenant*, 97. In *A Turning Point for Europe*, Ratzinger observed, "I would call this chronic defection from the one god to the many ambiguous powers in the history of religion paganism in the quantitative sense of the word. In this sense, we are threatened today by a new paganism in the enlightened Western world, but also for this reason in all other cultures too." 159.

425 Ratzinger, *Truth and Tolerance*, 128-129.

426 Ratzinger, *Truth and Tolerance*, 129.

427 Jeffrey Stout, *The Flight from Authority: Religion, Morality and the Quest for Autonomy* (Notre Dame, IN: University of Notre Dame Press, 1981), 9.

428 Thomas B. Ommen, "Relativism, Objectivism and Theology," *Horizons* 13:2 (1986), 291-305, here 294.

429 Ommen, "Relativism, Objectivism and Theology," 292.

[430] Peter Berger, *A Rumor of Angels: Modern Society and Rediscovery of the Supernatural* (New York: Doubleday Anchor Books, 1970), 1.

[431] Berger, *A Rumor of Angels*, 6.

[432] Stout, *Flight from Authority*, 146.

[433] Berger, *A Rumor of Angels*, 6.

[434] Ratzinger, "Relativism: The Central Problem for Faith Today," 236.

[435] Ratzinger, "Relativism: The Central Problem for Faith Today," 237.

[436] Ratzinger, *Many Religions – One Covenant*, 18.

[437] Ratzinger, *Many Religions – One Covenant*, 19; this question of dialogue with Judaism is treated in much more depth in pages 22-46 of this book.

[438] In Kant's book *Religion Within the Limits of Reason Alone* (New York: Harper & Brothers, 1960), especially Book Four, "Concerning Service and Pseudo-Service under the Sovereignty of the Good Principle, or, Concerning Religion and Clericalism," Part Two. "Concerning the Pseudo-Service of God in a Statutory Religion," pp. 156-179.

[439] Ratzinger, "Relativism: The Central Problem for Faith Today," 237. See also Geoffrey W. Bromiley, professor of Church history and historical theology at Fuller Theological Seminary, who notes: "God is absolute. If there is relativism in regard to him, it is because we are relativized by God, not because he can be relativized by us. God does indeed meet us in the changing circumstances and experiences of life, so that we can see new facets of him and correct our imperfect ideas. He himself, however, does not change. When the relation between God and man is at issue, only one of the factors is mutable and relative. There can be no greater mistake than to attempt to bring God himself under a principle of relativism." In "The Limits of Theological Relativism," 823.

[440] Ratzinger, "Relativism: The Central Problem for Faith Today," 238.

[441] Ratzinger, "Relativism: The Central Problem for Faith Today," 238.

[442] Brevard S. Childs, "On Reclaiming the Bible for Christian Theology," in *Reclaiming the Bible for the Church*, Carl E. Braaten and Robert W. Jenson, eds. (Grand Rapids, MI/Cambridge, UK: William B. Eerdmans Publishing Company, 1995), 1-17, here 5.

[443] Childs, "On Reclaiming the Bible for Christian Theology," 10. See Joseph Ratzinger, "Interpretation – Contemplation – Action: Consideration on the Task of a Catholic Academy," *Communio* 13:2 (1986), 139-155 where Ratzinger invites reflection on St. Teresa of Avila as one who developed a balanced approach to the dialogue between interpretation and contemplation.

[444] Childs, "On Reclaiming the Bible for Christian Theology," 15.

[445] Fahey in his article "Joseph Ratzinger as Ecclesiologists and Pastor," 79 observed that Ratzinger together with Hans Urs von Balthasar, in his "Why I Am Still in the Church," in *Two Say Why* (Chicago, IL: Franciscan. Herald Press, 1971), 65-91, here 67-69, again "worried about the simple faithful who have no voice. They are the ones who exercise the true mission of the Church: prayer, bearing daily life with patience, always listening to the word of God."

[446] Ratzinger, *Milestones*, 9.

[447] Ratzinger, *Milestones*, 9.

[448] Ratzinger, "Review of the Post-conciliar Era – Failures, Tasks, Hopes," 373.

[449] Nichols, *The Thought of Pope Benedict XVI*, 43.

[450] Ratzinger, "Relativism: The Central Problem for Faith Today," 239.

[451] Ratzinger, "Relativism: The Central Problem for Faith Today," 239.

⁴⁵² Ratzinger, "Relativism: The Central Problem for Faith Today," 239; For a further discussion on this issue, Ratzinger mentions in references former student H.J. Verweyen's *Gottes letztes Wort* (Düsseldorf, 1991), where he finds many important and valid elements, in its author's position. However, he thinks that the "essential philosophical error consists in attempting to offer a rational foundation for the faith that is independent of the faith, an attempt that cannot convince in its pure abstract rationality." Ratzinger, "Relativism: The Central Problem for Faith Today," 436; footnote 20.

⁴⁵³ Ratzinger, "Relativism: The Central Problem for Faith Today," 240. John Hick made the following comment: "In Humanity there is, as Cardinal Ratzinger says, an inextinguishable yearning for the infinite and I believe that the infinite divine reality is present equally to us all throughout the world, when our hearts are open to that presence. For it does not seem to me that Jews, Muslims, Buddhists or Hindus are in general less good human beings, or less responsive to the Transcendent, than are Christians in general–as, however, surely they ought to be if we alone are able directly to encounter God and feed on the divine substance in our Eucharistic worship." Hick, "Ratzinger absolutely wrong on relativism." 3.

⁴⁵⁴ Ratzinger, "Relativism: The Central Problem for Faith Today," 240.

⁴⁵⁵ Ratzinger, "Relativism: The Central Problem for Faith Today," 240.

⁴⁵⁶ Ratzinger, "Relativism: The Central Problem for Faith Today," 236.

⁴⁵⁷ Ratzinger, *Milestones*, 139. Allen states that *Introduction of Christianity* was "no legalistic manual stuffed with rules and regulations; it was a meditation on faith that reached into the depths of human experience, a book that dared to walk naked before doubt and disbelief in order to discover the truth of what it means to be a modern Christian." *The Rise of Pope Benedict XVI*, 152.

⁴⁵⁸ Edward T. Oakes, "Reconciling Judas: Evangelizing the Theologians," *Crisis* (October 2004): 31-35.

⁴⁵⁹ Nichols, *The Thought of Pope Benedict XVI*, vii; Corkery notes that in Ratzinger's Preface to the new German edition of *Introduction to Christianity* "there are many 'enemies sighted' and there is much 'impassioned countering,'" which Corkery attributes to the Augustianian influence. In "Joseph Ratzinger's Theological Ideas 1–Origins: A Theologian Emerges," 12, footnote 13.

⁴⁶⁰ Ratzinger, *Introduction to Christianity*, 11.

⁴⁶¹ Ratzinger, *A Turning Point for Europe*, 154.

⁴⁶² Ratzinger, *Introduction to Christianity*, 11.

⁴⁶³ Allen notes, "Metz pioneered 'political theology,' arguing that Vatican II meant that Christians must read the 'signs of times' in social and political movements and align themselves with those seeking to better the human condition." 138. Later he "picked up a favorite theme of both Ratzinger and John Paul, arguing that an apocalyptic understanding of the preciousness of time should be asserted against 'an intoxicating relativism.'" *Pope Benedict XVI*, 126.

⁴⁶⁴ Ratzinger, *Milestones*, 136. Allen observes, "what really shocked Ratzinger, however, was that the theology faculties of Tübingen became the 'real ideological center' of the movement toward Marxism" in *Pope Benedict XVI*, 82.

⁴⁶⁵ Ratzinger, *Milestones*, 137-138; Florian Schuller in his foreword to Jürgen Habermas and Joseph Cardinal Ratzinger, *Dialectics of Secularization: On Reason and Religion* (San Francisco: Ignatius Press, 2006), 14, notes, "Both were directly involved–Ratzinger in Tübingen from 1966, Habermas in Frankfurt am Main from 1964 – in the initial dramas that were to lead to years of upheaval. Those

years saw uncontrolled, often irrational rejection of tradition and this led both men to a decisive clarification of their convictions." See Joseph Ratzinger, "On Hope," *Communio* 21:1 (1985), 71-84.

[466] Ratzinger, *Introduction to Christianity*, 15.

[467] Ratzinger, *Introduction to Christianity*, 15.

[468] Ratzinger, *Introduction to Christianity*, 16. In *A Turning Point for Europe*, Ratzinger also notes, "Both of these, technological progress and the belief that the new world can be constructed on its basis, quite logically involve the view that one must leave God out of what happens in history and assign the question of his existence and of who he is entirely to the realm of the private (and thus arbitrary)." 126-127.

[469] Allen, *Pope Benedict XVI*, 90. Also, on page 273 he states: "Millions of Catholics, reacting against that decision [*Humanae Vitae*], embraced what the new breed of moral theologians were telling them – that for good reasons, they could dissent from official Church teaching and remain Catholics." Vincent Twomey noted that 1968 "among other epoch-making events… saw the publication of *Humanae Vitae*, which almost split the Church in two.… It soon became clear that the crisis was not simply an internal affair of the Church. It reflected nothing less than the crisis of Western civilization itself caused by the threefold rejection of moral objectivity, tradition, and a common human nature.… The West Germany Bishops' Conference published their somewhat ambiguous response to *Humanae Vitae* in the *Königsteiner Erklärung*. They accepted the papal teaching, but at the same time they encouraged people 'to follow their own conscience,' which was understood to mean, acting, if one thought it right, in contradiction to the traditional teaching confirmed by Pope Paul VI." In Twomey's *Pope Benedict XVI*, 19-21f.

[470] See Charles Curran and Robert E. Hunt, *Dissent in and for the Church: Theologians and Humanae Vitae* (New York: Sheed and Ward, 1970). Allen notes: "Curran had been fired from Catholic University in 1967 for questioning the Church's absolute condemnation of practices such as birth control and masturbation, only to be reinstated after a wildcat student strike.… Curran eventually lost his license to teach Catholic theology after an exchange of correspondence with the doctrinal congregation and an 'informal' meeting with Ratzinger in Rome on March 8, 1986." *Pope Benedict XVI*, 257-258.

[471] Ratzinger, *Introduction to Christianity*, 18. Brown notes, "Anthropologists have long wrestled with the question of whether moral progress is evident in cultural evolution (see, e.g., Hatch 1983, 106-26) and it is fair to say that we remain more skeptical than other occupational groups about the moral virtues of life in large-scale, hierarchically organized societies." Brown, "Cultural Relativism," 370.

[472] Nichols, *The Thought of Pope Benedict XVI*, 76; Corkery also notes that in his writings Ratzinger insists "on the priority of receiving over making. For him, the hallmark of Christian existence is that it is first and foremost a receiving existence." In Corkery, "Joseph Ratzinger's Theological Ideas 2–The Facial Features of a Theological *Corpus*," 4.

[473] Ratzinger, *Introduction to Christianity*, 19.

[474] Ratzinger, *Introduction to Christianity*, 20. See Joseph Ratzinger, "The Theological Locus of Ecclesial Movements," *Communio* 25:3 (1998), 480-504.

[475] Ratzinger, *Many Religions – One Covenant*, 96.

[476] Ratzinger, *Introduction to Christianity*, 20.

477 Ratzinger, *Introduction to Christianity*, 21.

478 Ratzinger, *Introduction to Christianity*, 21.

479 Ratzinger, *Introduction to Christianity*, 22.

480 Ratzinger, *Many Religions – One Covenant*, 98.

481 Ratzinger, *Many Religions – One Covenant*, 76-77.

482 Ratzinger, *Introduction to Christianity*, 24.

483 Ratzinger, *Introduction to Christianity*, 25.

484 Ratzinger, *Many Religions – One Covenant*, 107.

485 "Exchange of Letters between Metropolitan Damaskinos and Cardinal Joseph Ratzinger," in Joseph Cardinal Ratzinger's *Pilgrim Fellowship of Faith: The Church as Communion*, Stephan Otto Horn and Vinzenz Pfnür, eds.; trans. by Henry Taylor (San Francisco: Ignatius Press, 2005), 220.

486 Ratzinger, *Introduction to Christianity*, 26.

487 Ratzinger, *Introduction to Christianity*, 24.

488 Brown, "Cultural Relativism," 364-365.

489 Ratzinger, *Introduction to Christianity*, 25.

490 Ratzinger, *Many Religions – One Covenant*, 26. Girard on the issue of ethnocentrism observed, "Why would you be a Christian if you didn't believe in Christ? Paradoxically, we have become so ethnocentric in our relativism that we feel it is only OK for others – not us – to think their religion is superior! We are the only ones with no centrism." Girard, "Ratzinger is Right," 45-46.

491 Ratzinger, *Introduction to Christianity*, 27.

492 Ratzinger, *Introduction to Christianity*, 29.

493 Corkery notes that "although it was a text that dealt much with interreligious dialogue and ecumenism, it was not intended as a document of dialogue, but rather as a kind of 'in-house' document for Catholics ('Bishops, theologians and all the Catholic faithful,' n.3)," Corkery's "Joseph Ratzinger's Theological Ideas 6–Resisting the 'Dictatorship of Relativism,'" 7. Additionally, Robert P. Imbelli observed, "It is important to note that the declaration is directed not to ecumenical dialogue partners, nor to all people of good will, but to the bishops of the Catholic Church, to be communicated especially to theological faculties and missionary congregations, as well as to the Catholic faithful. It intends to recapitulate the Church's faith in the uniqueness and universal salvific significance of Jesus Christ, the incarnate Word of God: the article of faith upon which the Church itself stands or falls. What is crucially important about this document is that this article of faith, everywhere professed and presumed by Vatican II, can no longer be taken for granted." In Imbelli, "Rome & Relativism: '*Dominus Iesus*' & the CDF," 13.

494 Joseph Cardinal Ratzinger, "Presentation of the Declaration *Dominus Iesus*," in *Pilgrim Fellowship of Faith: The Church as Communion*, Stephan Otto Horn and Vinzenz Pfnür, eds.; trans. by Henry Taylor (San Francisco: Ignatius Press, 2005), 209-216, here 209.

495 Congregation for the Doctrine of the Faith, "Declaration *Dominus Iesus* On the Unicity and Salvific Universality of Jesus Christ and the Church" (August 6, 2000) available from: http://www.vatican.va/roman_curia/congregations/cfaith/documents/rc_con_cfaith_doc_20000806_dominus-iesus_en.html; accessed 14 April 2008; nr. 4.

496 Ratzinger, "Presentation of the Declaration *Dominus Iesus*," 210; Ratzinger's point is repeated by Nichols: "Not only are the Jesus of history [Harnack] and

the Christ of faith [Bultmann] unthinkable without each other, but also: 'one is bound to be continually pushed from one to the other because in reality Jesus only subsists as the Christ and the Christ only subsists in the shape of Jesus.'" Nichols, *The Thought of Pope Benedict XVI*, 86.

[497] Corkery notes "Ratzinger's fight against the contemporary relativistic mentality can be seen, in the light of this key principle [Christianity's claim to truth], to be imperative. Were he to ignore the relativist challenge, he would simply be allowing Christianity to be demolished at its very centre." Corkery's "Joseph Ratzinger's Theological Ideas 6–Resisting the 'Dictatorship of Relativism,'"4-5.

[498] In *A Turning Point for Europe*, Ratzinger explains the true origins of the term *fundamentalism* which, "according to the word's original meaning, is a tendency that arose in Protestant America in the 19th century as a protest against evolutionism and biblical criticism. It attempted to supply a firm Christian foundation against both of these through the defense of the absolute inerrancy of Scripture." However, he says, "The series of supposed fundamentalisms has in the meantime passed from the Protestant over the Catholic to the Islamic and the Marxist fundamentalisms. The differences in content go utterly unheeded; one is a fundamentalist if one has firm convictions, for this is viewed as something that provokes conflict and is opposed to progress. In contrast, the 'good' is the doubt that takes up the battle against old certainties – that is, every modern undogmatic or antidogmantic movement." 166-167.

[499] Ratzinger, "Presentation of the Declaration *Dominus Iesus*," 212-213. Leszek Kolakowski, the Marxist humanist philosopher made a distinction between "pluralist tolerance"– the respect for other beliefs – and "indifferent tolerance," which refuses to believe there can be any superior Truth. In Leszek Kolakowski, "Revenge of the Sacred in Secular Culture," *Modernity on Endless Trial* (Chicago, IL: University of Chicago Press, 1990), 63-74.

[500] Ratzinger, "Presentation of the Declaration *Dominus Iesus*," 212.

[501] Jim Corkery, "Joseph Ratzinger's Theological Ideas 6–Resisting the 'Dictatorship of Relativism,'" 9; also cites Ratzinger's "Interreligious Dialogue and Jewish-Christian Relations," *Communio* 25:1 (1998), 29-41, here 38, where Ratzinger makes clear that "he does not think abandoning the quest for truth enriches the process of interreligious dialogue. The religions can encounter one another only by delving more deeply into the truth, not by giving it up. Skepticism does not unite. Nor does sheer pragmatism."

[502] Corkery, "Joseph Ratzinger's Theological Ideas 6–Resisting the 'Dictatorship of Relativism,'" 11 also cites Gerard Hall, "Catholic Church Teaching on Its Relationship to Other Religions Since Vatican II," in *Australian E-journal of Theology* 3 (February, 2003), 6-7. See also Martin Marty, who sees the declaration as "a missed opportunity" because "Catholic theologians in the East, with Asian spiritual environments in mind, were working to relate the truth in Christ to the light in the East. They were no doubt making some mistakes – how is a non-Catholic to adjudicate?– as they fumbled their way tentatively into new relations, but now they are to cut off efforts." "Rome & Relativism: '*Dominus Iesus*' & the CDF," 12-15, here 12.

[503] Ratzinger, "Presentation of the Declaration *Dominus Iesus*," 213-214.

[504] Second Vatican Council, "Declaration on the Relation of the Church to Non-Christian Religions, *Nostra aetate*," nr. 2 (October 28, 1965); available from: http://www.vatican.va/archive/hist_councils/ii_vatican_council/documents/vat-ii_decl_19651028_nostra-aetate_en.html; accessed 13 May 2007.

505 Ratzinger, "Presentation of the Declaration *Dominus Iesus*," 216; Corkery in his "Joseph Ratzinger's Theological Ideas 6–Resisting the 'Dictatorship of Relativism'" notes that "it was a central task of *Dominus Iesus* to provide a remedy for this relativism. The document said: 'As a remedy for this relativistic mentality, which is becoming ever more common, it is necessary above all to reassert the definitive and complete character of the revelation of Jesus Christ' *Dominus Iesus*, 5." 7; and "it was against christological and ecclesiological relativism that Prefect Ratzinger published *Dominus Iesus*," 10, "Joseph Ratzinger's Theological Ideas 6–Resisting the 'Dictatorship of Relativism.'"

506 Umberto Eco, *The Name of the Rose*, trans. by William Weaver (London: Picador, 1984), 491.

507 Twomey noted, "*Truth and Tolerance* is Cardinal Ratzinger's 284-page answer to the worldwide outrage at the publication of *Dominus Iesus* (August 6, 2000), the document issued by the Congregation for the Doctrine of the Faith, of which he was prefect at the time." *Pope Benedict XVI*, 40-41.

508 Ratzinger, *Truth and Tolerance*, 19.

509 Ratzinger, *Truth and Tolerance*, 23.

510 Ratzinger, *Truth and Tolerance*, 23.

511 Ratzinger, *Truth and Tolerance*, 23-24.

512 Ratzinger, *Truth and Tolerance*, 34.

513 Ratzinger, *Truth and Tolerance*, 47.

514 Ratzinger, *Truth and Tolerance*, 40

515 Jean Daniélou, German trans. *Vom Geheimnis der Geschichte*, p. 128, as it appears in Ratzinger's *Truth and Tolerance*, 40.

516 Second Vatican Council, "Constitution on the Divine Revelation *Dei Verbum*," available from: http://www.vatican.va/archive/hist_councils/ii_vatican_council/documents/vat-ii_const_19651118_dei-verbum_en.html; accessed 14 May 2006, 4.

517 John Paul II, *Redemptor Hominis*, available from: http://www.vatican.va/holy_father/john_paul_ii/encyclicals/documents/hf_jp-ii_enc_04031979_redemptor-hominis_en.html; accessed 15 May 2006.

518 Mircea Éliade, *Der Mythos der ewigen Wiederkehr*, German trans. p. 5, as it appears in Ratzinger's *Truth and Tolerance*, 40.

519 Ratzinger, *Truth and Tolerance*, 42.

520 Ratzinger, *Truth and Tolerance*, 40. [emphasis added].

521 Protestant theologian Martin E. Marty writes, "anyone who cares about the truth in Christ has good reason to fear relativism in an age where in too many minds and mouths 'we are all, after all, in different boats heading for the same shore'; a time when 'it does not make any difference what you believe, as long as you believe'; a place where 'spirituality' gets invented as a do-it-yourself alternative to churchly 'religions.'" "Rome & Relativism: '*Dominus Iesus*' & the CDF," 12.

522 John Paul II, *Redemptor Hominis*, available from: http://www.vatican.va/holy_father/john_paul_ii/encyclicals/documents/hf_jp-ii_enc_04031979_redemptor-hominis_en.html; accessed 15 May, 2006.

523 Ratzinger, *Truth and Tolerance*, 44.

524 Ratzinger, *Truth and Tolerance*, 51; Corkery writes, "the first 'facial feature' of Ratzinger's theology: namely, that the God of philosophy and the God of faith are *one*. This 'facial feature' constitutes a principle that expresses the radical monotheism of the Bible and ensures, thereby, that Christianity's claim to *truth*

stands and that the Christian faith tradition cannot simply be relegated to the status of 'one tradition among many'" in "Joseph Ratzinger's Theological Ideas 2–The Facial Features of a Theological *Corpus*," 4-6; Corkery also provides a reference to Joseph Ratzinger's "Faith, Philosophy and Theology" in *The Nature and Mission of Theology: Essays to Orient Theology in Today's Debates* (San Francisco: Ignatius Press, 1995), 24-27.

[525] Ratzinger gives his definition of the *anonymous Christian* being "the pagan after the beginning of the Christian mission, who lives in the state of Christ's grace through faith, hope and love, yet who has no explicit knowledge of the fact that his life is oriented in grace-given salvation to Jesus Christ." *Truth and Tolerance*, 51; Cf. Karl Rahner, *Theological Investigations*, Vol. 14; trans. by David Bourke (London: Darton, Longman & Todd, 1976), 283.

[526] Ratzinger, *Truth and Tolerance*, 51.

[527] Ratzinger, *Truth and Tolerance*, 215; where Ratzinger relies on the article written by J. Seifert, who in turn refers to Elizabeth M. Anscombe, "Paganism, Superstition and Philosophy," in *Menschenwürde und Ethik*, ed. Mariano Crespo (Heidelberg: Winter, 1998), pp. 93-105.

[528] Ratzinger, *Truth and Tolerance*, 216, footnote 11.

[529] Ratzinger, *Truth and Tolerance*, 216, footnote 11.

[530] Ratzinger, *Truth and Tolerance*, 72.

[531] Ratzinger in an address given in Hong Kong to the presidents of the Asian bishops' conferences and the chairmen of their doctrinal commissions during a March 2-5, 1993 meeting mentions, "In Latin America today there is a movement under way which calls itself 'teologia India,' the title referring to the indigenous peoples. The movement mourns the passing of the old religions of that continent and would like to revive them in some fashion." Available at: http://www.ewtn.com/library/CURIA/RATZHONG.HTM; accessed 14 November 2009.

[532] Ratzinger, *Truth and Tolerance*, 75.

[533] Ratzinger, *Truth and Tolerance*, 78.

[534] Encyclical of His Holiness John Paul II, *Fides et Ratio* (September 15, 1998); available from http://www.vatican.va/holy_father/john_paul_ii/encyclicals/documents/hf_jp_enc_15101998_fides-et-ratioen.html; accessed 12 May 2009; Virgil Nemoianu argues, "Of all the encyclicals signed by John Paul II *Fides et Ratio* is the one that is probably the most 'universalist.' In other words, one can think of few others that are equally broad, comprehensive and acceptable not only to all Christians of normal and balanced judgment but probably to a good number of thoughtful followers of various other faiths and perhaps even to many honest persons of doubt, to the extent to which they are not narrow and intransigent in their thinking." In "The Church and the Secular Establishment: A Philosophical Dialogue between Joseph Ratzinger and Jürgen Habermas," 16.

[535] Ratzinger, *Truth and Tolerance*, 184.

[536] Allen, *The Rise of Pope Benedict XVI*, 175.

[537] Ratzinger, *Truth and Tolerance*, 184-185; Ratzinger tells us, that following C.S. Lewis, *The Screwtape Letters* (Glasgow: Collins, 1955), 139f., "The younger devil has expressed concern to his superior that especially intelligent people, in particular, might read the books of wisdom of the ancients and might thus come upon the track of the truth. Screwtape calms him by pointing out that the 'Historical point of View,' with which the intellectuals of the Western

world have fortunately been inculcated by the devils, means in fact that 'when a learned man is presented with any statement in an ancient author, the one question he never asks is whether it is true. He asks who influenced the ancient writer and how far the statement is consistent with what he said in other books and what phase in the writer's development, or in the general history of thought, it illustrates and how it affected other writers,' and so on."

538 Ratzinger, *Truth and Tolerance*, 185; cites Josef Pieper in "Was heißt Interpretation?" [What does interpretation mean?], in his *Schriften zum Philosophiebegriff* [Writings on the concept of philosophy], Vol. 3 of his *Werke*, ed. B. Wald (Hamburg: Meiner, 1995), 226-227.

539 Ratzinger, *Truth and Tolerance*, 186. Allen summarizes Ratzinger's view in the following words, "Orthodox theology for Ratzinger presumes epistemic realism: the human mind is ordered to the truth, it can ascertain truth in nature and recognize truth in revelation. These truths become the basis for universally valid conclusions in anthropology, ethics and theology. Modern thinkers, as Ratzinger sees it, are too much under the spell of Kant and his distinction between the noumenal and the phenomenal. We never meet objective truth as such except as it is filtered through human consciousness. In the absence of objectivity, the only standard for judging propositions is their practical value (does believing this help us build a better world?). Thus modern theology stresses an instrumental view of the truth: truth is something humanity makes, not something it finds. Ratzinger sees this view of the truth as both a false humility and a false pride. The human person is capable of knowing truth, Ratzinger insists, and in that sense the truth-as-doing model gives up on humanity too soon; on the other hand, if humanity can invent truth, then there are no limits on our behavior, and in that sense it is a dangerously arrogant idea." *Pope Benedict XVI*, 263.

540 Ratzinger, *Truth and Tolerance*, 186-187; with a reference to Marius Reiser, "Bibel und Kirche: Eine Antwort an U. Luz" [Bible and Church: A reply to U. Luz], *Trierer Theologische Zeitschrift* 108 (1999). 62-81, here 63; who in turn references David Tracy, *Theologie als Gespräch: Eine postmoderne Hermeneutik* [Theology as Conversation: A post-modern Hermeneutic] (Mainz: Matthias-Grünewald-Verlag, 1993), 73-97.

541 O'Grandy, "The Ratzinger Round," 410.

542 O'Grandy, "The Ratzinger Round," 410.

543 "Thoth, the 'father of letters' and the 'god of time' once came to the Egyptian king Thutmose of Thebes. He taught this ruler about various arts he had invented and especially about the art of writing that he has thought up. In praise of his invention, he said to the king: 'This knowledge, o King, will make the Egyptians more wise and better able to remember things; for it has been invented as an aid to the memory as well as for wisdom.' But the king was not impressed. On the contrary, he foresaw as the result of the art of writing 'this will bring forgetfulness into men's souls… through the neglect of remembering, in that by trusting in writing they will draw remembrance from without… and not from within, from their own selves. You have not, therefore, invented a means of remembering but of recording and you pass on to your pupils only the appearance of wisdom, not the thing itself,'" in Ratzinger's *Truth and Tolerance*, 187-188; a reference to Plato's *Phaedrus*, 274d-225b.

544 Joseph Ratzinger, *A Turning Point for Europe*, 93-94. As Allen states, "Ratzinger also charges those such as Curran and Küng and their supporters with attempting to use the tactics of political pressure – the mass media, petition

drives, demonstrations – to force the Church to change its teaching. He sees this as further evidence of the extent to which modern Western theology has capitulated to the zeitgeist, in which truth has been replaced by power, and utterly lost the proper sense of the Church." *Pope Benedict XVI*, 267.

[545] Ratzinger, *Truth and Tolerance*, 194; Here Ratzinger also recalls the 18th century work *Nathan the Wise* by Gotthold Ephraim Lessing, who "represented the three great religions in the parable of the three rings, of which one is the genuine and true ring, though there is no longer any way to establish this genuineness." See also Ratzinger's "Christ, Faith and the Challenge of Cultures," available at: http://www.ewtn.com/library/CURIA/RATZHONG.HTM; accessed 14 November 2009.

[546] Ratzinger, *Truth and Tolerance*, 195. For more on the issue of cultural relativism see: Brown, "Cultural Relativism," 363-384.

[547] Ratzinger, *Truth and Tolerance*, 196; also cites Theodor Haecker, *Vergil: Vater des Abendlandes* [Virgil: Father of the West], 5th ed. (Munich: Kösel, 1947), 117; where Haecker spoke about the advent character of the pre-Christian cultures and also refers to Horst Bürkle's *Der Mensch auf der Suche nach Gott Die Frage der Religionen* [Man in Search of God. The Question Concerning the Religions], *Amateca*, 3 (Paderborn: Bonifatius, 1996), 14-40.

[548] John Paul II, *Fides et Ratio*, Nr. 72.

[549] John Paul II, *Fides et Ratio*, Nr. 72.

[550] Ratzinger, *Truth and Tolerance*, 201; Jim Corkery argues that for Ratzinger, "the faith is always his starting-point–frequently because its perspective is seen to be required to counter the false understandings of such things as salvation and humanity that are developing in secular philosophies and ideologies and that do not, in his view, speak the truth about our situation. Christian faith is the truth; and it presents our situation correctly. Passion for truth, an eye for the world's false wisdom, confidence that the perspective of the faith can–and must–cut through the perspectives of this world all give a critical, controversial, incisive edge to Ratzinger's theological writings in which, repeatedly, the 'wisdom of God' robustly confronts the 'wisdom of the world.'" Corkery, "Joseph Ratzinger's Theological Ideas 1–Origins: A Theologian Emerges," 8.

[551] Ratzinger, *Truth and Tolerance*, 202.

[552] Ratzinger, *Truth and Tolerance*, 203.

[553] Ratzinger, *Truth and Tolerance*, 204.

[554] Ratzinger, *Truth and Tolerance*, 205.

[555] As Murphy notes, "It is clear that truth and love, when completely realized, as they are in God, are identical." Murphy, *Christ Our Joy*, 55.

[556] Ratzinger, *Truth and Tolerance*, 206.

[557] Ratzinger, *Truth and Tolerance*, 206. Therefore, Ratzinger believes, "the trouble is that the organ of utility and the organ of power are more palpable and more immediate in their effects than the organ of truth. That is why the organ of truth needs assistance, needs support. This is what the Church's task ought to be: to give this otherwise all too easily suppressed faculty the strength it needs.... She must break open the prison of positivism and awaken man's receptivity to the truth, to God and thus to the power of conscience." 55. For the further discussion on the question of conscience Ratzinger refers to his book *Wahrheit, Werte, Macht* [Truth, Values, Power], new ed. (Frankfurt: Knecht, 1999), 25-62; and his "Conscience in Time," *Communio* 19:4 (1992), 647-657. See also Twomey's *Pope Benedict XVI*, 121-132.

558 Nichols, *The Thought of Pope Benedict XVI*, 76.

559 Henri J. M. Nouwen, Introduction to Yushi Nomura's *Desert Wisdom: Sayings from the Desert Fathers* (Garden City, NJ: Image Books/A Division of Doubleday & Company, Inc., 1984), xii.

560 Ratzinger, *Truth and Tolerance*, 208-209; the citation of Jaspers comes from a quotation by J. Pieper in "Die mögliche Zukunft der Philosophie" [The possible Future of Philosophy], in his *Schriften zum Philosophiebegriff*, 315.

561 Joseph Card. Ratzinger and Marcello Pera, *Without Roots: The West, Relativism, Christianity, Islam*, trans. Michael F. Moore (New York: Basic Books, 2006), 128.

562 Ratzinger and Pera, *Without Roots*, 139 note 8: "The term *pensiero debole*, or 'weak thought,' was coined in the early 1990s by the Italian philosopher Gianni Vattimo to denote his own brand of nihilism and has subsequently become a blanket term to describe Italian post-modern thinking."

563 Ratzinger and Pera, *Without Roots*, 11 [emphasis added].

564 Ratzinger and Pera, *Without Roots*, 5.

565 Ratzinger and Pera, *Without Roots*, 12.

566 Ratzinger and Pera, *Without Roots*, 13.

567 Ratzinger and Pera, *Without Roots*, 140 note 10: "The technique of *elenchos*, frequently used in both common and specialized argumentation, consists in trying to confute an interlocutor who, for example, may have argued thesis T, proving that from T derives consequence C and that since C is not true, or C has already been disproved by the interlocutor himself, or even since T was directly or indirectly disproved by another thesis, T1, which is accepted by the interlocutor. In each case, a rule of elementary logic is applied according to which if a thesis *p* implies a consequence *q* and *q* proves to be false, then *p* is also false."

568 Ratzinger and Pera, *Without Roots*, 14.

569 Ratzinger and Pera, *Without Roots*, 19.

570 Giovanna Borradori, *Philosophy in a Time of Terror: Dialogues with Jürgen Habermas and Jacques Derrida* (Chicago, IL: University of Chicago Press, 2003), 115, as it appears in Ratzinger and Pera, *Without Roots*, 20.

571 Ratzinger and Pera, *Without Roots*, 21.

572 Ratzinger and Pera, *Without Roots*, 6-7. One cannot help but think of Albert Camus (1913-1960) and the similar paradoxes he had faced in terms of expressing relativism when Pera writes of Derrida, "In the end, the true answer comes out, but it is the same exact answer you would have heard from a poor, maligned and much deconstructed enlightenment philosopher with his back up against the wall." *Without Roots*, 21. Camus eventually came to realize that "relative morality may not recommend crime, but neither can it argue against it." He learned this the hard way, being pushed so to speak 'against the wall,' by the plagues and tyranny of the Second World War, to which he responded by abandoning his earlier relativism expressed in *Le Mythe de Sisyphe* with his *L'Homme Révolté*, claiming universal moral values and a fixed human nature as their source. In Richard T. Lambert. "Albert Camus and the Paradoxes of Expressing Relativism." *Thought* 56/221: (June, 1981): 185-198.

573 Ratzinger and Pera, *Without Roots*, 21.

574 Ratzinger, *Truth and Tolerance*, 175.

575 Ratzinger and Pera, *Without Roots*, 25. Ratzinger has his own understanding of

the role of doubt in religious experience, as he talks about it in his *Introduction to Christianity*, pp. 39-47, especially with the examples he gives, of St. Thérèse of Lisieux and a Jesuit missionary brother Rodrigue from the play *le Soulier de Satin*, written by Paul Claudel.

[576] Paul Knitter, *No Other Name?*, 17 as it appears in Ratzinger and Pera, *Without Roots*, 24.

[577] Ratzinger and Pera, *Without Roots*, 24.

[578] Ratzinger and Pera, *Without Roots*, 26.

[579] Ommen, "Relativism, Objectivism and Theology," 296-297. See also Jacques Dupuis, SJ, *Toward a Christian Theology of Religious Pluralism* (Maryknoll, NY: Orbis Books, 1997).

[580] Ommen, "Relativism, Objectivism and Theology," 297.

[581] Ommen, "Relativism, Objectivism and Theology," 297.

[582] Peter Winch, *The Idea of a Social Science* (London: Routledge and Kegan Paul, 1958), 100.

[583] Martin Hollis and Steven Lukas, eds., *Rationality and Relativism* (Cambridge, MA: M.I.T. Press, 1984), 67-86 and 261-305.

[584] Ratzinger and Pera, *Without Roots*, 28 [emphasis in original].

[585] Ratzinger and Pera, *Without Roots*, 28.

[586] His Holiness John Paul II, *Redemptoris Missio* (December 7, 1990); available at http://www.vatican.va/holy_father/john_paul_ii/encyclicals/documents/hf_jp-ii_enc_07121990_redemptoris-missio_en.html; accessed 14 June 2006, article 55.

[587] Ratzinger and Pera, *Without Roots*, 30.

[588] Ratzinger and Pera, *Without Roots*, 45.

[589] Joseph Ratzinger, *Europe, Today and Tomorrow* (San Francisco: Ignatius Press, 2007), 20-21. This book contains the same lecture by Cardinal Ratzinger that was published in *Without Roots*.

[590] Ratzinger, *A Turning Point for Europe*, 107. Here, Ratzinger also notes, "the 19th century largely followed him [Schleiermacher] in this and found in this way its own kind of reconciliation between religion, which was wholly feeling, did not stand in its way and was for its own part free to express itself in the realm of feeling and to make its own position secure." 107.

[591] Ratzinger, *Truth and Tolerance*, 117. See also Joseph Ratzinger, "Il significato dei valori religiosi e morali nella società pluralistica," *Communio* 22:127 (1993), 72-89.

[592] Ratzinger, *Europe, Today and Tomorrow*, 21.

[593] Oswald Spengler, *Decline of the West* (Oxford: Oxford University Press, 1991).

[594] Ratzinger, *Europe, Today and Tomorrow*, 24.

[595] In *A Turning Point for Europe*, Ratzinger observed, "We must not let ourselves be affected by the superficial obligatory optimism of certain trends, but, equally, we must not yield to the temptation to overlook the positive elements in the total complex of our age." 17. At the same time, he is also concerned with the fact that, in the view of many modern thinkers, "there exists at the same time an obligation to be optimistic and failure to observe this obligation does not go unpunished. For example, anyone who expresses the view that not everything in the intellectual development of the modern period has been correct, that it is necessary in some essential areas to reflect on the shared wisdom of the great cultures, has chosen to make the wrong kind of criticism." 15-16.

596 Arnold Toynbee, *A Study of History: Abridgement of Vols. I-VI*, D.C. Somervell, ed. (Oxford: Oxford University Press, 1946).

597 Ratzinger, *Europe, Today and Tomorrow*, 25.

598 Ratzinger, *Europe, Today and Tomorrow*, 26.

599 Ratzinger, *Europe, Today and Tomorrow*, 28-29.

600 Weigel notes that perhaps "his father's anti-Nazi convictions and his own experience of the war suggested a truth that the French Jesuit Henri de Lubac had made the theme in his 1943 study, *The Drama of Atheistic Humanism*: 'It is not true, as sometimes said, that man cannot organize the world without God. What is true is that, without God, he can ultimately only organize it against man. Exclusive humanism is inhuman humanism.'" Weigel, *God's Choice*, 163.

601 Ratzinger, *Europe, Today and Tomorrow*, 41. See Joseph Ratzinger, "Man between Reproduction and Creation: Theological Questions on the Origin of Human Life," *Communio* 16:2 (1989), 197-211.

602 Ratzinger and Pera, *Without Roots*, 68.

603 Lambert, "Albert Camus and the Paradoxes of Expressing Relativism," 185-198.

604 Corkery, "Joseph Ratzinger's Theological Ideas 3–On Being Human," 12; cites Joseph Ratzinger, *Abbruch und Aufbruch. Die Antwort des Glaubens auf die Krise der Werte* (Munich: Minerva, 1988), noting in footnote 24, "This is the published version of a lecture given by Ratzinger in 1987 at the University of Eichstätt in which, drawing on C.S. Lewis' book *The Abolition of Man* (New York: Macmillan, 1947), he showed how Lewis had seen in the loss of 'the doctrine of objective values, which express themselves in the being of the world' (Ratzinger, p. 13) the deadly danger of abolishing the human being (pp. 12-13)." Also in his other text, Ratzinger cites the same book of C.S. Lewis, where the latter asserts "This thing which I have called for convenience the *Tao* and which others may call Natural Law or Traditional Morality or the First Principles of Practical Reason or the First Platitudes, is not one among a series of possible systems of value. It is the sole source of all value judgments. If it is rejected, all value is rejected. If any value is retained, it is retained. The effort to refute it and raise a new system of value in its place is self-contradictory." *A Turning Point for Europe*, 31.

605 Ratzinger and Pera, *Without Roots*, 84.

606 Ratzinger and Pera, *Without Roots*, 71.

607 Ratzinger and Pera, *Without Roots*, 71.

608 Ratzinger and Pera, *Without Roots*, 72-73.

609 Ratzinger and Pera, *Without Roots*, 73.

610 Ratzinger and Pera, *Without Roots*, 74.

611 Ratzinger and Pera, *Without Roots*, 77.

612 Ratzinger and Pera, *Without Roots*, 78.

613 Ratzinger and Pera, *Without Roots*, 78.

614 Ratzinger and Pera, *Without Roots*, 78.

615 Ratzinger and Pera, *Without Roots*, 78-79.

616 Ratzinger and Pera, *Without Roots*, 79.

617 Ratzinger, *Europe, Today and Tomorrow*, 33.

618 Ratzinger, *Europe, Today and Tomorrow*, 33.

619 Ratzinger and Pera, *Without Roots*, 80. Allen observes, "It's pointless to hope that Christianity will be a mass presence in this historical period. Instead, as

Ratzinger himself has said many times, the aim ought to be to make Christianity 'a creative minority.' The goal should be to defend Christian identity rather than to make it acceptable to a culture hostile on principle to what it stands for, concentrating on forming a new generation excited about the faith, however small in number they may be, who can emerge at a future point when the false promises of hedonism and secularism have run their course." In *The Rise of Benedict XVI*, 83-84. In an article in 1986 Ratzinger wrote that "we should not be disquieted by the word 'subculture.' In the cultural crisis we are experiencing, new cultural purification and unification can spring only from islands of spiritual concentration." Joseph Ratzinger, *Co-workers of the truth: meditations for everyday of the year*, Irene Grassl, ed. (San Francisco: Ignatius Press, 1992), 247.

[620] Ratzinger and Pera, *Without Roots*, 85.

[621] Ratzinger and Pera, *Without Roots*, 86.

[622] Ratzinger and Pera, *Without Roots*, 90.

[623] Ratzinger and Pera, *Without Roots*, 96.

[624] Ratzinger and Pera, *Without Roots*, 99.

[625] Ratzinger and Pera, *Without Roots*, 100.

[626] Ratzinger and Pera, *Without Roots*, 105.

[627] Peter Berger in his book, *The Heretical Imperative: Contemporary Possibilities of Religious Affirmation* (New York: Doubleday Anchor Books, 1980) speaks of three basic modalities of reasoning: deductive, inductive and reductive. Deductive leads from the general to particular, inductive toward the general from particular and reductive – from complex to more basic and simple. Berger argues that through history we can deduce different people predominantly employing one of these three modalities of reasoning. The deductive way can be seen in Plato, inductive in Aristotle, and reductive in the writing of the Sophists. Among the modern theologians, these three modalities of reasoning are respectively represented by Karl Barth, Rudolf Bultmman and Friedrich Schleiermacher.

[628] Ratzinger and Pera, *Without Roots*, 105, references Aristotle, *Nicomachean Ethics*, trans. David Ross (New York: Oxford University Press, 1984), III.3, 1112b11.

[629] Ratzinger and Pera, *Without Roots*, 104.

[630] Ratzinger and Pera, *Without Roots*, 104.

[631] "Just as the believer is choked by the salt water of doubt constantly washed into his mouth by the ocean of uncertainty, so the nonbeliever is troubled by doubts about his unbelief, about the real totality of the world he has made up his mind to explain as a self-contained whole. He can never be absolutely certain of the autonomy of what he has seen and interpreted as a whole; he remains threatened by the question of whether belief is not after all the reality it claims to be. Just as the believer knows himself to be constantly threatened by unbelief, which he must experience as continual temptation, so for the unbeliever faith remains a temptation and a threat to his apparently permanently closed world." Ratzinger, *Introduction to Christianity*, 45.

[632] Ratzinger and Pera, *Without Roots*, 103.

[633] Ratzinger and Pera, *Without Roots*, 106.

[634] Ratzinger and Pera, *Without Roots*, 108. In *A Turning Point for Europe*, Ratzinger critiques the pacifism of Europe, which according to him is based on financial utility, "this notion of law is matched by an idea of peace that one might sum up as follows: *Utilitas, non veritas facit pacem.* In similar fashion to Adam Smith, Immanuel Kant developed his doctrine of perpetual peace largely along these

lines: 'The spirit of commerce sooner or later takes hold of every people and it cannot exist side by side with war. And of all the powers (or means) at the disposal of the power of the state, financial power can probably be relied on most. Thus states find themselves compelled to promote the noble cause of peace…. and wherever in the world there is a threat of war breaking out, they will try to prevent it by mediation, just as if they had entered into a permanent league for this purpose' (H. Reiss, ed., *Kant's Political Writings* (Cambridge: Cambridge University Press, 1970), 114. In other words, it is a question of making egotism, man's strongest and most reliable power and the source of his conflicts, into a real instrument of peace, because it is precisely egotism that makes peace seem more useful than war." 51-52.

[635] Ratzinger and Pera, *Without Roots*, 115.

[636] Ratzinger and Pera, *Without Roots*, 116.

[637] Ratzinger and Pera, *Without Roots*, 117.

[638] Ratzinger and Pera, *Without Roots*, 120-121. For further discussion on the question of "creative minorities" read Peter Berger's *A Rumor of Angels*. About joy, Murphy notes, "St. Augustine's insistence on the inseparability of joy and truth, so well expressed in the memorable formula *'gaudium de veritate,'* finds a powerful echo in the writings of Joseph Ratzinger. Like the Doctor of Grace, Ratzinger knows that true joy can be found only in knowing and loving the God of truth, who alone satisfies the human longing for meaning and enduring happiness." Murphy, *Christ Our Joy*, 61.

[639] Ratzinger and Pera, *Without Roots*, 122. See Joseph Ratzinger, "The Ecclesiology of the Second Vatican Council," *Communio* 13:3 (1986), 239-252.

[640] See Joseph Ratzinger, "Christian Universalism: On Two Collections of Papers by Hans Urs von Balthasar," *Communio* 22:3 (1995), 545-557.

[641] Ratzinger and Pera, *Without Roots*, 125 [emphasis added].

[642] Ratzinger and Pera, *Without Roots*, 124. Otherwise, Ratzinger thinks that "the attempt to bring about a world-wide empire of peace through a world-wide union of religions is perilously close to the third temptation of Jesus: 'All the kingdoms of the world I will give you, if you fall down and worship me' (cf. Mt 4:9)." *A Turning Point for Europe*, 58.

[643] Ratzinger and Pera, *Without Roots*, 125.

[644] Ratzinger and Pera, *Without Roots*, 126. In *A Turning Point for Europe*, Ratzinger in speaking about contemporary perception of love also noted: "The capacity to love, that is, the capacity to wait in patience for what is not under one's own control and to let oneself receive this as a gift, is suffocated by the speedy fulfillments in which I am dependent on no one but in which I am never obliged to emerge from my own self and thus never find the path into my own self" 176.

[645] Ratzinger and Pera, *Without Roots*, 126.

[646] Ratzinger and Pera, *Without Roots*, 128.

[647] Ratzinger and Pera, *Without Roots*, 130.

[648] Ratzinger and Pera, *Without Roots*, 130.

[649] Ratzinger and Pera, *Without Roots*, 131. In *A Turning Point for Europe*, Ratzinger says: "But there is an objective connection between this and the conviction that was common to almost the whole of mankind before the modern period, the conviction that man's Being contains an imperative; the conviction that he does not himself *invent* morality on the basis of calculations of expediency but rather *finds* it already present in the essence of things." And that: "In reality, the fundamental intuition about the moral character of Being itself and about

the necessary harmony between the human being and the message of nature is common to all the great cultures and therefore the great moral imperatives are likewise held in common."28-30.

[650] "The session was moderated by the Academy president, Dr. Florian Schuller and the audience was restricted to about thirty persons, including two cardinals, a few Bavarian statesmen including the Land prime minister (Vogel) and some prominent intellectuals such as the essayist Robert Spaemann and the theologian Johann Baptist Metz"; Nemoianu, "The Church and the Secular Establishment: A Philosophical Dialogue between Joseph Ratzinger and Jürgen Habermas," 24.

[651] Ratzinger and Habermas, *The Dialectics of Secularization*, 11.

[652] Ratzinger and Habermas, *The Dialectics of Secularization*, 10.

[653] Ratzinger and Habermas, *The Dialectics of Secularization*, 11-12; Nemoianu noted, "Habermas was not the only intellectual in whom one can recognize some signs of 'turning.' Several prominent European figures sent out similar signals." Nemoianu mentions figures like Norberto Bobbio, Jacques Derrida and Emmanuel Lévinas. Cf. "The Church and the Secular Establishment: A Philosophical Dialogue between Joseph Ratzinger and Jürgen Habermas," 16-42.

[654] Ratzinger and Habermas, *The Dialectics of Secularization*, 15.

[655] Ratzinger and Habermas, *The Dialectics of Secularization*, 21.

[656] See Dulles, "John F. Scarpa Conference on Law, Politics and Culture," where he noted that the state most fundamentally "depends upon the ideas and behavior of its citizens, which it cannot exhaustively control," it also "lacks the moral vision needed to motivate citizens to labor for the common good." 245.

[657] Ratzinger and Habermas, *The Dialectics of Secularization*, 36-37. Girard employing his theory of "mimetic rivalry" that not differences drive conflict but the desire to possess what the other possesses, argues that "we live in a mimetic world" and "today, we are more realistic. We are aware that globalization does not mean global friendship, but global competition and, therefore, conflict. That doesn't mean we will all destroy each other, but it is no happy global village either." Also, in his theory he argues that "the dilution of difference doesn't end conflict. In some ways, becoming the same intensifies rivalry." Girard, "Ratzinger is Right," 47.

[658] Ratzinger and Habermas, *The Dialectics of Secularization*, 37.

[659] Nemoianu noted that the common denominator of the different usages of the term "post-secular" is "a denial of the ideologized claims of purely rationalistic science and a refusal to keep science on some kind of pedestal, as a supreme and unshakable expression of truth against any other type of discourse." In "The Church and the Secular Establishment: A Philosophical Dialogue between Joseph Ratzinger and Jürgen Habermas," 33.

[660] Ratzinger and Habermas, *The Dialectics of Secularization*, 41.

[661] Ratzinger and Habermas, *The Dialectics of Secularization*, 42.

[662] Ratzinger and Habermas, *The Dialectics of Secularization*, 46.

[663] Ratzinger and Habermas, *The Dialectics of Secularization*, 46-47.

[664] Ratzinger and Habermas, *The Dialectics of Secularization*, 51.

[665] "One may compare Habermas 'softening' on religion with that of Nietzsche, who in his *The Gay Science* confessed: Even we godless anti-metaphysicians still take our fire, too, from the flame lit by a faith thousands of years old, the Christian faith, which was also the faith of Plato: that God is the truth, that

truth is divine," as cited by Edward T. Oakes, SJ, "On Relativism," available on Internet.

[666] Ratzinger and Habermas, *The Dialectics of Secularization*, 55.

[667] Ratzinger and Habermas, *The Dialectics of Secularization*, 65.

[668] Nemoianu, "The Church and the Secular Establishment: A Philosophical Dialogue between Joseph Ratzinger and Jürgen Habermas," 29.

[669] Julia Kristeva, "Rethinking 'Normative Conscience': Task of the Intellectual Today," *A "Dictatorship of Relativism"? Symposium in Response to Cardinal Ratzinger's Last Homily, Common Knowledge* 13:2-3 (2007), 219-226, here 220.

[670] Julia Kristeva, "Rethinking 'Normative Conscience,'" 221.

[671] Julia Kristeva, "Rethinking 'Normative Conscience,'" 221.

[672] Ratzinger, *A Turning Point for Europe*, 21; he also argues that: "On the basis of its roots, terrorism is a moralism, albeit a misdirected one that becomes the brutal parody of the true aims and paths of morality. It is not by chance that terrorism had its beginning in the universities and here one again in the milieu of modern theology, in young people who at the outset were strongly influenced by religion" 21.

[673] Allen, *Pope Benedict XVI*, 139.

[674] Ratzinger and Habermas, *The Dialectics of Secularization*, 58.

[675] Ratzinger and Habermas, *The Dialectics of Secularization*, 58.

[676] Ratzinger and Habermas, *The Dialectics of Secularization*, 59. Dulles also noted, "The Encyclicals of Pope John XXIII and the documents of Vatican II seemed to favor something like the American democratic system, in which the government is accountable to the people, who actively take part in the political process." Dulles, "John F. Scarpa Conference on Law, Politics and Culture," 242.

[677] Weigel, *God's Choice*, 163.

[678] Ratzinger and Habermas, *The Dialectics of Secularization: On Reason and Religion*, 61. Allen notes that Ratzinger over the course of his intellectual career, "has identified many positive elements in the contemporary social order that should be defended and built upon, chief among them democracy, and the respect for human rights upon which it is based. Yet Benedict also believes that democracy is dependent for its vitality upon citizens with a sense of moral purpose and attachment to ultimate truths that democracy itself cannot supply, and it is precisely this sense of purpose, this awareness of an objective order that does not depend upon human subjectivity, that relativism saps." *The Rise of Pope Benedict XVI*, 173.

[679] Habermas and Ratzinger, *The Dialectics of Secularization: On Reason and Religion*, 69. See also J. Budziszewski, "Natural Law as Fact, as Theory, and as Sign of Contradiction," *Catholic Social Science Review* 12 (2007), 11-32.

[680] Allen pointed out, "A related danger is that relativism undercuts respect of human rights by treating rights claims as grounded in social convention rather than transcendent truth. Ratzinger unpacked this point in November 1999, when he was given an honorary *juris doctorate* by the LUMSA School of Law in Rome. In a culture dominated by relativism, Ratzinger warned, law becomes distorted and human rights are in jeopardy." *The Rise of Pope Benedict XVI*, 176.

[681] Joseph Ratzinger, *"In the Beginning...": A Catholic Understanding of the Story of Creation and the Fall* (Edinburgh: T&T Clark, 1995), 45. Also, in *A Turning Point for Europe*, Ratzinger noted: "If there is no longer any obligation to which he can and must respond in freedom, then there is no longer any realm of freedom at all." 36.

682 Bloor, "Epistemic Grace: Antirelativism as Theology in Disguise," 273.

683 Joseph Ratzinger's Homily, *Pro Eligendo Romano Pontifice*, in *The Essential Pope Benedict: His Central Writings and Speeches*, John F. Thornton and Susan B. Varenne, eds. (New York: HarperCollins Publishers, 2007), 21-24, here 21.

684 Ratzinger's Homily, *Pro Eligendo Romano Pontifice*, 22.

685 For more on the paschal theme see "Faith as Conversion – Metanoia," in Joseph Ratzinger, *Principles of Catholic Theology: Building Stones for a Fundamental Theology* (San Francisco: Ignatius Press, 1987), 55-67.

686 Already early on in his life, Ratzinger uses the image of a wind to describe the dangerous tendencies of his time. Pursell tells, "On May 24, 1952, Ratzinger wrote a short poem to a little girl, a student in one of his religion classes, who was maybe eight years old at the time. The two stanzas are set apart, probably showing that the first is a quotation, the second being his own composition: *However the winds blow/You should stand against them/When the world falls apart/Your brave heart won't despair//Without the heart's bravery,/which has the courage to withstand /unshakably/the spirits of the time and the masses,/we cannot find the way to God/and the true way of our Lord.* He signed it, "in remembrance of your catechist, Joseph Ratzinger." Pursell, *Benedict of Bavaria*, 80.

687 Barbara H. Smith notes that in his homily and especially in the reference to St. Paul's Letter to the Ephesians 4:14, Ratzinger may be suggesting that "certain more or less specific movements associated with such views – pragmatism, poststructuralism, constructivism and so forth – are among the 'new sects' that '[make] come true' Paul's saying 'about human deception and the trickery that strives to entice people to error'" in her article "Relativism, Today and Yesterday," 245-246.

688 Ratzinger's Homily, *Pro Eligendo Romano Pontifice*, 22; How Ratzinger interprets the term "libertinism" can be found in his book *A Turning Point for Europe?* 17, "But anyone who dares to say that mankind should set itself free from the chaotic sexual libertinism that gives AIDS its offensive potential is dismissed by public opinion as a hopeless obscurantist...."

689 Smith, "Relativism, Today and Yesterday," 245.

690 Stout, "A House Founded on the Sea; Is Democracy a Dictatorship of Relativism?" 387. Ratzinger himself answers the question of his possible participation in the Hitler-Jugend group, in *Salt of the Earth*, 52.

691 Robert P. Imbelli recalls the statement from "Call to Be Catholic," Cardinal Joseph Bernardin's Common Ground Initiative, where it said: "Jesus Christ, present in Scripture and sacrament, is central to all that we do; he must always be the measure and not what is measured," in "Rome & Relativism: *'Dominus Iesus'* & the CDF," 14.

692 Nichols, *The Thought of Pope Benedict XVI*, 61.

693 Corkery, "Joseph Ratzinger's Theological Ideas 3–On Being Human," 13.

694 Ratzinger's Homily, *Pro Eligendo Romano Pontifice*, 23.

695 Ratzinger's Homily, *Pro Eligendo Romano Pontifice*, 23.

696 Ratzinger, *Salt of the Earth*, 282.

697 Ratzinger's Homily, *Pro Eligendo Romano Pontifice*, 23.

698 Corkery, "Joseph Ratzinger's Theological Ideas 2–The Facial Features of a Theological *Corpus*," 8.

699 Corkery noted that in speaking about the love of God and the love of man, "Augustine's 'two cities' are in the background... and that it was not so much a matter of two competing loves as a struggle between love and not being able

to love – indeed refusing to love." In Corkery, "Joseph Ratzinger's Theological Ideas 3–On Being Human," 13.

700 Ratzinger's Homily, *Pro Eligendo Romano Pontifice*, 24.

701 Ratzinger's Homily, *Pro Eligendo Romano Pontifice*, 24.

702 Vattimo tells us that the founding members of this journal's editorial board were Richard Rorty and Paul Feyerabend and that the idea of this symposium developed in conversation among Clifford Geertz, Caroline Bynum and the present journal's editors, "only a few months after Ratzinger's homily on the 'dictatorship of relativism' was delivered" 214. Geertz was among the leading relativist anthropologists of the last century; however, his closest friends argue, he was a relativist only as it related to the diversity of cultures, thus, cultural relativism, but not ethical. See Clifford Geertz, "Anti-Anti Relativism," in Michael Krausz, ed., *Relativism: Interpretation and Confrontation* (Notre Dame, IN: University of Notre Dame, 1989), 12-34. David Perusek, an anthropologist at Kent State University also notes there is a difference between cultural relativism and all other kinds of relativisms and if that difference is not maintained it becomes erroneously perceived, "after having long been regarded by Western traditionalists as a gateway to an icon of moral degeneration, criticized by philosophers as a negation of the idea of universal truth in ethics and denounced as evil by clergy – most notably by Joseph Ratzinger, whose pontifications on the subject now carry the weight of his recent ascendancy to the papacy – cultural relativism is increasingly under fire from human rights activists, socialists, communists and left-leaning thinkers the world over." David Perusek, "Grounding Cultural Relativism," *Anthropological Quarterly* 80:3 (Summer 2007), 821-836, here 821.

703 Christopher Norris, "Dictatorship of the Professoriat? Antiobjectivism in Anglo-American Philosophy," *A "Dictatorship of Relativism"? Symposium in Response to Cardinal Ratzinger's Last Homily. Common Knowledge* 13:2-3 (2007), 281-314, here 314. Howard Lesnick, Professor of Law at the University of Pennsylvania, also critiques Ratzinger's definition of relativism: "Ratzinger's 'definition' of relativism is pure invective; few if any relativists think that all positions are equal, or regard 'one's own desires' as unquestionable; it is only that one's values or goals cannot be evaluated by an external standard of truth, for no such external standard exists." Howard Lesnick, "The rhetoric of Anti-Relativism in a Culture of Certainty," *Buffalo Law Review* 55 (December 2007), 887-928, here 894.

704 Gianni Vattimo, *A "Dictatorship of Relativism"? Symposium in Response to Cardinal Ratzinger's Last Homily:* Introduction: *Common Knowledge*, Vol. 13:2-3 (Spring-Fall 2007), 214-218, here 216.

704a Vattimo, "Surtout Pas de Zèle," 216; Another participant of the symposium, Jeffrey Stout in his article "A House Founded on the Sea: Is Democracy a Dictatorship of Relativism?" notes that "John Paul's references to totalitarianism and tyranny [in *Evangelium Vitae*] help make clear why Cardinal Ratzinger's homily referred to the dictatorship of relativism." 218.

705 Vattimo, "Surtout Pas de Zèle," 218.

706 Vattimo, "Surtout Pas de Zèle," 218.

707 Vattimo, "Surtout Pas de Zèle," 218.

708 Hick, *An Interpretation of Religion*, 380.

709 Vattimo, "Surtout Pas de Zèle," 218.

710 Cf. Simon Blackburn, "True Enough," *Times Literary Supplement* (September 1, 2006), 61.

[711] Perl, "T.S. Eliot's Small Boat of Thought," *A "Dictatorship of Relativism"? Symposium in Response to Cardinal Ratzinger's Last Homily, Common Knowledge* 13:2-3 (2007), 337-361, here 360.

[712] Perl, "T.S. Eliot's Small Boat of Thought," 361, references Charles Taylor, "Benedict XVI," *Public Culture* 18:1 (2006), 11-14.

[713] Perl, "T.S. Eliot's Small Boat of Thought," 361.

[714] Corkery, "Joseph Ratzinger's Theological Vision 6: Resisting the 'Dictatorship of Relativism,'" 5; where he also adds, "Indeed Ratzinger once pointed out, drawing on Romano Guardini, that humility consists here not in retreating from naming God and being voiceless before the ineffable (as is so fashionable today), but rather in bowing before the scandal that God can and does *do* the unimaginable: become human, now true God *and* true man, in the historical Jesus of Nazareth." See also Joseph Cardinal Ratzinger, "It is Arrogant to Say Christ is the Only Savior? Ask Cardinal Ratzinger," available from: http://www.zenit.org/article-5964?l=english; accessed 15 November 2009.

[715] Vattimo, "Surtout Pas de Zèle," 218.

[716] Smith, "Relativism, Today and Yesterday," 228.

[717] Smith, "Relativism, Today and Yesterday," 230.

[718] Smith, "Relativism, Today and Yesterday," 234.

[719] Nichols comments that for Ratzinger "the setting of theology in the midst of the Church ought not, he says, to deprive it of its vigor or close off its openness to new style of thought." in *The Thought of Pope Benedict XVI*, xiii.

[720] Ratzinger, *Pro Eligendo Romano Pontifice*, 22.

[721] Smith, "Relativism, Today and Yesterday," 248.

[722] Bloor, "Epistemic Grace: Antirelativism as Theology in Disguise," 251.

[723] Bloor, "Epistemic Grace: Antirelativism as Theology in Disguise," 252.

[724] Bloor, "Epistemic Grace: Antirelativism as Theology in Disguise," 252.

[725] Corkery, "Joseph Ratzinger's Theological Ideas 2–The Facial Features of a Theological *Corpus*," 2-12.

[726] However, as Murphy notes, "Agnosticism, though initially appealing because of its lack of dogmatic commitment and its recognition of the limits of human scientific knowing, is no solution to the God-question." Murphy, *Christ Our Joy*, 63; also cf. Ratzinger, *Pilgrim Fellowship of Faith*, 286.

[727] Available at: http://www.uoregon.edu/~dlutz/webquotes/michelangelo.htm; accessed 13 June 2009.

[728] Bloor, "Epistemic Grace: Antirelativism as Theology in Disguise," 254.

[729] Bloor, "Epistemic Grace: Antirelativism as Theology in Disguise," 263. Nemoianu notes, "Nobody (least of all Catholic *Weltanschauung*) denied that religion is endowed with an incarnational and thus sociohistorical dimension, the side with which the Church responds to matters and issues of practical concern in the world. Although, in a way, such an approach is precisely the side where the Church is most vulnerable and most likely to err occasionally." In Nemoianu, "The Church and the Secular Establishment: A Philosophical Dialog between Joseph Ratzinger and Jürgen Habermas," 34.

[730] Bloor, "Epistemic Grace: Antirelativism as Theology in Disguise," 263.

[731] Bloor, "Epistemic Grace: Antirelativism as Theology in Disguise," 258.

[732] Bloor, "Epistemic Grace: Antirelativism as Theology in Disguise," 273.

[733] Bloor, "Epistemic Grace: Antirelativism as Theology in Disguise," 274.

[734] Austin Dacey, "Believing in Doubt," *The New York Times* (February 3, 2006),

cited in Corkery, "Joseph Ratzinger's Theological Ideas 6–Resisting the 'Dictatorship of Relativism,'" 19. In addition, Lawrence Hinman proposes a third way, a sort of pluralism, which he terms a "middle ground" between relativism and absolutism, one that "incorporates insights from both": "From relativism, it retains the sensitivity to the contextuality of our moral beliefs and the recognition that moral disagreement and conflict are permanent features of the moral landscape. From absolutism, it retains the commitment to the relevance of reasoned discourse in the moral life and the belief that some moral positions are better than others." Lawrence M. Hinman, *Ethics: A Pluralistic Approach to Moral Theory* (Fort Worth, TX: Harcourt Brace College Publishers, 1994), 48.

735 Bloor, "Epistemic Grace: Antirelativism as Theology in Disguise," 274-275.

736 Austin Dacey, "Believing in Doubt," *The New York Times* (February 3, 2006), available at: http://www.nytimes.com/2006/02/03/opinion/03dacey.html; accessed 7 November 2009.

737 Corkery, "Joseph Ratzinger's Theological Ideas 6–Resisting the 'Dictatorship of Relativism,'" 20.

738 Bloor, "Epistemic Grace: Antirelativism as Theology in Disguise," 276.

739 Nichols, *The Thought of Pope Benedict XVI*, 78. René Girard adds, "The whole point of Incarnation is to say that the human and divine are interrelated in a way that is unique to Christian theology, unthinkable in any other religion and, in my view, absolutely superior. Whether in the case of Muslims focused on martyrdom or the fundamentalist Christians focused on the Apocalypse, the old Greek conception of a God apart from man is not enough." Girard, "Ratzinger is Right," 48.

740 Bloor, "Epistemic Grace: Antirelativism as Theology in Disguise," 279.

741 Bloor, "Epistemic Grace: Antirelativism as Theology in Disguise," 279.

742 Julia Kristeva, "Rethinking 'Normative Conscience,'" 225. Twomey allows Ratzinger to respond: "As we will see, Ratzinger demonstrates how frankness (or boldness) is an essential component of that biblical understanding of freedom which truth engenders in the human heart: 'The apostle's frankness consists of saying the truth to a world dominated by appearance, even though this involves him in conflict (1 Th 2:2).' Ratzinger is no stranger that conflict." In *Pope Benedict XVI*, 29.

743 Kristeva, "Rethinking 'Normative Conscience,'" 221.

744 Kristeva, "Rethinking 'Normative Conscience,'" 226.

745 Ratzinger, *A Turning Point for Europe*, 36.

746 Daniel Boyarin, "The Scandal of Sophism: On the Epistemological Seriousness of Relativism," *A "Dictatorship of Relativism"? Symposium in Response to Cardinal Ratzinger's Last Homily. Common Knowledge* 13:2-3 (2007), 315-336, here 316.

747 Boyarin, "The Scandal of Sophism: On the Epistemological Seriousness of Relativism," 332.

748 Boyarin, "The Scandal of Sophism: On the Epistemological Seriousness of Relativism," 333.

749 Ratzinger, "The Church on the Threshold of the Third Millennium," especially see pages 286-287.

750 Boyarin, "The Scandal of Sophism: On the Epistemological Seriousness of Relativism," 333.

751 Corkery notes that for Ratzinger we are "beggars before God, stretching out

our hands to *receive* what only God can give. Indeed, we are first and foremost *receivers*, not 'do-ers.' But we forget this." In Corkery, "Joseph Ratzinger's Theological Ideas 3–On Being Human," 9, where he references Joseph Ratzinger, "Beten in unserer Zeit," in *Dogma und Verkündigung* (Munich: Wewel, 1973), 123; also David L. Schindler, "Is America Bourgeois?" in *Communio* 14 (Fall 1987), 262-290, especially 267-271.

[752] Boyarin, "The Scandal of Sophism: On the Epistemological Seriousness of Relativism," 334. Allen states, "In the Athens of Plato's era, Sophists believed that truth was meaningless and the only thing that mattered was the exercise of power, hence their preference for rhetoric over metaphysics... Platonists resisted that conclusion, Ratzinger says. By insisting on objective truth, Plato put limits to power and hence relativized all human regimes." *Pope Benedict XVI*, 101.

[753] Norris, "Dictatorship of the Professoriat?" 290.

[754] Boyarin, "The Scandal of Sophism: On the Epistemological Seriousness of Relativism," 324.

[755] Boyarin, "The Scandal of Sophism: On the Epistemological Seriousness of Relativism," 333.

[756] Boyarin, "The Scandal of Sophism: On the Epistemological Seriousness of Relativism," 336. René Girard, an emeritus professor of anthropology at Stanford University, argues against relativism, in terms of commitment: "Because all truths are treated as equal, since there is said to be no objective Truth, you are forced to be banal and superficial. You cannot be truly committed to anything, to be 'for' something – even if only for the period of time being. Like Ratzinger, however, I believe in commitment. After all, we are both convinced by the idea that responsibility demands we must be committed to one position and follow it through." Girard, "Ratzinger is Right," 43.

[757] Perl, "T.S. Eliot's Small Boat of Thought," 337.

[758] Perl, "T.S. Eliot's Small Boat of Thought," 338.

[759] Jeffrey M. Perl, *Skepticism and Modern Enmity: Before and After Eliot* (Baltimore, MD: Johns Hopkins University Press, 1989).

[760] Ratzinger argues that conversion is the fundamental Christian act and that "Readiness to be changed by Christ has nothing to do with that indecisiveness about existence, that facile conformity, that can be pushed in any direction." In Ratzinger, "Faith as Conversion – Metanoia," in *Principles of Catholic Theology: Building Stones for a Fundamental Theology*, 55-67, here 62.

[761] T.S. Eliot, "Demon of doubt": Eliot, "The Pensées of Pascal" (1931), in *Selected Essays* (New York: Harcourt Brace Jovanovich, 1978).

[762] Perl, "T.S. Eliot's Small Boat of Thought," 341, also references "Systole and diastole": Eliot, "Goethe as the Sage" (1955), in *On Poetry and Poets* (New York: Noonday, 1957).

[763] Ratzinger's best treatment of doubt is given in his *Introduction to Christianity*, 39-81; also Ratzinger, *God and the World*, 35-41.

[764] Gergen, "Relativism, Religion and Relational Being," 363-364.

[765] Gergen, "Relativism, Religion and Relational Being," 364.

[766] Gergen, "Relativism, Religion and Relational Being," 364-365.

[767] Gergen, "Relativism, Religion and Relational Being," 371.

[768] Gergen, "Relativism, Religion and Relational Being," 376.

[769] Richard Shusterman, "Fallibilism and Faith," *A "Dictatorship of Relativism"? Symposium in Response to Cardinal Ratzinger's Last Homily. Common Knowledge* 13:2-3, (2007), 379-384, here 384.

770 Bromiley, "The Limits of Theological Relativism," 823.

771 Ratzinger and Habermas, *The Dialectics of Secularization*, 76.

772 Ratzinger, "Relativism: The Central Problem in Faith Today," 239.

773 Ratzinger and Habermas, *The Dialectics of Secularization*, 79 [emphasis in original].

774 Ratzinger, *A Turning Point for Europe*, 108-109.

775 Nemoianu, "The Church and the Secular Establishment: A Philosophical Dialog between Joseph Ratzinger and Jürgen Habermas," 33. See also Alasdair MacIntyre, "Relativism, Power and Philosophy," *Proceedings and Addresses of the American Philosophical Association* 59:1 (September 1985), 5-22.

776 Baghramian, *Relativism*, 30. More about this criticism can be found in Chapter 1, pages 30-41 of Baghramian's book. See also I.C. Jarvie, "Relativism Yet Again," *Philosophy of the Social Sciences* 23 (1993), 537-547, here 546.

777 Richard Bernstein, *Beyond Objectivism and Relativism: Science, Hermeneutics and Praxis* (Philadelphia, PA: University of Pennsylvania Press, 1983), 109.

778 Ommen, "Relativism, Objectivism and Theology," 299.

779 Richard Rorty, *Philosophy and the Mirror of Nature* (Princeton, NJ: Princeton University Press, 1979), 377.

780 Ommen, "Relativism, Objectivism and Theology," 301-302.

781 Ommen, "Relativism, Objectivism and Theology," 302.

782 Ommen, "Relativism, Objectivism and Theology," 303.

783 Ommen, "Relativism, Objectivism and Theology," 303.

784 Hans Georg Gadamer, *Truth and Method* (New York: Seabury, 1975), 305-341.

785 Ommen, "Relativism, Objectivism and Theology," 303.

786 Berstein, *Beyond Objectivism and Relativism*, 154.

787 David Tracy, *The Analogical Imagination: Christian Theology and the Culture of Pluralism* (New York: Crossroad, 1981), 447.

788 Francis Schüssler Fiorenza, *Foundational Theology: Jesus and the Church* (New York: Crossroad, 1984), 302.

789 Ommen, "Relativism, Objectivism and Theology," 305.

790 Ommen, "Relativism, Objectivism and Theology," 305.

791 Ratzinger, *Truth and Tolerance*, 144.

792 Rowland, *Ratzinger's Faith*, 5. Cf. Ratzinger, *Truth and Tolerance*, 136. See also Brad Kallenber, "The Gospel Truth of Relativism," *Scottish Journal of Theology* 53:2 (2000), 177-211.

793 Ratzinger, *Christianity and the Crisis of Cultures*, 18.

794 Ratzinger, *Christianity and the Crisis of Cultures*, 18-19.

795 Ratzinger, *Christianity and the Crisis of Cultures*, 28.

796 Ratzinger, *Christianity and the Crisis of Cultures*, 28-29.

797 "Liberalism and Marxism were in agreement in refusing religion both the right and the capacity to shape public affairs and the common future of mankind. In the maturation process of the second half of this century, religion has been discovered anew as an ineradicable force both of individual and of social living. It has become clear that one cannot plan and shape the future of mankind while prescinding from religion. This process gives comfort to faith, but faith will not fail to recognize at the same time the dangers inherent in it, for the temptation is obvious on all sides to take in religion as an instrument to serve political ideas." Ratzinger, *A Turning Point for Europe*, 8.

[798] Ratzinger, *Christianity and the Crisis of Cultures*, 31.

[799] Ratzinger, *Christianity and the Crisis of Cultures*, 40.

[800] Ratzinger, *Christianity and the Crisis of Cultures*, 40.

[801] Ratzinger, *Christianity and the Crisis of Cultures*, 49.

[802] Ratzinger, *Christianity and the Crisis of Cultures*, 50. Murphy observes, "The question of God is, in fact, eminently practical, because it affects all spheres of life. While one could accept agnosticism as a theoretical position, in practice we must decide between one of the two possibilities: to live as though God exists or to live as though he does not. Hence, the question of God is not a neutral one, for the way we live our lives depends on our answer to it." Murphy, *Christ Our Joy*, 63.

[803] Edward T. Oakes, "Pascal: The First Modern Christian," *First Things* 95 (August/September 1999), 41-48, here 46.

[804] Marvin R. O'Connell, *Blaise Pascal: Reasons of the Heart* (Grand Rapids, MI: William B. Eerdmans Publishing Company, 1997), 184.

[805] Pascal, *Pensées and Other Writings*, 5.

[806] Pascal, *Pensées and Other Writings*, 8.

[807] Pascal, *Pensées and Other Writings*, 123.

[808] Pascal, *Pensées and Other Writings*, 161.

[809] Pascal, *Pensées and Other Writings*, 38.

[810] Pascal, *Pensées and Other Writings*, 72-73.

[811] Rick Wide, "Blaise Pascal: An Apologist for Our Times," Probe Ministries, 1998; available from http://www.probe.org/; accessed 21 October 2005.

[812] Frederick Copleston, *A History of Philosophy*, Vol. 4 (Garden City, NY: Doubleday, 1963), 170-171.

[813] Pascal, *Pensées and Other Writings*, 62.

[814] Pascal, *Pensées and Other Writings*, 35.

[815] Pascal, *Pensées and Other Writings*, 158.

[816] O'Connell, *Blaise Pascal: Reasons of the Heart*, 169. Allen states, "Ratzinger knows people are not led to God primarily through intellectual curiosity but through a burning need in their hearts. Loneliness and emotional impoverishment lead people to hunger for something more, and even happiness points beyond itself by posing the question of its source." *Pope Benedict XVI*, 94.

[817] Pascal, *Pensées and Other Writings*, 24.

[818] Pascal, *Pensées and Other Writings*, 79.

[819] Pascal, *Pensées and Other Writings*, 140.

[820] Pascal, *Pensées and Other Writings*, 63.

[821] Wide, "Blaise Pascal: An Apologist for Our Times," available on internet.

[822] Corkery, "Joseph Ratzinger's Theological Ideas 6–Resisting the 'Dictatorship of Relativism,'"18-19.

[823] Ratzinger, *Truth and Tolerance*, 136.

[824] Ratzinger, *Christianity and the Crisis of Cultures*, 113.

[825] Pascal, *Pensées and Other Writings*, 5.

[826] Pascal, *Pensées and Other Writings*, 53.

[827] Pascal, *Pensées and Other Writings*, 8.

[828] Pascal, *Pensées and Other Writings*, 8.

[829] Thomas V. Morris, *Making Sense of It All: Pascal and the Meaning of Life* (Grand Rapids, MI: William B. Eerdmans Publishing Company, 1992), 184-185.

830 Pascal, *Pensées and Other Writings*, 7.

831 Ratzinger, *Christianity and the Crisis of Cultures*, 93.

832 Pascal, *Pensées and Other Writings*, 7.

833 Ratzinger, *Christianity and the Crisis of Cultures*, 115-116. Edward T. Oakes, SJ summarizes what he calls Pascal's best recommendations for dealing with the challenge of relativism, by saying and eventually quoting Pascal, "Admit the hatred Christianity inspires and then meet that hatred with reason, love, and, above all, confidence in the 'absolutely' *beneficial* implications of Christianity. His advice could not be simpler: 'Men despise religion. They hate it and are afraid it may be true. The cure for this is first to show that religion is not contrary to reason, but worthy of reverence and respect. Next, make it attractive, make good men wish it were true, and then show that it is. Worthy of reverence because it really understands human nature. Attractive because it promises true good." In "On Relativism,"*First Things* (September 2007), available at: www.firstthings.com/onthesquare/?p=840; accessed 6 March 2009.

834 Ratzinger, *Milestones*, 20.

835 Ratzinger, *Salt of the Earth*, 47. Bardazzi recalls Ratzinger saying "Beauty is knowledge... a higher form of knowledge, since it strikes man with all the grandeur of truth." In Bardazzi's *In The Vineyard of the Lord*, 29, where he cites Joseph Ratzinger, "La corrispondenza del cuore nell'incontro con la bellezza," *30 Giorni* (August 2002); available at http://www.30giorni.it/it/articolo.asp?id=57; accessed 14 June 2009.

836 O'Grandy, "The Ratzinger Round," 411.

837 Ratzinger, *Many Religions–One Covenant*, 38. Allen observes that "Ratzinger regards Guardini's thinking on the liturgy as one of his most important contributions. In his 1992 introduction to the reissue of *The Lord*, Ratzinger says that by focusing on the liturgy as the arena in which believers meet the living Christ, Guardini pointed a way out of the radical skepticism that had gripped liberal Christianity under the influence of scientific biblical criticism." *Pope Benedict*, 39.

838 Fahey, "Joseph Ratzinger as Ecclesiologist and Pastor," 79; cites Ratzinger, "What will the Church Look Like in 2000," *Faith and the Future* (Chicago: Franciscan Herald Press, 1970), 89-106, here 105; for a comparison see also Ratzinger, "The Church on the Threshold of the Third Millennium," in *Pilgrim Fellowship of Faith: The Church as Communion* (San Francisco: Ignatius Press, 2005), 284-298.

839 Geoffrey Wainwright, "A Remedy for Relativism: The Cosmic, Historical and Eschatological Dimensions of the Liturgy According to the Theologian Joseph Ratzinger," *Nova et Vetera* Vol. 5, Issue 2-Spring 2007, 403. Wainwright bases his article on Ratzinger's book *The Spirit of the Liturgy* (2000), whose title recalls the classic text by Romano Guardini, *Vom Geist der Liturgie* (Freiburg im Breisgau; St. Louis: Herder, 1922); English translation: *The Church and the Catholic and the Spirit of Liturgy* (London: Sheed & Ward, 1935). Wainwright also states that the similarity of the titles "may be taken as a hint that Cardinal Ratzinger judged the Catholic Church itself and its liturgical practice to be in need of a recovery of certain qualities and even particular features, that had been lost to 'the spirit of the age' in an over-hasty rush to reform on the alleged basis of the Second Vatican Council," in "A Remedy for Relativism," 403.

840 Ratzinger, *The Spirit of the Liturgy*, 128.

841 Ratzinger, *The Spirit of the Liturgy*, 129.

842 Wainwright, "A Remedy for Relativism," 406.

843 Ratzinger, *The Spirit of the Liturgy*, 130.

844 Ratzinger, *The Spirit of the Liturgy*, 146.

845 Ratzinger, *The Spirit of the Liturgy*, 154. Ratzinger said in 1996 of Mozart: "The largest and most important and best part of my youth I spent in Traunstein, which very much reflects the influence of Salzburg. You might say that there Mozart thoroughly penetrated our souls, and his music still touches me very deeply, because it is so luminous and yet at the same time so deep. His music is by no means just entertainment; it contains the whole tragedy of human existence." Ratzinger, *Salt of the Earth*, 47.

846 Ratzinger, *The Spirit of the Liturgy*, 155. "The marketing of vulgar art, music, and literature and the generation of a very low, even barbaric, mass culture is seen by Ratzinger to be one of the serious pathologies of contemporary mass western culture." Rowland, *Ratzinger's Faith*, 9.

847 Wainwright, "A Remedy for Relativism," 408; cites Ratzinger's *The Spirit of the Liturgy*, 131 and 155.

848 St. Irenaeus, *Adversus Haereses*, 4.20.7.

849 Wainwright points to Ratzinger's *The Spirit of the Liturgy*, 45-50.

850 Wainwright, "A Remedy for Relativism," 415.

851 Wainwright, "A Remedy for Relativism," 415.

852 Geoffrey Wainwright, *For Our Salvation: Two Approaches to the Work of Christ* (Grand Rapids, MI: B. Eerdmans, 1997), 18.

853 Ratzinger, *The Spirit of the Liturgy*, 18.

854 Ratzinger, *The Spirit of the Liturgy*, 18. Ratzinger also speaks of man being degraded if he cannot know truth, "if everything, in the final analysis, is just the product of an individual or collective decision." In *Salt of the Earth*, 67. Also in *A Turning Point for Europe*, Ratzinger notes, "If truth is inaccessible,… then there is no distinction in reality between right and wrong, no distinction between rightful and wrongful power, but only the pressure of the momentarily stronger group, the supremacy of the majority." 51.

855 Ratzinger, "Guardini on Christ in Our Century," 55; also Ratzinger says, for Romano Guardini – himself in search of a new path for theology – the experience of liturgy was the place of encounter with Jesus, "it is above all in the liturgy that Jesus is among us; here he speaks to us, here he lives." 53f. Jim Corkery says that "The priority of *logos* over *ethos*, of receiving over making, of being over doing lies at the heart and center of Joseph Ratzinger's theological synthesis." In Corkery, "Joseph Ratzinger's Theological Ideas 2–The Facial Features of a Theological *Corpus*," 6. As Nichols puts it, "At the same time, the developed Christological orthodoxy of the Church also acknowledges and no less resolutely, that in this radical service of sacrificial love, Jesus is 'the most human of men' and it thus subscribes *to the identity of theology with anthropology* [emphasis added].'" Nichols, *The Thought of Pope Benedict XVI*, 87.

856 *Dominus Iesus*, 4; cited in Wainwright, "A Remedy for Relativism," 426. See also Raphael Jospe, "Pluralism out of the Sources of Judaism: Religious Pluralism without Relativism," *Studies in Christian-Jewish Relations* 2:2 (2007), 92-113 where Jospe confronts Ratzinger's equation of relativism with religious pluralism. He proposes his own thesis, basing it on an argument of employing the correctly understood Jewish concept of the chosen people, where it should be understood not as directed externally, but internally, saying that Jews in fact are not better than other people, but rather, this idea is challenging Jews

to become better people. This is compatible with religious pluralism, based on "the paradigm of the Jewish obligation to live in accordance with the commandments of the Torah while accepting the legitimacy of other ways of life in accordance with the paradigm of the universal 'seven commandments of the children of Noah.'" Consequently, Jospe states, "what I propose is a reversal of traditional claims. Instead of spiritual exclusivity (the notion that there is only one truth and that one group has exclusive possession of the truth and of the key to salvation, however understood), which logically leads to ritual inclusivity (the impulse to proselytize and include others in one's own religious community with its ritual obligations), we should attempt to work for spiritual inclusivity (recognition that different groups are capable of understanding the truth, albeit frequently in diverse ways), which logically leads to ritual exclusivity (or pluralism, namely that the existence of different religious approaches and ritual practices is both legitimate and desirable and that there is no reason to seek to proselytize others)."

857 Ratzinger, *The Spirit of the Liturgy*, 183.

858 Ratzinger, *The Spirit of the Liturgy*, 201. See also Ratzinger's "Christ, Faith and the Challenge of Cultures," available at: http://www.ewtn.com/library/CURIA/RATZHONG.HTM; accessed 14 November 2009. Allen notes: "Ratzinger says the oft-repeated buzzword of 'inculturation' is actually a misnomer, because it implies that a religion shorn of culture (Christianity) meets a culture independent of faith (for instance, Asia).... Ratzinger proposes instead 'interculturality' to capture the actual process of 'reciprocal refinement and combination' that should occur when Christianity meets another culture." *Pope Benedict XVI*, 237.

859 Encyclical of Pope Pius XII, *Mediator Dei* (November 20, 1947); available from: http://www.vatican.va/holy_father/pius_xii/encyclicals/documents/hf_p-xii_enc_20111947_mediator-dei_en.html; accessed 24 August 2009; 48.

860 Wainwright, "A Remedy for Relativism," 429.

861 Helmut Richard Niebuhr, *Christ and Culture* (New York: Harper, 1956).

862 Wainwright, "A Remedy for Relativism," 429.

863 Wainwright, "A Remedy for Relativism," 429. Allen observes that in Ratzinger's view "One cannot apply pluralism inside the Church, forgetting it is not a state but a communion." *Pope Benedict XVI*, 267.

864 George Weigel, *God's Choice: Pope Benedict XVI and the Future of the Catholic Church* (New York: Harper Perennial, 2006), 140.

865 E.J. Dionne, Jr., "Cardinal Ratzinger's Challenge," in *The Washington Post* (April 19, 2005), 19.

866 Weigel, *God's Choice*, 151.

867 Weigel, *God's Choice*, 211-212.

868 The expression "dictatorship of relativism" up to January 12, 2010 appears only twice in the official records of Pope Benedict's speeches: the first time on January 8, 2007 during his address to the diplomatic corps accredited to the Holy See for the traditional exchange of New Year's greetings, where the Pope noted that "the practice of democracy must not be allowed to turn into a dictatorship of relativism, by proposing anthropological models incompatible with the nature and dignity of the human person," available from: http://www.vatican/va/holy_father/benedict_xvi/speeches/2007/january/documents/hf_ben-xvi_spe_20070108_diplomatic-corps_en.html; accessed 12 January 2010; and the second time during his apostolic journey to the United States of

America in the responses he gave to the questions posed by the bishops at their meeting in the National Shrine of the Immaculate Conception in Washington, D.C. (April 16, 2008), where the Pope argued that "the 'dictatorship of relativism,' in the end, is nothing less than a threat to genuine human freedom, which only matures in generosity and fidelity to the truth," in James Corkery, SJ, *Joseph Ratzinger's Theological Ideas: Wise Cautions and Legitimate Hopes* (New York/Mahwah, NJ: Paulist Press, 2009), 29.

[869] Weigel, *God's Choice*, 215-216.

[870] Weigel, *God's Choice*, 216.

[871] Benedict XVI, *Christ Our Hope: The Papal Addresses of the Apostolic Journey to the United States* (Mahwah, NJ: Paulist Press, 2008), 46.

[872] Weigel, *God's Choice*, 216-217.

[873] Alasdair MacIntyre, *After Virtue: A Study of Moral Theory* (Notre Dame, IN: University of Notre Dame Press, 1981), 245 as referenced in Weigel's *God's Choice*, 217, footnote 4.

[874] Weigel, *God's Choice*, 217; Weigel also adds: "The crisis of the post-modern world is only slightly different in that it is a world in which 'true' and 'false' have lost their meaning, excepts as verbal signals of personal preferences. Yet it seems to him [Benedict XVI] just as unlikely that decent human communities can be built on foundations of determined ambiguity as on foundations of deliberate falsehood" 217.

[875] Appendix I in bibliography.

[876] (Emphasis added).Benedict XVI, *Address of His Holiness Benedict XVI to the Participants in the Ecclesial Diocesan Convention of Rome* (June 6, 2005), available from: http://www.vatican/va/holy_father/benedict_xvi/speeches/2005/june/documents/hf_ben-xvi_spe_20050606_convegno-familia_en.html; accessed 12 January 2010. On another occasion the Pope noted: "The dynamic between personal encounter, knowledge and Christian witness is integral to the *diakonia* of truth which the Church exercises in the midst of humanity." In Benedict XVI, *Christ Our Hope*, 44. Also, Benedict XVI uses that same expression "particularly insidious obstacle" when addressing the bishops of Canada-Ontario on their *ad limina* visit December 8, 2006, as referenced by James Corkery, in *Joseph Ratzinger's Theological Ideas*, 93.

[877] Benedict XVI, *Angelus* (December 4, 2005), cites *Dignitatis Humanae*, n. 2, available from: http://www.vatican/va/holy_father/benedict_xvi/angelus/2005/documents/hf_ben-xvi_spe_20051004_en.html; accessed 12 January 2010.

[878] Benedict XVI, *Angelus* (December 4, 2005), available on internet.

[879] Benedict XVI, *Message of His Holiness Benedict XVI to His Eminence Card. Antonio José González Zumárraga, Archbishop Emeritus of Quito, President of the Central Commission of the Third American Missionary Congress* (August 12, 2008), available from: http://www.vatican/va/holy_father/benedict_xvi/messages/2008/documents/hf_ben-xvi_spe_20080812_antonio-gonzalez_en.html; accessed 12 January 2010.

[880] Benedict XVI, *Address of His Holiness Benedict XVI to the Roman Curia Offering them his Christmas Greetings* (December 22, 2005), available from: http://www.vatican/va/holy_father/benedict_xvi/speeches/2005/december/documents/hf_ben-xvi_spe_20051222_roman-curia_en.html; accessed 12 January 2010. The Holy Father also noted that at the youth gathering in Cologne he was most impressed with the unforgettable *intense silence* of that million young people, "a silence that united and uplifted us all when the Lord in the Blessed Sacrament

was placed on the altar." Benedict XVI, *God's Revolution: World Youth Day and Other Cologne Talks* (San Francisco: Ignatius Press, 2006), 94.

881 Pope Benedict XVI, *God's Revolution*, 95.

882 Pope Benedict XVI, *God's Revolution*, 95.

883 Benedict XVI, *Receive the Power: World Youth Day, Sydney Australia 2008* (WYD 2008: Catholic Press Newspaper Company Pty Ltd., 2008), 78.

884 Benedict XVI, *Receive the Power*, 78.

885 Benedict XVI, *Receive the Power*, 78.

886 Benedict XVI, *Address of His Holiness Benedict XVI to H.E. Mrs. Anne Maree Plunkett, New Ambassador of Australia to the Holy See* (May 18, 2006), available from: http://www.vatican/va/holy_father/benedict_xvi/speeches/2006/may/documents/hf_ben-xvi_spe_20060518_ambassador-australia_en.html; accessed 15 January 2010.

887 Benedict XVI, *Receive the Power*, 78.

888 *Encounter of His Holiness Benedict XVI with the Youth of Rome and the Lazio Region in Preparation for the XXI World Youth Day* (April 6, 2006), available from: http://www.vatican/va/holy_father/benedict_xvi/speeches/2006/april/documents/hf_ben-xvi_spe_20060406_xxi-wyd_en.html; accessed 24 January 2010.

889 Benedict XVI, *Receive the Power*, 79.

890 Benedict XVI, "Address of His Holiness Benedict XVI to Young People and Seminarians, April 19, 2008" in *Christ Our Hope*, 105-116, here 109.

891 Benedict XVI, *Receive the Power*, 147.

892 *Homily by the Holy Father at Mass in Pilsudzki Square during Pastoral Visit of His Holiness Pope Benedict XVI in Poland* (May 26, 2006), available from: http://www.vatican/va/holy_father/bencdict_xvi/homilies/2006/documents/hf_ben-xvi_spe_20060526_varsavia_en.html; accessed 24 January 2010.

893 *Homily by the Holy Father at Mass in Pilsudzki Square during Pastoral Visit of His Holiness Pope Benedict XVI in Poland* (May 26, 2006), available on internet.

894 *Address of His Holiness Benedict XVI at his Meeting with Clergy and Men and Women Religious during Pastoral Visit of His Holiness Benedict XVI to Assisi on the Eighth Centenary of the Conversion of St. Francis* (June 17, 2007), available from: http://www.vatican/va/holy_father/benedict_xvi/speeches/2007/june/documents/hf_ben-xvi_spe_20070617_clero-assisi_en.html; accessed 12 January 2010. See also *Message of His Holiness Benedict XVI to Bishop Domenico Sorrentino on the Occasion of the 20ᵗʰ Anniversary of the Interreligious Meeting of Prayer for Peace* (September 1, 2006), available on internet; where Benedict XVI noted: "The witness Francis bore in his time makes him a natural reference point today for people who are fostering the ideal of peace, respect for nature and dialogue between people, religions and cultures. It is important, however, to recall, if one does not want to betray his message, that it was Christ's radical decision that provided him with a key to understanding the brotherhood to which all people are called, and in which inanimate creatures – from 'brother sun' to 'sister moon' – also in a certain way participate."

895 *Address of His Holiness Benedict XVI to the Roman Curia Offering them his Christmas Greetings*, available on internet.

896 *Address of His Holiness Benedict XVI to the Roman Curia Offering them his Christmas Greetings*, available on internet.

897 *Address of His Holiness Benedict XVI to the Roman Curia Offering them his Christmas Greetings*, available on internet.

⁸⁹⁸ *Address of His Holiness Benedict XVI to the Roman Curia Offering them his Christmas Greetings*, available on internet.

⁸⁹⁹ *Address of His Holiness Benedict XVI to the Roman Curia Offering them his Christmas Greetings*, available on internet.

⁹⁰⁰ *Address of His Holiness Benedict XVI to the Roman Curia Offering them his Christmas Greetings*, available on internet.

⁹⁰¹ Pope Benedict XVI, *The Church Fathers: From Clement of Rome to Augustine* (San Francisco: Ignatius Press, 2008), 17.

⁹⁰² Pope Benedict XVI, *The Church Fathers*, 19. During this audience Benedict XVI also recalled his predecessor Pope John Paul II and quoted his encyclical *Fides et Ratio*, n. 38, where the latter described St. Justin as a "pioneer of positive engagement with philosophical thinking – albeit with cautious discernment.... Although he continued to hold Greek philosophy in high esteem after his conversion, Justin claimed with power and clarity that he had found in Christianity 'the only sure and profitable philosophy' (*Dial.* 8:1)," 19.

⁹⁰³ Pope Benedict XVI, *The Church Fathers*, 20.

⁹⁰⁴ Pope Benedict XVI, *The Church Fathers*, 20.

⁹⁰⁵ Pope Benedict XVI, *The Church Fathers*, 20.

⁹⁰⁶ Benedict XVI, *Address of His Holiness Benedict XVI at Inaugural Session of the Fifth General Conference of the Bishops of Latin America and the Caribbean during Apostolic Journey to Brazil* (May 13, 2007), available from: http://www.vatican/va/holy_father/benedict_xvi/speeches/2007/may/documents/hf_ben-xvi_spe_20070513_conference-aparecida_en.html; accessed 12 January 2010.

⁹⁰⁷ Benedict XVI, *Address of His Holiness Benedict XVI to the Bishops of Malaysia, Brunei and Singapore on their "Ad Limina" Visit* (June 6, 2008), available from: http://www.vatican/va/holy_father/benedict_xvi/speeches/2008/june/documents/hf_ben-xvi_spe_20080606_bishops-malaysia_en.html; accessed 24 January 2010.

⁹⁰⁸ Benedict XVI, *Address of His Holiness Benedict XVI to the Bishops of Malaysia, Brunei and Singapore on their "Ad Limina" Visit* (June 6, 2008), available on internet.

⁹⁰⁹ Benedict XVI, *Address of His Holiness Benedict XVI to H.E. Mr. Geoffrey Kenyon Ward, Ambassador of New Zealand to the Holy See* (June 16, 2005), available from: http://www.vatican/va/holy_father/benedict_xvi/speeches/2005/june/documents/hf_ben-xvi_spe_20050616_ambassador-new-zealand_en.html; accessed 12 January 2010.

⁹¹⁰ James V. Schall, SJ, ed., *The Regensburg Lecture* (South Bend, IN: St. Augustine's Press, 2007), 139.

⁹¹¹ Schall, ed., *The Regensburg Lecture*, 140.

⁹¹² Schall, ed., *The Regensburg Lecture*, 141.

⁹¹³ Schall, ed., *The Regensburg Lecture*, 142-143.

⁹¹⁴ Schall, ed., *The Regensburg Lecture*, 144. Dale T. Irvin (Baptist) argues that Benedict in his lecture insisted that Christianity achieved a decisive synthesis of faith and reason by a joining of Greek philosophy and biblical faith, and that makes it related to Europe's history in a unique way that is not true of any other culture. Cf. Dale T. Irwin, "Benedict XVI, the End of European Christendom and the Horizons of World Christianity," in *The Pontificate of Benedict XVI: Its Premises and Promises*, ed. William G. Rusch (Grand Rapids, MI: William B. Eerdmans Publishing Company, 2009), 1-20.

915 Schall, ed., *The Regensburg Lecture*, 144.

916 Schall, ed., *The Regensburg Lecture*, 146-147.

917 *Address of His Holiness Pope Benedict XVI to the Diplomatic Corps Accredited to the Holy See for the Traditional New Year Greetings* (January 8, 2007), available from: http://www.vatican/va/holy_father/benedict_xvi/speeches/2007/january/documents/hf_ben-xvi_spe_20070108_diplomatic-corps_en.html; accessed 12 January 2010.

918 *Address of His Holiness Benedict XVI to the Delegates of the Academy of Moral and Political Sciences of Paris* (February 10, 2007), available from: http://www.vatican/va/holy_father/benedict_xvi/speeches/2007/february/documents/hf_ben-xvi_spe_20070210_academy-paris_en.html; accessed 24 January 2010.

919 Benedict XVI, *Address of His Holiness Benedict XVI to the Men and Women Religious, Members of Secular Institutes and Societies of Apostolic Life of the Rome Diocese* (December 10, 2005), available from: http://www.vatican/va/holy_father/benedict_xvi/speeches/2005/december/documents/hf_ben-xvi_spe_20051210_religious-rome-diocese_en.html; accessed 12 January 2010.

920 *Address of His Holiness Benedict XVI to the Delegates of the Academy of Moral and Political Sciences of Paris* (February 10, 2007), available on internet.

921 *Address of His Holiness Benedict XVI to the Delegates of the Academy of Moral and Political Sciences of Paris* (February 10, 2007), available on internet. Benedict XVI also speaks of "cultivating a Catholic identity which is based not so much on externals as on a way of thinking and acting grounded in the Gospel and enriched by the Church's living tradition." In *Christ Our Hope*, 30.

922 *Message of the Holy Father Benedict XVI for the 42nd World Communications Day:* "The Media: at the Crossroads between Self-Promotion and Service. Searching for the Truth in order to Share it with Others." (January 24, 2008), available from: http://www.vatican/va/holy_father/benedict_xvi/messages/communications/documents/hf_ben-xvi_mes_20080124_42nd-world-communications-day_en.html; accessed 12 January 2010.

923 *Message of the Holy Father Benedict XVI for the 42nd World Communications Day:* "The Media: at the Crossroads between Self-Promotion and Service. Searching for the Truth in order to Share it with Others." (January 24, 2008), available on internet.

924 *Message of the Holy Father Benedict XVI for the 42nd World Communications Day:* "The Media: at the Crossroads between Self-Promotion and Service. Searching for the Truth in order to Share it with Others." (January 24, 2008), available on internet.

925 Schall, ed., *The Regensburg Lecture*, 133-134, the Pope said of the emperor: "Without descending to details, such as the difference in treatment accorded to those who have the 'Book' and the 'infidels,' he addresses his interlocutor with a startling brusqueness, a brusqueness that we find unacceptable, on the central question about the relationship between religion and violence in general, saying: 'Show me just what Mohammed brought that was new, and there you will find things only evil and inhuman, such as his command to spread by the sword the faith he preached.' The emperor, after having expressed himself so forcefully, goes on to explain in detail the reasons why spreading the faith through violence is something unreasonable. Violence is incompatible with the nature of God and the nature of the soul. 'God,' he says, 'is not pleased by blood – and not acting reasonably is contrary to God's nature. Faith is born of the soul, not the body.

Whoever would lead someone to faith needs the ability to speak well and to reason properly, without violence and threats... To convince a reasonable soul, one does not need a strong arm, or weapons of any kind, or any other means of threatening a person with death....'"

[926] Ian Fisher, "Many Muslims Say Pope's Apology Is Inadequate," *The New York Times* (September 18, 2006), available from: http://www.nytimes.com/2006/09/18/world/18cnd-pope.html?_r=1&hp&ex=1158638400&en=09867eb4bf0ed8e6&ei=5094&partner=homepage; accessed 12 February 2010.

[927] *Address of His Holiness Benedict XVI to the Writers of the College of "La Civiltà Cattolica"* (February 17, 2006), available on internet.

[928] *Address of His Holiness Benedict XVI to the Writers of the College of "La Civiltà Cattolica"* (February 17, 2006), available on internet.

[929] *Encounter of His Holiness Benedict XVI with the Youth of Rome and the Lazio Region in Preparation for the XXI World Youth Day* (April 6, 2006), available from: http://www.vatican/va/holy_father/benedict_xvi/speeches/2006/april/documents/hf_ben-xvi_spe_20060406_xxi-wyd_en.html; accessed 24 January 2010.

[930] *Letter of His Holiness Benedict XVI to Cardinal Walter Kasper on the Occasion of the Second Conference on Peace and Tolerance Organized by the Ecumenical Patriarchate of Constantinople in Conjunction with the Appeal of Conscience Foundation* (November 4, 2005), available from: http://www.vatican/va/holy_father/benedict_xvi/letters/2005/documents/hf_ben-xvi_let_20051104_kasper-istanbul_en.html; accessed 12 January 2010.

[931] *Address of His Holiness Benedict XVI to H.E. Mr. Antoni Morell Mora, Ambassador of the Principality of Andorra to the Holy See* (December 1, 2005), available from: http://www.vatican/va/holy_father/benedict_xvi/speeches/2005/december/documents/hf_ben-xvi_spe_20051201_ambassador-andorra_en.html; accessed 24 January 2010.

[932] Twomey, *Pope Benedict XVI: The Conscience of Our Age*, 63.

[933] *Address of His Holiness Benedict XVI to H.E. Mr. Noel Fahey, New Ambassador of Ireland to the Holy See* (September 15, 2007), available from: http://www.vatican/va/holy_father/benedict_xvi/speeches/2007/september/documents/hf_ben-xvi_spe_20070915_ambassador-ireland_en.html; accessed 24 January 2010.

[934] Benedict XVI, *Christ Our Hope*, 28.

[935] *Address of His Holiness Benedict XVI to Members of the International Theological Commission* (October 5, 2007), available from: http://www.vatican/va/holy_father/benedict_xvi/speeches/2007/october/documents/hf_ben-xvi_spe_20071005_cti_en.html; accessed 12 January 2010.

[936] *Catechism of the Catholic Church*, n. 1955.

[937] *Address of His Holiness Benedict XVI to Members of the International Theological Commission* (October 5, 2007), available on internet. In an interview during his flight to the U.S. in 2008, Pope Benedict was asked about the role of the United Nations in safeguarding the "non-negotiable" principles, that is, the principles founded on natural law, to which the Holy Father responded: "I think it is very important that the United Nations be founded precisely on the idea of human rights, rights that express non-negotiable values, that precede all the institutions and constitute the foundations of all the institutions. And it is important that this should be the convergence between the cultures that have achieved

consensus on the fact that these values are fundamental, that they are engraved in man's very being." In Benedict XVI, *Christ Our Hope*, 7.

938 Weigel, *God's Choice*, 219 (emphasis in the original). See also Benedict XVI, *Christ Our Hope*, 37, where in a homily delivered during the Mass at Nationals Park in Washington, D.C. the Holy Father spoke of "a growing forgetfulness of Christ and God."

939 Benedict XVI, *Christ Our Hope*, 28.

940 *Address of His Holiness Benedict XVI to Members of the International Theological Commission* (October 5, 2007), available on internet.

941 *Address of His Holiness Benedict XVI at the Meeting with the Members of the Roman Clergy* (March 2, 2006), available on internet.

942 *Address of His Holiness Benedict XVI at the Meeting with the Members of the Roman Clergy* (March 2, 2006), available on internet.

943 *Address of His Holiness Benedict XVI at the Meeting with the Members of the Roman Clergy* (March 2, 2006), available on internet. Also, the eschatological dimension is extensively addressed in Benedict XVI's encyclical letter *Spe Salvi* (San Francisco: Ignatius Press, 2008). See also Benedict XVI, *Christ Our Hope*, 31.

944 Benedict XVI, Encyclical Letter "Charity in Truth," *Caritas in Veritate* (Washington, DC: United States Conference of Catholic Bishops, 2009), 1.

945 Benedict XVI, *Caritas in Veritate*, 2.

946 Benedict XVI, *Caritas in Veritate*, 25.

947 *Letter of His Holiness Benedict XVI to the Participants in the Third European Ecumenical Assembly organized by the Council of European Episcopal Conferences and by the Conference of European Churches* (August 20, 2007), available from: http://www.vatican/va/holy_father/benedict_xvi/letters/2007/documents/ hf_ben-xvi_let_20070820_assemblea-sibiu_en.html; accessed 24 January 2010.

948 *Address of His Holiness Benedict XVI to the Ambassadors of Countries with a Muslim Majority and to the Representatives of Muslim Communities in Italy* (September 25, 2006), available from: http://www.vatican/va/holy_father/benedict_xvi/ speeches/2006/september/documents/hf_ben-xvi_spe_20060924_ambasci- atori-paesi-arabi_en.html; accessed 24 January 2010.

949 *Letter of His Holiness Benedict XVI to Card. Paul Paupard on the Occasion of the Pan-Asiatic Meeting of Members and Consultors of the Pontifical Council for Culture and Presidents of the National Episcopal Commissions for Culture* (Denpasar, Bali, 26-30 November 2006), available from: http://www.vatican/va/holy_father/ benedict_xvi/letters/2006/documents/hf_ben-xvi_let_20061115_pan-asiatic- meting_en.html; accessed 12 January 2010. The Pope also adds that "evangelization and inculturation constitute an inseparable pair, both elements which must be present if the Gospel of Christ is truly to become incarnate in the lives of people of every race, nation, tribe and language." (Cf. *Towards a Pastoral Approach to Culture*, 5).

950 Cf. *Address of His Holiness Benedict XVI to the Participants in the Plenary Session of the Congregation for the Doctrine of the Faith* (January 31, 2008), where the Holy Father noted that "confronted by the risk of persistent religious and cultural relativism,… in the age of interreligious and intercultural dialogue the Church does not dispense with the need for evangelization and missionary activity for peoples, nor does she cease to ask men and women to accept the salvation offered to them all. Recognition of elements of truth and good in the

world's religions and the seriousness of their religious endeavors, together with dialogue and a spirit of collaboration with them for the defense and promotion of the person's dignity and the universal moral values, cannot be understood as a limitation of the Church's missionary task, which involves her in ceaselessly proclaiming Christ as the Way, the Truth and the Life (cf. Jn 14: 6)." Available from http://www.vatican/va/holy_father/benedict_xvi/speeches/2008/janu-ary/documents/hf_ben-xvi_spe_20080131_dottrina-fede_en.html; accessed 24 January 2010. See also Congregation for the Doctrine of Faith, "Doctrinal Note on Some Aspects of Evangelization" (December 3, 2007) in *Origins* 37:29 (2007), 457-463.

[951] Benedict XVI, *Caritas in Veritate*, 25-26.

[952] Corkery, *Joseph Ratzinger's Theological Ideas*, 136.

[953] Allen, *The Rise of Benedict XVI*, 9.

[954] Cicero, *De Oratore*, II.9.

[955] Murray G. Murphey, *Philosophical Foundations of Historical Knowledge* (New York: State University of New York Press, 1994) 318.

[956] Ratzinger, "Faith as Conversion – Metanoia," in *Principles of Catholic Theology: Building Stones for a Fundamental Theology*, 55-67, here 57. Allen adds: "Ratz-inger has said, rightly, 'We ought to have the courage to rise up against what is regarded as 'normal' for a person at the end of the 20th century and to rediscover faith in its simplicity.'… Should we strive to make liturgy more relevant, moral teachings more achievable, catechetics more fun? Or do we need, in at least some of these cases, to be less accommodating, to insist upon inconvenience and discomfort in order to reawaken our people to the 'sign of contradiction' that Christian faith is supposed to be? Shouldn't we be fostering our ability to resist? These are judgments that cannot be made without an intimate knowledge of a particular community and its needs, but they are questions that I fear are too infrequently asked," *Pope Benedict XVI*, 305-306.

[957] Allen, *Pope Benedict XVI*, 44.

[958] Ratzinger, "Christ, Faith and the Challenge of Cultures," available at: http://www.ewtn.com/library/CURIA/RATZHONG.HTM; accessed 14 November 2009.

[959] As Allen noted about Ratzinger: "He realized that it is far easier to entice young people to disengage themselves from the dominant ethos than adults, who are often less open to significant change in world-view and lifestyle." *The Rise of Pope Benedict XVI*, 230.

[960] Ratzinger, *Truth and Tolerance*, 254.

[961] Homily of His Eminence Card. Joseph Ratzinger: Mass *Pro Eligendo Romano Pontifice*. See also Corkery, "Joseph Ratzinger's Theological Ideas 3–On Being Human," 13-14.